In the Shadow of Silence

Gertrud Mackprang Baer

IN THE SHADOW
OF SILENCE

From Hitler Youth to Allied Internment:
A Young Woman's Story of Truth and Denial

HarperCollins*PublishersLtd*

In the Shadow of Silence: From Hitler Youth to Allied Internment: A Young Woman's Story of Truth and Denial
Copyright © 2002 by Gertrud Mackprang Baer.
All rights reserved. No part of this book may be used or reproduced in any manner whatsoever without prior written permission except in the case of brief quotations embodied in reviews. For information address
HarperCollins Publishers Ltd.,
55 Avenue Road, Suite 2900,
Toronto, Ontario, Canada M5R 3L2

www.harpercanada.com

HarperCollins books may be purchased for educational, business, or sales promotional use. For information please write: Special Markets Department,
HarperCollins Canada,
55 Avenue Road, Suite 2900,
Toronto, Ontario, Canada M5R 3L2

First edition

Canadian Cataloguing in Publication Data

Baer, Gertrud Mackprang, 1925–
In the shadow of silence : from Hitler Youth to Allied internment : a young woman's story of truth and denial

Includes bibliographical references and index.
ISBN 0-00-200093-8

1. Baer, Gertrud Mackprang, 1925–   .
2. Germany – History – 1933–1945.
3. Hitler-Jugend.
4. National socialism and youth.
5. Political prisoners – Germany – Biography.
6. World War, 1939–1945 – Personal narratives, German.
I. Title.

DD247.B3154A3 2002   943.086'092   C2002-900563-9

HC 9 8 7 6 5 4 3 2 1

Printed and bound in the United States
Set in Granjon

*We do not have a mandate to establish the moral respons-
ibility of those who saw things happen and did nothing,
including people who might have had the capacity to stop
the process and did nothing. But we have to be careful in
thinking that just because we focus on individual criminal
guilt we therefore absolve the community. The old distinctions are too simplistic when we move up the chain of
command and witness the merging of the collectivity into the
personae of these charismatic political and military leaders.*

Louise Arbour,
Justice for the Supreme Court of Canada,
formerly the Chief Prosecutor for the International Criminal
Tribunal for the Former Yugoslavia,
in an interview with Erna Paris.

*A totalitarian system shapes all citizens within its sphere of
power. Nobody remains untouched. No-one is safe from
repression. Everyone is a potential victim — unless he
complies with the regime, becomes a collaborator and
thereby a potential perpetrator.*

Judith Belinfante,
former director of the Jewish-Historical Museum
in Amsterdam and member of the Labor Party (PvdA).

CONTENTS

AUTHOR'S NOTE

In 1938, after the Anschluss of Austria, a great national fervor gripped the German people. With the slogan *"Ein Volk, ein Reich, ein Führer"* (one People, one Reich, one Führer) a powerful trinity was invoked that hinted at Germany's aggressive policies for the territorial reconstitution of the Reich. *Ein Volk, ein Reich, ein Führer* became the mantra of the Third Reich, an ideological vision of a German state that was totalitarian and confrontational by nature, directed by the *Führerwillen* (Führer's will) and legitimized by the enthusiastic support of tens of millions of ordinary people. As the First Reich had been defined by the power of the papacy and the Second by emperor and cabinet, the Third Reich was defined by the masses. Never before had German politics been so inclusive, so populist, so blatantly seductive of the *Volk*.

After Germany's collapse in 1945, reality replaced ideology: The *Führer* became a non-entity overnight, the *Reich* returned to its medieval origins, and the *Volk* was left with Hitler's monstrous legacy.

I was one of the ordinary German *Volk*. I witnessed the entire Third Reich and its cataclysmic collapse, the early years of the war's aftermath, and the birth of the new German state. I never voted for any German government, nor was I a target of either state's legal or arbitrary powers. I did, however, trip up over my own folly, for which I paid dearly. This book is about my extraordinary experiences during the last weeks of the tottering Reich and the chaotic months that followed, as well as the disturbing insights they engendered over the ensuing years.

This was not an easy book to write. Indeed, it took decades to make a start, and years of rewriting, with the urge to sanitize the text, perhaps to scrap it altogether, was ever present. There is an inescapable logic that haunts everyone brave—or naive—enough to discuss the Nazi state from first-hand experience rather than through the detached lens of the historian: If Hitler's Third Reich derived its immense power from the collective will of the people, then the people, in turn, bear a collective responsibility for the aims and means of the Third Reich. It is a disturbing truth that is easy to state, but painfully difficult to define, let alone accept.

After the war, the Hitler generation—*das Volk*—instantly and collectively repudiated any personal knowledge of, let alone involvement in, the crimes of the Third Reich. Huge sums were paid by the new German government against the state's outstanding material and moral debts. Yet the thorny question of the political accountability or moral responsibility of the ordinary German remained unresolved. For decades, it has influenced the country's political culture and marred its tireless efforts to come to terms with the past. It became the defining issue for writing this book.

PROLOGUE

The war had been over for a little more than a year. On the evening when the doorbell rang, I answered it, as I always did. With the economic circumstances the way they were, my parents expected no visitors, no social calls. Outside stood a man I had known throughout my school years. Now in his early fifties, with a Roman nose, grey eyes and a deeply lined, swarthy complexion, he could still be considered good-looking. Maybe somewhat slighter in build than I remembered him, yet still with the authority that comes naturally to certain people.

The last time I saw him had been three-and-a-half years earlier, the day of my *Abitur*, the final oral examination before graduating from high school. He had been the school's principal and my Latin teacher. His enthusiasm for the classics and their larger-than-life characters had been inspiring at times, intimidating and tiresome at others. We had read about the Gallic campaigns of Caesar, whom he had liked to compare to Hitler, who had liked to be compared to Caesar.

During the exam he sat next to a short, muscular woman in her mid-thirties, with a mop of kinky hair complementing remarkably un-Nordic features. Years back, she had been a teacher herself; now she was our *Bannführerin*, the highest-ranking district leader in the girls' Hitler Youth movement. Seated at the principal's right, her presence was neither announced nor explained. Whether she watched him or the proceedings remained unclear, yet ominous.

She remained silent during my oral examination. No hint of recognition, no sign of either satisfaction or dismay that I took part at all. Yet, it was only a few months earlier that, in the presence of the principal, she had threatened to force me out of school. Her scorn had been justified, if disproportionate: During the past three or four years, I had allowed my membership in the Hitler Youth to lapse, simply by neglecting to pay my dues and quietly ignoring meetings and assignments. Given the ideological climate of the times, this was not a crime, but still a serious misdemeanour by any Nazi standard. I had made myself an outsider in a German community fighting for its very life. Why? There was no acceptable answer, since teenage ennui, the only true explanation, would have been incomprehensible to a society collectively sworn to fanatical activism.

Yet, the *Bannführerin* had made it clear that there was no way to finish high school and pass my *Abitur*, the prerequisite for admission to German universities, unless I immediately re-enrolled in some Hitler Youth organization. Demonstrating the appropriate remorse, I joined an innocuous branch of the girls' movement with the bizarre name of *Glaube und Schönheit* (Faith and Beauty), where once a week during the next three months I dutifully discussed works of Nazi-approved literature.

"Good evening, *Herr Direktor*." I tried to conceal my surprise and embarrassment at the sight of my former principal standing like a beggar at our door. In earlier times, I had greeted him with a snappy *Heil Hitler*, and outside classes avoided him altogether. Now I had to decide whether to ask him to come into our apartment, which was overcrowded and run-down by the forced billeting of three refugee families. I decided against it.

"I'm no longer *Direktor*," he replied with a wry smile, pulling a document from his briefcase. "I would like you to testify that I always protected the school against the arbitrary powers of the Party," he continued. "Many of my former students have already signed. Would you mind adding your signature?" His voice was level, but lacked the authoritarian edge that he, like so many other civilians in positions of power, had adopted during the war. "As you may have heard, one needs these signatures for the process of denazification."

I was stunned. I had, of course, heard about *Denazifierung*, but had never expected to be approached about it myself. Its purpose, to track down and unmask large numbers of Nazi criminals, appeared to most people to be the farcical exercise of a clueless Allied bureaucracy.

I didn't reply. I don't remember how long I just stood there, one hand on the doorknob, desperately searching for some suitable words, some explanation for why I could not possibly do what he expected as a matter of course, a natural act of loyalty for a fellow German. "I'm terribly sorry, *Herr Direktor*, but I can't—"

He looked at me, more surprised than hurt. I wanted to say: Yes, I know, you were not bad, probably better than most. Certainly an excellent teacher, a teacher we respected.

"I was never a Nazi," he said.

The arrogance that his students had known and feared had faded from his eyes, which studied me with a calm intelligence. He had an air of dignity, despite the worn jacket, that seemed to evoke happier times. Every nerve in my body urged me to grab the paper and be done with it. After all, what difference would it make? The war was over, and all the bad things that had happened to me afterwards were over too. Besides, many Nazis were getting off these days. Why shouldn't he? He had never been a fanatic, as far as I knew. Perhaps he had even stood up for me against the *Bannführerin* who, people now claimed, hadn't been so bad herself; she had been under tremendous pressure, they said. So, probably, had he; so had everybody. They all now had reasons for the way they had acted.

I shrugged helplessly. Whatever my inclination, I felt paralyzed, mute, unable to reach for the paper, unwilling to sign one of those obscene documents, mockingly called *Persil-Scheine* after a popular German detergent that could cleanse all Nazi-brown whiter than white. I was numb with embarrassment and regret. Avoiding the gaze of my former teacher, I reluctantly closed the door in his face.

I don't know what ever became of him. He probably got back into his former position. And why not? Others had.

Others, like Joseph Müller, or Jupp to his friends—PhD, former high school history teacher, *SS-Hauptsturmführer* (captain), leader of the local SD (*Sicherheitsdienst,* or secret service), leader of the *NS-Studentenwerk* (student union) and commanding officer of the *SS-Studentenkompanie* (student company), all in the university town of Marburg, in the province (now state) of Hesse. Müller, who had drawn me into the filth of the dying Reich, and into the net of the Allied Nazi hunters. The man in whose tracks I was brought to Iserlohn, the idyllic little Westphalian city where a select group of British Secret Service personnel held an equally select number of former Nazi brass for interrogation. Müller, the man who in his glory days bred fear and trust, yet deserved neither, and whose erstwhile bravado dissolved into cowardly flight, imperiling others, while the system he had so zealously served vanished as though it had never existed.

ADOLF-HITLER-PLATZ 13

There have to be mental markers, imaginary little flagpoles that clearly say "from here you may go to there"; and that resist all impulses that want to divert the mind from the outlined road.

My first "memory pole" stands on a small public square in the well-to-do west end of Marburg, an old and dignified university town in the centre of Germany. Before 1933, and again after 1945, the square was called Friedrichsplatz. Whether in honor of the hapless Emperor Friedrich III (son-in-law of Queen Victoria), or Friedrich Barbarossa of crusader fame, or Friedrich the Great of Prussia, I don't know. There have been many Friedrichs; so far, there has been but one Adolf. In 1933, Adolf Hitler—dubbed "the Greatest Name in German History" by his minister of propaganda, Joseph Goebbels—replaced the names of Friedrich and other worthies, not only in sleepy little Marburg, but in public spaces all across Germany.

Well-treed with a neat lawn, Marburg's Adolf-Hitler Square was surrounded by upper-middle-class buildings that dated back to the turn of the century. Their inhabitants, mostly elderly people who in 1933 would still have remembered Kaiser Wilhelm II or even Bismarck, may have felt a certain lack of urgency about the name of their square. As a street address, "Friedrich" probably served just fine, as evidenced by the fact that they reverted to it as soon as the Greatest Name in German history shot himself in the head. In 1933, of course, no one thought to consult them; everyone was in an awful rush to join the Thousand-Year Reich, an urgency justified in retrospect, given its meager twelve-year-life.

My memory pole stands at the northwest corner of Adolf-Hitler-Platz, in front of number thirteen, a genteel, stuccoed building which, in 1944 when my story begins, could have done with a fresh coat of paint, like most buildings in this fifth year of war.

I wonder now whether even a modest amount of political smarts might have raised in me second thoughts about moving to an address that combined the inauspicious number thirteen with the name of Germany's Führer, whose legendary fortunes were beginning to show alarming signs of exhaustion. Political savvy was not my strong point, however, and the consequences of that will soon become plain. Besides, jokes, let alone doubts, about Hitler were strictly *verboten*.

In any case, I did not hesitate even for a moment. At a time when every square foot of residential space was registered, administered and jammed to capacity, I considered myself lucky beyond belief to have found residence in a large furnished room facing the square.

"Found residence," of course, is a manner of speech only. In 1944 no one "found residence." One neither searched, nor found. There must have been cases of bribery, but that was a deadly dangerous game. And besides, I had nothing with which to bribe. On the other hand, I did have connections; naive as I was at the time, though, I recognized neither their character nor their cost.

After registering for my second year of medical school at the University of Marburg, I moved my things into that superb room with its imposing oak desk and elegant Chippendale furniture. My friend Alexander, Alex for short, accompanied me to the registrar's office and to my new home at Adolf-Hitler-Platz. He told me about my landladies, an elderly widow of a *Geheimrat* of theology—a venerable professorial title going back to imperial times—and her daughter, a spinster and nurse. The latter would take my rent money over the subsequent months and speak to me only when contact was unavoidable.

Alex carried my suitcase to the second-floor apartment, but didn't wait around, and thereafter, he never entered the building again. I thought he was protecting my reputation as a *höhere Tochter*, a girl brought up in a respectable family who, in 1944, still risked social opprobrium by receiving a young man alone in her apartment. To some extent, I was right about this. But, having procured the room for me through high official connections, Alex may have simply wanted to avoid a run-in with the more traditional ladies.

Although I didn't know it at the time, the man with all the influence was his boss, *SS Hauptsturmführer* Dr. Joseph Müller. Whether Alex, a humble *SS Sturmmann* (corporal), had used his own name to requisition the place or posed as the *Hauptsturmführer*, or whether Müller had made the call to the landladies himself, I don't know. Like most Germans, including myself, the widow and her daughter had probably never had anything to do with the SS, and would hardly have noticed the difference.

In the end, of course, it didn't matter how I got the place; I got it, and eleven months later I lost it. As did my landladies, and everybody else at Adolf-Hitler-Platz 13.

*   *   *

The best way to describe Alex is to quote a friend of his: "Alexander," this friend declared with a grand gesture, "was born to wear white tie." Years later, while reading Thomas Mann's *Confessions of Con Man Felix Krull*, I was reminded of him and the pivotal role he played in my life during the 1940s. Alex wasn't exactly a con man. He merely exploited talents he had acquired through some kind of osmosis while growing up in the Balkans, that vexatious and impenetrable web of Europe's most unassimilated tribes stuck in the mountains or lost in the plains since the times of the Great Migration. Whatever the cause or process, the product was a man of extraordinary charm.

He was born near the end of World War I in a distant corner of the Austro-Hungarian empire that, in 1919, became part of the kingdom of Romania. Ignoring the social and political changes brought about by Austria's breakup, the German-speaking minority continued to represent the cultural elite within its new borders. Educated in private institutions, Alex acquired, in addition to his German mother tongue, an easy familiarity with French and Latin. Five-foot-ten, athletic, blond, with grey mocking eyes, a strong nose and long, dimpled chin, he oozed quaint old-world courtliness, a trait further emphasized by the fact that he was a *Volksdeutscher*, or ethnic German.

In contrast to most European countries, which preferred to ignore their nationals abroad, or at least avoid stirring in them any desire to return to their homeland, Hitler's Germany pursued an aggressive *Volkstumspolitik* aimed at repatriating into the Reich ethnic Germans "wilfully excluded" by the Treaty of Versailles. By September 1, 1939, and the outbreak of war, this policy had successfully "brought home" the Saarland, Austria, Sudetenland, and the Memel territory; within days it would add Danzig and the parts of Poland that were formerly German. The policy would also invite Alex and thousands of other ethnic Germans to leave their native lands to report for voluntary military service in the German army.

Not surprisingly, most of these homelands promptly withdrew the citizenship of their departed German minorities. Conversely, the Reich, notwithstanding its welcoming propaganda, refused to grant its returning expatriates the justifiably expected German citizenship, leaving thousands of young patriots baffled and stateless. What seemed like a minor glitch in 1939 would later prove to have disastrous consequences for many of these ethnic volunteers.

At the time, Alex's feelings over the statehood issue were negligible compared to his bitter disappointment on learning that the Wehrmacht, the regular German army, rejected all *Volksdeutsche* as a matter of policy, unceremoniously handing them over to the Waffen SS, the military arm of the SS. Whether his loyalties and convictions became elastic as a result, or whether they had always been that way, I never found out. The fact is, he was surrounded by a mysterious aura of invincibility, which protected him from the perils and adversities experienced by most Germans during and after the war. And in the end, in spite of the telltale SS tattoo under his arm, he would slip through the net laid out by the Allies to catch members of the former Waffen SS and other outlawed organizations.

But I am getting ahead of myself.

In 1941, when our paths—or lucky stars, as I saw it then—crossed at some seaside resort on the Baltic Sea, Alex was clad in the humble *Feldgrau* (field-grey uniform) of the ordinary German soldier, with one modest bar on the sleeve for the rank of *SS Sturmmann*. With his *Käppi* (forage cap) set at a rakish angle, and a mischievous smile and engaging jauntiness, he was the picture of the happy warrior about to win the war all by himself. Luckily for him, that chance had dissolved early in his military career. When we first met, he was walking with a slightly awkward gait, recovering from surgery to his ankle after an accident that took him out of basic training, rendering him permanently unfit for frontline duty. Later, he would enter medical school, where there was little military supervision, but for some loose attachment to an *SS Studentenkompanie*.

In that golden summer of 1941, Germany was still winning the war, and winning it big. I was sixteen years old, carefree, and smitten by this man seven years my senior, who had been raised to a life of sophistication, worlds removed from my own puritanical North German upbringing.

Within days, Alex became the man of my wildest dreams, different from anybody I had ever met. Or, for that matter, would ever meet.

In the following years, while I attended high school, our holiday flirtation developed into a charming, though infrequent, correspondence. His cocky self-confidence leaped from his hurried pages, while his precise whereabouts remained a mystery. I knew he had been transferred from Berlin to sleepy little Marburg, home to one of Germany's oldest and most highly acclaimed universities. But his letters usually came stamped with some cryptic *Feldpost* number. Did he actually work in a field hospital between terms, as he later claimed, with lots of big tales to tell? I wasn't sure. From his letters, it all sounded like great fun and adventure, though.

Meanwhile, my own life progressed, however hesitantly, from adolescence to adulthood. Graduation from high school in the spring of 1943 was followed by seven months of *Arbeitsdienst*, the compulsory labour service for all eighteen-year-olds—both men and women. From the beginning, I proved a thoroughly unhappy misfit within the jolly camaraderie and rustic wholesomeness of it all. Later in the summer, I developed a bad case of scarlet fever, which sent the whole camp into quarantine and further reduced my popularity among the leadership. These were pre-penicillin times in Germany, and the infection left me with some complications. When the lab results came in, however, leading to my unexpected and unlamented release, I was ecstatic. Five days later, I was out of uniform and enrolled for the 1943–1944 winter semester in Hamburg's medical school, free again while most of my generation were busy saving the nation.

Not so free, of course. There was no real freedom.

Living under a dictatorship that was fighting for its survival, an unguarded word, an untimely quip could mean instant imprisonment, or even death. By this time, there were no more military victories either, no more conquests of vast enemy lands. Only "orderly retreats," in the official parlance, along the Russian and Italian fronts. And, in the newspapers, ever more black crosses alongside soldiers' names, challenging the official optimism and rattling public morale.

At the end of July 1943, while I was still doing service in the *Arbeitsdienst*, my hometown, Hamburg, was destroyed by three days and nights of sustained bombing that left forty thousand dead and hundreds of thousands homeless. The deliberate targeting of densely populated parts of the

Reforestation work during the *Arbeitsdienst* in 1943. *(left):* Author is on the right.
(right): Author right front

inner city, combined with the meteorologic fluke of hot, sticky weather, plus the use of "canister bombs" filled with highly flammable phosphorus, produced the first man-made firestorm in the history of war. The brain-child of British Air Chief Marshal Arthur Harris, the raids resulted in unparalleled human disaster, immediately dubbed by Germans *die Katas-trophe* (the catastrophe).[1] With tornado-strength winds, several-hundred-degree temperatures, and people welded to the melted asphalt, the *Katastrophe* is still debated today by historians and strategists for its rela-tive military value. At the time, if nothing else, it changed the human landscape in wartime Germany for good: As streams of refugees from the stricken city spread deep into southern and eastern parts of the country, and every square foot of undestroyed living space was forcibly filled with the homeless, the public mood changed from demonstratively victorious to quietly defiant.

My family was unharmed. Together with my *Arbeitsdienst* comrades, I watched the red sky of the burning metropolis one hundred and fifty kilometres to the south. When I came home three months later, my father took me on a tour of the worst-hit areas. We stood in front of a primitively constructed wall, restricting access to—what? Four square kilometres? Ten?[2] How large does a square kilometre of built-up city appear after it has been flattened into rubble? There were a few tall buildings left, some steeples, forlorn between the ragged silhouette of debris. No trespassing. "The whole area has been declared 'a dead city,'" my father explained. "They say they couldn't get them all out. And the weather was so hot. So the soldiers went in with flame throwers to incinerate the bodies."

There are mass graves at Hamburg's largest cemetery, wide grassy areas divided into former boroughs. The *Katastrophe*, just like the war itself, the great equalizer. At a time when the Americans still believed in the precision-targeting of German production lines, "Bomber" Harris believed in killing morale by killing civilians. He was the only Allied general later blamed on moral as well as strategic grounds. His strategy was successful, of course—after the *Katastrophe*, morale never fully recovered, even if Albert Speer, Hitler's armaments minister, could proudly point to ever-rising production figures of new weapons and materiel.

*   *   *

By late 1943, the sirens in Hamburg wailed almost daily, harassing citizens and robbing them of their sleep. Their terror was compounded by an ever-vigilant Nazi party, hunting for any emerging signs of collapsing loyalty and defeatism.

Befitting all that gloom and doom, I quickly discovered that I hated university. I hated the classes where I understood little, and I hated the professors, who hated women. I forced myself to smile nonchalantly at their sexist remarks, and stared them down for their crude jokes, but my unfortunate habit of blushing impaired all acts of defiance. I vomited frequently from the bad cafeteria food and the stench of formaldehyde in the dissection hall, which had no shortage of corpses.

During the two-month spring holiday, I signed up for nursing duties at a local hospital. I was assigned to a large ward of twenty or so prostate patients, fitted with long catheters in old penises, plus a number of patients undergoing general surgery—all cared for by one registered nurse and one student nurse. Needless to say, their happiness to see me outstripped my own enthusiasm. We were on twelve-hour shifts. If there were regulations about do's and don'ts, nobody had the time to tell me. After all, there was a war on and most of the staff had been called away for more exciting service at field hospitals.

In hindsight, though, I doubt I saw things in such patriotic terms. Reality for me was not a war some thousand kilometres away, but the ugliness right in front of me: the prompt and rude dispatch of my amazing innocence; the necessity of doing things for which I was completely untrained. There were the horrifying situations that trapped me, by fate or by ignorance, as when, on a quiet Sunday afternoon, one of those human scarecrows in their ridiculous nightgowns accidentally ripped the catheter from his bursting bladder. I was alone on the ward as he hopped around, tube in hand, his senile shrieks demanding action. I tried my best, but skill was not on my side.

During all that misery, Alex's infrequent letters were like missives from another planet—read and reread and read once again, until I knew every word by heart; I quoted them like pearls of wisdom to impress my friends. In the end, that long-standing infatuation probably had more than a little to do with my decision to enter medicine, a rather eccentric choice in the eyes of my merchant-class parents. And, it most likely was Alex who subsequently persuaded me to transfer my studies from Hamburg to Marburg.

Once there, all my troubles were instantly blown away by the unfolding romance. I was happy, and I didn't care how he had managed to get that exceptional room, when there were no rooms to be had. I never asked him how he had "pulled rank," or, more accurately, used his SS credentials. My landlady, the tight-lipped *Geheimratswitwe*-widow never spoke to me. I thought her odd. She may have been odd, or she may have just been prudent.

In the summer of 1944, the Allies landed in Normandy; all major and many minor cities were bombed to rubble. The Red Army drew closer to German territory, and in August, propaganda minister Joseph Goebbels closed the universities to all but a few students. In an act of frenzy, the German people had demanded "total war," and total war was what they got. Not only from enemy aircraft, now dominating the skies almost unchallenged, but from the ruthless powers of the Nazi regime and its increasingly fanatical supporters.

None of these calamities touched me, not really. In addition to studying for a minor exam, I was involved in a high-minded and ritualistic courtship. It was all very charming, very romantic—and very silly.

Yet, given the contradictory social climate of the Third Reich, such puritanical conduct was by no means exceptional: National Socialist propaganda to the contrary, class structures in the Third Reich were rigidly maintained by most major institutions such as high schools and universities, the highly trained public service, and the military and diplomatic corps, whose upper ranks read like the Who's Who of old German nobility. It may even be noted that Himmler's SS patterned its prototypical officer after the strapping, blond, East-Elbian Junker. The *Ordensburgen*, Nazism's three elite academies teaching Party ideology and fanatical devotion, were conceived as modern revivals of the castles of the Teutonic Knights (*Deutschritter*), one of the highest orders of medieval German aristocracy.

Alex was no Junker, much less a spic-and-span German officer, SS or otherwise. His appearance was happily relaxed, even a bit rumpled. Thanks to his old-Austrian background, stiff-backed Prussian deportment wasn't his style. Observing the exigencies of one's class, however, was, resulting in a courtship resplendent in all the romantic impediments of a Victorian novel. Still, by the end of the term, we had arrived at some sort of betrothal, terribly secret of course, and without any thoughts of a precipitous marriage. Not because of any sinister foreboding about Germany's future—such thoughts didn't occur to us, not yet—but because it would have been completely out of character in light of both our upbringings. One married in style, or one didn't marry at all, lest there arise some unwelcome rumor about the hastiness of it all.

Needless to say, there were still plenty of people who, even at that late stage in the war, decided to tie the knot, either because the girl wanted a child from the man she loved—even though he might not live to see it—or, as a couple, they expected to stand a better chance of staying together or finding each other after the final collapse, whenever that occurred.

But did we really think of collapse in 1944? The German soldiers and civilians in occupied Poland, who were already retreating from the approaching Red Army, may have thought about it. I did not. I still believed in the "miracle weapons" that Goebbels had promised so many times. Because not to believe would have been nearly impossible for a person who had been eight years old when Hitler had come to power, and who had never been taught to think very differently from the prescribed line of thought.

As for what Alex or his friends in the *SS Studentenkompanie* thought, I didn't know. We never talked about it. Strange as that sounds, we never discussed the possibility of losing the war. Not seriously. There was a wisecrack, though, that I remember suddenly being on everybody's lips: "Folks, enjoy the war, the peace will be terrible!" Where did it come from, and how could it have spread so fast? Maybe its cynicism was sufficiently ambiguous to prevent it from turning perilous. Or control was beginning to crack.

Something else I remember from those darkening weeks was the tremendous relief we felt upon hearing that the Führer had survived an attempt on his life by a group of high-ranking army officers. Later on, I will discuss this event, its immense moral implications, and the political exploitation of it by postwar Germany. Here, I will simply relate how things happened when they happened, without the benefit of hindsight. The way we saw it then, Hitler stood out amidst a bunch of vain and stupid Party members as the only great leader who could save Germany. Thanks to his military genius, some grand scheme would still evolve that would stop the advance of enemy troops and bring a peace that would leave German lands intact.

There isn't a shred of doubt in my mind that this is what I believed, what most Germans (certainly the young ones) believed, regardless of what they would later tell their children or write in the history books. Did my parents believe it? Maybe, but probably not, although they were far from any inside knowledge. But they had lived through World War I, and instinct must have told them that the war was lost.

Certainly, the honest and upstanding gentleman who, twelve years later, would become my father-in-law, harbored profound doubts about the outcome of the war. Then a high-ranking civilian administrator in a provincial government, he must have known the true numbers of destroyed buildings, industries, and lives in his area. And he must have had at least a vague idea of the number of Jews who had disappeared, perhaps even where they had gone. If he ever mentioned the things he knew, he almost certainly did so under the most circumspect and self-censoring terms. No German would speak openly about some terrible secret he happened upon, whether by virtue of his office or sheer bad luck, and expect to survive unscathed.

So what did we talk about during that final summer of the war? About ourselves, most likely; about our friends. We laughed a lot, like young people do. On our bicycles we toured the charming Hessian countryside. And we were happy. There were no bombers yet over Marburg, my classes seemed suddenly more comprehensible, my professors less prejudiced, and even my nervous vomiting stopped.

But it all ended with the last day of the term, when the German universities closed down—not to reopen for a very long time.

*   *   *

Two years would pass before I saw Alex again; he was wearing dark glasses and a beard, like a character from a movie. It was September 1946, and he came to our house in Hamburg one day, just as I was about to leave for my sister's engagement party. I cannot remember whether the cane he used was part of a disguise, or whether he had some injury. He stayed for a day or two, never explaining where he had been or how he had avoided internment camp. But the plucky bravado and charming self-confidence were gone. Without citizenship or a place of residence, he was a non-person in a country desperately trying to re-establish its social order.

What it all came down to, of course, was a plea for help—from me, from my family—any kind of help. None of us was able to deliver—not physically (we were struggling to survive ourselves) and certainly not emotionally. When my father, in his gentle manner, finally turned him away, I didn't object. Too much had happened since we had last seen each other. Too much fear and hunger, too much betrayal and cowardice, too many revelations.

*   *   *

At this point Alex disappears from my narrative. His name will come up, though; and so will his friends and his boss, all connected with me—or I with them—through him. Had I never met him, chances are that I would never have gone to Marburg, never met Müller, never known a thing about the SD or its local office, the *SD Dienststelle*. It was nobody's fault but my own. Ignoring all warnings, I acted out of infatuation and ignorance—as most nineteen-year-olds are wont to do.

My story picks up again in Marburg, where, throughout the late summer and fall of 1944, my memory pole has remained faithfully staked at Adolf-Hitler-Platz 13, while the city changed its face, becoming dark and joyless like the rest of Germany. Three months had passed since the universities closed down, during which time I worked at an army hospital in Styria in the southeast corner of Austria, a couple of kilometres away from the Yugoslavian border. The German-occupied area beyond was one of the most unpacified regions and riddled with partisan peril.

Nevertheless, it had been a rather pleasant time for me, all things considered. I was well-fed, well-housed and reasonably well-treated, in spite of the fact that all personnel from the "Reich"[3] (as the Austrians

Author on the left with nurses at an army hospital in Styria in the fall of 1944.

called Germany proper) were exposed to some measure of disdain. Part medical student, part nurse, I worked in any capacity required by the authorities or dictated by the ever-increasing emergencies. By the time the Russian front had closed in and people were called up for trench-digging, I had learned a few things about the dirtier aspects of wounds and war that my later civilian studies would never expose me to again.

During the last days of October 1944, as the relentless rumble of guns became clearly audible over the hospital's daytime noise, I decided to head for home without waiting for any official release. After forty-eight hours of changing trains, and countless detours and delays, I reached Marburg. I was hungry, exhausted, and badly shaken by the brutally revealed evidence of a devastated country.

Arriving alone, with nobody to welcome me at the station, I felt terribly downhearted. Back at Adolf-Hitler-Platz 13, I met nobody on the stairs or in the hall as I repossessed my cold, dusty, but otherwise undisturbed apartment. I suddenly felt very lonely. Why had I returned here? Whom had I expected to see? I knew nobody in a university town which had shut down its only important activity, where I had no fuel to heat my room, nothing to boost my meagre rations.

I thought of my mother's preserves, the potatoes, fruits and vegetables from our garden. And there was the wood and coal that arrived mysteriously at our house in Hamburg, despite stringent rules forbidding illicit provisions. Managing a grain-storage enterprise deemed "vital to the war effort," my father possessed a modest ability to "divert"; not much and never to an extent that might alert the ever-vigilant Gestapo, but enough to keep us from starving in the cold.

That night I felt so lonely and frightened that I would have welcomed even a chat with my landladies. Neither of them showed up; there was no sign that they had noticed my return. During the long, dark hours, I made up my mind not to stay in a town that had lost all its charm and appeal. Instead, I would board yet another train, one that was heading for Hamburg and the comfort and security of my family's home.

The next morning, as I stood in line at the post office waiting to place a call to my parents, I happened to run into Alex's boss, *SS Hauptsturmführer* Joseph Müller. A sturdy man in his mid-thirties, Müller was five-foot-ten, but looked taller in his uniform. His strutting gait and habit of turning smartly on his heels further conveyed a sense of superiority and self-assurance. The straight black hair that covered his square cranium was cut short and parted on the left, framing a broad face with heavy brows under a low forehead. The clear blue eyes, strong nose, and full lips suggested a man of purpose, in strange contrast to his pasty skin, which looked poorly shaved and somewhat sickly.

It was a chance encounter, and without his uniform I probably would not have noticed him. Müller, however, had recognized me, even though we had met only once or twice before. After an exchange of banalities, he inquired whether I had heard from Alexander. I said, No, I hadn't, and he said that he couldn't tell me where he was, either. Whether he couldn't or wouldn't was unclear.

"What are you doing in Marburg all by yourself?" he continued.

"I'm just back from service at an army hospital in Austria."

He made a great act of how impressed he was. "Excellent. I'm sure you showed *Kamerad Schnürschuh* ("Comrade Laced-shoe," a derogatory term for Austrian soldiers from World War I) how Germans win a war. How close are the Russians down there, anyway?" It sounded aloof, almost indifferent as though things "down there" didn't make much difference up here.

"Very close. One could hear the guns."

He shook his head. But then, remembering his position, he added hastily, "They'll never tread on German territory."

I couldn't think of a response, if indeed one was expected.

"What are you going to do now? Did they give you new orders?"

I replied that I didn't have any, and that I was going back to my family in Hamburg, where I would report for further duties.

"They may draft you into a munitions plant," he warned, his tone stressing the ominous nature of that prediction.

"I once worked in a factory that builds the 'Big JU,'" I remarked. "I was still in high school then. I must admit I'm not particularly eager for more of the same." We both laughed. The JU 52 was one of Germany's most reliable transport planes. But, despite the plane's merits, it was no secret that work in an armaments factory—any armaments factory— was extremely unpleasant and to be avoided at all costs. "Perhaps I can get a job as a ticket collector on a streetcar. It's surely more fun than working on an assembly line."

"But it's more dangerous, too. If there's an air raid, you'd be the last to get out." He was right, of course. I had also heard about conductors who failed to hear the sirens on those long stretches through thinly populated industrial areas, running their dimly lit cars until stopped by bombs or fighter bullets.

"You should stay away from Hamburg altogether," Müller said in a tone that was authoritative, though not unkind. "There must be something more agreeable for you to do." He paused while his eyes studied me. "Maybe I could try to get you a job as a student at my office," he said, adding: "I'm sure we've got something interesting for you to do. I may even be able to squeeze out a small salary. Can you type?"

"No."

One hand in the pocket of his breeches, the other clamped over his belt buckle in the typical German officer's pose, Müller grandly dismissed that minor shortcoming.

"Doesn't matter, we have secretaries." He seemed increasingly enamored of his plan. "When you come back from Hamburg, I'll personally see to it that you are okay. For Alexander's sake. We old comrades must stick together, eh?"

"I'll let you know," I said with just enough enthusiasm to sound polite.

"Sure. But don't wait too long." He shook my hand, then raised his: "*Heil Hitler!*"

"Thank you. *Heil Hitler!*"

After talking to my mother over a buzzing telephone wire, I returned to my room, packed my bag, made arrangements with the landladies for another indefinite absence, and set out for the station. The train wasn't due for several hours. But I was nervous and wanted to leave myself ample time.

In the end, the train came precisely on schedule. It took all night to get to Harburg, the suburb at the southern approaches of Hamburg where my family lived. There were no incidents.

But when I got off the train, things looked dismal. The streetcars didn't work for lack of electricity, and the station was so badly ruined that nobody could tell me where to leave my suitcase. In the end, I just dropped it in a corner and attacked the four or five kilometres to the house on foot.

It was nearly ten in the morning when I arrived home. Because I had phoned the day before, my mother had prepared breakfast. The food was cold by then, but ever so welcome. We exchanged news about all the things that had happened since we had seen each other last; and I remember my mother joking about my expanded girth, telling evidence of the generous provisions allocated to an Austrian army hospital. When the wail of the air-raid sirens sounded later that morning, we were in a happy mood as we left the house to take shelter in our backyard dugout.

Nobody had actually ever used the shelter, everybody preferring the house. So why did we go there that day? I don't remember.

There had been some bombing the night before; perhaps my mother had suddenly become fearful of being buried alive underneath her own home. Maybe she had wanted to please her husband by giving his cherished dugout a try. My father had always been proud of the structure, built by his workers according to the best specifications available at the outbreak of the war. Visitors had been led into the garden to view and admire it, though that had been years back, when nobody could have foreseen the intensity of future air attacks.

Or, perhaps my father had suggested the dugout earlier in the day. The three-story house with its glass roof and split-level basement didn't provide much protection. In any case, when the time came, my mother simply said, "Let's go to the bunker." It is unlikely that I had any opinion myself, one way or the other.

The shelter was a four-by-eight-foot hole in the ground, lined with railway ties and reinforced with steel beams. Two benches afforded a modicum of comfort, but there was no door—the idea being that if it wasn't there, it couldn't block the exit. Instead, a passage of narrow steps met the bunker at a certain angle meant to ward off fragments from nearby explosions.

Despite the attack the night before, we were surprisingly relaxed. There hadn't been a lot of heavy bombing in recent months. According to my mother, rumour had it that the Allies, for their own purposes, wanted to spare the ultra-modern oil refineries down at the harbour, the giant rubber plant, and other valuable factories to be dismantled and shipped abroad as soon as the hostilities ended. Whether anybody really believed those tales, I don't know; looking back, they certainly made a lot more sense than the events that actually unfolded.

That day, the dugout wasn't hit, although it did not survive the war. But the air pressure resulting from hundreds of explosions around us was such that it would have blown in the door, had there been one. Judged from that standpoint, the shelter was a success, having been designed, I assume, according to the trench war experiences of World War I. On the other hand, little thought had been spared for sissy considerations like the psychological fallout of modern warfare. Indeed, my mother and I were exposed to an acoustic assault far exceeding anything Dante, creating brilliant verses about God, men and hell, could ever have imagined. The physical results of the raid—the flattened buildings, the wounded and dead—we didn't learn about until later.[4]

"When you hear them, that means they are going to hit somewhere else," my mother explained. Now, as I coax my mind back into that horrid bunker, time and details become vague. How long did it last? One hour? Two? How many hits were nearer than, say, two hundred metres? I cannot even remember with certainty whether the walls of the dugout shifted, although I do remember the strong tremors and the sand that rained in from the roof and through the cracks between the ties.

There is one image, though, that I will never forget: my mother, then forty-nine years old, wrapped in an old wool coat with a black Persian lamb collar, clutching a handbag containing her papers and other vital belongings, while keeping a small overnight suitcase stashed beneath the bench. She probably looked like any other middle-aged housewife dressed in clothes worn down by five years of rationing. What was so different that day was the way she conducted herself.

To say that her behavior was extraordinary would miss the mark. My mother was never "ordinary," so the term would start from a faulty premise. In fact, she was, and would remain, the most fearful and insecure person I have ever known. Minor things like the purchase of a dress—worse, the wearing of it later—caused her painful anguish. All year, every year, she was haunted by the thought of having to choose yet another birthday present for her wealthy sister-in-law. When the momentous occasion neared, she would visit the most exclusive china shop in town and, after a lengthy discussion with the manager, invariably end up with a gold-crusted vase that was vulgar, unwanted, and way over budget. To be fair, her sister-in-law tried hard to press a somewhat overly energetic solicitude upon the much younger woman. But her husband's great wealth always got in the way.

It all started during the Great Depression, when my father, an independent businessman, had been forced to accept employment from his brother Paul. Ever since, my mother had been withering away. From fine stock herself, she felt oppressed by the ostentation of the nouveaux riches and pressured by the need to reconcile the limits of her middle-class budget with the exigencies of an upper-middle-class lifestyle.

All this analyzing is merely hindsight. At the time, I saw a father who seldom spoke and, if not provoked, was a kind and gentle family man, and a mother unable to express her own needs and desires for fear of making the wrong choices. Maybe she had long since convinced herself that there wasn't any real need for decision-making, that her husband, Walther, was there to protect her. And protect her he did. He was her knight and slave; within the privacy of their home, Helene became queen. It was a unique relationship, a kind of love for which I felt nothing but contempt. Perhaps there were many like them. Perhaps they were not unique at all; today I wonder.

That particular morning, my mother turned into a different person—a person I had never met before and whom she herself, at any other time, might have found difficult to recognize.

"Calm down, please, do calm down," she insisted, again and again. "You must calm yourself. All that racket, it's from bombs that have already passed us, that can't hit us anymore." Her voice was quietly pleading, soothing as though directed at a baby woken by a bad dream. It betrayed no fear, just the desperate desire to reassure. The thing about hearing only bombs that had passed, she must have picked up somewhere;

it had stuck in her mind and it was all she could think of. It was an absurd effort to distract me from the screaming, roaring reality of thousands of bombs tumbling from wave after wave of four-engine planes. There was no respite from the terror, just the same empty words, like a mantra, a lullaby. "Please, be calm. Please."

It's that completely out-of-character picture of my mother, to whom I had never felt particularly close, that has etched itself into my mind: that self-effacing, always wavering, and frequently depressed woman quietly taking charge, defeating hysteria, hers and mine, transforming herself into a font of solace, when solace was far beyond ordinary human strength.

I cried. I don't think I sobbed or did anything theatrical. The tears simply spilled down my face while my chin, hands, legs trembled as though nothing could ever stop them. As it turned out, my mother's naive reassurances proved true: none of the bombs hit us. We heard their piercing shrieks as they passed over our heads, and their violent explosions a few hundred meters further on. The one we wouldn't have heard, because its trajectory would have taken it to the top of our dugout, never came.

The trembling stopped some time later, but I didn't "calm down." Not then, and not for many years afterwards. Perhaps I never got the experience entirely out of my system. They called it shell shock in soldiers who hadn't been able to stand an artillery barrage, who had screamed or run away or shown all sorts of irrational behavior for which they got shot on the spot or sent home, depending on whether they were German or Russian or from some more tender-hearted country.

We never returned to the dugout. At the first sign of an approaching raid, we would run as fast and as far as we could. I ran. Sometimes with my mother trying to catch up, sometimes alone. I couldn't always wait. I wanted to survive, I had to survive. There's nothing in the world as powerful as a young person's will to live.

*   *   *

The raids on our suburb of Harburg continued day and night, and lasted about a week. By the time Allied Bomber Command set its sights on a different target, we had decided to leave town. That is, my mother and I were to leave, while my father would move to the basement of the grain elevator down at the harbour. There were fifty metres of concrete above it, a unique kind of protection from a structure that would turn out to be one of a handful in the area to survive the war. Before our departure there had been some argument about my planned return to Marburg.

"What do you mean, Müller can employ you? What does he want you to do?" my father demanded.

"I have no idea. Writing stuff, probably."

"What 'stuff'?"

I shrugged.

"He's SS or SD, isn't he?"

"Both, I guess. He is branch leader. He's Alex's boss, commander of the *SS Studentenkompanie*. He wants to help me. Can't you see that he's simply trying to be kind?"

"*I* am trying to be kind ... I am trying to help you."

"By sending me with Mami to Bad Pyrmont."

"Exactly."

"I don't want to go to Pyrmont. Or, for that matter, to any other boring spa. Besides, I'll never get permission. They'll come right after me to draft me for some munitions factory probably back at the *Niedersachsenwerk* where I already got that wonderful experience with those thousands of stupid little pieces for our precious J U 52, lining them up for anodizing. Wouldn't that be great—getting killed from noxious fumes before getting killed by the bombs. A hero in the service of the fatherland."

My father, who had always been too preoccupied or indifferent to oppose any of my personal decisions, suddenly became difficult.

"Do you know *anything* about the SD?"

"No. Not a thing. It stands for *Sicherheitsdienst*, security service, I suppose. It's not the Gestapo, if that's what worries you." I had found it necessary to go on the offensive, because although it was true that I didn't know what the SD did, it was also true that I didn't have an entirely good feeling about it.

"I'm not sure either," my father said, "but I believe they spy on people."

I felt the heat rising to my cheeks. Spying. I didn't know what to say.

"Whatever they're doing," my father continued, "I don't think it's such a good idea to get mixed up with these people, now that the war is almost over. What do you think will happen to them once the enemy gets them?"

"They never will!" Young people in Germany still thought reflexively, in terms drilled into them during twelve years of indoctrination. "They won't come *here*, certainly not Marburg."

"I don't know." My father gave up.

He had done—even exceeded—his duty by speaking so openly about things I had never heard mentioned before. Given the political situation, this was quite a brave act. It occurred to me that in his cautious way, he had really gone out on a limb; that in order to protect me, he had put himself into my hands. After all, couldn't I go to Müller and repeat what he had said? Either from stupidity or ideological zeal? It may sound unthinkable now; it surely wasn't then. Children did tell on parents, friends or teachers, or anybody else who provoked them. There were clandestine powers everywhere, watching, whispering, conspiring to trap anybody not totally committed to the Führer and Nazi ideology.

*   *   *

Just before midnight, my mother and I set out for the railway station. Although the trains were still running more or less on time, they were badly overcrowded and largely scheduled for night travel. The drizzle from the cloudy sky turned the dust and debris under our feet into a slippery mush. We were guided by one of my father's workers, who pulled a wooden handcart loaded with our bags. The man carried a flashlight, blacked out but for a narrow slit. By its feeble beam he guided us around craters that blocked the sidewalks, past piles of rubble and ripped-out tramway tracks tangled into grotesque sculptures.

The streets were deserted, their eerie silence assailed by the insensitive clatter of the cart's iron-shod wheels. Nobody spoke, lest we miss the sound of some fast-approaching plane, a fear that was real enough under a warning system that had pretty much broken down. It wasn't the only fear. As the Reich's final collapse drew nearer, and public hysteria grew, the act of leaving a city, though not prohibited, could well be seen as defeatism. Somebody might stop us, question us, demand to see our papers. Nobody did.

We were to part ways in Hanover. From there my mother would board a local train to Bad Pyrmont. My sister Caroline was coming up from Freiburg, where she had almost finished her studies, and would meet her there. Pyrmont was one of Germany's famous health spas, whose palatial hotels had once housed Europe's most prosperous citizens. Until now, I had resisted my mother's pleas to accompany her. The way I imagined the place, it would be filled with elderly people enduring an assortment of balneal tortures, sipping sulphurous water, and offering gratuitous advice to their fellow sufferers.

I was partly right, but mostly I was wrong. I had never been to this or any other spa, but I must have picked up enough tidbits of information to form a pretty accurate picture of things as they once were. They had changed, of course, like everything else.[5] By late fall of 1944, all spas had long been transformed into military hospitals, with huge red crosses on the roofs of their formerly fashionable hotels, demanding protection from enemy action according to the Geneva Convention. Any civilian fortunate enough to find accommodation in a private *Pension* nearby could hope for some degree of safety.

"Why don't you change your mind? I simply cannot understand you." My mother made a last effort as the train slowed on its approach to Hanover station.

"You know my reasons. I want to keep that room." I tried to sound bored; after all, we had been over the same ground many times. "If I'm away for too long, it'll surely be requisitioned. On top of that, I may find a chance to get back into university."

"All you want is to be with Alex."

"And would that be such a crime? Anyway, he isn't even there."

"If he's as noble as you say, he'll be glad to know you are somewhere safe."

"Marburg is as safe as it comes. Besides, it's at least 300 kilometres further south."

"It's not a military hospital town protected by the Red Cross."

"It is so. All the big university clinics have red crosses on their roofs. And anyway, I can't imagine what kind of target there is to bomb in that old place."

She gave up then. Would I have been more vigorous in her stead? More insistent? I doubt it. After all, there were no bets on the relative safety of any particular spot. By now, almost everybody had heard of incidents where people had been hit in the most unlikely hideouts, while their homes in the city remained untouched. My mother had one parting shot left, though.

"I don't like that Müller thing. You have enough money to carry you through until Christmas. Dad will send you more. You don't *need* to go there."

"Sure," I replied with faked indifference.

"Promise?"

"I can't make promises about things I know nothing about. I'll have a talk with Müller and look around, and if I think there's anything spooky about the outfit, I'll find some excuse to get out."

She shrugged. I knew she doubted my bravado, because I did so myself. But I had resolved to be in town if Alex should happen to return. That was really all there was to it, which seemed easy enough to understand.

I stood at a crossroads and made a decision. As it turned out, the road I chose would lead to disaster. It would lead me to Müller and Josephine, to being bombed, imprisoned, and stripped of my dignity as well as my health. It would force upon me some late but authentic insights into Hitler's perfidious Reich, the stench of its disintegration, and, incidentally, an early discontent with the new Bundesrepublik

In 1955, six years after the country's constitutional birth, and well into its rapidly growing prosperity, the government would introduce rearmament and general conscription for the new Bundeswehr. *"I'm not going to America— I'm leaving Germany," I would say in 1957. A harsh assessment then, and still true today. Earlier that year, I had given birth to a son, who would never, never serve in another German army.*

INTERLUDE I
The Nazi Paradox

Historians have collected thousands of facts on Nazi perpetrators, the SS, SD, Gestapo, SA, and other organizations of the Hitler era, as well as on their victims, the persecuted, the dead, and the damaged. Weighty as these accumulated facts and testimonies are, they ignore about sixty to sixty-five million people out of a population of eighty million citizens of the *Grossdeutsche Reich* (Greater Germany) who never experienced anything extraordinary in the villain/victim category. One may have to deduct children under the age of fourteen, but one would still be faced with about two-thirds of the population who, by sheer numbers, would have to be considered the "body and soul of the Third Reich." Out of their ranks came the wildly cheering enthusiasts on the town squares, the marchers on May Day, the civil servants and employees of the national government and of all levels of the Nazi administration, the bloc and air-raid wardens, the leaders of the Hitler Youth, the *Reichsarbeitsdienst*, and hundreds of other Nazi organizations. They were the minor leaders, functionaries, caretakers, watchers, and informers. They were relatively harmless, yet never entirely so, because they possessed what was seen as the highest good in the Third Reich: power. "Small" power, to be sure, but power just the same in a state where "Big" power was always ready to be called upon.

One may assume that these *Mitläufer*, or "fellow travellers" (lowest category in the denazification process), comprised about one-fifth of "ordinary Germans," which still left half the adult population who, during twelve of the most extraordinary years in German history—1933 to 1945—somehow succeeded in avoiding active politics, the affairs of the state, and trouble with its more odious organizations. (I have mentally integrated the German army, the Wehrmacht, into all of the above, since its members—whether professional officers or drafted civilians—fell into the same categories as everybody else.)

After the Hitler-Reich was gone, those forty-or-so million people would claim they had never known anything about Nazi crimes, but had hated the Nazis just the same. The vast majority of my relatives, friends and schoolmates, colleagues and neighbours were among them, as were all of my next of kin. There is no other group of German Hitler contemporaries that, by number and conformity, can be so easily identified— and about whom so little has been told. No Allied court had to deal with them, few biographies or autobiographies emanated from their ranks (though many of the more thoughtful ones put down their memories in privately kept scripts). They were the inconspicuous, hardworking, obedient masses; they went along, when called, and stayed away, when not. On May 8, 1945, they cut the umbilical cord that had tethered the "ordinary German" to the Führer state, and started a new life, as though the old one had never existed. They rejected the concept of collective guilt by the sheer size of their collective innocence—forty million "exonerated" (an official term—if not an official number—of the denazification process) Hitler contemporaries, many of whom would later say: "Not everything was bad under Hitler."

What influence did National Socialism have on their professions, incomes, families, hobbies? Which programs did they like beside such well-known achievements as the *Autobahn*, full employment, order, cleanliness, and the absence of crime? What did they feel about *Gleichschaltung*, the enforced submission of all political, social, or cultural diversity to prescribed standards of National Socialist ideology, which, within one year, had conquered every aspect of German life? There are no statistics, there was no polling. What did they really think about the Party's outlawing of strikes and assemblies, its policy of frozen wages and fixed ties to the place of employment? Did these measures split the famous *deutsche Volksgemeinschaft*, the new "community of the people," by favoring the capitalists at the expense of the workers, allegedly the most steadfast supporters of the National Socialist German Workers' Party, NSDAP? As Engelmann writes, steel giant Krupp paid its 43,400 workers sixty-seven million *Reichsmark* in 1933, two million less than it paid 36,000 workers in 1932, the last year of the strike-ridden Weimar Republic. In 1937, despite greatly increased productivity and a sixty-hour workweek, wages were still below those of 1931/32, the worst winter of the Depression.[6] Protected by the new government's harsh labour laws, industrialists enjoyed a rapid recovery. Was National Socialism, that new political concept, oriented towards the right or left? Who among the new leaders was nationalist, and who was socialist? Hitler? Röhm? Strasser? Were people confused? These were complex questions; they still are.

There can be no doubt that the nationalist component of the new National Socialist German Workers' Party was extremely popular, particularly among the broad middle class. It was the driving force that united Germany after years of political paralysis during the multi-party Weimar Republic and made it "so powerful that it took the unnatural and temporary alliance of Liberal Democracy and Russian Communism ... to defeat and conquer it. Neither side could do it alone."[7] Although the Hitler party called its new program *Nationalsozialismus* (National Socialism)—for merely euphonic reasons or because of different priorities at the time[8]—it might perhaps have been more truthful to speak of *Sozialnationalismus* (Social Nationalism), a name that would have made things clearer about Hitler's intentions. (It also might have soothed the fears of the bourgeoisie about the disappearance of private property and class barriers.) Between 1933 and 1945, the German people were gripped by nationalism in a way that is impossible to imagine in any Western democracy. Millions of pictures and documents attest to this phenomenon, which can hardly be denied or belittled by any Hitler contemporary. Whether it was a singular outbreak of passionate fervor provoked by the devilish nature of National Socialism and the demagoguery of the Führer (as many Germans maintain), or whether it was due to some special German character inclined to bring forth strange and dangerous political cultures (as non-Germans have feared), goes beyond the scope of these discussions.

It seems worthwhile, however, to reflect on the second component in *Nationalsozialismus*, which has been much less investigated, but played such a tremendous role in people's lives during the pre-war years and well into the early 1940s. I don't know what people expected—or feared— from *Sozialismus*, a word that carries such an ominous political weight today. As it turned out, the Nazi version had little in common with what the true socialists, who desperately battled the Nazis' ascent to power, had in mind. *Gleichschaltung* aside, there was no effort to purge capitalism. Rather than expropriate private companies, the state built and ran huge new enterprises like the *Reichswerke Hermann Göring*. With one million employees it was the largest industrial enterprise in Europe.

Between 1933 and 1939, Roosevelt's New Deal restored the American economy and helped thirteen million unemployed people to get back into the mainstream of society. Similar programs were introduced in Germany soon after Hitler's *Machtergreifung* (seizure of power)—albeit brought in and enforced by dictatorial powers rather than legislated against a resisting Congress. Hitler started his government on January 30, 1933; Franklin D. Roosevelt followed suit five weeks later on March 4. Who emulated whom at the time is hard to decide; it may well be that the terrible economic conditions in both countries simply forced the hands of both. The German programs do not easily fit today's public image of Nazism, yet they created the very foundation on which Hitler's early successes rested. Indeed, one might argue that it was the linkage of a fervent nationalism (mostly gripping the middle classes) with a number of progressive social programs (directed foremost at the lower classes) that brought about the National Socialist "conditioning" of millions of ordinary Germans—even if those millions never saw themselves as Nazis and later refused to accept responsibility for a part they had played without ever having realized they were playing it.

On the surface—meaning without the "deep mystery" of the Führer cult—everyday life under National Socialism was ordinary enough, and largely unaffected by the ideological "Nazi stuff" that, if truth be told, most people were unable to define. Ordinary Germans disliked and distrusted the faceless bureaucrats, the same as citizens everywhere have always done.

For the more specific questions about their thoughts and attitudes under Nazi rule, there are probably few answers that wouldn't immediately be contested dependent on what people like to remember or prefer to forget.

How, for instance, did they feel about the daily barrage of propaganda, the ever more shameless grab for control over their personal lives? Did they notice it while it went on, or only much later after having lived through the consequences? Did people object? Most, I suspect, were taken too much by surprise by the stream of new directives that demanded careful attention and observance. Amazed and intimidated by the activism of the National Socialist "revolution," all they could do was hope that it would lead to a better Germany. And in a way it did. The rich got richer, the middle class—after the ravages of the Depression—regained its prosperity, the industrial proletariat became the self-respecting *Deutsche Arbeiterschaft* (German community of workers), while (non-Jewish) private ownership remained generally untouched. If those were the economic conditions, they would certainly go a long way towards explaining the rapidly growing Hitler cult. We know about the huge rearmament programs and subsequent full employment that generated much national pride. But seeing one's own pockets getting fuller surely meant a lot more to ordinary Germans than dry statistics, however pleasing. Were people happy?

Sebastian Haffner,[9] a German writing for *The Observer* in England between 1938 and 1961 and certainly no admirer of Hitler, credits the Führer with the "economic miracle" of the 1930s. "The transition from depression to prosperity had been accomplished without inflation at perfectly stable wages and prices." The years 1935 to 1937 were the "good" Nazi period: Germany did not produce cannons *instead* of butter, but cannons *and* butter, he writes. I agree. A child then, I clearly remember the pre-war tables at Christmas laden with luxury items, from cameras and opera glasses to gold watches and jewellery.

The word "inflation" was never mentioned in our merchant-class family. Later, say after 1941, the growing scarcity of goods made people realize that they had more money than there were things to spend it on. Yet no one used the dreaded I-word. After Germany's catastrophic experience in 1923, when billions of *Reichsmark* would no longer buy a loaf of bread and all private savings were wiped out, it became an article of faith that the National Socialists would never cause another inflation (just as they would never cause another Versailles). That conviction was so deeply rooted that even towards the end of the war, when soldiers lit their cigarettes on paper money, inflation remained a non-issue. Was there inflation? Yes and no. At that time, a huge cash supply faced almost no goods, which raised the black market value of government-rationed items by a factor of more than one hundred.[10] Yet store prices, wages, and rents remained unchanged. No new bills with large numbers of zeros were printed, thereby masking the true state of Germany's bankruptcy and keeping the I-word out of people's minds. How could that have happened?

The answer probably lies in the combination of a collective, anti-inflationary mindset that subconsciously welcomed the deception, with years of sophisticated management by the *Reichsbank*. I grew up in Flensburg next to the Danish border and the respectable Danish Crown, and I remember the Nazi government's tight currency controls, which allowed us the purchase of only ten crowns (six *Reichsmark*) per person per day for our frequent excursions to Denmark's lovely sandy beaches. Larger sums, say for a holiday, required formal applications that could take weeks or months to be approved and were limited to the smallest possible amount. Was the *Reichsmark* soft? The official slogan at the time "The value of the *Reichsmark* is backed by the value of the German labor" probably meant that the currency was artificially stabilized under full employment and strict import/export controls. Of course, once half of Europe had been conquered, the *Reichsbank*, after appropriating huge amounts of foreign gold, simply dictated all terms of payment.

Although most members of Hitler's cabinet had no popular profile, there were a few who gained public respect, popularity (Göring), hatred (Goebbels), or contempt (Ley, Sauckel, Streicher). Among those who were highly regarded was the president of the *Reichsbank* and the general director for wartime economy, Hjalmar Schacht. Hitler allegedly had little interest in, or knowledge of, the country's economic affairs, but he was fortunate enough to attract talented financiers and bankers whom he allowed to do their jobs. (Schacht later established contacts with the resistance movement and, in July 1944, was imprisoned by the Nazis. The judges at the International War Crimes Tribunal in Nuremberg declared him "not guilty," but, in 1946, a German court sentenced him to eight years in a labor camp. He was released in 1950).

While Schacht was respected, the young and good-looking *Reichsminister* for armaments and munitions, Albert Speer, was popular. He took over from the highly regarded Fritz Todt, who built the *Autobahn* and the *Westwall*, and was killed in a plane crash in 1942.

The *Autobahnen* were probably Hitler's most celebrated innovation. Esthetically pleasing and well engineered, the modern road system engendered the new image of the Führer as a forward-looking man who took a keen interest in advanced technologies and rapid progress. This was in stark contrast to the artistic elite's perception of Hitler as a mediocre painter and petit-bourgeois, who had purged Germany's galleries of all modern art, notably Expressionism, which he considered "degenerate." The next logical step to make use of those fabulous new highways, was the design of a car that would be inexpensive enough to find a mass market. Bohemian-born Austrian Ferdinand Porsche was the gifted designer who came up with the prototype of the Volkswagen "Beetle" that, after the war, would become a cult item for 20 million buyers. During the thirties, however, the Porsche-team, despite much redesigning and fiddling with numbers, never succeeded in bringing down the estimated production cost to Hitler's suggested retail price of 1,000 *Reichsmark*. Before the new *Volkswagenwerk* was ready to build the first mass-produced civilian automobile, it was caught up by the war. Instead, the factory constructed the *Kübelwagen*, a lightweight kind of Jeep, whose air-cooled engine made it ideal for the Russian winter. Meanwhile, 300,000 "Volkswagen-savers" paid five *Reichsmark* every month towards the future ownership of a car. Their RM 18 million yearly savings disappeared in the construction and operation of the *Volkswagenwerk* and, after the war, were lost like most other German savings. (In 1961, *Volkswagenwerk* finally settled the claims of former *Volkswagensparer* by allowing a discount of 15 per cent, or DM 600, against the purchase price of a new "Beetle.")

Whereas Hitler's popularity was boosted by the construction of the *Autobahnen* and the design of the "people's car," the hoped-for infrastructural benefits of the new roads did not materialize. The *Autobahn* network was spotty at best and existed in mostly unconnected stretches of not always primary importance. Though construction was accelerated in the late 1930s to prepare for the forthcoming war, the military preferred the safe and reliable German railways for the mass transport of their troops and materiel. Once the war had been declared, gasoline controls and the requisition of privately owned cars put a quick end to civilian road transportation. Not until six years later, with the German rail system more than seventy per cent destroyed, did the *Autobahnen* finally come into their own, when heavy enemy armor and huge motorized convoys enjoyed the smooth penetration of German lands.

Generally speaking, little was planned or achieved by the government's national programs that was not, in the minds of the population (as well as in fact), directly or indirectly connected with the preparations for an inevitable war. But as long as the Führer, in his widely publicized speeches, claimed only peaceful intentions, Germans considered it prudent to keep their fears to themselves.

Certainly among the most beloved social programs were the heavily subsidized group travels offered by *KDF,* or *Kraft durch Freude* (literally: Strength through Joy), for workers and low-ranking employees. Encouraging people who never ventured outside their immediate neighborhoods to discover and enjoy faraway parts of their country created a great deal of pride in the fatherland. It also brought new wealth to often poorly developed resort areas. Nowadays, wherever one ventures, one is likely to encounter some well-heeled, well-guided German travel groups, the more sophisticated descendants of the still fondly remembered *KDF* program. In fact, mass tourism was the one Nazi achievement that Germans quickly reactivated after the war, polishing that gem into the obsessive wanderlust of today's entire population.

But the ever-present war rumors were linked even to such heartwarming programs as *KDF*: When its fat and ugly patron, labor minister Robert Ley (who later committed suicide in his Nuremberg prison cell by hanging himself from the toilet pipe), commissioned two large passenger ships to the *KDF* program, people immediately recognized in them future troopships. I don't remember what happened to the *Robert Ley*. Her sister vessel, the *Wilhelm Gustloff*, however, became tragically famous when, overloaded with six thousand desperate refugees, she was sunk by Russian submarines near the East Prussian coast in April 1945.

Certainly the most important social initiative of the new Hitler government was the *Winterhilfswerk* or, for short, *Winterhilfe*, "Winter Relief," a giant relief program not unlike today's welfare programs, soup kitchens, the United Way, and dozens of other charitable organizations all rolled into one. In the early and mid-1930s, the need for such broad-ranging assistance was urgent and huge. I clearly remember the beggars who regularly came to our house. There were chalk marks on the pavement outside, directing the unfortunates to homes of some proven charity. When the bell rang at our house, it was the maid who answered the door. But I must have peeked many times, because in my mind I can still see those silent figures and the humble movements of their hands. The maid, young and from a working-class background herself, nodded, closed the door, and, after a couple of minutes, returned with a rye-bread sandwich thickly covered with lard. The beggar would tip his rumpled cap and depart. The maid closed the door. No words were spoken.

After Hitler seized power on January 30, 1933, begging became *verboten*. It was considered as beneath the dignity of the reconstructed *deutsche Arbeiter* (German worker). With or without the individual worker's consent, the country's labor force collectively bade farewell to the *proletarian Internationale* by turning itself into the backbone of the new *national-sozialistische Bewegung* (revolutionary movement). Instead of their former militant unions, the workers now had the NS *Arbeitsfront* to look after their affairs. They were promised—and soon got—employment and protection against layoffs in return for loyalty to the employer, frozen wages, and laws against strikes and assemblies. This guaranteed a stable work force for the country's rearmament industry. As a bonus, workers were granted what they had long been pining for: a free, fully paid holiday on May 1, *Der Tag der deutschen Arbeit* (Day of German Labor), celebrated with marches and speeches under a canopy of swastika flags.

One small but highly visible part of the multifaceted *Winterhilfe* was the *Eintopf-Sonntag,* the once-a-month Sunday, when every family was supposed to eat one of those famous German stews (cooked in "one pot") and donate the saved amount of one *Reichsmark* to the *Winterhilfe*. I also remember the *Arbeiterkinder*, (unemployed) workers' children who, one shy little kid at a time, came to us regularly for Sunday dinner. I can still hear my mother on Christmas Day urging us to put away our presents, lest the poor child be saddened by the absence of gifts in his or her own home. I tell myself that we were encouraged to part with something, though I cannot recall any details. Maybe we weren't—or didn't. I was eight or nine years old then, but remembering those intimidated kids and our childish efforts at "socializing" still makes me feel embarrassed.

Winterhilfe crept into people's lives and pockets with never-ending demands for money and volunteering, demands that were impossible to reject. Once economic recovery had become universal, people saw it simply as another means of raising money for armament. The *Arbeiterkinder* stopped coming, but there were still the "one-pot Sundays" and the subsequent collection of the saved *Reichsmark*. Voluntary donations for all kinds of purposes—familiar to every North American, but then and still today, much less customary in socially pampered Germany—became a growth industry, something between a secondary tax and state-sanctioned extortion, executed and closely monitored by Party functionaries. These were the dreaded *Senftöpfe,* or "mustard pots" (for their brown uniforms), canvassing on Sunday mornings, the collected amounts clearly marked beside every name. My father was always number three on their list, after the *Kreisleiter* (regional Nazi leader) and the president of the police, our next-door neighbor. Like them, he "voluntarily" donated RM 50, one-twelfth of his monthly salary or almost half our rent.

For the children there were the *Sammeltage*, the days when we were excused from school in order to collect money on the streets by selling small pins for ten *Pfennig* (cents) each. Invariably, at Christmas we were out hawking sweet little ornaments for the tree. Artfully carved and gaily painted, they were produced in cottage industries in the country's most depressed villages in the hills of east-central Germany. It was the first make-work program I encountered, meant to revive and cultivate traditional skills before they became extinct because of mass production elsewhere.

A different kind of *Winterhilfe*, one the population responded to with a truly heartwarming readiness, was the collection of fur coats, woollen blankets and all sorts of warm clothes for the German army, which had become stuck outside Moscow without the necessary supplies during the winter of 1941 to 1942. After more than two years of overrunning, encircling and destroying the enemy, Germany had experienced its first reality check. Grim comparisons with Napoleon's dreadful retreat from Russia preoccupied all of us.

By now, there was no doubt that a high percentage of all that collected money no longer went to the needy, but into armament payments. Yet, while every thinking person must have had some notion of the tremendous cost of the *Blitzkriege,* which eventually engulfed most of Europe, the subject was never officially mentioned. There were no war bonds for people to buy—and lose, as there were in World War I. Did my father ever say: "Who in the world is going to pay for all this?" He probably did, but not in my presence. In Nazi parlance, the German soldier, united in courage and selflessness with the German worker, was winning the war. There was heroism and sacrifice, and even death (the toll rapidly increasing after Stalingrad in January 1943); but, in the end there could only be victory. Merely to hint at something as prosaic as huge—and possibly unpayable—production bills came dangerously close to questioning the invincibility of the Wehrmacht and the omnipotence of the National Socialist Reich.

If large programs such as *Winterhilfe, Kraft durch Freude,* or the construction of the *Autobahnen* were ultimately connected with the war effort, there was one social initiative that, even in hindsight, could probably have stood on its own merits: The home building program that had already been planned or started during the Weimar Republic. These were massive projects, frequently, but not always, directed at large factory populations. Today, whenever I see rows and rows of smart little single-family homes, I am reminded of *Hermann-Göring-Kolonien.* There were, of course, many other names for these tidy colonies, but this one stuck as utterly typical for Nazi-built lower-middle-class developments featuring little white houses with red-tiled roofs and symmetrically arranged windows, all neatly arrayed in proper little gardens suggesting uniformity in body and soul. At the time, they created tremendous pride—for those who built them and for those who bought them at artificially low mortgages that kept the construction industry abuzz. In 1942, three years into the war and during my last year of high school, my entire grade was taken out of school for four months. Our orders were to help the mothers of large working-class families by allowing the poor women a bit of a breather. I was lucky. My employer had once been a maid herself; now, she simply refused to see the tables turned. Mama Eggers was a very small, very sweet woman, old before her time and stricken with a heart ailment. But what I remember most, was her truly boundless delight when she and her family of four little carrot-topped kids were allotted a brand new three-bedroom apartment with a private washroom, playgrounds nearby, and clean air to breathe.

Was she grateful? Of course, though I doubt she knew to whom. Was she a Nazi? Or better yet, was she a true believer in National Socialist ideology? Were she and her husband rewarded as good Party members, or bribed to become such? I can't tell. What I do remember, though, is my father's dry observation: "My workers hate Hitler."

In twelve Nazi years, I had never heard anything so outspoken, so unequivocal. That statement was simply and totally impossible, and it bowled me over. It must have been as late as 1944, when workers in big industrial cities were fed up, overtired and overworked from long shifts and endless air raids, not to mention constantly worried about their homes, which were usually located in the densely populated and heavily bombed areas of the inner core. At least one specimen of the celebrated *deutsche Arbeiter* had let it be known that he hated Hitler. It was like something to chew on, too big to be swallowed. My father didn't elaborate, neither did he repeat his remark. Whatever else I thought of him, that moment of revelation—of insight into something utterly mysterious and unfathomably dreadful—could never be taken away from him by the passage of time.

One last anecdote about the success or failure of National Socialism's massive social scheme to entice the German worker: On March 13, 1939, the famous battleship *Bismarck* was launched from Hamburg's shipyard Blohm & Voss. The event was to be attended by Hitler himself on his private yacht *Aviso Grille*. To allow us a better view of the momentous spectacle, my uncle had rented a harbor launch to bring family and office staff as close to the site as possible. It probably wasn't all that close. We never saw Hitler, and the monstrous ship, not yet outfitted with all its mighty superstructure, looked rather unimpressive. But it is something entirely different that I remember—unremarkable at the time, but crystallizing later as a drop of unsoiled truth: "Hitler hates coming to Hamburg," someone remarked. "The workers in this town are still red, and he knows it. That's why he doesn't like to show his face." Not only were most of Hamburg's thousands of dock and shipyard workers unreformed Social Democrats in the late 1930s, they remained that way throughout the war; they still are today.

After the launch, Hitler never visited Hamburg again

* * *

In recent decades, two closely related terms have entered the German vocabulary to describe a state governed by criminals along unlawful or outright criminal lines: *Verbrecherstaat* (criminal state) and *Unrechtsstaat* (unlawful state)[11] refer almost exclusively to the moral and political aberration called the Third Reich that emerged in 1933 and collapsed after a dozen years of unspeakable crimes and horrors. It was succeeded by the legally constituted Federal Republic of Germany, the new German *Rechtsstaat* (lawful state),[12] also referred to as *Verfassungsstaat*, a state identified by its exemplary legal constitution.

There is little in my memory to suggest that during the Third Reich a significant number of my contemporaries saw the NS state as it is described above. Were we all blind? Were we simply *Mitläufer* (followers), active or passive collaborators in an all-embracing criminal system? Or were things much more ambiguous and complicated? I feel I have to give a troubled nod to all of the above. At the same time I hear the distant echo of my father's quiet voice: *"Das sind alles Verbrecher"* (They are all criminals). When did he say this? On June 22, 1941, when Hitler attacked an unprepared Russia? When he declared war on America six months later? Or, a year after that, when he turned down General Paulus's reasonable request for withdrawal from Stalingrad to save his troops from certain disaster? Did my father say it *during* the Nazi Reich, when it would have been an enlightened, but life-threatening remark? Or afterwards, perhaps during the Nuremberg Trials, when it had long become the expected thing to say? I can't remember. It would be interesting though, even important, to know what an "ordinary" German thought. I know what many of the famous and erudite thought from their later autobiographies; what they claimed to have observed and analyzed, even prophesied from the late-1920s on. They were people with high connections and deep insights, worlds removed from my own middle-class environment.

Rechtsstaat and *Unrechtsstaat* are terms that refer to the constitutionality of a state and its willingness or unwillingness to uphold, and adhere to, universally recognized legal standards. Having given that definition, I will now draw a general picture of the legal circumstances of the Third Reich, and—more importantly—the people's feelings about them.

The Hitler state was born on January 30, 1933, under the constitutional laws of the tottering Weimar Republic. (The Nazis themselves boasted about their *Machtergreifung*, or seizure of power, suggesting a bold coup d'état instead of a rather bourgeois act of state.) The state died on May 8, 1945, exactly twelve years, three months and one week later, after the unconditional surrender of the once mighty Wehrmacht to the Allied commanders of Britain, the United States, and Russia. Between 1933 and the beginning of World War II on September 1, 1939, the Nazi government maintained diplomatic relations with every important state in the world, including the Vatican. It recognized—but often ignored—sovereignty rights, and signed—but frequently broke—international agreements.[13] In short, Hitler's Germany behaved like a legitimate and powerful, though ill-mannered and arrogant, state, which other governments tried in vain to soothe through flattery or appeasement.

From the outset, its greatest asset was its bureaucracy. Germany's highly educated public service, superbly trained according to Prussian standards of civil morality and informed by the legal principles handed down from the Kaiserreich, reassured people inside and outside the country. Murder, robbery, theft, rape, child abuse, and other crimes were duly punished the way they had always been, though frequently now under more strictly applied laws or a less lenient judiciary, resulting in lengthy prison terms. This "making the streets safe again" activism (which included harsh penalties against abortion and homosexuality) was clearly welcomed by the population. It is less clear, however, how many people knew, or cared, about the Gestapo's arbitrary interference with the civilian justice system when it sent prisoners to concentration camps for indefinite stays, often after they had served their time in a regular penal institution. (For many years, the population readily accepted the Nazi propaganda that the concentration camps were mostly intended for habitual criminals and communist rabble rousers who could not be let out on the streets.)

After the failed attempt at democracy by the Weimar Republic (the German governing system between 1919 and 1933), with its frequent elections, liberal mores, social unrest and political polarization, a great number of people were highly appreciative of the political and social peace promised and delivered by the new National Socialist leadership. It may be worth mentioning that the law-enforcing institutions of the Weimar Republic had already shown a strong bias towards the national parties on the right. Assassinations (Rosa Luxemburg, Karl Liebknecht, Matthias Erzberger and Walter Rathenau, to name only a few of the victims), illegal marches and bloody brawls—including Hitler's own failed Munich putsch on November 9, 1923—had often been treated with a great deal of leniency not granted perpetrators on the political left.[14] After January 30, 1933, the new Hitler government quickly released previously convicted Nazi brawlers and killers, while their own murdered comrades were elevated to the status of national martyrs.[15] Meanwhile, Nazi Storm Troopers (SA) carried out vicious purges against old-time Communists. Many left-of-center moderates and intellectuals were also denounced as enemies of the people and held responsible for the "political and moral decay"of the previous two decades. Thus, tens of thousands were dragged from their homes, away from their typewriters and printing presses, their labs and pulpits, and sent off to concentration camps. Another group that had been singled out long before 1933 was Germany's Jewish population. The "non-Aryan" blood of half a million Jews made them "undesirable and undeserving" of full German citizenship and protection. Though the far-sighted ones recognized the writing on the wall and left the country early, the majority stayed put, hoping that things would calm down. And they did calm down—for a while. The introduction of the Nuremberg Laws on September 15, 1935,[16] and the Olympic Games in Berlin and Garmisch-Partenkirchen in 1936 (attended by tens of thousands of foreigners) put a temporary restraint on the all-out persecution already waiting in the wings.

"Quiet and order" (*Ruhe und Ordnung*) have traditionally enjoyed an extraordinary status in German society. While hundreds of thousands feared for their welfare and freedom, even their lives, a rapidly increasing number of ordinary citizens wholeheartedly supported the rough measures of the new Nazi government, which was intent on cleansing Germany of her unsavory, "un-German" elements. These undesirables included communists, socialists, trade unionists, criminals, perverts, libertarians—and, of course, the Jews, though, as Peter Novick points out, during the first years of the Hitler regime, they were, for whatever reason, not at the top of the Nazis' long list of enemies.[17]

It would be nice to be able to tell today's readers that people were upset, that they banded together to protest, to protect their friends, colleagues and neighbors, whose lives or careers were suddenly in danger. Surely, such things happened; here and there, they may even have done some good. But, by and large, "quiet and order" ruled the day. After all, Hitler had been elected to do *something* about the dissolving political, social and moral order, and—to quote a much-loved German idiom—*Wo gehobelt wird, da fallen Späne*, or "You can't make an omelette without breaking eggs." Everybody understood that simple wisdom, and most were willing to accept its consequences. Indeed, the aggressive, even ruthless measures of the new government were seen as reassuring rather than alarming by the ordinary—that is, politically and racially "uninvolved"—German. Together with the rapidly growing prosperity and social stability described earlier in this chapter, this new experience of order and safety, even predictability, soon created a wave of optimism, a sense of feeling good that was quite alien to the habitually skeptical German spirit. It did not take long for the government to exploit this new confidence, stirring it up into a huge wave of enthusiasm and national pride that generated the euphoria of the 1936 Olympics. The triumphant mood would culminate at victory in France in June 1940, after which it would only slowly and reluctantly abate until the fall of Stalingrad in January 1943, when it would drop dramatically, never to recover.

How could that kind of collectivism, conformity of thought and ambition, the need to belong, and to fall in line, occur so quickly among a people of seventy million, historically plagued by more tribal and religious differences than any other major European country? The answers are difficult and varied, depending on whether one blames the naivety of the people, the timidity of the opposition parties, the aloofness of the churches, or the instability of Germany's first democratic system which, in 1933, yearned for a "firm hand" at the levers of power. In addition to those opinions, there are also a number of irrefutable facts: Years before the Hitler government attained power, an elaborate National Socialist party network had been established to organize marches, rallies, demonstrations, and speeches attended by ever-increasing numbers of Party faithfuls. Since the early 1920s, their brown uniforms and red swastika flags had fought for the domination of all public spaces, forcing themselves into the public consciousness as a new and powerful phenomenon that could be admired or feared, even despised—the initial reaction of many—but not ignored. When Hitler's long-anticipated *Machtergreifung* on January 30, 1933, finally occurred with a minority cabinet of only two Nazi ministers besides Hitler himself as Reich Chancellor,[18] the huge party organization was well-established and prepared for instant action. I was seven at the time, but clearly recall the long torchlight procession that wound along the narrow street where I was allowed to watch from the window of our nanny's home. This happened to be in Flensburg, then a city of 60,000, but similar demonstrations of the new Nazi might took place all over Germany. There would never be another Nazi event watched *live*—and remembered with so much enthusiasm or foreboding—by so many.

It wasn't a one-off extravaganza, though. Suddenly, the brownshirts were everywhere. Within months, new Nazi hierarchies began to duplicate, penetrate, supersede, or supplant all functions and structures of the German *Rechtsstaat* with its affiliated organizations and institutions, nationally, provincially and—most perniciously and in-your-face—locally. Their stream of new rules and regulations—enforced, if necessary, by thuggish storm troopers, but mostly followed by a docile and somewhat stunned population—soon reached into every citizen's private life, interfered with industry and commerce, influenced education, science and technology, controlled the media, and dictated all standards for literature and the arts. Had the nation's economic recovery been the initial excuse for all this planning, organizing, rationing, and restricting, extensive preparations for a possible war, and eventually the war itself, soon created an ever-increasing pressure to co-operate. Mild jokes and guarded complaints directed at the Nazi system were tolerated, but not everywhere and less so after the war broke out; they became life-endangering as defeat drew nearer. But, whatever the reason or depth of such personal resentment, it seldom gelled into a concerted revolt by even a handful of ordinary people. As time went on, the frightening image of tens of thousands of Nazi informers and SS enforcers implanted itself in people's minds. Yet, did I ever hear a remark, even a carefully worded one, that we were actually living in a "police state"? I did not. Did any of my friends or family ever allude to Himmler's "state within a state"? They didn't, ever. After more than five decades, I may be vague about many things; but of those I am quite certain. The reason is that these expressions were well-known to every German high school student duly instructed about Joseph Fouché, the dreaded Minister of Police of French revolutionary infamy. *They* had their *Schreckens-herrschaft* (reign of terror)—*we* had a law-and-order Führer state. The vast majority of ordinary Germans, regardless of what they would later claim, never made the connection, never recognized what was right before their eyes. The relentless indoctrination by the schools, universities, media and, of course, Goebbels's Ministry of People's Enlightenment and Propaganda had long succeeded in *Gleichschaltung*, in having the masses march to the tune of one single piper. There were few, indeed, who managed to keep their minds unspoiled by the pressures and exhortations that excluded every uncontrolled information or social association, let alone political alternative.

With even more fury and bluster, that hypothetical ordinary German would have rejected the notion of living in a *Verbrecherstaat*. Though many had heard the word "gassing,"[19] and everybody knew about the deportations of the Jews and other atrocities inside and outside the concentration camps, a large majority of the people, if asked, would almost certainly have insisted that they were living in a *Rechtsstaat*, a law-abiding state. After all, they had voted for Hitler to give them quiet and order, and quiet and order they had got. There were no known incidents of civic unrest during the mass flight from German-occupied Eastern territories, no wide-scale looting in the chaos of area bombings; even the military surrender of one German city after another occurred in an orderly manner. The Third Reich stood on a mountain of regulations and legal orders; nothing could possibly happen that had not been previously endorsed by some authorized official. As the vast majority of civil servants would later insist, none of them had ever experienced feelings of guilt for their part in the atrocities, since everyone had done his duty, stood his place, followed the law, and executed rules and orders that were carefully filed in stacks of binders, every text clearly indicating its origin and signed and stamped by someone higher up.[20] In Prussian-styled Germany, an order was an order; like a dogma, no questions asked. Unless you were the Prince of Homburg—the hero of Heinrich von

Kleist's famous eighteenth-century drama, who attacked *against* his sovereign's express order, won the battle, and was *pardoned* for his unpardonably un-Prussian action—you did as you were told.[21]

The term *Verbrecherstaat* is a postwar invention. Though linguistically it does not exist, it has become a cliché that tends to simplify, even trivialize, the crux of a Nazi paradox that must perplex everyone who makes a serious stab at understanding Nazi Germany's ethical and legal mechanisms. It is a fact that the Third Reich was served by an army of well-trained officials, a great number of whom possessed multiple law degrees and had distinguished careers, an upper middle-class background (many with aristocratic titles), and a worldly culture. Collectively, they observed and executed not only the traditional laws of the land written at the start of the century, but also the large body of orders introduced by Hitler's government. If *Verbrecherstaat* conjures up an image of murderous warlords rampaging the land, this image is dead wrong: Nobody under German jurisdiction "rampaged"; indeed, nobody who carried arms moved outside a tight web of orders and directives. As Hannah Arendt describes in her remarkably astute analysis of "the banality of evil,"[22] Himmler's killing commandos, the SS *Einsatzgruppen* in Poland and Russia, were "terrifyingly normal" people, who, in their own eyes and in the eyes of their superiors in Berlin, acted in a perfectly disciplined fashion and just followed orders. There were records kept for every slaughter, turning the genocide of the "inferior races" (Jews, Slavs, gypsies) into a well-planned, well-organized military action ordered by some highly trained, well-educated officer,[23] probably married with children.

The Nazi state, with its legions of diligent, loyal servants, where everybody and everything was subjected to the most stringent rules and controls, worked like a conjuror's stage: Behind the smoke and mirrors of the perceived *Rechtsstaat*, which the vast majority of Germans respected, trusted, and relied upon for the orderly guidance of their ordinary lives, existed another stage where the directives for unspeakable horrors were planned and executed by yet another army of duly appointed *Amtsträger* (civil servants and Party functionaries), or their perfectly groomed, academically titled SS counterparts.

German philosopher Karl Jaspers, a close friend of Hannah Arendt, calls the horrors of the Hitler state *staatliche Verwaltungsmassenmorde*— state-administered mass murders.[24] Given that there was something inherently contradictory between the Third Reich's reality and the people's perception, the Nazi paradox would at least begin to explain one of the greatest riddles of the Hitler era: How could one of the most highly educated nations, with its penchant for culture and learning, its thousands of humanist high schools (based on a classicist education), its dozens of world-leading academics, so rapidly lose all its moral bearings, Christian sensibilities, ethical standards, and legal principles? By skilfully co-opting and surreptitiously corrupting their own loyal servants, the Nazi ideologues succeeded in devaluing what should be any country's most prized possession: the very morality of the state itself. And yet, if ordinary Germans suspected something foul in their Führer state, even fouler than the whispered rumors would suggest, they could immediately reassure themselves with a glance at their decent fathers and brothers, their respectable uncles, trusted friends and neighbors, who had faithfully applied the laws of the land since the Weimar Republic, or even the Kaiserreich, loyally soldiering on for Führer and fatherland, obedient, diligent people—who had *legally* usurped an entire nation's righteousness.

Notes to Chapter 1

1   The term *die Katastrophe* expressed the unspeakable shock and terror of the victims of this unprecedented event. Later generations dropped the spontaneous word coinage in favor of the German translation of "firestorm" (*Feuersturm*) or, occasionally, *Operation Gomorrah*, the official designation of the series of attacks by British Bomber Command. See also Chapter Two, fn 2.

2   W.G. Sebald, writes in *Luftkrieg und Literatur* (Air War and Literature): "Within a few minutes, huge fires burnt on the estimated 20 square kilometers of attack area…" creating a firestorm with flames 2,000 meters high and winds of hurricane strength that pulled in all oxygen. (Munich: Hanser, 1999) 36.

3   Literally translated, *Reich* means "empire." The First Reich, the Holy Roman Empire of the German Nation, lasted from the ninth century to 1806, when it was dissolved by Napoleon. Lengthy power struggles between the German emperors and the Roman popes (who insisted on their privilege of crowning the emperors) had long since weakened the empire. The Second Reich was founded by Bismarck in 1871, and lasted until 1918 and the end of

World War I. It was strictly secular and, after Bismarck's dismissal by Kaiser Wilhelm II, aimed for world power status. Hitler's Third Reich (1933–1945) had undisguised hegemonic ambitions. Unification (*Anschluss*) with Austria in 1938 was the first step in building a Greater German Empire, rectifying Bismarck's "small-German solution" (Germany *without* Austria). With the annexation of Czechoslovakia in 1939, the *Grossdeutsche Reich* contained a non-German "protectorate" within its borders, becoming "supranational" as the Holy Roman Empire had once been.

4   Martin Middlebrook writes in *The Battle of Hamburg: Allied bomber forces against a German city in 1943* (London: Allen Lane, 1980), 360: "One of the American raids caused the greatest loss of life experienced in Hamburg after the summer of 1943. On 25 October 1944, 455 American bombers set out to bomb three oil refineries in Hamburg but cloud covered their targets and the Americans bombed through this cloud on radar. Most of the bombs fell into the township of Harburg, which had remained relatively undamaged thus far. Much of Harburg was destroyed and 750 people were killed."

5   They would change again after the war: At the first signs of a rebounding economy, spas would recover quickly and, over time, develop into one of Germany's most successful industries.

6   Engelmann, Bernt, *Einig gegen Recht und Freiheit* (Gütersloh: C. Bertelsmann, 1975), 337.

7   Lukacs, John, *The Hitler of History* (New York: Vintage Books, 1998), 263.

8   According to Ian Kershaw in *Hitler, 1889–1936* (London: Penguin Press, 1998) 144, the Party's program went back to the early years of 1919–20, but was later largely ignored.

9   Haffner, Sebastian, *Anmerkungen zu Hitler* (Munich: Kindler, 1978), 37.

10 Prior to currency reform in June of 1948, a pound of butter cost 600 *Reichsmark* on the black market, while the controlled store price for the tiny rations (100 grams per person per week) remained stable at about RM 4 a pound. With the introduction of a hard currency, the supply of goods returned to normal almost overnight, the black market disappeared, while store prices, now in Deutschmarks, remained the same.

11 Neither of these terms is applied to present-day "rogue-states," the German translation of which is *Schurkenstaat*.

12 The distinction between the *Unrechtsstaat* and the *Rechtsstaat* not only facilitated the political and mental distancing of the successor state from the Hitler state, but was also helpful during the 1950s and 1960s to justify West Germany's political and social ostracism of its East German brother state. These rigid atti-

tudes slowly began to change in the 1970s under West Germany's Federal Chancellor Willy Brandt and his Social Democratic government.

13 On September 30, 1938, Hitler signed the Munich Agreement with the leaders of England, France, and Italy. It ceded the Sudetenland to Germany in return for no further territorial claims in Europe. He broke the agreement on March 15, 1939, when German troops entered Czechoslovakia.

On August 23, 1939, Hitler signed a Non-Aggression Pact with the Soviet dictator Joseph Stalin which enabled Germany to attack Poland one week later, starting World War II. He broke the pact on June 22, 1941, when the Wehrmacht assaulted Russia.

14 In March, 1924, Hitler was convicted to five years imprisonment at the Bavarian Fortress Landshut, but was released after only eight months. At Landshut, he dictated a first draft of his book *Mein Kampf* to his co-prisoner and deputy, Rudolf Hess.

15 Munich's *Feldherrnhalle*, where on November 9, 1923, Hitler's "March on Berlin" ended under the fire of the police, became the most sacrosanct place of Nazidom, decorated with the sarcophagi and flags of its fallen heroes.

November 9 is a date laden with historical significance for twentieth-century Germany: On November 9, 1918, revolution broke out in Berlin, Kaiser Wilhelm II was forced to abdicate, and the country changed from a constitutional monarchy to a republic. Two days later, Germany signed the armistice treaty that ended World War I; *Kristallnacht*, when Nazi thugs destroyed synagogues, stores, and properties, took place on November 9, 1938; and it was on November 9, 1989, that the Berlin Wall came down.

16 The race laws "for the protection of German blood" forbade marriages or sexual relations between Jews and non-Jews. Jews were no longer "citizens of the Reich," but second-class "citizens of the state" with far fewer rights. According to Hannah Arendt in *Eichmann in Jerusalem: Die Banalität des Bösen* (Munich: Piper, 1964), 114, many Jewish leaders initially saw the laws, though restrictive, as something positive, since they defined the Jewish minority's exact place within the German majority. From then on, they hoped, a more peaceful co-existence could be worked out.

17 Novick, Peter, *The Holocaust in American Life* (New York: Houghton Mifflin, 1999), 21.

18 The two were Wilhelm Frick, Minister of the Interior, and Hermann Göring, Minister without portfolio. On February 28, 1933, triggered by the fire of the Reichstag building (parliament), which was alleged to be caused by a Communist conspiracy, the "order for the protection of people and state" abolished the

political basic rights of the Weimar constitution. Less than four weeks later, on March 24, 1933, through the infamous Enabling Act (*Ermächtigungsgesetz*), the Reichstag practically disenfranchised itself. It was the end of the legally constituted state, and the beginning of the Hitler dictatorship. It had taken the Nazis exactly fifty-three days to achieve their goal.

19 It is difficult to determine who actually knew what and when; yet, it seems almost certain that the term *vergasen* was well-known long before the end of the Hitler regime.

20 The highest order was a *Führerbefehl* (Führer's order), which overruled any military order or civilian and criminal law. Even if nobody had ever seen the alleged *Führerbefehl*—as happened with the order for the "Final Solution," which may actually never have been put on paper—the "perceived" *Führerwille* (Führer's will) was authoritative enough to make people perform the most horrible acts.

21 Actually, no case of death penalty for refusing to participate in a mass execution has become known; however, the resisting German officer or soldier could expect to be transferred to a *Strafbataillon* (delinquent battalion) with its high rate of fatalities.

22 Arendt, Hannah, op. cit., ref.16.

23 The leaders of the *Einsatzgruppen* were chosen specifically for their postsecondary degrees, frequently in law.

24 Jaspers, Karl, *Wohin treibt die Bundesrepublik?* (Munich: Piper, 1966), 58.

2

DIENSTSTELLE

I have to go back to my memory pole to recall the events that led me to Josephine—a woman five years my senior who, though largely a stranger at the time, selflessly took me into her home and gave me shelter and friendship. And who, unwittingly and innocently, became the cause of my personal catastrophe.

In early 1945, despite the darkening clouds over Germany, I had no premonitions, saw no sinister omens while living at Adolf-Hitler-Platz 13. It was just another place in a country awash with Hitler-designated streets, squares, monuments, schools, and other public installations. Still, fate would not be denied: On March 12, after a number of insignificant bombings (unremembered by me, but assiduously documented in the city's archives), a group of enemy aircraft circled in over undefended Marburg. A few dozen bombs, strategically aimed at the railway station, hit the tracks and a number of buildings nearby. Only one, mysteriously attracted to a more provocative, albeit entirely civilian, target more than a mile away from the station, crashed through the roof of No. 13 Adolf-Hitler Square. It wiped out the offensive address. It also robbed me of my home.

I wasn't there when it happened. I had been busy dragging Müller's child to the air-raid shelter, my privileged job now that the air-raid sirens were sounding in Marburg almost as often as they had done for years in the big cities. On any clear day, 800 to 1,000 American bombers would stream across the sky like invading legions. In awesome precision they left in their wake fifty-mile-long vapor trails, making them easy-to-detect targets for German anti-aircraft guns. There was little flak, however; only scattered salvos that left pitiable puffs of smoke well below the monstrous columns. German fighter planes had long been grounded for lack of fuel, and many of the high-precision anti-aircraft guns had been redirected at Russian tanks, or concentrated around Berlin and other sensitive targets.

Much to my disgust, many people in Marburg, particularly those whose allegedly vital occupations allowed them to avoid being drafted into the army, made a great show of ignoring the planes, as if the roar of their hungry engines and the terror they carried beneath their wings belonged in someone else's war. These draft dodgers strutted about with an air of invincibility that hinted at some special connection to the Party hierarchy and—by extension—to God. The way I saw it, they were not brave but stupid, and there was no merit in being either.

I was different, even acknowledged by the office staff to be different, which in practical terms meant that what would have been seen as cowardice in others was simply caution with me. After my Hamburg bombing ordeal, I had become a veteran of all-out air war and, as such, was granted special status: Rather than mocking my undisguised terror (a no-no among steadfast Germans still determined to win the war), they considered me prudent, my comportment acceptable under the circumstances. Circumstances, by the way, that conferred on me some aura of "expertise," which, in turn, led *Hauptsturmführer* Müller to entrust me with the safety of his adopted child. She was a blonde, somewhat pale two-year-old girl. Whenever the sirens went off, I would race upstairs from the first-floor *Dienststelle* to the Müllers' apartment, grab the child, and then flee down to the basement, where we would crouch under some narrow arch that I judged to be the most reinforced spot under the four-storey structure. It was better than nothing, but not by much.

On the morning of March 12, I was at the office, as I had been more or less regularly for the past three and a half months. It was a day like any other, with nothing much happening, if indeed anything exciting had ever happened at that place. No one took work seriously anymore. One of the three secretaries, the recently hired wife of a wounded army major, kept to herself, quietly knitting a sweater for her baby. Müller, the man who had never seen frontline duty, treated her with a reverence usually reserved for the wives of generals. The rest of the staff busied themselves doing nothing, trying to be not too obvious about it. One was a desiccated redhead in charge of bookkeeping and personnel. A spinster in her mid-thirties, she devoted her affection and loyalty to her boss. She was assisted by Käthe, a young, heavily permed blonde who openly flirted with Rolf, a good-looking young man of about twenty-five. Though he appeared healthy enough to me, the reason for his noncombatant status was not disclosed. Neither was the nature of his present duties. Another student named Rita completed the staff. She was a very pretty girl of about twenty-one, whose frequent and unexplained absences nobody bothered to question.

While we amused ourselves with idle chit-chat, we each kept an eye on the door in case Müller should return. I don't know where he was; his comings and goings were never discussed. He cannot have been in his own office, though, or else we would have been more careful. The way I remember the scene, we had draped ourselves across the Spartan furnishings, once again irreverently discussing Frau Müller's unfulfilled womanhood. Rumor had it, her husband's tuberculosis, in total disregard of the requirements of SS ideology, had afflicted the regenerative faculties of his otherwise sturdy body. One of his kidneys was infected, too, though I learned that only later.

I heard the high-pitched crescendo seconds before the others had even stopped chatting. Nobody who had ever experienced that earsplitting terror could fail to recognize it instantly.

"*Bomben!*" I flew out of the room and up to the apartment, two bounds for each flight of stairs. With the child under my arm like a parcel, I was back down in seconds. Everybody else was still in the office when the building was hit. Nobody was killed, though some were slightly hurt. The *SD Dienststelle* Marburg, the local branch of the dreaded *Sicherheitsdienst*, however, had become non-operational.

The office had been located at Bahnhofstrasse 1, directly opposite the railway station. Given the less-than-accurate science of air war, this had been an extraordinary hit, though nobody up in the air or down on the ground would ever know its significance—save the people who had worked there, of course, and their superiors. The staff was ordered to move their files to another of Müller's offices at the *NS Studentenwerk* (National Socialist student union) in the Wettergasse, a steep and narrow cobblestoned street in the old part of town. I should have helped them, but I didn't. I have already explained how I got into their company; I now have to describe how I got out—or tried to. But first I have to go back a step.

*   *   *

By now, more than three months had passed since I had bid farewell to my mother—she, on her way to the anticipated safety of Bad Pyrmont, and I, on my way back to Marburg, to my apartment and my meeting with Müller. I don't remember much about that job interview, except that the question of salary never came up. As a result, my duties remained undefined, my presence largely unsupervised, and my services, if any, unpaid. To be frank, it was a *Druckposten*, a cushy job at a time when the whole population was being incessantly exhorted to put in its collective oar for the Great War Effort. With airtight Party controls watching, harassing everyone, the *Dienststelle* was probably the safest place to hide. That it would soon turn out to be the dumbest place, I didn't foresee—or perhaps refused to recognize.

Müller had wanted to do me a favor; I'm sure of that. He wasn't a bad man, all things considered, just a weak one who would neglect honor and decency just when those qualities were of paramount value to my fortunes. They might have spared my freedom. Or maybe he had tried, but nobody had listened on that fateful day, six months after the war ended. There had been so much confusion and zeal in the British effort to connect Müller and myself to the "Werewolf," an alleged conspiracy by a bunch of former SS officers determined to continue their fight underground. All the while, the ex-*Hauptsturmführer* had been too sick to stand up for himself—let alone for me.

I return to the winter of 1944–45, when, during the daytime, the American "Flying Fortresses" of the 8th Army Air Force were able to bomb any city in Germany, while the four-engine British and Canadian Lancasters terrorized the same air space at night. Breslau, Pforzheim, Graz, Nürnberg, Freiburg, Würzburg, and many other cities became targets, often for no other military objective than the demoralization of a population exhausted from more than five years of war. It was the Allies' not unreasonable hope that the German people, fed up with a government that had nothing left to offer but lies and threats, would finally resist any further demands for ever more sacrifices. But as the unique medieval and baroque culture of their cities collapsed in ashes, the German people's despair gelled into a defiance that would keep the Nazi war machine humming, generating record numbers of weapons that lacked nothing but fuel and manpower for delivery. The reason for this incomprehensible and reckless display of bravado were two Allied strategies that were somewhat contradictory and therefore easily exploitable by the Hitler government: In January 1943, during the Casablanca Conference, President Roosevelt had proclaimed his adamant demand for Germany's unconditional surrender. Half a year

Marburg railroad station after an air attack on March 12, 1945. *(left front)* The former *SD Dienststelle*. (BILDARCHIV FOTO MARBURG LA I.497/39)

earlier, in Moscow, Churchill had been under heavy pressure by Stalin to open up a second front. Knowing that the Western Allies were not ready for an invasion for at least another year, the British prime minister promised massive American and British bombing attacks against German cities and industries, an offer the Soviet dictator happily accepted.[1] Roosevelt's argument that the total crushing of the Third Reich was necessary to ensure that all the roots of National Socialism were destroyed would, of course, turn out to be correct. Equally correct, however, was Churchill's belief that, by excluding all possibility of a partial settlement, the Allies would never succeed in making the German people rise up against Hitler to force him to make peace. Indeed, his prophesy came true almost instantly: Goebbels's triumphant speech in the huge *Sportspalast* in Berlin after the Casablanca Conference still rings in my ears: *"Wollt ihr den totalen Krieg?"* (Do you want total war?) And the crazed shouts of the fanatical masses: "Ja! Ja!" Nothing could have played into Hitler's hands better, in his quest to mobilize the entire population for the ultimate self-sacrifice, than Roosevelt's (militarily unconventional) demand for unconditional surrender.

As far as the Nazis were concerned, Casablanca would prolong their

dominance over a cowed and resigned people. As for the people themselves, they didn't quite believe or understand what was coming their
way. Not yet. Not until the summer of 1943, the fire bombing of
Hamburg, and the all-out air war that followed. In 1944, as the Russian
front drew ever closer, they would bravely say "Better dead than red" in
full support of the Wehrmacht's desperate struggle to stave off the Red
Army's advance. At the same time, they—and secretly the entire Nazi
elite—were anxiously waiting for a separate peace with the Western
powers, never quite able to believe in Roosevelt's determination. Why
didn't the Americans recognize the strategic and political consequences
of their foolish policy, the Germans asked each other? (For decades after
the war, Germans remained doubtful about America's strategic wisdom:
The refusal to recognize their "real" enemy not only prolonged the terrible blood letting in Europe, but later forced the Americans to pay the
high price of the Cold War—with the help of a remilitarized Germany.)
The common hysteria reached its climax on April 12, 1945. On hearing
of President Roosevelt's death, Goebbels triumphantly cried out: "*Die
Zarin ist tot!*" (The Czarina is dead!) Few Germans who did not immediately understand the meaning of those words; and there may have been
many who shared the Minister's excited hopes that history would repeat
itself: In 1762 the Prussian King Frederick the Great, facing final defeat
in the Seven Years' War by the coalition partners Austria, France and
Russia, was miraculously saved when the Russian Czarina Elisabeth
suddenly died and her son turned the tables by becoming Frederick's
ally. The Nazi brass, and Hitler in particular, had been anxiously waiting
for just such a gift from heaven. Had providence finally taken a hand?
Would Roosevelt's successor, President Harry Truman, show a better
understanding of the political and military consequences of Germany's
unconditional surrender? Would we all be saved? Well, as things turned
out, he didn't and we weren't.

While the war over Germany's cities unfolded with ever-increasing
brutality, I hardly took notice. I had never been to any of those places
mentioned in the news. Their names didn't register, not really. With so
much horror to go around and a person capable of concentrating only on
so much, I waited for news from Hamburg and ignored the rest.[2] At a
certain hour every night, I would hide under a heavy duvet, clutching my
Braun radio close to my ear. It was a small, precious instrument that Alex
had lent me. I don't know where he found it or "confiscated" it. He had

left it for me to use the day he departed. He hadn't mentioned its range or other details, and I was too uninformed to inquire.

Sure, I had heard rumors which were invariably much more grim than the daily *Wehrmachtsbericht*, the official military bulletin. Nobody knew, or would say, where these rumors came from. There was a law against listening to enemy broadcasts; people were denounced by their neighbors for doing so, and were picked up by the Gestapo to deter others from following suit. I cannot remember how I discovered the *Voice*.

Perhaps I had played with the dial on my radio, idly turning it from the *Deutschlandsender*, the official German radio station with its mix of carefully edited news, propaganda, and light entertainment. Suddenly it was there. A strong and confident male speaker had clearly mentioned Harburg, the highly industrialized suburb of Hamburg that happened to be my home: Phönix, Hobum, Esso, Shell, a long list of huge industries, mostly refineries, all bombed. The *Voice* spoke an impeccable German without emotion or hype. It called itself *Soldatensender West*,[3] the "Soldiers' Radio Station West," and it spoke of "our" retreats, "our" losses. It listed all the cities that had been bombed during the past twenty-four hours, their particular industries, as well as the presumed loss of lives; and it gave a meticulous account of the "enemy's" progress. It was a masterful instrument of enemy propaganda, and it fooled me, as it was meant to, just long enough to catch my interest. Conditioned to the heavily censored Nazi broadcasts that left a widening margin of doubt, the authenticity of the *Soldatensender*'s detailed news became immediately apparent.

I was hooked. From then on, I tuned in every night. After the broadcast, I turned the dial back to the *Deutschlandsender*. I listened only to the news that was of interest to me personally, filtering out all other events and places: It was Hamburg, or more precisely Harburg, that I wanted to hear about. I was lonely and scared. Looking back, it seems that we had all become like that, horror-story zombies. After years of news overkill, at first greatly victorious, then distorted and increasingly terrifying, the collective mind had shut itself off, absorbing only matters of pressing personal concern.

So near the end of the war, while the Allied troops concentrated on the Rhine as Germany's last major line of defence, my whole being was motivated by one single dread: the fear of being caught in another bomb attack. I wasn't hysterical; quite the contrary. I was totally rational, to the point of scheming. But it was all one-track, all directed at protecting myself, saving myself, *surviving*. Mentally and physically, no other exigencies existed. I don't know how far this "total motivation" might have carried me, whom I might have betrayed or abandoned, had it been necessary. Had I reached the stage where I would have run from battle had I been a soldier? More and more were deserting now, rumor had it. And most of those who were caught were summarily shot or strung up from trees.

Would I have had the will to desert? I don't know. Maybe not. That would have taken courage, and I wasn't courageous; I was frightened like a hunted animal, terrified by the revolting senselessness of it all. Any self-sacrifice now, any act of patriotism, would have been sheer lunacy or suicidal, or both. I could see no connection between my being killed by a bomb and the survival of the fatherland by even one minute.

When the *Soldatensender* spoke about Harburg, as it now frequently did, the memories came rushing back: the tight web of railroad tracks branching off to the refineries, the office buildings with their windows boarded up, the warehouses and factory halls clad in dark brick and sooty plaster, the rain-filled potholes, the weeds between the debris from earlier bombings, the lonely chimneys that had miraculously survived, the high fences and closed gates, unmanned while everybody hid in some shelter. I couldn't get rid of those images: Again and again, I saw myself standing outside one of those locked gates, alone, not more than 200 meters away from the safety of my father's silo—frozen while the inferno unfolded.

In comparison, the raid on Marburg on March 12, 1945, was a minor event, both at the *Dienststelle*, where people were knocked around while Müller's daughter and I were safely underground, and at No.13 Adolf-Hitler Square, where fire had caused most of the damage. By the time I found out about the errant hit on my home, the flames had been brought under control. Boys from the Hitler Youth were inside, throwing people's belongings out of the windows for others to collect and pile up on the square.

I had never expected an attack on Marburg, and I was completely unprepared. Where would I spend the night? Where would I live, knowing nobody, and with every square foot of extra living space occupied by the flood of refugees streaming in from the East? Where were my possessions? And if I managed to find some, who would guard them while I continued the search?

In the end, I did lose a few things, not many, just those irreplaceable items like my Voigtländer camera, my electric iron, and, of course, my precious Braun radio. So close to the Third Reich's final demise, honesty, like so much else in Germany, had taken a hit.

Heartbroken, I kept watch over my pitiful pile of belongings gathered in the square. Not knowing what to do next, I was suddenly addressed by a tall, dark-haired woman. In her mid-twenties, she stood out from the crowd with her fine posture and simple, yet elegantly tailored, good-quality attire. When I recognized her and learned that she had come especially for me, I broke into tears and clung to her as to a rescuer, which indeed she was. Living in the center of town, Josephine had heard about the bombing. In her practical way, she had brought along a laundry basket, in the unlikely event I might be among the unfortunate ones who had lost their homes. She calmly helped me gather what could be salvaged, then took me to the safe haven of her apartment.

I had met her and her husband, Karl, a graduate of the Munich Academy of Arts and presently a dentistry student and older member of the *SS Studentenkompanie*, only once. That had been almost a year before, when Alex and I had been invited to their home. Müller, a regular guest of theirs, had been there as well. I hadn't taken much notice of him then, never suspecting that a time would come when he, Josephine, and I would be thrown together by circumstances as bizarre as they were perilous.

I clearly remember that evening. I had been deeply impressed by the natural dignity of the older woman. Despite her advanced pregnancy, she had generously provided for all, while charming the men with her wonderfully mature sexuality. I had felt envious then and incredibly childlike and insecure. It was a feeling that would never quite leave me in Josephine's presence, though when she rescued me from my bombed-out home, I felt nothing but overwhelming gratitude.

Later that night, the couple and I shared the matrimonial bed, with Josephine in the middle and all of us giggling and feeling naughty and daring like schoolchildren. The following day, Karl was called up for military duty, allowing the two of us to spread out, with Baby Dieter, rosy and content in his crib, at the foot of the bed. For the next four months Josephine gave me shelter, food and motherly warmth, asking for nothing in return but my friendship. Together we lived through strafing attacks from low-flying planes, the arrival of the American army in Marburg, the last drawn-out weeks of the Reich's demise, and the first months of military occupation.

*   *   *

It must have been around midnight, two weeks after I found shelter in Josephine's small, second-floor apartment in a creaky old house in the medieval part of town. Being a mother, Josephine was easily alarmed by the slightest noise and was the first to be aroused.

"Wake up," she whispered as she shook me. "There's somebody down there throwing pebbles against the window."

Numbed by sleep, I got up and looked out. "It's somebody from Müller's office," I said, shocked and now fully alert at the sight of Rolf, the young man whose exact functions had always been a mystery to me. "He hasn't seen us. Let's pretend we didn't hear anything."

But Josephine opened the window. "We can't have the whole neighborhood wake up."

"The boss wants you at the *Dienststelle*," Rolf called up to me in a sharp whisper, his hands cupped like a megaphone. "*Sofort*—now! Highest orders!" He was gone before I could collect my wits to ask questions. Stunned, Josephine and I stared at each other.

"Do I have to go?" In my nightshirt at the open window, I trembled with cold and fear.

I hadn't been back to the office since the bombing. The first two days I considered myself officially excused, as was customary for people who had lost their homes. But, when nobody objected to my extended absence, I allowed myself the cautious hope that my misfortune would permit me to inconspicuously extricate myself from any further contact with the *Dienststelle*. Müller himself, in a fatherly sort of way, might have followed the same reasoning. Or so I had hoped. Well—he hadn't. Whatever fantasies I had harbored about Müller's personal concern for my welfare were wiped out in seconds. The long tentacles of the *Sicherheitsdienst* were dragging me back into their loathsome embrace.

"I guess you have to go," replied Josephine, closing the window.

"What if I don't want to?"

She suddenly looked worried. "As long as he has power, he can be a threat. To all of us." She gestured to include her child. I wanted to say that I wasn't afraid of Müller and didn't think him particularly dangerous. But she silenced me with her look. And by then, I was no longer too sure about him myself.

We did not speak while I dressed. I felt bitterness welling up, suffocating any plea for help. My only friend, the woman I adored and trusted for her motherly wisdom and gentle patience, had suddenly shown herself unable or unwilling to protect me. I felt vulnerable and in desperate need of somebody to blame. There was nothing rational in this; the *Hauptsturmführer* was beyond reach, and my resentment had simply spilled over on an innocent bystander.

The cobblestoned streets were dark and deserted. Not a soul, not even a patrolling policeman, soldier returning to his quarters, or air-raid warden monitoring the blackout, crossed my path. It was as though the whole town had shut down, aware of the impending change and numbed by fear of the precarious balance between the unpredictable forces of a collapsing regime and the unknown powers of the new masters. The final outcome was not in doubt; time was the only variable. Not much time—days, perhaps hours. Even so, mere minutes could bring sudden disaster on the crazed order of some hysterical Nazi functionary.

My spine tingled. Any moment I expected the horrible whine of the sirens. All day there had been the roll of distant artillery fire. Low-flying fighters had crisscrossed the sky, spewing bullets at non-existent targets, withdrawing after dark like naughty boys tired of taunting their victims.

From Josephine's apartment it was only a few blocks to the Wettergasse, where the *Dienststelle* had relocated to an upstairs floor. That night the short walk felt like a long and dangerous trek. Even before I arrived, I noticed the smell of something burning; a fire truck pulled away from the curb as I entered the building.

The new office looked like it had been hit by an earthquake. Drawers, shelves, the safe—everything had been pulled open, rummaged through and partly emptied, with documents strewn all over the floor. The windows in the back stood open. Two secretaries rushed back and forth, dropping armloads of documents into the yard, where some Hitler Youth boys threw them on a heavily smoking bonfire.

"We tried to burn the stuff in the coal furnace in the basement," the senior secretary explained. She had been friendly enough when she greeted me, making no reference to my extended absence. "The furnace got completely plugged up, which created an enormous stink," she continued.

"Somebody must have called the fire department. When they got here and started to ask questions, the boss just sent them away." She laughed, proud of her master's authority. I looked around; Müller was nowhere to be seen.

"Where is he?"

She shrugged. "He left right after. You must have just missed him. His wife phoned. She wanted him back to protect her."

"*Him* protect *her*—?" Our eyes met. For a second I was shocked by my audacity. It was the first time I had dared to allude to the imminent collapse of power and authority.

Indicating some shelves, she ordered me to pull out files for inspection by Rolf, who would then bring the most important papers to Müller's office. I set to work alongside the others. There was little talk; everyone was silenced by the urgent secrecy of the operation and the sense of dread rising up from the darkened town like an unredeemed sin.

It was close to daylight when Rolf told us to leave what remained for the cleaning women, since everything important had been dealt with. Outside, the fire still smouldered, but the boys were getting ready to leave. One man, possibly the building's caretaker, was standing by the fire. Otherwise the yard was empty; there was nobody curious—or imprudent—enough to linger or ask questions. Up in the office, somebody had made a pot of ersatz coffee. The four of us sat down together, trying to relax after the hectic hours.

Käthe, the pretty secretary with the mop of blonde curly hair, was the first to ask: "What now? Can we go home?"

"The boss wants you to stay," replied the young man, whom I have referred to as Rolf, although nobody but Käthe called him that—everybody else in the office maintained the customary use of family names. The two had done away with that formality since the Müllers' two-week vacation, when the young lovers had taken advantage of the free, if risky, comfort of their master's connubial bedroom and later told everybody about it.

"Why? There's nothing more to do here." Käthe gestured dismissively. Nobody spoke. We were all too tired even for the usual small talk. Suddenly Käthe sat up, her eyes wide. "Quiet!" She held a finger to her lips.

"What's the matter?"

She motioned for everybody to listen. "I can hear them—"

"Hear what?"

"The tanks—"

"Good God—" We all crowded around the open window, straining to hear the ominous rattle none of us had ever experienced. Outside, the streets were empty, the dairy and bakery still closed. Was there a brooding quality to the quiet of the early hour, or was this just a trick of my imagination?

The atmosphere in the room was charged, but nobody mentioned it. After all, we had just burned highly secret government documents, an act which only yesterday would have been utterly unthinkable, condemned as sabotage and punishable by death. Yet, the destruction had been carried out on the highest orders of the very same government. Nothing could be more foreboding, more revealing of the desperate state of the Nazi leadership than the spooky scene in which we had just participated. I hated the thought of having allowed myself to be drawn into the sordid affair, which had all the characteristics of a "cowardly retreat," the very salvation Hitler and his generals, time and time again, had denied their exhausted and outnumbered troops.

But those in charge of the *Dienststelle*, and of all the other branches of the SS and SD bureaucracy right up to the top where the order to destroy had originated, were probably never engaged in a battle. They were the thousands of officials and agents in a spidery organization that had watched and encircled and ruthlessly crushed anybody deviating even an inch from the National Socialist course.

I was appalled. I should have followed my instincts earlier that night and refused to go. Where, by the way, was Rita, the other student? Had they given up on her, or she on them? I shivered. "Please close the window. I'm freezing."

Rolf clowned around, leaning out of the window with both hands to his ears. "No tanks," he declared grandly, "Käthe suffers from hallucinations." He closed the window and threw himself into a swivel chair, making it spin while he hugged his legs.

"What are you going to do when they do come?" demanded the older secretary in a sober, no-nonsense tone that sliced through the posturing.

Rolf got up and stretched, still reaching for a smart-alecky retort. "Stick on a beard and slip through the lines, I suppose. There are people in Holland who owe me. They've been hiding Jews for years, and we have let them. Maybe I'll work in the fields, growing lettuce and radishes." In spite of his efforts, his cockiness sounded contrived.

Käthe asked: "And what's going to happen to us?"

"You'll all get raped." Rolf shot back without a moment's hesitation.

I never got that answer out of my head. Rape was something not usually mentioned within the highly puritanical mindset of Nazi literature and education. But it was plain that Rolf was not trying to be daring or funny. The viciousness of his remark was clearly meant to jolt, to evoke intense fear of the most degrading punishment systematically to be perpetrated on German women. Given his highly confidential position at the *Dienststelle*, one may well assume that he was propelled by the wish to unload on others some of his own well-justified fears. I was shocked, and for the first time I was truly afraid that something terrible would happen.

But how? And why? Though I would never have confessed this to anybody, I had secretly wished for the arrival of the American army sooner rather than later, to end the harrowing attacks from the air. Besides, with the image of clean-shaven German soldiers who sang and marched, danced with their girls, or took part in national ceremonies as my only notion of the military, I found it impossible to conceive of American troops drunkenly roaming the streets, looting, burning and raping like Mongol hordes—or their latter-day descendants in Red Army uniforms.

Before anyone had time to react, the door was flung open and Müller stormed in, black leather boots shining, green uniform buttoned up to the silver-lined collar, his unshaven chin framed by SS runes. His pistol holster hung open, and the gun was in his hand. He stood legs apart, eyes scanning the room without seeming to fix on any particular thing. We all leapt to attention and watched in terror as he began to march about, his boots stomping the floor and kicking up papers. For a second he paused at the window, then turned back to us.

"You should all be shot," he shouted. "The whole *Scheisse* that Germany is in is the fault of people like you. Cowards, traitors, deserters—all of you." He held the gun aimed at the ceiling, as though he had not made up his mind whom to shoot first. Or maybe from caution— God knows what went on in his head. I had never seen a pistol up close; or a man in such a dangerous rage. I can't remember whether I was afraid. Perhaps there was no time. We were shocked by the scene, which was as terrifying as it was preposterous. It was also very bad theatre, of course, which is easy to say in hindsight; at the time, I am sure nobody in the room felt that way.

He suddenly stopped. He put the weapon back in its holster and spoke in a more normal voice: "Go home. You can all go home. It's over." With long strides he marched towards the door, then turned around. Echoing the immortal words of his Führer, he added: "I'll join the troops; I shall die on the field of honor."

After he left, Rolf went over and quietly closed the door. He took Käthe's hand; she had started to cry. Nobody spoke. Finally, with a sigh that sounded more like a sob, the older secretary got up and left.

We all filed out. Rolf was last.

I never saw any of them again.

*   *   *

I have to move my memory pole one more time, though only for a short period, a few hours or so. It now stands on top of the Schlossberg, outside Marburg's ancient castle, which guarded the old city for hundreds of years.

I returned to the castle again, not long ago. Pure chance directed my itinerary in a way that brought me back to Marburg on March 28, 1995, fifty years to the day after the events I am about to relate. So much had changed during that half century that I had trouble finding my way around the entirely unfamiliar scene. At the castle, there were signs giving directions and others with regulations for the dozens of visitors. There were guards and guides and a museum with a large collection of artifacts. I had not come for the museum, which surprised me by its existence. Following the arrows, I moved upstairs and downstairs, feeling increasingly bewildered: Where were those vast ancient vaults I so clearly remembered? Had they just been in my imagination? Caring hands had repaired broken stairs, leveled the naturally uneven floors and plastered the raw masonry of the old walls, fine improvements to make the castle safe for the modern-day tourist. Following the staircase to its lowest end, my search was rewarded: There, unmolested by visitors and still in an unfinished state of "upgrading" were those impressive walls. Ten feet thick and surmounted by several stories of heavy stonework, they had offered sanctuary against enemy invaders throughout the centuries. Even in 1945, they looked wonderfully secure and protective against the rigors of modern warfare.

Deep underneath the chattering tourists, five decades of a busy lifetime suddenly dissolved. I saw myself again, frightened out of my wits, climbing the steep cobblestoned incline up to the castle several times a day. The sirens having become unreliable, I was off and running as soon as I heard the telling roar of approaching aircraft. What normally would have been a half-hour stroll became a ten-minute sprint, without even a glimpse at the lovely mansions of ancient student fraternities lining the path.

I had been deep inside the vaults when the first American tanks entered the town. There were tiny windows at the far end of those immense walls, but they were too distant and at too steep an angle to make out what was happening down in the valley. Other people milled about, went outside and came back to report. I stayed put. I can't remember for how long. When everything was quiet, I left. I was one of the last. Slowly I crossed the cobblestoned yard, where in happier times young knights had pranced and galloped under gaily embroidered bunting to the sounds of hailing fanfares.

There were American soldiers in the streets, but nobody stopped me. In their tidy brown uniforms, round helmets and laced boots, they looked relaxed and aloof rather than belligerent. I passed a man lying on the other side of the road, his face concealed by his arms; nobody seemed to have decided yet what to do about him. I headed for Josephine's apartment at the bottom of the hill, not far from the meadows along the river Lahn, where huge army tents were already being erected. From here, the luxurious smells of food Germans had long forgotten existed would soon emanate. As their own supplies became ever more scarce in the months to come, men, women and children, regardless of background, would part with their dignity to satisfy hunger and habit. They would hang around those sites of great splendor, begging and scrounging for scraps, for yesterday's bread or wilted greens. They would scavenge around the tents, hustling for cigarette butts carelessly tossed away.

I walked without haste; there was no more need to run. I looked up at the sky, which was overcast, and I breathed deeply the air that already smelled of spring. In four days I would be twenty. I did not know what those days would bring, what the next week or year would hold. Was there any truth to the Nazi propaganda that had painted such horrible pictures of the things the enemy would do, if we ever allowed him to step onto our sacred soil?

Well, we had; the sacred soil was now his to do with as he liked.

I remembered what Rolf had said. Had it really been just this morning that we had left the *Dienststelle* for good? Time seemed to have stopped during those painful hours, while the defeated remnants of the Wehrmacht had retreated from yet another part of our battered land. I dismissed the possibility of the Americans being raping marauders. As I looked around the narrow streets and crooked houses with their small windows and firmly closed doors, everything seemed the way it always had been. How many wars and invaders had this old town endured? Yet, in the end it had survived, while all the intruders had returned home.

It would be the same again. So much propaganda, so many speeches, threats and lies. Now they were all gone, dissolved into thin air, stripped of whatever power and importance they once had held. Held yesterday? Just a few hours ago? But already as passé as last year's fashion. There was a new feeling instead. Unfamiliar still; it should have come slowly, gradually, but didn't. Instead, it was there suddenly, with breathtaking impact. From one minute to the next it had become the only thing that mattered, unbelievably precious, never to be let go of again: I was alive.

It was over at last—and I had survived.

I knew there would still be reasons for fear. Too many unknowns lurked in these ancient lanes, now filled with the awesome rattle of tanks. But the terror was over—the senseless destruction, the uncontrollable fear of death. Or was it?

Walking back to Josephine's apartment, I was blissfully unaware of the frightening events I was yet to encounter.

INTERLUDE II
The Organizations

I remember a little verse. It was part of a longer poem that I heard first in 1941 or 1942. At the time, we thought it very amusing, even a bit daring, since it poked fun at something as magnificent and awe-inspiring as National Socialism's ever lengthening list of organizations:

Ein Bäumchen steht im Walde,	A little tree stands in the forest,
Es ist organisiert;	It is organized;
Es ist im NS Waldverband,	It is in the NS forest union,
Damit ihm nichts passiert.	So that nothing will happen to it.

It was recited by one of my uncles in an exaggerated conspiratorial manner and with a mocking imitation of the *deutsche Blick* (the furtive glance Germans used to throw over their shoulders). Though harmless enough for today's reader, for anybody living under the Third Reich its satirical message was immediately clear: Within a few years, National Socialism's insatiable hunger for power and total control had succeeded in casting a tight organizational net over a population that rapidly became obsessed with uniforms, ranks and titles, and whatever personal advantage and protection their new membership could afford. Boys and girls from age ten were in the Hitler Youth, women could join the *Frauenschaft*, the women's organization,[4] workers were in the *Arbeitsfront* (labor front), a Nazi-controlled variant of their former unions, and professionals, students, farmers and other independents had their own associations, all with the prefix NS- or Reichs- for official sanction.

The largest organization, of course, was the Party itself, with a membership of 10.7 million men and women. Though one usually spoke only of the *Partei*, its full designation was the National Socialist German Workers Party, or NSDAP. If party membership was not exactly compulsory for all civil servants, it certainly came close. Anybody aspiring to a career in the military, the diplomatic service, industry or finance could expect faster advancement as a party member, even if he refused to stick the swastika pin to his lapel. To obtain government grants or supply orders, patronage appointments or titles—not to mention promotion to powerful Nazi ranks—membership was next to indispensable. It should not come as a surprise, then, that the vast majority of *Reichstag* delegates for the National Socialist German Workers' Party (the only political party remaining in Germany) were anything but *workers*, or even petits bourgeois, but members of the old German elites from the aristocracy, the military, academe, industry and finance, now frequently also the holders of high SS or SA ranks.

Apart from their ideological zeal, most of the Nazi organizations were relatively harmless and membership in them was something "that simply came with the job." Others, particularly the SA and SS, were not. Nobody in my family belonged to either; and had I not met Alex, I would have sailed through the entire period of the Third Reich without ever having personally met any of their hundreds of thousands of members. I am sure that such a statement sounds surprising today after the notoriety accorded them through fifty postwar years. Yet, it is safe to say that a great number of Germans could give similar assurances without telling a lie.

Very little about the inner workings of the SA, and even less about the SS, was known by a population that, generally speaking, felt well-advised to stay out of the way of these groups. Indeed, over time, the structures of the SS State[5] became increasingly byzantine and almost completely obscure to the German public. Here then are just a few remarks concerning the National Socialists' two most infamous organizations.

The *Sturmabteilung* (Storm Troopers), or SA, was founded in 1920, as the paramilitary force of the National Socialist German Workers' Party. Dressed in brown shirts, brown breeches and pillbox hats, SA members were the most raucous and in-your-face expression of the new Nazi movement. Many were former soldiers and officers of the Kaiser's army who, after World War I, had banded together in more or less privately financed *Freikorps* (volunteer corps) that had strong anti-republican agendas. As part of their new vocation, they marched through every town in Germany, protected the Party's activities from communist interference, and spread Nazi propaganda. Their rallies, *Saalschlachten* (meeting hall brawls), and street fights were legendary, as was their verbal and physical abuse of Jews and political opponents.

In the summer of 1934, seventeen months into the new Hitler government, the power of the 4.5-million-strong Storm Troopers was broken
literally overnight by charges of conspiracy and high treason. Their
homosexual leader, Ernst Röhm, was assassinated, along with more than
150 other SA leaders and some civilian "undesirables," in what became
officially known as the Röhm Putsch. (In fact, though trying to move the
Nazi revolution further to the left, neither Röhm nor any of the other
leaders had planned a putsch at the time.) Dithering through days of
indecision and close to a hysterical collapse, Hitler feared for his personal
prestige among his followers if he allowed his best and only friend, a
comrade-in-arms-of-the-first-hour to be liquidated. However, he finally
threw Röhm to the murderous wolves, partly to distance himself from
the wide-spread homosexuality among the SA leadership, but primarily
to respond to the strong pressures from the conventional army (*Reichswehr*) which had looked with increasing suspicion on the fast-growing
powers of the rival SA. To handle the dirty work, Hitler, eagerly
supported by Himmler, Göring and Goebbels, called on his most trusted
guards, the SS.

Rather than creating a shock among the population over the (mostly
rumored) multiple killings, the putsch—the first true hint of the regime's
ruthless brutality—was welcomed for putting an end to the aggravating
expressions of Nazi vulgarity and street power. Only nine years old at the
time, I don't remember anything about the bloody event. Actually, it may
not have been all that bloody in Flensburg, the small city by the Baltic Sea
where I lived at the time. Two years later, however, when my family
moved to Hamburg and I was enrolled in a new school, the mysterious
incident suddenly came up. "Addy has no father," somebody whispered
into my ear while pointing at a small, dark-haired girl with a plump nose
and full lips. "He had something to do with the Röhm Putsch." I didn't ask
what she meant, and she didn't elaborate, probably knowing nothing
more about the affair. But the tone of her voice hinted at something dreadful and forbidden, an imitation of the way she must have heard the rumor
herself. Throughout our school years, Addy was well-liked by everybody.
Never rising above the lower third of the class, she was witty in a quiet,
non-sarcastic way, friendly and good-natured. She was also clearly disad-
vantaged—though nobody used that expression at the time or commented
on the fact—with her single mother not able to provide her with the
clothes or entertainment enjoyed by most of the other students.

After the putsch, the SA continued to exist under a new, yet impotent leadership until the end of the Third Reich, their popular regard low and their power as a paramilitary force permanently broken. (The SA was called up for "heavy duty" one more time, on November 9, 1938, for *Kristallnacht*, the bloody attack on Germany's Jewry.) SA membership rapidly declined from a high of 4.5 million in 1934 to 1.6 million in 1935, 1.2 million in 1938, and 900,000 in 1940, while the *SS-Staat* established itself as the new political order in Germany.

With the worst manifestations of Nazi vulgarity silenced, the public may have become more aware of, though certainly never fully informed about, the presence and purpose of the "black" SS, or *Schutzstaffel* (Protective Squad). Founded in 1925 to protect Hitler and the leadership of the NSDAP, they were fewer in numbers and generally better educated and disciplined than the SA, to which they originally belonged. In 1929 Heinrich Himmler became their leader as *Reichsführer SS*. Five years later, in recognition of their co-operation during the Röhm Putsch, Hitler gave his permission to have the SS turned into an independent organization. Its taller-than-average members with their certified Aryan backgrounds were smartly dressed in black tunics, black breeches and shiny black boots, the famous death's head insignia and SS runes blinking like warning symbols from caps and collars.

Their rigid demeanor and ideological zeal set them apart from all other party organizations, clearly marking them as Germany's new elite. So did their often extraordinarily distinguished backgrounds, reaching up to the highest circles of aristocracy (including the imperial Hohenzollern) and to the leaders of industry, commerce, and finance. Beginning at 250, membership grew rapidly to 2,000 in 1930, 10,000 in 1931, 90,000 in 1934, and reached 200,000 by 1936. Their true place within the Nazi hierarchy remained a mystery to the average person; it also remained more than slightly sinister. Apart from guarding the Führer, their protective functions were expanded to include ministries, important Nazi functions, events and rallies, and concentration camps. Their connection with the deportations of the Jews was generally known, though detailed knowledge was seldom demanded and virtually impossible to obtain.

By 1936, *Reichsführer SS und Chef der Deutschen Polizei*, Heinrich Himmler, was the supreme commander of the entire SS and the police forces. Most notorious were the *SD* (*Sicherheitsdienst*), or Security Service, under Reinhard Heydrich, and the *Sicherheitspolizei*, or Security Police, combining the Criminal Police (*Kripo*) and the Secret State Police (*Gestapo*) under Ernst Kaltenbrunner. In addition, Himmler had control over 210,000 Waffen SS (in 1939), which included the *Leibstandarte Adolf Hitler*, the Führer's personal bodyguard, and the brutal *Totenkopfverbände* (Death's Head units), specially trained guards for the concentration camps. Through their aggressive recruiting system parallel to, and often in competition with, the Wehrmacht, the Waffen SS counted thirty-eight divisions with close to one million men by the end of the war. A voluntary military ground force, they were extolled for their bravery and endurance by German war propaganda. In contrast, very few civilians had any notion of the activities of the *SS Einsatzgruppen*, special task forces of the SD, Gestapo and Order Police, who followed closely behind the advancing Wehrmacht in Poland and the Soviet Union. They became responsible for the rounding-up and mass executions of East European Jewry and large numbers of the Polish civilian elite, for the murder of Bolshevik commissars and the killing of a great many Russian POWs.

Each Waffen SS division carried its own patriotic name: *Das Reich, Deutschland, Hitlerjugend, Adolf Hitler,* to name just a few. After the conquest of western and northern Europe, the SS recruited large numbers of volunteers from France, the Netherlands and Scandinavia, creating ethnic brigades and divisions named *Wiking, Charlemagne, Wallonien, Nederland,* and *Nordland.* The largest contingent, 25,000 men, came from Holland, the homeland of Anne Frank, a detail of that country's history we usually hear little about. Fiercely believing in their "crusade against Bolshevism," these units fought to the very last.

Throughout the war, the members of the Waffen SS were touted as Germany's military elite, troops who were especially well-trained and equipped for tough assignments and heavy losses. (They were the first who were outfitted with camouflage uniforms, which the Wehrmacht ridiculed, but later also introduced.) It can be assumed that in most people's minds, their connection to the ideologically obsessed SS leadership in the *Reichssicherheitshauptamt* in Berlin, the *Totenkopf SS*, the concentration camps, and the persecution of the Jews remained unclear, if irksome, and was, I suspect, largely ignored. After the war, it was difficult to reconcile the reputation of the Waffen SS for heroism and sacrifice with the shocking new image of murderers who had gassed millions of Jews, burned thousands of synagogues, and—with a debatable amount of co-operation by the Wehrmacht—starved or shot millions of Russian POWs.

That conceptual dualism—heroes or criminals—still exists today: While the spirited reunions of aging SS veterans may be tolerated as old men's follies, the 1985 handshake between President Ronald Reagan and Chancellor Helmut Kohl at a military cemetery at Bitburg near the Luxemburg border, was condemned by many German and American writers and journalists. The occasion was the celebration of the fortieth anniversary of the end of World War II, and of postwar Germany's firm integration into the alliance of Western democracies ever since. The president's well-intended gesture turned into a major scandal when reporters discovered forty-nine graves of members of the Waffen SS among the 1,995 soldiers buried at Bitburg.[6,7]

Details about the various Nazi organizations were easy to keep away from public scrutiny because of a lack of interest by a population traditionally disdainful of politics, which it considered vulgar and uncultured. As to the activities of the SS, including the SD and the Gestapo, people's curiosity instinctively shied away from any more intimate knowledge. For proof, I only have to turn to my own family.

It may be impossible to understand today, but the truth is that my gentle and decent father, who had no military background and whose civic principles were never bent to Nazi demands, was immensely proud of being a *Förderndes Mitglied* of the SS. Literally a "promoting" or "sponsoring member," in practical terms it meant that by paying a small monthly amount he was rid of all further obligations. There were no requirements to join the SS, attend their rallies or speeches, or wear a uniform. In fact, his status as *FM* spared him from joining any other organization. That's what made him so proud. "*Ich bin ein feines Mitglied,*" he used to boast, making fun of the initials FM; I'm a "fine member." He kept a silver pin with the letters FM in his drawer, but was never required to wear it. He had become a "sponsoring member" soon after the Nazis attained power. A couple of good-looking, polite young men in smart uniforms had visited him in his office and had made their pitch. It seemed a small thing at the time in exchange for being left alone. As far as I know, my father never regretted it, never saw himself as anything but a successful dodger of the enforced expressions of Nazi enthusiasm all around him. Though he closely followed the Nuremberg Trials, which declared the SS a criminal organization, I am sure he never made a connection between his modest monthly dues and the terror of the concentration camps, the Gestapo or the SD, not to mention the *Einsatzgruppen*, about which he probably had never heard when he died in 1969 at the age of eighty.

While the SD worked quietly behind the scenes to ferret out even the slightest hint of opposition, discontent or defeatism, the Gestapo's methods of punishment for such behavior were very often much in the public eye for purposes of intimidation and deterrence. Arrests were frequently followed by the proceedings of a *Volksgerichtshof* (People's Court), which operated in open disdain of the legal rights of the accused.

Gathered under the umbrella of Reinhard Heydrich's *Reichssicherheitshauptamt* (RSHA)—one of twelve "Main Offices" of Himmler's SS empire[8]—the powers and jurisdictions of the various security organizations frequently overlapped within a bewildering array of infrastructures and commands. Such notorious names as Heinrich Himmler (who killed himself in British captivity) and Reinhard Heydrich (assassinated in Czechoslovakia in 1942) may sound immediately familiar, as would Ernst Kaltenbrunner (chief of the Gestapo, hanged in Nuremberg) and Adolf Eichmann (in charge of Jewish Affairs and the Final Solution; kidnapped, tried and hanged in Jerusalem by the Israelis in the early 1960s). But, beyond that, the image of the Nazis' murder machine dissolves into an organizational blur of offices, divisions and subdivisions, sections and subsections, Roman numerals, letters, departments, and branches led and staffed by an army of anonymous SS leaders.

The lines of authority between Himmler's SS organizations and the Wehrmacht, judiciary and government ministries, were often poorly defined and highly contentious. Historians have speculated on the reasons for this near-impenetrable maze, which existed in some strange disregard of the traditional German love of bureaucratic order. One explanation has been the explosive growth of the Nazi bureaucracy, which never had the time to sort itself out before the Reich collapsed. Others have suggested that Hitler himself masterminded the deadly jealousies among his mightiest lieutenants in the army, SS, and Party to give himself, the supreme commander, the power "to divide and conquer." He certainly must have recognized those fierce animosities as the best insurance on his own life. That the only full-fledged assassination attempt against him failed, was at least partly due to a lack of co-operation among the various military and civilian conspirators.

Yet, if public intimidation by the Gestapo[9] and by a wide-ranging net of secret surveillance by the SD[10] were the tools of a state obsessed with its own security, few people were truly aware of their extent or felt personally threatened. Sure, one was careful in a general way; more so as the war turned against Germany and controls and restrictions became ever tighter. But to imagine a whole population shaking in their collective boots would be a gross distortion. Things were much more subtle and layered, which is why so many contradictory analyses exist about conditions in the Third Reich. People without Jewish or left-wing backgrounds did not consider themselves physically in danger during the "good years" of the 1930s and early 1940s. Granted, many Germans who prided themselves on their refinement and high level of culture, felt provoked by the brassy side of National Socialism, which continued to emphasize the Party's revolutionary origins through its crude preference for too much noise, and too many flags, marches, and speeches. Indeed, more than anything else, it was the sheer vulgarity of National Socialism that repelled the people, particularly the *Gebildeten*, the large middle-class group of educated Germans. They were contemptuously dubbed *die Intellektuellen* by Joseph Goebbels, whose truly obscene hatred of intellectuals found an enthusiastic response among the tens of thousands of low- and middle-rank party hacks happy to bait and badger anybody not totally immersed in the *Deutsche Volksgemeinschaft*, the German People's Community.

But such mutual disdain rarely led to open conflict. Most citizens abhorred the notoriety that came from speaking out and feared the trouble it might cause. The press in particular soon felt the heavy pressure of *Gleichschaltung*, of being forced to sing from the prescribed hymn book and to withhold opinions not officially sanctioned. Barred from more informed, more varied sources of information, the middle classes were soon drawn into the same process of ideological *Gleichschaltung*, even if they recognized what was happening and tried to resist. In 1933, the highly public *Bücherverbrennungen* (book burnings) of Jewish and leftist writings certainly shocked and disgusted a great number of people. But, since these acts were widely seen as further proof of the vulgarity and the poor level of education of the SA, people turned up their noses, feeling contempt for, rather than fear of, the Nazis' attempts at mind control. Many, I suppose, acted like my parents by keeping their cherished authors hidden behind officially acceptable books, considering themselves clever and superior—this may well have been the extent of their anti-Nazi resistance.

Organized protests by the left quickly ceased when the Communist party was outlawed, its members sent to prison or concentration camp. Social Democrats were harassed into silence or emigration; those who refused to "reform" were frequently taken into "protective custody," a euphemism for the growing number of concentration camps. Outside the political left, this energetic cleansing process was highly popular. Indeed, most people, blissfully ignorant or only vaguely aware of the increasing power of the SS state, felt proud to be part of Germany's great renewal and optimistic about its future.

There are many explanations for the quick surrender of the country's middle class to the rapidly developing totalitarianism of the new *Führerstaat*—the one-party government under its dictatorial *Führer*—but these may be completely incomprehensible to anybody living in a Western democracy. One of the reasons was that *Demokratie* (democracy) was a dirty word in Germany, standing for a political system which was as much abhorred by the Nazis as Communism was by the Western world during the Cold War. Democracy had been attempted, with disastrous results, during the Weimar Republic, the short pluralistic interval between 1919 and the advent of Hitler's Third Reich a mere fourteen years later. Though democratic reforms had timidly knocked on the doors of Imperial Germany prior to World War I, the majority of the Kaiser's citizens lived willingly enough in a spirit of deference to authority, or *Untertanengeist,* which Nazi ideology later quickly moulded into the *Deutsche Volksgemeinschaft,* a community of seventy million people (after Austria's Anschluss in 1938 eighty million), obedient by habit and inclination, and too politically naive to resist the leveling forces of National Socialist ideology. *Führer befiehl, wir folgen dir* (Leader, give us orders, we will follow you) was shouted in mighty choruses at countless ceremonies, a commitment to blind allegiance known to all who ever wore a uniform during the Third Reich. Traditional subservience to power, which had kept generations of Germans neatly in line, became "ennobled" to *Führer-Gefolgschaft*, a close, almost personal loyalty to "our Führer, Adolf Hitler," only to be exploited by a fanatical leadership.

Hitler's attack on Poland in September 1939 was followed by the Wehrmacht's invasion of France in May 1940, and of Russia in June 1941. The German population, each time, was deeply shocked, but always recovered quickly upon hearing reports of Germany's amazing *Blitzkrieg* successes. Until the catastrophic defeat at Stalingrad in early 1943, the growing restrictions on personal freedom had been readily accepted by a population optimistic about the outcome of the war, and only too happy to make personal sacrifices. Things began to change in 1943: As military losses rose, and more and more ancient cities fell into ruins under heavy bombing, enthusiasm became silent resignation, and concern about losing the war entered people's hushed conversations. The SS state, fearing defeatism, perhaps even revolt, responded by strengthening its already pervasive security systems. Controls over all aspects of life tightened, while the notion of being watched by a network of insidious informers made Germans mindful of every spoken word. Critical or derisive remarks about the ever-worsening war, the *Luftwaffe*'s disastrous failure to protect the homeland, or the dwindling chances for "final victory" were never spoken outside the circle of trusted friends and family. Everyone knew the penalty for *Zersetzung der Wehrkraft* (corrosion of the fighting spirit): concentration camp or death.

Is that a reasonably accurate picture of how ordinary people thought and acted under the Nazi dictatorship? Looking back over five decades, I find it almost impossible to peel the unsung "ordinary German," the young one in particular, out from under the layers of postwar assumptions and reformed thinking. Over the years, like most of my contemporaries, I had fabricated a nicely sanitized version of myself, only one day to discover an old exercise book from my high school history class with handwritten notes dripping with Nazi ideology. Hot with shame, I threw out the incriminating object, lest it would sear my mind. I should not have done so, of course, because this was precisely the type of document of the "ordinary people" we are so clearly missing today.

I return to my subject: Did we, the young ones, look over our shoulders in fear of being overheard by a surreptitious informer? Were we *aware* of that army of secret collaborators who provided the Gestapo and SD with observations and denunciations about their colleagues, neighbors, students, bosses? The answer cannot be better than a cautious Yes, and No. One sensed the danger in the presence of certain people, even if one wasn't entirely certain about it. Party bosses and functionaries kept to their own company. Never having to worry about election results, they cared little about their popularity among the rest of the population. There was little social intercourse between the Nazi hierarchy and ordinary

Germans. Fear and distrust kept both groups apart. Certainly, one had to be careful at Hitler Youth meetings, and even more so during the months at the *Arbeitsdienst*, where a radically National Socialist leadership watched over us every minute of the day.[11] But, until graduation from high school, things had been more relaxed. One *knew* one's family, friends and foes, teachers, cousins, and neighbors. Then came 1943, the year of the fateful turnaround, when our parents realized that the war could no longer be won. Did we share their somber views? Almost certainly not. I try to detach today's knowledge of the miles of single-file German soldiers of General Paulus's beaten 6th Army dragging themselves over the snowy ground into Russian captivity and to almost certain death (*verboten*, of course, to show in Nazi German newsreels), from Goebbels' propaganda version: Paulus, a coward and defeatist, had capitulated against Hitler's orders. Did Goebbels succeed? Were people convinced that the Battle of Stalingrad *could* have been won with just a bit more stamina and trust in the *Führer*? Did he overcome people's gloomy apprehensions? He did not, at least not quite. For the first time in ten years, cracks had opened up in the relationship between the regime and the people. Meanwhile, after a few days of mourning, dancing lessons for high school students were allowed to go on, movie theaters favored comedies and the radio broadcasts returned to their diet of light entertainment. After all, in spite of 250,000 German soldiers dead or captured at the Volga, we were still winning the war! And we believed, had been trained to believe. We were the bearer of the Great Faith.

Clearly, there were differences in our attitudes and commitments towards National Socialism: Like every schoolchild, I had grown up with Nazi ideology, knowing no other alternative. But instructions in *Weltanschauung* were dull and compulsory and rather peripheral to our adolescent concerns, something one "endured "—like school, or church, or any other adult institution one had to observe. I was not a fanatic; none of my friends or family were. I never stood in a marketplace waving the swastika flag and shouting slogans. (I once waved at Hitler, as his car passed me and a group of children on a Bavarian country road. It was in 1937, and he was still riding in an open Mercedes.) And yet, there is also the fact that for half the life of the Third Reich there was a war on, a great national conflict. To cheer for one's country during such dazzling times is simply a matter of course. I happened to be German; it would have been the same had I been British, American, Russian, or Japanese. And for the first three years there had been a lot to cheer about. Hitler was sacrosanct, of course, and a number of his marshals, admirals and generals, such as Göring,[12] Rommel,[13] Dönitz[14] and Guderian,[15] were very popular figures. *Luftwaffe* aces like Galland, Moelders, and Marseille were venerated like film stars, their pictures decorating the rooms of the adoring girls in my class. Together with U-boat captains Prien, Kretschmer and others, they were our heroes: their fates were of Homeric proportion and heart-rending tragedy. Adolescent and kitschy, of course—and entirely disconnected from the SS state. Like most Germans, we had learned to compartmentalize—here Germany, the Wehrmacht and, of course, the Führer; there his minions with their impertinence, their stupid pressures, and idle harassments; somewhere—though we never quite knew where—the SS and Gestapo.

Notes to Chapter 2

1 Overy, Richard, *Das Reich des Bösen* (The empire of evil). *Spiegel special*, No. 1, 2001, 96.

2 For the technical and strategic details of the Allied air war—particularly Operation Gomorrah, the fire bombing of Hamburg—refer to Greenhous, Harris, Johnston and Rawling, *The Crucible of War, 1939–1945: The Official History of the Royal Canadian Air Force,* Volume III. (Toronto: University of Toronto Press, 1994), 689ff.

3 Christof Mauch—in *Schattenkrieg gegen Hitler: Das Dritte Reich im Visier der amerikanischen Geheimdienste 1941–1945* (Stuttgart: Deutsche Verlags-Anstalt, 1999), 211—explains that the *"Soldatensender Calais,"* installed in 1943 and renamed *"Soldatensender West"* after the Allied conquest of Calais, was actually located in Milton Bryant, England. Its powerful 600-kilowatt transmitter could broadcast all over central Europe. The program was designed so that Germans could claim they had *assumed* it was German, thereby making listening less dangerous than to the BBC or the *Voice of America*.

4 Most non-working women were able to avoid membership in the *Frauenschaft*,

which was not compulsory. Some joined the Red Cross or other charitable organizations, but the majority simply stayed home and away from politics which were considered "unwomanly."

5 The "SS State" is a term coined by Buchenwald survivor and author Eugen Kogon (Eugen, *Der SS-Staat: Das System der deutschen Konzentrationslager* [Munich: Kindler, 1974]).

6 Numbers from the *Stadtverwaltung* (city administration) Bitburg, which has no information about the soldiers' military units. They cannot confirm the allegation by Canadian writer Erna Paris that those forty-nine members of the Waffen *SS* belonged to the 2nd SS Panzer Division, "Das Reich," responsible for the murder of 642 men, women, and children at the French village Oradour-sur-Glane on June 10, 1944. Paris, Erna, *Long Shadows* (Toronto: Knopf, 2000), 68.

The massacre, executed by the 3rd Company of the SS regiment *Der Führer* (of the 2nd SS Panzer Division "Das Reich") under its leader *SS Obersturmbann-führer* Diekmann, has been recorded as the worst in the Western theatre of war. At the time, immediate demands for an investigation by SS and Wehrmacht officers, as well as French officials, were turned down by Hitler. During the days and weeks following the Oradour slaughter, Diekmann and large parts of his regiment were killed in action.

On March 12, 1953, a French military court in Bordeaux sentenced two of the surviving men to death and twelve to prison terms. Since a third of the men of the regiment *Der Führer* were Alsatians who claimed to have been drafted into the SS, there was a great deal of controversy and dissatisfaction in France about the trial, which led to an early release of all defendants. (Cartier, Raymond, *Der Zweite Weltkrieg* [Munich: Piper, 1979], 799ff.)

7 According to Peter Novick's *The Holocaust in American Life* (New York: Houghton Mifflin, 1999), 227, half of Americans surveyed, when asked whether their president should go through with the visit, approved; half disapproved.

8 Other greatly feared *Hauptämter* (Main Offices) were the *Rasse- und Siedlungs-Hauptamt* (Race and Settlement Main Office) and the *Wirtschafts-Verwaltungs-Hauptamt* (Economic and Administration Main Office), which administered the concentration camps. After Reinhard Heydrich's murder in Prague in January 1942, Ernst Kaltenbrunner took over the RSHA.

9 In 1943, the Gestapo (*Geheime Staatspolizei* or Secret State Police) consisted of 31,000 men and women. Their relatively small number sufficed because of the many denunciations they received from a co-operative public. *Enzyklopädie des Nationalsozialismus* (Stuttgart: Klett-Cotta, 1997), 481.

10 The work of the SD (*Sicherheitsdienst*, or Security Service) was discreet and almost unknown. Its 6,500 active members and 30,000 informers were organized in fifty-one main offices with 519 branches. (ibid., 728.) According to Eugen Kogon (op. cit., ref. 5, 50) those numbers were much higher: 100,000 to 120,000 in 1939, twice as many during the war.

11 On this particular issue, opinions may differ, depending on camp leadership, year of recruitment, or labor conditions. Generally speaking, however, compulsory labor service was one of the most hated Nazi institutions for both men and women.

12 Reich Marshal Hermann Göring, once the most popular man in the entire Nazi system, lost much of the people's admiration when his *Luftwaffe* fighters proved unable to stem the attacks of the British and American air fleets. Forced out of his drinking and drug problems while in captivity, he regained much of his former popularity during the Nuremberg Trials, when he proved himself a formidable adversary to the Allied prosecutors.

13 Field Marshal Erwin Rommel, the famous "Desert Fox," was commander of the Africa Corps and later of Army Group B in Italy and France. After the failed attempt on Hitler's life, he was forced to commit suicide in October 1944.

14 Grand Admiral Karl Dönitz, chief of the U-boat fleet and later commander-in-chief of the entire navy, headed the last Reich government, May 5 to 23, 1945.

15 Colonel General Heinz Guderian was the Inspector General of the Panzer Troops, the mainstay of the Wehrmacht's *Blitzkrieg*.

3

ENGLÄNDER

It was late one evening near the end of October in 1945 when I arrived in Osnabrück. Three months earlier, I had finally returned to Hamburg, located in the British zone of occupation, and, as far as traveling from American-occupied Marburg was concerned, as difficult to enter as a foreign country. Now I was back on the road again—or on the rails, as it were. My destination was Dülmen, a small town in Westphalia, also within the British zone and therefore "legally" accessible.

Almost six months had passed since the guns had fallen silent; World War II, having left Europe in ruins, was finally over. Moving around had become possible again, provided one was willing to accept any kind of conveyance, no matter how crude. There were no timetables, no assurance of services upon arrival. But there were no restrictions either, as long as one stayed within one's own zone of occupation.

After East Prussia and the areas east of the rivers Oder and Neisse were awarded to Poland and Russia, the remaining German territory was split into four zones of military occupation and governance. The Soviet zone east of the river Elbe was the largest, followed by the American zone in the beautiful southern half of the country, which included Bavaria. The British zone was the third largest, located in the highly industrialized, densely populated, but badly destroyed north and northwest region. Finally, a narrow strip in the southwest was handed to French general Charles de Gaulle as a last-minute sop for his support of the Allied cause after France's defeat in 1940. Bremen, Germany's second-largest port, was, like its larger rival Hamburg, located within the British zone, and became an American enclave in order to connect the landlocked American troops with their overseas supply lines.

A few weeks earlier, Josephine's father had arrived in Marburg, after driving his old tractor trailer over 200 kilometers of broken roads to pick up his daughter and her two small children and take them back to safety on his farm in Dülmen. To clear the place out, they had simply added my meager belongings, left behind when I set out for Hamburg, to everything else on the truck.

Now I was on my way to Dülmen for a reunion with Josephine, and to make arrangements, if at all possible, for the return of clothes, books, and whatever else might have survived from my former student existence. That, at least, was the official version, the one I had given my parents when they tried to talk me out of yet another traveling adventure. I hadn't listened, of course. My real intentions—or hopes, as it were—the ones I didn't mention, were contained in a crumpled letter from Josephine that had arrived only a couple of days earlier, and which I now carried in my pocket like a precious nugget. I had read and reread the letter dozens of times, savoring the casual message that was really a hidden message to me personally and only to be understood by me.

My route, to the extent that it could be planned at all under the still chaotic conditions, was to take me through Osnabrück, a mid-sized city where I intended to stay overnight at my godmother's house. Aunt Hilde was my last relative in a city where a small steel-processing plant had afforded my maternal grandparents a comfortable existence, until the Great Inflation of the early 1920s wiped out all their savings and securities.

Having traveled all day at a snail's pace, stopping at every village and town and frequently in-between, the train now approached its final stop. I peered into the darkness, but all I could see was the familiar sight of ruins and rubble. My heart sank as I realized how difficult it would be to locate my aunt in a city that had lost all points of orientation, and that was about to shut down for the night.

The long line of freight cars came to a clanging stop. After more than fourteen hours in an open coal wagon, I was cold and stiff. I anxiously clutched my jute bag, as strong arms lifted me out of the car and down onto the gravel.

The moment I hit the ground, my worst fears were confirmed. Under the dim light of the open sky, the station erupted in bedlam. Shouts and whistles pierced the air, as the rough hands of military police herded and shoved hundreds of confused passengers away from the train through an unlit underpass and out of the station. Our arrival had been delayed by hours, leaving just fifteen minutes to curfew, the nightly period of confinement for all Germans that was strictly enforced by the occupying armies.

I glanced at my watch, then hastened along the dark underpass, pushed along by a panicky crowd. The shrieking whistles echoing from the walls made my jaws cramp with fear.

"You have a place to stay?" A fat old woman in shabby clothes with a working-class accent nudged my shoulder. Instinctively I pulled back.

"Yes—at Heinrichstrasse," I answered reluctantly, giving her my godmother's address. "Much too far—you'll never make it. You'd better come with me." It sounded more like an order than an offer. I didn't know what to say. I tried to put some distance between the woman and myself, but I knew she was still behind me when we reached the exit.

The crowd dispersed, swallowed up by empty streets that spread out like ribs in a lady's fan. An eerie silence rose from the dark. There were no lights, no signs to direct me. Just the dim outlines of shell-pitted facades, now a common sight throughout Germany. I was still unsure of which way to turn when the woman grabbed my hand.

"Come along—never mind you don't know me." When I didn't respond, she added more kindly: "It's all right. You needn't be afraid."

She must have sensed my reluctance, which was really a strong personal aversion. In the social confines in which I was raised—and which stubbornly resisted reform while everything else collapsed—women like her had never touched me. I had encountered her kind before, when I accompanied my mother to the harbor to buy fresh crabs right off the boat, or handed out rags from our back door—a long time ago, before the war, when there were still rags to collect or crabs to catch in unmined waters.

We crossed the square fronting the station, then lost ourselves in the darkness of the city. The woman hurried along. "Watch that rubble," she warned as we passed piled-up debris. And shortly after: "Won't be long now." A real fear of being kidnapped or violated prevented me from taking stock of where we were going. I thought of my mother and the many times she had warned me never to go with strangers, wondering what she would have done in my position. We didn't meet a soul. Whether we went a thousand metres or twice as far, I didn't notice.

The woman stopped. She pushed open a door and dragged me into an unlit hall.

"It's four flights up. Stay close." I couldn't see a thing as we shuffled up the stairs. "Careful, the rail is gone."

Not only was the rail gone, but the outside wall as well. We stood again in the cold air, grey light drifting in from the open sky. The woman groped for her keys and opened a door to what must have been the surviving back portion of the top floor. "You must be quiet. My husband is asleep," she whispered. "He doesn't need to know."

A grizzled figure snored in one of the beds as we tiptoed through the cluttered room to a narrow chamber behind. The woman lit a candle. The chamber was empty but for a bed and a night table. A comforter and a plump pillow were piled on an uncovered mattress; there was no linen. The woman puffed up the pillow.

"When does your train go?" she asked, after I told her I had given up hope of finding my godmother in the shattered city. "Seven o'clock," I replied, and she promised to wake me. She closed the door, then returned once more with a chamber pot, which she placed inside the night table. "If you have to go—"

"I never have to," I said, embarrassed, hoping it would be true.

I decided to stay awake in case something happened; I certainly would not undress. God only knew what kind of people had slept in that bed.

When the woman returned, I couldn't believe that almost eight hours had passed. I still felt uneasy, but also ashamed about my poor self-control. What if she had really intended to harm me? Who would ever have heard from me again? The woman showed me the communal toilet that was down two flights of stairs. It was old and water-stained but otherwise clean. There were squares of newspaper stuck on a nail and a long chain with a wooden grip that reluctantly released water from a tank above.

Afterwards, she let me out onto the street, shoving a molasses sandwich into my hand. "Just follow this road till you see the tracks. Then turn left until the crossing. The station entrance is on the other side." She withdrew into the house. I wanted to thank her, perhaps say something more, I'm not sure. The door had already closed, leaving me with an odd sense of abandonment.

Recalling the scene today, I still feel ashamed. Why hadn't I said some kind words, or thanked her properly? Why was I so stuck up, a captive of my prejudices?

I hadn't even asked her name.

A dense fog pressed down on the street like steam trapped under the roof of a station. It picked up the sound of my steps, and threw it back, as though the steps belonged to somebody else. Within minutes I had lost all orientation; I wasn't sure about the other side of the road, whether I had already passed that pile of rubble the woman had warned me about the night before. Suddenly, two men emerged like ghosts from the fog, right at my side. Relieved, I asked them for directions. When it turned out that they, too, were heading for the station, I gratefully fell in with their rapid stride.

"Where are you going?"

"Dülmen. And you?"

"Cologne." We would be traveling together.

Our train was late and hopelessly overcrowded with people crouching on top of the wagons, hanging from the doors, or trying to find a precarious foothold on the bumpers. One of my companions headed straight for the car at the end, then beckoned us when he found its brake cabin empty. There was no glass in the windows, and it seemed draftier even than the open car the day before. Perhaps it was the early hour, or a colder day—I shivered.

The men had brought along some lengths of canvas, which they quickly draped over the missing glass. They seemed remarkably astute in matters of transport for reasons they didn't explain and I didn't ask. I knew, however, that there were people who made a living by being habitually on the road; like gypsies, but for more dubious reasons and greater profit. We huddled in a tight knot under army blankets the men provided.

In hindsight, I often wonder about the situation I so willingly put myself into. How dangerous was it really? After all, there was nothing in that closed room of a moving train to stand between me and any act of violence. And yet, I hadn't hesitated for a second. While I had entertained all sorts of sinister fantasies about the kind old woman, no doubts crossed my mind that morning. Was I just terribly naive? More enlightened about the subject of class than sexual assault?

Sure, those men hadn't looked particularly villainous, but neither had the woman. Besides, how was one to recognize a villain at a time when everybody was dressed in old, shabby clothes suitable for traveling in a boxcar?

Perhaps I had simply been lucky. Still, I am convinced that things were different then, that despite six years of a violent war and the breakdown of all civil niceties, people were generally quite safe. Even with living conditions as bad as they were, I do not recall a single report of murder, rape, or robbery perpetrated by Germans on Germans during those early postwar years. There were alleged isolated cases at the hands of Allied soldiers, but they were quickly hushed up and dealt with in military style.

This stood in marked contrast to the grim conditions in the Soviet zone, where, in the early months of occupation, Red Army soldiers assaulted Germans almost at will. Also vulnerable were people living in isolated locations in both the Eastern and Western zones—farmers mostly—who were frequently attacked by roaming bands of displaced persons or former concentration camp inmates. Often of non-German origin, and with no place to go, these formerly oppressed individuals took easy revenge against their oppressors. When things threatened to get out of hand, British field marshal Bernard Montgomery commanded his troops to restore order.

*   *   *

I was cold and miserable when I climbed out of the train in Dülmen. Like the rest of the city, which had stood in the way of the invading troops, the small station had been razed by bombs and artillery shells. There were few shoppers in the street at this early hour. I asked for directions, then crossed the town towards the open countryside. Whether there was a bus or a streetcar to take me part of the way, I cannot remember.

It was a dreary walk. Not knowing how far I had to go, it seemed very long. The farmhouses on both sides were large and well-maintained, with a hint of parsimony in the severe lines of their architecture and in the frugal order of the unadorned yards, as though the owners were trying to conceal their wealth. I studied the square little windows with their muslin curtains and small potted plants, and wondered about the people within, whose famed prosperity had been built by generations working the Westphalian soil, the richest in all of Germany. Were they deliberately shutting themselves off from the starving urban population?

I had to fight a rising unease. It was a damp morning and I wore no coat. It had been sunny and unusually mild when I left Hamburg. I had easily persuaded myself that it would be all right to travel in my new suit with its three-quarter-length jacket of bottle-green Loden over a skirt of heavy grey tweed. The pieces had been cut from my father's old hunting outfit by a seamstress who had bartered her time and skills in exchange for a few days of food and warmth in our house. The suit, my first ever, had filled me with extravagant pride. I hadn't wanted to spoil its effect with a coat that, after years of wear and war, was frayed at the cuffs and inches too short.

The fog had lifted and a light wind had sprung up. The cool air smelled of earth and dung and life. I stopped to wipe the mud off my shoes, my eyes roaming over the land that stretched vast and flat and sated to the distant horizon, where a dark line of soil welded itself to the heavy clouds. A farm wagon, drawn by two horses, passed me, bearing a load of turnips. I beckoned to the driver, but he looked away without offering a lift. A flock of crows rose from the field and circled overhead, their petulant cries piercing the melancholy of the day.

I recognized the Hilltrupp farm with its high lilac hedge from photographs Josephine had shown me in Marburg. During those first uncertain weeks of American occupation, we had often consoled each other with reminiscences about our families, our homes, and whatever else had filled our days during a past that, even then, seemed far removed and forever gone.

Many times back then, Josephine had talked about her years in school, where strict, if not unkind, nuns had filled her young mind with stories of Sweet Jesus and the glory of service in the bosom of the Holy Church. Over the years, as Josephine moved from one convent school to the next, loved and expelled and loved again, her teachers' gentle insistence had followed her, never relenting. In the end, she had resisted all their appeals, just as she had resisted the best hopes of a mother who prayed a lot, but rarely praised. And yet, Josephine was a true believer in Christ, the Holy Spirit, the sanctity of the Virgin Mary, and an eternal life. To me, a lapsed Protestant, such unquestioning acceptance and observance of a string of incomprehensible dogmas sounded utterly incompatible with the idea of a free spirit like Josephine's; moreover, it seemed entirely irreconcilable with her razor-sharp mind. But, whenever I gave voice to my iconoclastic thoughts—naive and uninformed, perhaps even insulting, as they most likely were—Josephine would throw back her head in mocking laughter, which started out on a very high note and shimmied down the scale like a hammer over a child's xylophone. She never got angry, never scolded me for my ignorance; neither did she try to convert me. Perhaps even then, the doubts had begun to nestle deep within her soul.

The memories came back like the scenes of an old film. Until I met

Josephine, church to me had meant Protestant confirmation in Hamburg by a young pastor who, one year later, had volunteered for service at the Russian front and had been killed within three months. Dark-haired and dark-skinned, he had blue eyes and a hard Baltic accent. He hadn't brought me much closer to God, but he had been the first man to whom I had, at age fourteen, linked myself in romantic fantasies. I had cried when I learned of his death. I found God unjust and wilful, and I banished him from my life, a life he had never fully entered.

The Hilltrupp house was a large two-story building with narrow windows and a black slate roof. I knocked, but there was no answer. I tried the knob, and when the door proved unlocked, I stepped over the stone threshold into a long hall extending down the width of the building. The floor was covered with red tiles, uneven from a century of use. On the dark wall hung a mirror in a gilt frame with a slim rest at the bottom and a bunch of dried flowers decorating the ledge. There was a door with a small window, leading outside, at the opposite end of the hall, and two more doors to the right and left with crucifixes on top. At the far side, a staircase led up to the second floor. A faint smell of oil-painted walls and newly waxed floors mingled with the scent of fresh dung from outside, a comforting and familiar reminder of the farms my father had taken me to as a child. Through the low ceiling came the loud tick-tock of a grandfather clock. Otherwise, the house was completely silent.

Wondering what to do next, I walked slowly down the hallway, trying both doors. To the right, the large kitchen with its wood-burning stove was empty; so was the living room across the hall. Without much hope of a response, I called out: "Hello—?" Immediately a door on the second floor opened and closed, and hurried steps descended the stairs. The light from the window in the rear silhouetted a woman's tall, slim figure, dressed in a hand-knitted sweater and heavy woollen frock.

"Gerti! How wonderful to see you." Josephine spread her arms wide to embrace me. Her joy was huge and genuine. So was her surprise. "How in the world did you manage to get here?"

"By train. All day yesterday in a coal wagon."

"You poor girl. How absolutely dreadful."

"It wasn't too bad. Lots of soldiers around, back from POW camps."

"I bet they kept you warm!" Once more we hugged and laughed with the warm old intimacy, as though we had never parted.

*　　*　　*

After five decades, I still cannot think about the way I left Josephine in Marburg without hating myself: Perhaps because I had been completely penniless, with no more cash transfers from my father since Christmas, when the mail had come through for the last time; or, because I had grown tired of being so dependent, so inferior by reasons of age, status, and experience; or, because I was overwhelmingly homesick, not knowing whether my parents were alive or dead. Whatever the reasons I gave to myself or her at the time, I had suddenly decided to try the risky border crossing from Marburg in the American zone to Hamburg in the British. There had been rumors about a large truck destined for the port city that would take a few passengers, provided they had the proper papers. When I heard about it, my mind was made up: I had to go—I simply had to.

When I left Josephine, it was the end of July, a little over a month before her second baby was due, her first child still being only a year old. I felt profoundly guilty for abandoning her in that condition. Yet, she insisted that I leave, that she would be all right. She made it so easy for me, too easy.

When I had not returned after a few days, she decided that I had reached my destination or perished in the process. It was only reasonable for her then to ask another student to move in with her, though she hadn't mentioned her plans to me. The girl stayed with her throughout the time of her hospitalization and until the day when Josephine's father came down from Dülmen to pick up his daughter and grandchildren. I never learned whether the girl had approached Josephine, or whether Josephine had sought her out deliberately. I was surprised when I heard about it, even a bit annoyed; actually, I was fiercely jealous. Because, of all the girls in the world she could have chosen, the one she did choose was Rita, the other student from Müller's office, the one whom nobody had liked, and whom I, being her equal, had liked—or trusted—even less. Josephine had surely known what I thought of Rita, and she must have known that I knew she knew. Had this been her subtle way to teach me some manners?

With a chunk of bread in my rucksack and a few items of clothing, plus a crudely faked travel permit, I got across the border into the British zone. After two days of hiking, and the occasional haphazard transportation, I finally made it home. When I arrived, at seven o'clock in the morning, the streets were empty and the house was very quiet. At sunrise, my last transport had let me off near the bridge over the river Elbe, after a wild eight-hour ride in a car crammed with boxes of schnapps, whose weight had broken the car's axle, which, in turn, had caused so many bottles to crack that their fumes had lulled the driver (a specimen of the new security police allowed to drive during curfew) into a semi-comatose state. Grateful for the transport and glad to have survived its erratic course, I set out on foot. I passed the railroad station (crumbled), my father's grain elevator (still standing), the *Niedersachsenwerk*, where I had helped build the Big J U (crushed). And later, as far as the eye could see, the bent skeletons of the oil refineries and the flattened bodies of burnt-out oil tanks. An eery sound of moaning hung over the deathscape as the morning breeze playfully pushed and twisted huge sheets of ripped metal dangling like grotesque sculptures.

At the house, I tried the bell. It didn't work, so I called my parents' names and knocked on the plywood that covered the broken windows. The sudden shock of hearing my voice after nine months of separation badly confused them. First they couldn't find the key to the outside door; and, after they had found it and let me in, they were still running back and forth, babbling and shaking their heads, my father searching for his pants and my mother fussing over her hair. We embraced in a tight knot and we laughed, and then we cried. I cried as though I would never be able to stop, as though mountains of fear and despair needed to be washed away. When it was over, so much else seemed to be over, too. Like a terribly difficult book one has neither had the strength to finish, nor ever fully understood, but has finally decided to close.

*   *   *

"Take off your jacket and make yourself comfortable. You must be starving." Josephine reached for my bag and led me to the living room, where I recognized most of her old furniture. "This is where we live now. It's not grand, but it's better than Marburg. Remember?" She nudged me playfully. "The bedroom is just behind. Come on, I'll show you." She held a finger to her lips. "The baby is asleep." We tiptoed into a half-darkened room where the first things I noticed were two prints in stark colors. One showed a bearded Jesus with long wavy hair and soft, red lips, carrying his heart in one hand and pointing to the blood on his shirt with a white and effeminate finger. The second was of a sweet-faced, very young Mary, smiling down on an oversized infant.

We bent over a laundry basket in which a small bundle lay hidden beneath a cloud of white muslin and tulle. Little hands clasped into fists were pressed against both sides of his tiny head. His skin was rosy and smooth, and he looked healthy and content. Josephine's face was filled with motherly pride. "Isn't he adorable?" she whispered, leading me back to the living room. "Our Manfred," she announced proudly. "He's almost as much yours as mine." I was touched and immensely relieved that she seemed to have accepted my former desertion in such a generous way. Suddenly, all the shame and bitter jealousy that I had lugged around right up to this moment dissolved in a wave of gratitude. "We'll all sleep together again—you and Karl, with me in the middle, like in the olden days." We both giggled, remembering my first night at Josephine's apartment.

"Is Karl all right? When did he come back?"

"Didn't I tell you in my letter? My goodness, there'll be so much to talk about. We'll need ages. I hope you can stay a couple of days?"

I didn't know how to answer. Hadn't she realized I wasn't there for just an overnight stay? Whatever the duration, I certainly hadn't planned on going anywhere else. Sure, I wasn't exactly dressed for a three-week holiday late in fall. But if the weather turned cold, or walks around the farm were too messy, Josephine would certainly supply me with everything necessary. After all, she had done the same in Marburg.

She seemed not to notice my silence, but kept talking as she set the table for lunch.

"We'll eat late today. I hope you don't mind." She reached into the sideboard to bring up a poundcake wrapped in oilcloth. "Home-baked. To tide you over till one-thirty. That's when Karl and Jupp should be back."

"Jupp—?"

"Jupp Müller. You know—your old boss." She smiled at her choice of words, then paused. "Didn't I mention him in my letter?"

I froze. There was a buzz in my ears and my throat felt dry. In a split second I recognized the horrible mistake I had made. *Should you be able to visit us, you will meet somebody else you know.* How on earth could I have mistaken that casual remark for a secret message meant to reconnect me with my fugitive fiancé, Alex? Yet, not a shred of doubt had marred that agreeable illusion, which I now realized had been nothing but wishful thinking. I was mortified by this latest demonstration of my immaturity and impulsiveness. It was utterly unthinkable that I should let Josephine in on that ridiculous misunderstanding and the childish haste in which I had acted upon it. I struggled to regain control.

"Sure you did. For the moment I had forgotten all about it."

She looked at me with concern. Something in my voice must have sounded a bit off. And my hot cheeks may have given me away. "You weren't expecting someone else, were you? Alex maybe?"

"No, no, of course not."

"What did I write?"

"I can't remember exactly. That Karl was back. And somebody else I knew—"

"Müller."

"Yes, sure."

"You do remember Müller, don't you?" she inquired, rather archly I thought.

"Of course." I laughed derisively, signaling an end to whatever embarrassment the name might have caused me. "What is he doing here? After all, you weren't all that close. Did you invite him?"

"Heavens, no. He was here when I came back. Let me think: Manfred was born on August 25. My father came to Marburg to pick us all up when the baby was five or six weeks old. It was terrible—two days on the road with the children. Dieter was sick most of the time, then my milk blocked up, just like the first time. Without my father, we'd never have made it. He was so patient, much more patient than Karl could ever have been.

"Anyway, we must have gotten here around the first week of October. Müller was already here. He'd arrived while my father was on his way to Marburg. He told my mother he was a friend of Karl's, and Karl, of course, was too spineless to throw him out. My mother hasn't spoken to either of them since. Not a word. She tells me they're all a bunch of criminals, and a plague sent from God to punish us for our sins."

"You and sin!" The suggestion was plainly absurd. To me, Josephine was the most devout person on earth.

"Oh yes. She does have a point." She giggled mischievously, then confided in a hushed tone: "I baptized Manfred in the Protestant faith."

"No—you didn't." I was shocked, horrified. "Why—?"

"I don't know." Her voice became serious, revealing the trace of a sigh. "Since I've been here, I've found it hard to remember exactly why. Back then in Marburg, it somehow seemed the natural thing to do. After all, we had talked so much about the craziness of it all, the straitjacket the Church puts on people, its lack of true charity, its total failure during the war and the things the Nazis did. You know …" She suddenly sounded lost and sad.

"Sure, I understand." We embraced again in a tight, warm hug, two souls who had been through a lot, shared a lot. Lost a lot. "Did Karl object?"

"Of course not. He doesn't care one way or the other. I guess anything that upsets my bigoted mother is fine with him." The teasing little laugh was back and I joined in, relieved that she was climbing out of her mood.

"She won't be too happy having another infidel under her roof now," I remarked.

"She knows about you. I think she'll accept you as one of my closest friends. Anyway, we live pretty separate lives in this house. My parents have the upstairs and we are down here. Only the kitchen is for everybody."

"Still, you have to introduce me."

"Of course. But later." She looked at her watch. "Karl and Müller are in Münster at the university clinic. They both needed checkups for their tuberculosis. You know that Karl picked up TB in the Polish campaign?"

"I thought he was okay now."

"He is. But he needs regular checkups. Anyway, he wanted to go with Müller, who is still pretty weak after they removed one of his kidneys in Switzerland."

"How did he get there?"

"I have no idea. Illegally, of course. Somehow he must have had the good fortune to have an operation before they shoved him back across the border. He was still terribly weak afterwards, and the only place he could think of to hide until he got better was—guess where?"

I nodded.

"Good food and plenty of space to stay out of sight. He also rediscovered his old faith."

"You've got to be kidding!"

"I'm not. He used to be a choirboy; or so he told my mother. He even wanted to go to mass, but my father forbade him to show his face in public."

Josephine turned away, as though she was trying to make up her mind about something. "I guess I should keep quiet about this, but you won't tell?" Her eyes searched mine.

"Of course not."

"There are more people here than just Karl and Müller," she began in a voice so low and tentative, that I had to strain to make out her words. She had stopped working around the table and sat down in the rocking chair, where I remembered her so well with her swollen belly, forever knitting sweaters and pants for Dieter, and jackets and little bonnets for the baby she was expecting. "I don't know how many. One or two, I guess. They're all from Müller's old *Studentenkompanie*, and they've all miraculously turned up here on Dad's farm."

I was dismayed, but tried not to show it. "Did Karl invite them?"

"I doubt it. I can't image him doing a thing like that. He's unhappy enough about the way my mother goes on about him never doing an honest day's work, and stealing the Lord's time, and lying in bed till eleven in the morning—well, you get the idea."

"I know him so little. After all, he was away most of the time." Which was true. I knew much more about him from her stories than from personal contact. "Who are these 'others'?"

"I don't know and I don't want to know. They sleep in one of the hay barns and, with the exception of Müller, help with the work. For Dad it's not too bad a deal, and Mother never sees them."

"It's terribly dangerous, though."

"I know, I know. It's illegal to shelter any of them." She shrugged. "I guess many people do it, though."

She stood up resolutely, indicating the subject was closed. "You know nothing about this."

"Of course not. I would be crazy if I did." I meant it.

"I think I hear the tractor—that would be my father. He took Dieter with him this morning. They're all working at the wintering pits to get in the potatoes and turnips." Her laugh was good-natured. "Of course, that's all Greek to you, coming from the big city."

"It is not," I protested. As we headed out to look for little Dieter, I reminded her of the seven miserable months I had spent in 1943 in the *Arbeitsdienst*. For eight to ten hours a day, I had worked for peasants who would sooner have died than force a smile to their embittered lips. I hated farm life; I still do. I hated all those primitive, thankless, and unending tasks in an environment that seems hard to imagine now, but which, by 1943, had already vastly improved when compared to the early 1930s and the Great Depression. Strange as it may sound, there existed a direct connection between the post-Depression recovery of those indebted farmers and my own family's life, a connection that bears recounting for what it says about my father's earliest experiences with the Nazi dictatorship.

*   *   *

In the spring of 1943, immediately after my high school graduation, I received my draft papers for the *Arbeitsdienst*. The first thing I noticed was the coincidence that had me enlisted in a camp near Schobüll, smack in the area where my father had served his customers during the 1920s and early 1930s. There was hardly a village, peasant, or miller he didn't know. He had been an independent grain dealer then, making a good living by buying grain for bread, seed, and feed from major importers, and selling it to millers and local farmers. His office had been in Flensburg, a charming old city of 60,000 people and the commercial center of Angeln (Angul), a fertile peninsula formed by the lovely firths of the Baltic Sea. The farmers of Angul were proud of their solid history of homesteading, which went back centuries to early Germanic settlements. Thus, when they lost their sons in World War I, their savings in the disastrous inflation of 1923, and their farms and livestock in the Great Depression, their tragedy affected everybody in nearby Flensburg.

One of my earliest memories is of a large herd of beautiful cattle being hustled by its indebted owner through the narrow streets to the slaughterhouse. I can still remember the tears in my father's eyes as he tried to explain all this while we watched from his office. I thought that he cried for those poor cows, and he may well have. But he was really grieving for us—his family—and the comfortable lifestyle that was coming to an end right before his eyes.

It would take me a lifetime to understand the wider economic picture of the Great Depression and its consequences for my family, in order to judge with tolerance my father's actions, which I found so easy to condemn as a young person. Having alluded in a previous chapter to the unhappy climate in our house, I now find a chance to trace things back to their early beginnings.

Business transactions between a retailer and his client, or a retailer and his wholesale supplier, were traditionally sealed with a three-month promissory note. The system worked fine as long as everybody paid up on time. Once a link in the chain broke, and a promissory note went unredeemed, things came unstuck and the person in the middle got squeezed. My father, like many other grain dealers in Germany, was the one in the middle who lost his business through the prolonged insolvency of the farmers. A few merchants, my father not among them, were able to hold on until the government stepped in to help.

In order to save the country's endangered agricultural class, the Hitler regime acted boldly (many might say ruthlessly). Soon after coming to power, it disencumbered the farmers of much of their debt, while protecting land ownership through a new *Erbhofgesetz*, or Farm Inheritance Law. For the first time in several decades, farmers could breathe more freely. A secure line of inheritance was established, while pawning farms to creditors or parceling them up among quarreling siblings was outlawed. It was a Draconian measure, by no means welcomed by every peasant, but probably the most effective one, given the economic circumstances. By improving the country's domestic food supply, the government cut down on costly imports. It also created one of the Nazi party's most loyal group of supporters.

Understandably, there were others who were less happy. By a stroke of the government's pen, creditors were no longer permitted to squeeze any money or collateral from their insolvent debtors. If the creditor happened to be Jewish, his credit holdings were declared usurious and instantly forfeited. Non-Jewish merchants were eventually compensated by the government, at least in part, but only after much delay and uncertainty.

By 1936 our situation had become desperate enough for my father to concede defeat. After weeks of soul-wrenching debates and in the absence of any other long-term alternative, he finally reached for the life preserver thrown out to him by his brother, Paul, a wealthy grain importer and wholesaler in Hamburg—thrown to him after having refused to extend the terms of the promissory notes in his hand. The job my uncle offered his younger brother, Walther, was director of a brand new and ultra-modern grain elevator in Hamburg.

Was Paul a power-driven man who couldn't tolerate his younger brother's independence? There are sibling rivalries, certainly, but was this one excessively vindictive? And if so, why? The brothers were only one year apart, and the younger no threat to the elder. Personally, I had always had an excellent relationship with my uncle, whose wit and pluck

I admired. Had he recognized a weakness in his younger brother that would presage failure? Maybe all he ever wanted to do was rescue Walther from himself. Perhaps that's what he truly thought to be best.

Ironically, my father's final "surrender" came in November 1936, just when things in Germany were turning around. Primed by a huge rearmament effort, the Nazi economy was changing depression-ravaged Germany into that fully employed, well-organized, ultra-clean country the world had admired during the Olympic Games in Berlin earlier that year. Soon, our personal finances were improving also, though the mood in our home was not. It would never become cheerful again over the ensuing thirty-three years—my father, long having recovered his middle-class comforts, would carry his bitterness to his grave.

*　　*　　*

Little Dieter didn't recognize me. After all, he was not even two years old and couldn't be expected to remember people he hadn't seen for months. Still, I felt disappointed by his rejection. Josephine laughed as she scooped him up. "Give Auntie Gerti a hug, Dieterle." She pressed him into my arms, then left us struggling while she went out to call everybody for lunch.

"Down in a minute." I recognized Karl's voice with its delightful accent of an educated Franconian. It made my north-German idiom ring flat and graceless, even to my own ears. He entered, spreading his arms wide, his warm and dimpled smile charming me off my feet as it always had. He was tall and slim, with straight black hair greying at the temples. The skin on his face was tanned and creased around his dark brown eyes. "What a surprise! When did you get here? Did Josephine know anything about it? Josephine?" He turned to his wife as she entered with a huge tray. "Did you have any idea?"

"Of course not. She surprised us all." She took us both in with her engaging, motherly smile, happy to have her loved ones united under one roof.

"Jupp will be down in a minute. He apologizes, but one of the men is trying to get into the American zone and will take a letter along for Jupp's wife. He's just about finished it."

"If he doesn't mind a cold meal." Josephine shrugged.

The three of us took our seats around the table, with little Dieter elevated on a stack of dictionaries. There was a large platter of pork boiled in white cabbage, with a bowl of peeled potatoes to go with it.

"Help yourself, Gerti—I bet you haven't seen anything like this in a long time." She was right.

"Josephine is stuffing us all like the—" Karl stopped in mid-sentence as ominous sounds drifted in from the yard.

We all fell silent. Everybody strained to listen.

"*Engländer!*" Karl leaped from his chair and flung open the door. "Englishmen." He ran down the hall, a door banged, then several other doors opened and shut.

Silence.

Josephine stood at the window, careful not to be seen from outside. "There are two or three trucks with soldiers. They all have rifles."

I moved over beside her. "What do they want? Have they been here before?" I was too surprised to be scared. But the child, upset by the commotion, began to cry. Josephine picked him up and cradled him. "Shh-shh—they won't do anything to us, they'll go away." But her voice was tight. There was a loud knock on the front door, then the sound of heavy boots in the hall. Two men, an officer and a corporal, stood at the threshold to our room.

"Your name, please," the officer demanded. He spoke in English and the corporal translated.

Josephine replied.

"And yours?" I told him. He consulted a paper, then looked up, annoyed. "You live here?"

"No."

"Your ID, please." I rummaged in my purse, and when I couldn't produce it, he became impatient.

"*Es muss in meiner Reisetasche sein.*" The corporal translated, and the officer allowed me to search through my travel bag. When I found my identification papers, he wrote the information carefully down, then directed his attention back to Josephine: "Where is your husband?"

She shrugged. "Not here."

"But he was just here." He gestured sternly at the half-eaten lunch plate. "He may try to run away, but we'll catch him in no time." He made some more notes, then looked up again. "You know a man by the name of Joseph Miller?" Josephine, even then the teacher at heart that she would later become for life, couldn't resist correcting him:

"Müller. His name is Müller. Yes, I know him."

"And where is he?"

The low ceiling suddenly made the room feel stuffy, as though the silence had used up all the air. Everybody looked at Josephine, who picked up the whimpering child.

I realized that I had not yet seen Müller, and that I didn't know where his room was exactly. If it was here in the house, the situation for all of us might be difficult. The officer's voice was still quiet but contained the trace of a threat as he repeated: "Where is Joseph Müller?" The empty plate on the table sat in silent reproach.

Apparently Josephine had decided that a good offence might be the best defence. "It's been months since I last saw him. In Marburg, where my husband studied. Do you expect me to keep track of everybody I've met, even in the American zone?" For a moment the British officer seemed disturbed by the mention of his powerful ally's zone of control. But it took him only a second to recover.

"We'll get him, don't kid yourself. He's a sick man—he won't get far."

So they knew that too. Josephine must have had the same worrisome thought, because she started fussing with the child.

The officer handed back my ID and turned to Josephine: "What is she doing here?" Clearly, he had decided that she was the more intelligent one, the person in charge of the situation.

"She's visiting me."

His lips curled. "Just like that."

"Yes."

"Why?" Again, there was that underlying menace in his tone. But Josephine seemed not to have noticed, or else to have decided that I really was an innocent bystander and she could abandon her former caution: "To eat. To get her fill from the Westphalian pork pots." It was a good answer, and the corporal seemed to think so too, grinning while he translated.

There was no reaction from the officer. He merely nodded, then left.

*   *   *

Nothing much happened during the next hours, at least nothing that we could see from our rooms. Ordered to remain in our quarters (which, by special licence, included the kitchen across the hall), we were physically cut off from the world. I hadn't even had a chance to see the rest of the house, its layout, its entrances and exits, not to mention the rest of its inhabitants. I therefore didn't have a clue how Josephine managed to pick up various rumors, that sounded increasingly ominous. But somehow she did.

From the window, I could see a large yard bordered in front by the familiar lilac hedge, a low barn to the right, which probably housed pigs, and a two-story structure to the left, with a hayloft over what presumably were stalls for cattle and horses. The center of the yard was covered by lawn with an oak tree in the middle. The tree was one of those immense specimens symbolizing, in national imagery and literature, the German people's most cherished virtues: indestructibility, reliability, and resilience. It was a man-woman image suggesting strength as well as survival, the very essence of Germany's ideological credo, if not necessarily its reality.

There were no flower beds to cheer things up, only a wooden bench under the thick oak canopy. A circular driveway led around the perimeter of the lawn, bisected by a footpath. Apart from an empty army Jeep, and the occasional British soldier roaring in and out on his motorcycle, the place looked deserted.

Yet, there had to be guards posted somewhere. The heavy silence that hung over the farm was clearly artificial and the result of orders from higher authorities. Knowing since earliest childhood the various routines of the hired hands, Josephine worried whether everyone who belonged to the farm was still permitted to be there. But, what concerned her even more was the fate of her father, who hadn't been back to the house since noon, when he had delivered little Dieter—less than thirty minutes before the place became "occupied."

And occupied it was; there could be no doubt about the seriousness of the operation, its organized character, or the secrecy of its execution. The last was what really disturbed us—it suggested some political, rather than military, connection. Though neither Josephine nor I knew much about the size and depth of the ongoing operations to clean up the collapsed Nazi system, we had heard enough to make us squirm at the prospect of being drawn into some sinister process of political reckoning.

Later that afternoon, after an unexplained absence of over an hour, Josephine reappeared in the living room, stone-faced. She closed the door and leaned against it.

"Where have you been?" I tried to suppress the anger I had nourished since discovering that she had slipped out without a word. "I've worried myself silly. Why didn't you tell me where you were going? What if somebody had checked? What was I supposed to say?" My resentment slipped through despite the effort to control it.

During her absence, I had stewed over the situation and my unfortunate and ill-timed part in it. The longer I thought about it, the more annoyed I had become: After all, the whole thing didn't concern me, and I was beginning to feel rather unjustly done by.

Josephine ignored my outburst. In a hushed and urgent voice she explained: "They've taken my father. They told him it would only be for some interrogation, but the man I talked to is sure they've put him in jail."

"Why?" I, too, kept my voice down, although there was nobody around to hear. "What does your father have to do with them?" My selfish anger burst like a bubble as our worst fears became shockingly real. Clearly, what we were faced with was not a hare-brained military exercise on someone's private grounds—after all, Germany was conquered and occupied and, at least in theory, any officer could do as he pleased—but rather a serious danger, lurking somewhere in the fields and barns of that pastoral scene.

"The man said they had searched the buildings and found an army pistol."

"What man? Where have you been?" She still hadn't answered that question.

For the first few hours after the initial shock, we had tried to behave as normally as possible, so as not to upset the children. Josephine had breast-fed the baby, and I had renewed my friendship with Dieter. Now and again we ventured into the kitchen, opened some doors and peeked through, playing silly games to entertain the children and ourselves. There were no soldiers in the main building, we discovered, nobody to enforce orders. So Josephine had sneaked up to the second floor to look in on her mother. But the old woman, kneeling before a small shrine, had turned her away with some bitter words. Her father hadn't been there, and when Josephine asked where he was, her mother hadn't answered.

Now Josephine said: "I didn't want to upset you, that's why I didn't say anything. But I simply had to know what's going on. And if it's true that Papa has been taken away—"

She left the sentence unfinished, but its implication was clear. We locked eyes, panic welling up between us like the rancid stench of a cornered animal. Dieter started to whine, but for once his mother showed no patience. She marched him into the adjoining room and closed the door. When his whining escalated into screams of protest, she let him back out again so the baby would not wake up. She sat down in the rocking chair, trying to soothe the child and herself, while tears gathered in her eyes.

"My father—the kindest, most generous man in the world."

For a while she let the tears run freely, then wiped them away with her sleeve. "In the barn are crates and bags from all sorts of people who have stored them there to protect them from the bombs."

"They should have picked them up a long time ago."

"Of course they should. But you know how people are. The man I talked to thought the box or crate with the pistol had belonged to some officer who was killed or taken prisoner by the Russians or something, and his parents, who had asked my father to keep his stuff, perhaps don't even know where he is, or have forgotten that they left his things with us."

"But that shouldn't be too difficult to prove." I felt relieved. After all, there must have been witnesses; the owners of those boxes could be located and all accusations dropped.

"You're probably right. But he says there's no name, and nobody knows who really owns the pistol." While talking, she caressed Dieter, whose dark eyes were round with fear. He was sitting on his mother's lap with a rigid back, as though no longer daring to entrust his fear to the one person who had always been able to make it fly away. Absentmindedly, she stroked his fine brown hair. "We'll put him to bed and then we can talk," she said.

With less than her usual resolve, she got up to fix supper for the boy, and I followed her into the kitchen.

"Who did you talk to?"

"A Frenchman. He used to work here as a prisoner of war. But when they came to send him home, he decided to stay. He said he really liked farm work—he was a teacher in France before being drafted. He has been with us all these years, since 1940. He adores my father, and my father has always treated him like a son."

"By the way, where are your brothers?" I knew that she had two younger brothers, though I'd never met them.

"Still with the Russians. We hope that at least the younger one, Hermann, will be home soon. He wasn't even eighteen when he was drafted, just weeks before the end of the war."

I wanted to know more about the things she had learned: "That Frenchman—"

"Jacques."

"Whose side is he on, really? Do the British trust him? Do they let him move around?"

"He cannot leave the farm—nobody can. The people who come every day to help all have to stay overnight." She pushed her hair back in an angry gesture. "Jacques says they are furious about it and that they blame us. They have been working here for ages, and now they've suddenly turned against us. There are three—two men and a woman—and none of them wants to do any more work. Jacques does everything. The others would like to get back at him for it, but they don't really know where he stands with the soldiers."

"To stand with you may hurt him," I said. It was an unpleasant thought: One of the victors becoming ostracized for his loyalty to the vanquished. Officially it was called "fraternization" and frowned upon by all sides.

"I know—I warned him. He doesn't care."

"How did you manage to talk to him?"

For a second, the old mischievous laugh was back in her eyes. "I put a big apron on, and clogs, and a scarf over my head. Anybody who saw me would have thought I was one of the laborers."

"Not your own people."

"No, they wouldn't have. I don't think any of them saw me, though. I went straight for the barn, where I knew Jacques would be milking at that time. With my stool and pail, I clamped myself under the next cow and milked away, like any old farmhand. Thank God for having learned that little part of peasant routine!"

"And there you talked."

"Whispered."

"What else did he know?"

"It seems they're looking for somebody."

"Whom?"

"Müller, perhaps?"

"God—that guy! He seems to be nothing but trouble. Why did he ever come here?"

Josephine shrugged. She took a tray from the shelf and carried milk and tea and slices of smoked sausage to the living room. I followed her with butter, cheese, and a huge loaf of sourdough bread. For a moment, I forgot my worries as my eyes feasted on the food, which seemed like a three-month supply from a whole family's ration cards—if there were such delicacies to be had on the cards, which, of course, there weren't.

"Maybe you didn't lie to that officer when you said I'd come here to get fat."

"Fine with me—stay as long as you like." We ignored the irony of her words. For a while, neither of us spoke. Then, Josephine continued: "Isn't it strange that fate always brings us together when something really bad has happened?"

"Or is about to happen."

"What do you mean?"

"I don't know. But instinct tells me that this thing isn't over by a long shot."

She sighed. "Much as I hate to admit it, I have the same feeling." She reached for my hand and squeezed it. Then she turned to Dieter, who had been playing quietly with his toy soldiers, arranging them in a long single file that wound around the legs of the dining room table. "Come on, let's eat—no good has ever come of an empty stomach." The boy climbed onto his stack of books, angrily pushing away his mother's helping hand.

Nobody ate much, despite Josephine's encouragement. She herself took only a few bites, mostly rejects from Dieter's plate. After twenty minutes, we got up and cleared everything away.

It must have been after seven, the children safely in bed, when we again heard steps enter the hall and stop outside our room. Josephine opened the door, but when she tried to look out, a soldier barricaded her path with his rifle. Without explanation, he reached around to pull the key out of the lock, closed the door, and locked us in. Josephine hammered against the door, but there was no reaction. About an hour later, the officer returned with his interpreting corporal and advised us to use the second-floor bathroom immediately, because our room would be locked for the night. The officer tapped his cap in a mock salute, and departed. One at a time, we were chaperoned upstairs, the corporal standing guard outside the door. He marched us back to our quarters, turned the key and joined his superior in the Jeep outside.

We tried to stick to some semblance of normalcy in order to control our mounting fears. Josephine fed and diapered the baby, while I gathered up Dieter's toys in a big wooden box. Earlier, he had allowed me to put him into his pyjamas without protest. In fact, he had been so quiet, so obviously aware that something was terribly wrong, that it only added to our depressed mood. Later, we carried the two sleeping angels into the living room, then crept into bed ourselves.

Outside, things seemed to have arranged themselves according to some prescribed order. The front yard was brightly lit by two heavy spotlights, mounted on an army truck. The lights penetrated the blinds that covered our windows. There were soldiers somewhere; we couldn't see them, but we could hear their laughter. A radio played American jazz.

"We are prisoners," Josephine whispered. "I'm a prisoner in my own house, and you, my guest, have been made a prisoner too." It sounded like a declaration of protest over some intolerable conduct for which one would only have to complain to the proper authorities for things to be straightened out. She was play-acting, of course. Although we didn't know the exact circumstances of our predicament, we were only too aware that under the laws of occupation, every German was subject to whatever military rule happened to apply in his sector. We were in the British sector and, for all practical purposes, anybody wearing a British uniform held absolute power. There was no civilian recourse whatsoever.

"I wonder where Karl is?"

It was the first time she'd mentioned him, as though she had intentionally distanced herself from the thought.

"He must have gotten away. Otherwise, your Frenchman would have said something."

She agreed. "Karl knows a lot of people. The funny thing is, although he's so different from anybody around here, they all like him."

"He's an extremely likeable person."

"He's a fool. A nice fool, maybe, but a fool. And most people like nice fools, because they're no danger to them." Her voice, which usually had a motherly tone when she spoke of Karl, sounded bitter. "Without Karl, there would be no Müller, or any of the others. How could he have let them come here?"

"I thought you said he had nothing to do with it?"

"He may not exactly have sent around written invitations. But it stands to reason that without Karl, nobody would ever have dreamed of showing up here."

I suddenly felt uncomfortable. The thought that good old Karl (at thirty-six, he really did seem "old" in comparison to my twenty) should have been responsible for the mess we all found ourselves in just didn't seem right. I tried to change the subject. Remembering the big slices of meat I had witnessed at lunch and for supper, I said: "Do you remember the last time we feasted together?"

Josephine laughed, then abruptly turned serious: "Don't remind me. I'll never get that thing off my conscience. Poor Mrs. Heise—I believe we truly destroyed something deep in her heart. I can still hear her: 'And I'd always thought you such a good woman...'" She mimicked the whiny voice of her former landlady, from whom we had stolen at a time when it was difficult to replace even a half-loaf of bread.

"Did you make it up to her later?"

"Of course. My father brought her all sorts of good things, and in the end she was so moved, she cried every time she saw me. I was glad when we finally left." She paused, reflecting: "Still—I broke something deep inside her."

"We did."

She didn't answer. For a while, both of us were silent, remembering the day the war ended, when the last remnants of the German government surrendered and, after six years of terror, the killing in Europe finally stopped.

*   *   *

Following Hitler's suicide on April 30, 1945, Josephine and I listened to the radio almost incessantly. When on May 8 the momentous news finally came, the announcement was solemn, yet short and anticlimactic: The German army had surrendered, unconditionally, at such and such a time, to such and such a general. There was more, of course: serious music, commentaries, calls for calm. But the facts themselves were short, just a line marking the conclusion to a long and brutal story: Hitler was dead, the Third Reich was dead, Germany was dead.

That, then, was it. After six years of the most excruciating suffering by hundreds of millions of people, it was over. What no radio could report, was the tremendous sigh of relief—everywhere, in all of Germany, Europe, the world:

IT WAS OVER!

Sitting in Josephine's small Marburg kitchen, we duly shed a few tears, feeling sentimental as one does when a close relative, lingering too long at the brink of death, demanding endless sacrifices from all around, finally passes away. The dead relative was Germany—the Third Reich, which they claimed would live for a thousand years, had lasted only twelve. Torn between relief and brief, though sincere, attacks of *Weltschmerz*, we vacillated between outbursts of laughter and sobs like any person in shock. In the end, of course, our youthful optimism—if not callousness—got the upper hand, allowing us to begin to take stock of our situation.

We had survived, even if Germany had not. Sure, there were changes to come, but life would go on. It had to. After all, there were seventy million Germans who had to be fed and housed. They couldn't all be packed off to some kind of Babylonian Captivity, with no Babylon to take them in.

Were we afraid of retaliation? Did we talk about such things already then? It is a question I have often pondered, because it ties in directly with another question which, in turn, lies at the heart of this book: What did we, ordinary citizens, really know about the crimes of the Hitler regime and, by extension, the German people? How far had we been brainwashed into accepting as normal or necessary what, by every moral standard, should instantly have been recognized and condemned as inhuman? How far were we all involved, all guilty?

As night fell, we began to feel better. The worst of our fears had been debated out of the danger zone of irrational panic and down to the familiar level of wartime problems. Tomorrow would be another day, and another would follow after that, each with new challenges and different ways of coping. None would bear the significance of this particular day, when the mighty Nazi state had finally and simply dissolved into thin air without causing the earth to split, as had so often been prophesied. Nor had Wotan, Grand Master of Germanic Valhalla, hurled his fearsome spear in anger. Actually, it had been a sad little no-show, endlessly anticipated, endlessly postponed. When at last it did happen, the *Götterdämmerung*'s grand finale had fallen flat. All that would remain after twelve years of mystic bonding with, and ecstatic worship for, the Führer was instant ridicule that would immediately be overtaken by yet another, equally shocking phenomenon: the collective amnesia of an entire population. But I digress. I have yet to finish relating the events of May 8, the day on which liberated Europe, Russia, and North America triumphantly celebrated victory in Europe.

Josephine got up and untied the strings that released the roll of blackout paper over the window, as she had done for years, night after night. Midway, she stopped. "It's over, Gerti," she said without turning around. There was the hint of a question, as though she couldn't quite believe her own words. Then, with one vicious movement, she ripped down the whole ugly contraption. "It's over!" she shouted. "Can you believe it? No more attacks, no more blackouts." She opened the window and leaned out. "Come here. Look."

There were lights everywhere. A city filled with people who, after years of darkness, celebrated life as though they were living it for the first time. People, cowed into silence only yesterday, were daring to breathe again, repeating to themselves, to each other, like a mantra: It's over, it is finally over …

Josephine clapped her hands. There was that charming twinkle in her eyes and the familiar energy with which she had managed both our lives during those past difficult weeks. "You know what we need?" She looked at me expectantly, then answered her own question: "A *Festessen*, of course, a great feast in honor of the occasion. After all—how often in one's life does one get conquered?"

She whirled around and left the room with a roguish grin that invited complicity. When she returned, she held up a huge preserving jar, like a cross in a holy procession.

I couldn't believe my eyes. "We can't do that!" I was shocked. "It's Frau Heise's precious duck."

"So?" She placed the glass jar in the middle of the table. "Frau Heise has left us without so much as an explanation or a word of farewell, expecting us to defend her apartment. Without us, I'm sure it would be requisitioned in no time." This was, at best, a lie of convenience.

Frau Heise, an elderly widow, positively adored the young family who had rented two rooms of her apartment. She hadn't liked me, though. "You are too generous," she had reproached Josephine after she brought me home when my place had been bombed. "You shouldn't be picking people up in the street." To me, Frau Heise looked quite old; in fact, she may have only been in her late fifties or early sixties. She had a daughter and three grandchildren in Giessen, a small university town twenty miles south. Not having heard from them in weeks, she had finally decided to look for them herself. Josephine had done her best to dissuade her with stories of fighter planes machine-gunning everything that moved, and bombing the rest. But the woman was not to be deterred. She quietly slipped out of Marburg early on March 28, the day that was to see the arrival of the Americans and the occupation of the city. All civilian traffic stopped; there were no more communications, by wire or without, no travel by rail or road during the weeks that followed, up to and after Germany's final surrender on May 8. It would be false to pretend that

Josephine or I had felt unduly anxious about our landlady's fate, which, as we saw it, had to be ascribed entirely to her own folly.

"Frau Heise may be dead by now," Josephine pointed out. "Or imprisoned. Or missing in action. God knows what has become of her. Right now the two of us have an obligation to survive, and that's all there is to it." Her obvious insincerity—all in the name of getting a grip on our emotional volatility—was touching for the effort it must have cost her. Knowing her as I did, I was stunned by her phony recourse to petty larceny.

She held the jar firmly to her bosom, then opened it with a sharp pull to the rubber ring. There was a hiss, and then a delicious aroma wafted through the kitchen, the likes of which I hadn't experienced in years. Josephine forked some pieces of roasted duck into a saucepan and covered them with thick gravy. There were no delicate side dishes to embellish the menu, just our usual diet of potatoes and carrots. While we waited for them to cook, we set a festive table with Josephine's finest silver and porcelain, lovingly arranged on white damask.

We had a marvelous feast. We ate and talked and laughed, and we were drunk with happiness. We even had a bottle of Franconian Bocksbeutel from Karl's little store, which he maintained for those "special occasions" he loved to celebrate.

Now, half a year later, under house arrest in Dülmen, Josephine reminisced: "We really had a ball."

"We sure did. One of the truly great experiences of my life."

"You sound cynical."

"I do?"

"Yes. Why?"

"You know why."

"Yes, I do." She became serious. "Mind if I smoke?"

"Of course not."

"Karl knows some supplier on the black market—he himself doesn't smoke, of course. With his lungs, he can't. But I took it up again right after Manfred was born. I've never been much of a smoker, but now, with the stuff so scarce and expensive, I've become quite addicted." She opened the drawer of her night table and pulled out a pack. "Sometimes I get a real craving for it." She shook out two cigarettes. "You want one?"

"Thanks. What a treat." With a single pack of Camels costing several hundred *Reichsmark* on the black market, I hadn't smoked in months.

We silently watched the white curls, illuminated by the glow of the tobacco as we inhaled deeply.

"You know," Josephine continued, "the thing that's really been bothering me is that we kept on stealing till everything was gone."

"Why did we start in the first place?"

She took a while to answer. "I'm not sure. I've wondered about that myself. Perhaps at that moment I wanted to break with everything that had been important before." She spoke in a voice so low that I could barely hear her. "I knew that after that day, nothing would ever be the same again. Or I thought I knew. That I had Manfred baptized as a Protestant fits, of course, under the same heading."

Once more, I had nothing to say about that particular decision, which troubled me all the more because I felt vaguely responsible for it.

"The war and everything that happened was so wrong that for a while I had an almost perverse urge to challenge every moral principle that was ever drilled into me." She gave a bitter little laugh. "Stupid, I know. You don't have to say it."

"I didn't say it. Personally, I don't believe you have a nasty or perverse bone in your body. But even if I was sure that that's what motivated you, I would still admire your decision to take a stand."

"It's nice of you to say so. But you don't get it."

Rightly or wrongly, I understood her remark as another reference to these five years that separated us in age, and in so much else. When all was said and done, I was just another one of her kids. I struggled not to let on how hurt I felt by the person I so desperately wished to equal. She didn't seem to notice, and continued: "What I'm afraid of is that all this time I've been lying to myself—no, don't interrupt—"

I hadn't even tried.

"—the disgusting truth is, we didn't stop after that first night, but instead ate up all her preserves—"

A giggle slipped out, I simply couldn't help myself; it happened on cue every time the subject of Mrs. Heise's duck came up.

"—because of greed, plain and simple," Josephine finished in sudden anger.

"Look, there's really no need to blame yourself—not for the stupid duck, and certainly not for pilfering Mrs. Heise's kindling wood," I interrupted, trying to steer the conversation to a safer track. "We had no more fuel for the stove, and you know what happened when we tried to gather some sticks in the woods." We had been out in a nearby forest busily piling small branches into a handcart borrowed from a kind neighbour, when we suddenly found ourselves surrounded by a half-dozen American soldiers. As though that wasn't scary enough, the men were black, something we had yet to get used to. In any case, we didn't stick around to find out what their intentions were. With one hand grabbing little Dieter and the other the wagon, Josephine determinedly thrust out her belly and ploughed through the line of approaching soldiers. By the time I had assessed the situation, she was already yards ahead.

Josephine was unimpressed: "Didn't you know that Mrs. Heise found the theft of her kindling wood even more offensive than the loss of her meat?"

"She did? Why?"

"Because her son had cut it all up for her. She was prepared to forgive us for what we did to her. It was different with him."

"Come on. Was she that scared of him?"

"He never found out. Missing in action—somewhere at the Eastern front."

She fell silent and I was afraid she was going to cry. I tried to think of something to say. "We didn't use it all up."

In a burst of anger she replied, "Not from the goodness of our hearts, we didn't, but because Mrs. Heise came back before we had the chance." Actually, I had left before her return, but that was a minor detail that didn't really bear on the matter.

It was now long past midnight. From time to time, searchlights swept across the yard, while gentle jazz seeped into the pristine night.

"I still think you're being too hard on yourself," I said, in an effort to placate her and find a peaceful way to end the conversation. But Josephine would not be so easily distracted from her contrition.

"Why? We were stealing from a defenceless old woman. Can't you see that?"

"Of course. But everybody's doing it. You should be in the city for just one day. You live out here like in some kind of wonderland: plenty to eat, room for everybody, warmth, security. You have no idea how things are in other places. Just look at the coal trains—most of them arrive so heavily looted that it hardly pays to bring them in."

"You still come up with the same old rationalizations. It's like you're saying it doesn't matter if one apple is bad, if the whole bushel is rotten.

You're suggesting that stealing from Mrs. Heise is no different from stealing public property, which is not really an offence because everybody does it. A circular and self-serving argument if ever I heard one."

I could tolerate Josephine's anger; what I couldn't bear was that note of condescension. "You're right, as always, and I'm sorry," I answered, more demurely than I felt, if only to end the matter before it slid further out of hand.

She drew me close and stroked my face. "Don't be. I'm the one who should be sorry. I'm older than you and I took the first step. Without the bad example I set, you'd never have thought of attacking Mrs. Heise's treasures in the first place."

It was, of course, the truth, so I didn't answer directly. "It helped us survive the worst."

Josephine had only one more thing to add: "I wish to God we hadn't been so quick to fall from grace. Just six hours after our glorious liberation, we had already thrown away all moral restraint." Though it was dark and I couldn't see it, I knew that the familiar twinkle was back in her eyes.

After that we slept through the night, undisturbed.

*   *   *

The next morning began with shocking news: The previous day, Müller had been caught hiding in a ditch less than a mile from the farm, and taken to prison in nearby Coesfeld. There was no further news about Mr. Hilltrupp. The hired farmhands had somehow managed to get away and stay away without explanation, and the Frenchman was the only one left to look after the livestock. Once again, it was he who supplied the information.

Our confinement was lifted at daybreak, after the officer and his interpreting corporal had made their rounds. The officer allowed Josephine to procure some milk from the barn; there were even hints that things would soon get back to normal, and that I might be allowed to return to Hamburg.

Unfortunately, these predictions were premature or ill-informed. By nightfall, the military surveillance on the farm would be increased, and all communications cut. Müller and Josephine's father would remain in jail, out of contact, and I would be sharing their fate in the otherwise empty women's wing of the same penal institution.

INTERLUDE III
The Great Führer

Any historian or political commentator writing about the Third Reich sooner or later has to tackle the one big question: What did Hitler possess that enabled him to infatuate an entire nation to the point of ecstatic idolatry? Why did his people keep their faith long after it had become obvious that it held no promise but the total abyss?

In her book *Ich denk so viel an Euch* (I think of you so often), Hedda Kalshoven has published the correspondence (1920–1949) between her mother in Holland and her aristocratic German grandmother, Minna von Alten-Rauch, then living in Braunschweig, Germany.[1] Four months after Hitler attained power, the grandmother writes: "Something so big, so edifying has seldom been experienced by a people." Referring to "our Hitler," she confides: "Can you believe that today I can hardly think of that man without tears filling my eyes? And imagine … a simple man of the people … a simple soldier … He will become the leader of the world."

After the German occupation of Holland in May 1940, von Alten-Rauch writes: "Here, everybody is confident; the Führer's spirit infects the people." In another letter about "the Jewish question" she opines: "The persecution of the Jews is mean and disgusting … [But] it is world history in which we live and world history treads on the fate of individuals; that makes this time so difficult, which otherwise is so noble and pure in its goal. [It is] compassion with the individual's fate [one feels], besides the joy. But that does not change one's view of the Jewish question as such. The Jewish question is a world question, the same as Communism." (My translation.)

Superb contributions to the portrayal of Hitler, the man, his spectacular successes and horrendous failures, the extraordinary phenomenon of the Führer cult, and the explosive creation of the Third Reich and the SS state have come from biographers Alan Bullock (1952), Joachim Fest (1973), Sebastian Haffner (1978) and, most recently, Ian Kershaw (1998/2000), as well as journalist William Shirer and psychoanalysts

Alexander and Margarete Mitscherlich. With the notable exceptions of the Mitscherlichs and Fest, almost all important authors were ex-Germans or non-Germans, a fact that should not surprise, since ordinary Germans—together with serious writers and historians—sealed their collective lips the day after the fall of the Third Reich. If I were to speak for them, I would bypass some of the experts' more esoteric discourses and head straight for the basics. I would make three key observations:

First, Germans were impoverished by the Great Depression and deeply resentful of the *Schandvertrag von Versailles* (the "shameful" Treaty of Versailles). They felt alienated by the political instability of the new multi-party democratic system of the Weimar Republic, which Nazi propaganda later disdainfully labeled *Systemzeit*. Demonstrations and strikes by the left, and the marches and brawls of the right, frightened the population and made people long for the "firm but just" hand of a government that knew where it was going. Repulsed by the endless quarrels and frequent changes of the governing parties, the country's middle and upper classes felt drawn to the fledgling National Socialist German Workers' Party and its charismatic leader, Adolf Hitler.

Second, with his compelling oratory, Hitler—the former front-line soldier who was gassed and temporarily blinded in WW I—instinctively zeroed in on people's grievances. His voice, low and tentative at the beginning of a speech, gradually amplified using measured cadences, pauses, repetitions, and crescendos, until it reached a thundering climax, whipping up mass sentiments of betrayal, humiliation, and exploitation by the country's enemies, while viciously lashing out at the un-Germanness of the new democratic system of the Weimar Republic. That his promises for law and order and a return to German traditions under the rule of National Socialism were invariably mixed with fanatical accusations against "Jewish bloodsuckers" and the "international conspiracy of Bolshevik Jewry" was largely ignored by the majority of citizens, including many from the Jewish community themselves.

Hitler was arguably one of the greatest public speakers of modern times; he was an even greater demagogue. Bound together in fervent nationalism, his immense radio audiences were captivated by that deep Austrian-accented voice with its hard consonants and rolling "rrr's." A closer scrutiny of his texts might have revealed that they rarely contained any new messages, but were the same harangues and vilifications of his enemies that people had heard from him before. Yet, nobody dared to question such passionate convictions which, even if exaggerated, had to be true, if for no other reason than the sheer force of their delivery. During this brief period in history, when radio had become universal, and television, with its lethal effect on bombast, did not yet exist, the power of his rhetoric had a unique opportunity. It became inescapable.

The first two points address the creation of the Führer image and Hitler's early and extraordinary sway over his subjects, from which the emergence of the Führer cult was only a short step. Tales about certain idiosyncrasies and habits that underlined Hitler's ascetic lifestyle were deliberately spread by Goebbels in order to emphasize the Führer's "otherness," even his "chosenness." They included long working hours with hardly any need or time for sleep (a blatant lie; Hitler was a late riser who never shed his Bohemian distaste of systematic work); a vegetarian diet (with lots of creamy pastry), no smoking, no drinking, and, of course, no sexual relationships. The stunning revelation of his last-minute petit-bourgeois marriage to unassuming Eva Braun, followed by the couple's suicide, toppled the Führer cult faster than any other single aspect of his violent career.

Give or take some degrees of emphasis, these historical and personal circumstances surrounding and shaping Hitler's life, are largely uncontested. But it is a third point, the old truism that "nothing succeeds like success" which, I believe, stands as the decisive reason for the people's unswerving loyalty, even in the face of horrifying rumors and impending defeat. Hitler's successes were enormous: They surpassed all expectations, baffled his (often overruled) advisers, scared his enemies, and endowed his name with near-mythical powers. I have mentioned the social accomplishments and the "economic miracle" (Sebastian Haffner) of the 1930s. In the eyes of the vast majority of contemporary Germans, Hitler, between 1933 and 1941 (and even into 1942), led his people from economic depression and shame to prosperity and military victory over most of Europe. Whatever the Macedonians or Romans had felt about their armies' distant conquests, modern transmission technologies and propaganda (selecting, exaggerating, or downright faking the facts) turned the Second World War into the first war-as-popular-drama, played out in weekly newsreels and over radio waves right into people's daily lives.

The magnitude of Hitler's triumphs, which spanned close to a decade, subsequently blocked the enormity of his failures from penetrating people's souls, if not their minds. Between the surrender of the 6th Army at Stalingrad on February 2, 1943, and Germany's unconditional surrender two years, three months and six days later, hope remained alive, even in the face of mass bombings at home, rumors about huge German losses at the front, retreating armies, and dwindling oil supplies for tanks and planes. This hope, together with the people's unswerving sense of loyalty, was pinned on one name only: Adolf Hitler, the great Führer who had done so much for his *Volk* and whom his *Volk* could not, and would not, abandon now that the Goddess of Fortune had temporarily shrouded her face.

How could there be so much shortsightedness and self-delusion, or— even more perplexing—such total disregard for the dark side of National Socialism, about which a great deal more was known or suspected by Germans than they were later willing to admit?

Stalingrad and the retreat in Russia—reminiscent of Napoleon's defeat—played against Victory in France, a triumph of legendary proportions. Admittedly, the escape of almost 400,000 British and French troops across the English Channel at Dunkirk—despite Göring's assurances that his *Luftwaffe* would be able to stop them—caused a great deal of embarrassment among the German military leadership. But this was a setback that did little to mar an extraordinary triumph: *Der Erbfeind Frankreich*—France, the eternal foe—which had dominated German military strategy and inspired countless patriotic songs and poems for more than 200 years, had been conquered within six weeks. The symbolism of *Compiègne*, where, in 1940, France's generals surrendered in the same Pullman car in which Germany had surrendered in 1918, was something the German people could not forget. After all, the generation that had fought in World War I was by then only middle-aged, many of them officers still in the field; their pride was boundless. *La grande nation* had been vanquished, the dreaded Maginot Line had proved a sham. Trench war with its unspeakable horrors was out, blitzkrieg and panzers were in—the sacrifices of Langemarck and Verdun and the shame of Versailles were redeemed. Any historian who overlooks the momentous emotional impact of Victory in France is bound to miss one of the most significant, most deeply rooted motives for the people's undying belief in Hitler's military genius and Germany's ultimate victory.

Also contributing to the country's almost maniacal euphoria were the

Sondermeldungen, special radio bulletins from Wehrmacht headquarters. Introduced with the bombastic fanfares of Liszt's *Préludes*, the clipped-language reports spoke authoritatively of vast tonnages sunk, great battles won, huge enemy armies encircled and crushed. At times, the announcements came with such frequency that people began to take them for granted. They were the amphetamines of war, keeping eighty million people on a sustained high. When the *Sondermeldungen* became fewer in number and thinner in content, Germans kept their radios on anyway, longing for more fixes. Towards the end, as they listened to the continual warnings of approaching enemy aircraft (carried over radio from military radar stations), their hearts secretly longed for the familiar tunes of the *Préludes*. In the Reich's final days, people's hopes still clung to the crazed Führer in his Berlin bunker fifty feet below the Reich Chancellery, waiting with him for relief troops that were mere phantoms—armies that were cut off, decimated, or simply dissolved. The shot that ended Hitler's life also ended the *Sondermeldungen* addiction. The Führer was dead; there would be no more fixes.

Throughout the war, people tended to distance Hitler from the obnoxious and pompous behavior of his party hacks. And later, when the helpless exposure of German cities to Allied bombings became an ever-increasing political and military embarrassment, while Hitler refused to make even a token appearance among his stricken countrymen, people again found excuses, however far-fetched. Suggesting that his minions conspired to keep him ill-informed about the true suffering of his beloved *Volk*, Germans, in a mix of frustration and wishful thinking, would say: *Wenn das der Führer wüsste* (If only the Führer knew), the great man would immediately put an end to somebody else's scandalous blunders. Only towards the very end, as discipline began to crack and doubts were cautiously aired, did the widespread cliché acquire overtones of cynicism.

To be sure, the patriotic fervor and tribal fealty have long been forgotten, or replaced by more comfortable accounts of the political attitude of those ordinary Germans who, by chance of birth, were Hitler's contemporaries. What had been such a proud experience during twelve wildly exhilarating years, suddenly became a great embarrassment. From the day after their army's capitulation, Germans convinced themselves that they had never possessed any close ties with the Hitler regime, or knowledge of its widely rumored crimes. Neither had they liked the Nazis or their ideology. Hitler, the focus of twelve years of the most extraordinary personality cult—*"Heil Hitler!"*, the prescribed greeting, was said or signed a billion times a day—became a non-person overnight. There was no conspiracy, no agreement on some communal course of behavior. Every person acted individually and spontaneously. How was it that, like cattle before a storm, they all followed the same instinct?

Shocking rumors that Germany might actually lose the war began to be whispered after the fall of Stalingrad. Over the next two years, while the mighty Wehrmacht was pushed back relentlessly, dread about a terrible reckoning, should the Russians ever reach the Reich's Eastern territories, began to grip German residents and Nazi functionaries in occupied Poland. After all, these people had a better-than-average idea about the ideological subplot of the SS played out behind the Wehrmacht's battle lines—the murder and enslavement of what was then presumed to be thousands, but was in fact millions, of Jewish and Slavic "subhumans." For Germans in the West, such fears remained vague and were entirely overshadowed by the more immediate terror of daily air raids. But, with the arrival of the first refugee treks from the *Generalgouvernement* (German-governed part of Poland), the Baltic states, and East Prussia during the winter of 1944 to 1945, reality finally and brutally struck home. Tales of the most hideous acts of reprisal by the Red Army spread through the country like wildfire. Often having escaped mere hours ahead of the Russians, the terrified people told of torture, murder, and rape on an unimaginable scale, for the first and only time confirming the dire predictions of Goebbels's propaganda.

Granted, people felt less threatened by the possibility of physical abuse from Western armies. Yet, as the end of the war drew near, nobody entertained the slightest doubt that in the West, too, the day of reckoning would come.

Therein lies the contradiction: If no one had done anything bad, or knew about anything bad, and therefore had nothing to fear, why did they all feel compelled to amend their personal histories for the interval of the Hitler years? I am, of course, with great circumspection, leading up to the thorny issue of "collective guilt," whether such a thing existed and if it did, whether it touched all Germans, who then could or should be held morally responsible. For the large majority of Hitler contemporaries, these questions were resolved during the first years after the war: There was no collective guilt in Nazi Germany—end of argument.

Others, this writer included, have felt uneasy about a moral judgment that sounded all too facile and opportunistic at the time, and that, after more than five decades and a good deal of effort to keep it down, still pops up again and again to spook the younger generations. It also turns up repeatedly on these pages.

Over the decades, evaluations of Germany's total defeat and the extent of people's involvement in the crimes of their government have undergone strange historical revisions, all aimed at depersonalizing the guilt and the guilty, and putting a happier face on everything else. According to German Federal President Richard von Weizsäcker, speaking on the occasion of the fortieth anniversary of the end of the war, Germany, in 1945, was "liberated" by the Allies. The German people, he said, would never have been able to free themselves from the Nazi yoke, which is probably true, though hard to prove. There were certainly hundreds of thousands of Germans who, for years, had lived in terror of the SS, and who had hidden themselves or been detained in concentration camps. For them, the arrival of Allied troops was the ticket to freedom and survival. But did Germans in general feel liberated and, by implication, thankful towards their victors?

Granted, people were tremendously relieved that the bombing and killing had finally stopped. Given the choice between the daily terror and the harsh but tolerable conditions under the occupying forces, most people clearly preferred the latter. In that sense they were grateful: to be alive, to have survived. But to euphemize such basic human feelings along today's lines of political correctness sounds completely anachronistic. Germany had lost the war; four million were dead, eight million wounded; seventy per cent of the country had been laid to waste, and every square foot was occupied by the enemy; food, clothing, and shelter were at a premium, and so was hope. Uplifting concepts like "liberation" must have ranked on people's minds as high as the Second Coming. (I wonder whether the former German president ever heard of President Truman's directive JCS 1067 of April 26, 1945, which guided American occupation policies in Germany from 1945 to 1947. It stated that "Germany will not be occupied for the purpose of liberation but as a defeated nation." The order of the day was denazification, which, one hoped, would eventually lead to democratization.)[2]

*   *   *

Unfortunately, the instant and collective denial by a whole generation of Germans of any personal involvement with, or knowledge of, the state-ordered crimes of the Third Reich had serious consequences: Because all those potential witnesses fell silent, a vital archive of historical knowledge and personal documentation never materialized. That we, nevertheless, possess a reasonably accurate picture of the complex infrastructure of the Nazi dictatorship is, to a large extent, due to writer and former Buchenwald inmate Eugen Kogon. His unsurpassed book *Der SS-Staat: Das System der deutschen Konzentrationslager* (The SS State: The System of the German Concentration Camps)[3] recorded the extraordinary dimensions of Hitler's murderous empire, and the power and corruption of Heinrich Himmler, Hitler's chief of security forces. To what degree our knowledge is complete today, nobody knows. Though the bureaucratic "master race" generated mountains of paper, much of it was subsequently destroyed, or hidden and never found.

Not surprisingly, postwar Germany's new elites—who all too often had also been members of the old elites—were not eager to have personal files recording their activities during the Third Reich surface in the new Federal Republic of Germany. Between 1957 and 1994, consecutive West German governments resisted all offers of return of the largest collection of Nazi documents, which had been guarded and administered by the Americans at the Berlin Document Center (BDC) since the end of World War II. The center holds thirty million documents, weighing 450 tons and stored on twelve kilometers of shelving. Among its contents are the complete NSDAP membership files of a staggering 10.7 million men and women. Moreover, the BDC houses 600,000 applications for NSDAP membership that were turned down by the Nazi party for various reasons. Of these "rejects," the newspaper *Leipziger Volkszeitung* notes mockingly, quite a few may have reinvented themselves as resistance fighters during the intervening years.[4]

The BDC also contains the files of 600,000 SA men, almost 300,000 SS officers and men, 490,000 teachers, 185,000 members of Goebbels's *Reichskulturkammer* (artists), 72,000 physicians, as well as 238,000 documents from the *Rasse- und Siedlungshauptamt* (Race and Settlement Main Office, a branch of Himmler's Berlin headquarters), and 50,000 files of the dreaded *Volksgerichtshof*, the Nazi kangaroo court. As Germany's respected weekly *Die Zeit* observed: "Nearly 140 million pages on fifteen million German citizens who were loyal to the Hitler regime [represent] a heritage that quite a few would gladly have foregone."[5] (My translation.)

Obtaining information from the BDC has never been easy; it has become even more cumbersome since July 1, 1994, when the transfer of custody to German hands finally occurred. Already in 1988, in a precautionary act, the Bonn government passed the Federal Archives Law, which restricts access to personal data until after the individual's one-hundredth birthday, or thirty years after his death. Unlimited access to the files exists, however, at Washington's National Archives where, prior to the transfer, the entire contents of the BDC was stored on 50,000 rolls of microfilm.

Notes to Chapter 3

1   Kalshoven, Hedda, *Ich denk so viel an Euch: Ein deutsch-holländischer Briefwechsel 1920–1949* (Munich: Luchterhand, 1995). From a review by Gabriele von Arnim, *Die Zeit*, No. 8, 1996.

2   Herf, Jeffrey, *Divided Memory: The Nazi Past in the Two Germanys* (Cambridge, Mass: Harvard University Press, 1997), 202.

3   Kogon, Eugen, *Der SS-Staat: Das System der deutschen Konzentrationslager* (Munich: Kindler, 1974).

4   Wahl, Torsten, *Naziakten wechseln wieder den Besitz* (Nazi Files Change Hands Again), *Leipziger Volkszeitung*, May 28, 1994.

5   Albrecht, Jörg, *Das Erbe* (The Legacy), *Die Zeit*, July 1, 1994.

4

COESFELD JAIL

It was a Sunday afternoon in 1977. Spring had arrived. The weather was warm and dry. There was little traffic passing the grey stuccoed facades of buildings whose uniform blandness typified so many of West Germany's cities, flattened by war and all too hastily rebuilt during the early years of the country's "miraculous" recovery.

For several weeks I had been traveling across Germany, both East and West, enjoying its great temples of culture, visiting friends and relatives, and only now and then mustering the courage to make a tentative and half-hearted attempt to locate some of the sites mentioned on these pages. This now was Coesfeld, a little Westphalian town near the Dutch border, fifteen kilometers northwest of Dülmen—and, in 1945, home to the jail nearest to the Hilltrupp farm. I stopped my rented Volkswagen alongside a strolling policeman and asked for directions. He complied promptly. If he was surprised at my request, courtesy or discipline prevented him from showing it.

I had no trouble finding the place, a perfectly ordinary facility, three stories high, red-bricked—more like a German high school than a penal institution. A ten-foot wall extending along the pavement for some twenty yards was the only indication that circulation into and around the structure might be restricted.

Handsomely dressed people passed me on the sidewalk, enjoying their Sunday walks. Nobody stopped at the jail's entrance, nobody took notice as I got out of the car, walked to the door, and tried the handle. It was locked, but there was a bell with an intercom. I hesitated. Granted, my experience with German prisons was limited; nevertheless, I was convinced that none had entrances as harmless-looking and user-friendly as this one. With my confidence rapidly dissipating, I silently hoped to find no one in the building, my research efforts concluded, right then and there.

I pushed the bell.

"*Hallo?*"

I was speechless; intercoms always have that effect on me, and this one robbed me of my wits entirely. "Is—is this the jail?" I asked.

"Sure. Why?" A male German voice sounded confident and slightly challenging. Clearly, it was now or never.

"Could I come up and talk to you?"

There was a pause. For a moment I thought he hadn't understood me. Then he replied: "What about?"

This time, I paused. "Years ago I was a prisoner here," I began, probably sounding as if I was reading from a prepared text. With a bit more feeling, I continued: "Maybe you could let me see what it's like today." If my voice conveyed doubt, it was quite genuine.

"Okay. One moment." Loud steps came down the stairs. The door was opened by a strong, mid-sized man of about forty, dressed in something khaki-colored—whether civilian or uniform, I don't recall. But there was no doubt that this was the man in charge, whatever his charge was.

"*Guten Tag.*" He extended his hand German-style and stated his name and rank. Meanwhile, he sized me up, a fiftyish woman who probably looked more like the mayor's wife than a former jailbird. "*You* were here?" He emphasized the "you" with just enough incredulity to imply that he was ready for a little joke as long as it didn't impinge on his dignity. "When?" He even smiled.

"Right after the war."

"That long ..." I could see his mind working. Clearly he was too young to instantly scan the long list of possibilities that would automatically unfurl in the mind of someone my own age: war criminal, collaborator, resistance fighter, black marketeer, spy, Communist, fascist, Jew, gypsy, DP. At one time or another, all had populated Germany's prisons—patriots and swindlers, victors and victims, traitors and betrayed, the flotsam and jetsam of Europe's most deadly war.

Satisfied by my harmless appearance, he invited me upstairs. With each step, I grew more convinced that this couldn't possibly be the place I was looking for. "Is this Coesfeld's only jail?" A silly question, given the size of the town. Thankfully, the man appeared trained to handle all kinds of nuts: Yes, it was; no, he didn't know when it was built; yes, it had been there as long as he could remember; and yes, he had grown up in the region. Which still left plenty of room for doubt in my mind.

The answers I was searching for were probably available at the city archives, if—and what a big "if" this had become—I could ever bring myself to turn my timid queries into the serious research of a past nobody in Germany now gave a hoot about. To have come this far had been an excruciating experience, as it had forced me to own up to a truth that I had, until then, been unable to admit to anyone.

Why had I told this stranger? Why not simply pretend to be a reporter working on a story? Perhaps the thought hadn't occurred to me. Perhaps I had been too rattled by the voice through the intercom and the unexpectedness of it all. Whatever the reason for my confession, here I was, searching for a most unlikely connection between the nightmarish images still haunting my mind, and a public institution run by the masterfully restored, spic-and-span *Bundesrepublik*.

"What do you want to see?"

I shrugged. From the landing upstairs, I had already seen enough. There were clean, bright rooms—definitely not cells in the conventional sense—on both sides of a central hallway. As we continued down the hall, it filled with the noisy laughter of several young men, dressed in clean slacks and open-necked shirts, who gave the warden a friendly "*Tschüss*" as they clattered down the stairs.

"Sunday afternoon furlough," he explained.

"Those are prisoners—?"

"Yes. Quite a harmless lot. They'll be back all right."

"Things sure have changed," I said in an effort to sound casual, though I felt like a fool. I searched desperately for a tactful way to extricate myself from an altogether impossible situation. The warden, in contrast, was suddenly very eager to show me around, delighted by the unexpected intrusion. I edged back towards the stairs, murmuring: "You've been awfully kind." Still, I needed to ask one more question: "Do you have any cells in the basement?"

"No. Why?"

"Nothing. Just asking." Before he could say anything more, I stretched out my hand for a parting handshake. I assured him that our meeting had been a most valuable experience, even if it hadn't quite squared with my expectations. "It has been a long time," I said by way of apology.

"Sure has," he affirmed.

As I retreated to the car, I forced myself into a measured step as I sensed his eyes burning into my back.

* * *

The title of the book was *Via Mala*, its author John Knittel. Though his name sounded English, I now wonder whether he actually was, since I remember having read another of his books in high school. That one was called *El Hakim*, its main character an Egyptian doctor.

The first time the girl came into my cell she didn't have the book with her. Instead, she ordered me to pick up the pail and follow her to the row of toilets down the hall.

"I didn't go."

"The pail has to be washed every morning anyway. Regulations."

I tried to hide the bucket by holding it between us as we walked down the hall to the washroom, though there was nobody around to see. There were several basins with taps for cold water. She handed me a brush, then waited as I scrubbed the heavy zinc, stained by years of corrosive cleansers.

"May I use the toilet?"

She nodded. I slipped in and closed the door. In the privacy of the cubicle, I quickly rid myself of the crudely forged transit permit that had enabled me, when I left Marburg in July, to make the risky crossing from the American into the British zone of occupation. I had rediscovered the wrinkled document while searching my purse in early daylight, agonizing about its disposal ever since.

Back at the cell the girl explained: "I'm the warden's daughter. I'm the supervisor of women prisoners." She probably said her name, too. I asked her how many women were in her charge.

"Just you."

"And before?"

"Nobody." She was tall and strong-looking, though not heavy. Her fresh-colored face was broad and good-natured. She had dark brown hair done up in a tight Olympia roll. I guessed her to be four or five years my senior.

The warden's daughter made no effort to conceal her pride in her new job and its attendant authority. She told me that she knew Josephine from primary school, but that she herself hadn't gone on to high school because her parents were unable to pay the fees. She knew that Josephine had attended convent schools and had gone on to university. She didn't sound envious, just matter-of-fact.

When I asked for a towel, the girl brought one. It was clean and ironed but riddled with holes. I held it up accusingly, but she just shrugged. It didn't occur to me that it might have come from her mother's kitchen and that, after six years of rationing, all the family's towels probably looked the same.

When she left, she locked the door to my cell. She had just that one key. Not the bunch her father had carried when he shut me in the night before.

Later, the warden's daughter returned with the Knittel book. She asked me whether I had read it and I told her I had not. She said she had not read too many books, but had enjoyed this one.

When I was alone again, I tried to decide whether I liked or trusted her. I felt a desperate need to talk to somebody. There were dozens of questions for which, I was sure, everyone around me had answers. Maybe they all joked about my appalling ineptitude in handling my demeaning situation. I pictured them in the family kitchen, discussing what I had said or done or failed to do. The girl was a spy, I was now convinced, deliberately sent in to win my trust, to report my confidences. I decided not to talk to her again, not to answer any of her questions.

My resolve lasted a couple of hours, just until her next visit. Completely defenceless against my desperate need to speak, I talked to the warden's daughter every minute she spent in my cell. I told her everything that had happened at the Hilltrupp farm. And I kept asking her questions about my circumstances, which she could not, or would not, answer. I was longing for company, any company. Once a day she would lead me outside into the walled-in yard, where I was allowed to walk around. I never saw another person, staff member, or prisoner. There was no clanging of doors, or shuffling of feet. No cries, curses, shouts, or whatever one might expect from a prison. In fact, the place was completely silent, as though I was the only person in it. Somewhere, though, they must have been keeping poor Mr. Hilltrupp. And Müller, of course.

The cell was in the basement with a barred window, which I could reach by stepping on the pail. But the viewing angle was awkward and didn't allow for more than a slice of grey sky and the uppermost portion of the prison wall. The bed had a thin mattress and a lumpy pillow. A small table and a chair comprised the rest of the furniture. There were six paces of rough concrete between the door, with its peephole, and the pail beneath the window, which had a cover but no seat.

I spent eleven days in that cell; I marked the time with small pencil lines on the grimy wall beside my cot. Eleven days or twenty or 300—in some ways it didn't matter. Once the iron bolt had been rammed into place the first time and the rattle of keys swinging from the old warden's hand had retreated down the hall, I had been sullied for life. I had been stained by a shame that could never be washed away.

There was the shaking that couldn't be stopped, neither by will nor by force. It had sneaked under the skin of my thighs like a living thing. I could see it till the light was turned off, and then it kept going in the darkness—something forbidden and obscene. Like a traitor. My body betraying its own soul, or mind, day and night, whenever I lay down on the cot, confronting me with that visible, tangible, irrepressible proof of my own terror.

Is there such a thing as mortal shame? There is mortal fear and mortal danger, both implying death. There is no death by shame unless perpetrated by one's own hand, something having to do with loss of face, or fallen virtue and nineteenth-century novels. Surely, my kind of shame had nothing to do with virtue.

Instead, what it did have to do with was the careless destruction of the innermost niche that shelters a person's dignity, that single indispensable possession that, if taken away, makes the need to regain it as compelling as the need to survive.

What happened to German prisoners of the Allies? Political prisoners? How long did they remain in prison? What did the Allies do with them? All these stories about the Jews and what had been done to them came flooding back into my mind. How much of the horror reported by the Allied-controlled media had been propaganda, how much fact? How would whatever had happened to them bear on me and my freedom?

I thought of the people I had heard about, men (no women) who had been picked up and sent to prison. But their situation bore no resemblance to my own. They had been functionaries of the Nazi party. I hadn't been a member, nor had anybody else in my family. Then there was the Nazi brass, the hundreds, perhaps thousands, of former high-ranking officers or bureaucrats who, one by one, were snatched from their hiding places. The newspapers reported their capture. Some had been instantly court-martialed, particularly if they were caught in formerly German-occupied countries. Others sat in Allied camps or prisons, waiting for their day in court. And finally there was the Big One, the Nuremberg Trial, which was then just getting started.

None of these reflections could shed any light on my own case, which was as bewildering as it was ominous. I was 400 kilometers from home and under the present circumstances, as forlorn as on a desert island. There was no means of communication with my family. Besides, they most likely had no idea about my predicament and—assuming I was safe with Josephine—would not even begin to miss me for quite some time.

And finally there was that book, *Via mala*, about which I remember nothing except that it was the most sinister story I had ever read. It left me convinced that, either by accident or design, the warden's daughter had shown me the "bad path" that had been laid out for me. I tried to stop reading, but couldn't. By the time I finished the book, my nerves were shot. In the privacy of my cell, I was in a state of repressed hysterics, fully convinced of my sudden end between a wall and the muzzle of a rifle. (In 1989, I watched the execution of the Romanian dictator Nicolae Ceausescu and his wife on TV. At that moment, half a century dissolved and I was back in my cell. Villainous as they had been, I suddenly and totally identified with their terror. I can still see them slumping to the ground, their deaths covered live.)

I never undressed. There was nothing to change into. Also, I needed all my clothes to keep me warm. The girl had offered a cover of dubious material, which I promptly rejected for fear of bugs. All I had was my brown blanket, which was small and rather lightweight. Perhaps it wasn't even wool. But without Tall Guy, I wouldn't even have had that much.

*   *   *

It was the second day of our house arrest, and Josephine and I had just finished supper. We were beginning to relax and settle into some kind of routine. There had been no news from Karl, and, by now, Josephine was sure her husband had managed to escape the dragnet. On the whereabouts of her father or Müller, there had been no further information either. Even so, we were generally less concerned than the day before, and had even started to talk about my return trip home.

Suddenly, without knocking, two men entered the room. We froze in our seats. I can't remember whether a military guard was still outside the door. If so, he hadn't announced them, and now kept himself out of sight. Both men were German, both civilians. They wore coats and hats and, even allowing for the general poverty of the population, one couldn't help but notice their shabbiness. The men's faces were expressionless as they looked around the apartment. They opened the door to the bedroom, turned on the light, turned it off again, and closed the door. There were no introductions, no explanations. Satisfied that, apart from the children, we were quite alone, they asked for our names. One of them then turned to me: *"Ihr Personalausweis, bitte."*

I protested that I had already shown my identification card to the military authorities, who had found everything in order. Instinct told me it was safer to deal with the English than with these shady-looking members of my own country. They were working-class, most likely communists promoted to some position of power after their recent release from concentration camp. There were thousands like them, their ruthless exploitation of sudden influence making them a scourge all over Germany.

"We have to see it again."

I whipped out the document and held it under their noses. "There. It's quite in order. I'm here on a visit." I still felt no fear.

"Why?"

"Why what?"

"Why have you come all the way from Hamburg to visit her?" A curt nod in Josephine's direction.

So far, all the drama had revolved around her and her family. Now, suddenly, the spotlight was on me. Moreover, there was a palpable change of atmosphere from the clear rules of military control to a sinister cloud of unspoken threats. There was something dangerous about these two, their demeanor and undeclared purpose. Looking back, it seems strange that neither Josephine nor I thought of asking for their identification. Perhaps we were too stunned. More likely, it simply didn't occur to us. People in Germany were still a very long way from questioning authority.

When they told me I had to come with them, I felt more revulsion than fear. "You have to accompany us to Coesfeld in order to answer some questions," one of them said. We knew that Mr. Hilltrupp had been taken to the prison in Coesfeld, as had Müller. Before my arrival at the farm, I had never heard of the town. But during the past two days the name had come up repeatedly, and by now it sounded like an important city, the center of all the action. So I simply accepted the men's story that there was an officer in Coesfeld who wanted some information from me.

The strangeness of the request didn't strike me, at least not immediately, although I briefly wondered about the lateness of the hour. I didn't protest. I simply shrugged and got ready to go along. That's when the taller of the men, as though struck by a sudden thought, suggested I take a few personal things—"In case you don't get back tonight."

I went to the bedroom, packed my toilet case, and put it in the bag I had arrived with two days earlier. I still sensed nothing suspicious, had no particular fear or foreboding, even when the man suggested: "Maybe you should bring a blanket, too."

The car was some pre-war model, small and asthmatic. After thirty minutes it stopped. I was led into the poorly lit entrance of what looked like an old school or government building, its halls deserted at this late hour. We were met by a heavy-set man of about fifty. After a brief exchange, my two companions handed me over, then quickly left.

Still expecting to meet the person who was going to ask those questions, I followed the old man eagerly enough, down a flight of stairs, along an empty hallway, and through a door he held open. Only when the heavy bolt clanged into place and the door was locked with a rattle of keys did reality crash down on me with devastating force.[1]

*   *   *

I met the tall German once more. On day three of my imprisonment, the warden's daughter ordered me to put on my jacket and follow her up to the office where the man stood waiting. He told me to come along, and we left the building, walking side by side. I don't think we went very far. Still, I was allowed to walk among ordinary people. Nobody took any notice, there were no shackles at my wrists. I was like everybody else.

I was almost free.

I was going to see the British interrogator, who surely would just go through some stupid routine before handing me back my papers and allowing me to return home.

The officer was in his early thirties, and he stood up when we came in. His back was to the window of a drab, oversized room as he sat down and ordered me to take a seat across from his desk. Tall Guy remained on his feet, eager to please as he explained my presence in English.

I remember very little of the interrogation, which lasted about an hour.

But I do recall questions about my years at school, my membership in the Hitler Youth and when and why I had dropped out, and questions about people I had never heard of.

He also asked whether I knew Müller, to which I replied: "He was my fiancé's boss in Marburg, his commanding officer."

The only memorable exchange occurred when I asked to be allowed to answer his questions in English. My grasp of that language wasn't very good, but speaking it seemed vastly preferable to listening to the biased version resulting from the civilian's interpretation of my German. Frankly, I'm still proud of having spoken up against that hostile compatriot. Having never exceeded some middling marks during six years of high school English, I still marvel at the mind's ability to instantly adjust to a dangerous situation, to bring up reserves one never knew one possessed.

I felt no fear during the interrogation. Clearly, the officer had no idea why I was there or what he was supposed to get out of me. After it was over, I asked to be allowed to go home. I was dismissed with a kindly nod, which I interpreted to mean that my release from prison was imminent. When it finally came on day eleven, I eagerly grabbed my bag and blanket and ran up the stairs.

Outside stood a pickup truck, and in the open back sat Müller, his face badly swollen with one eye half-closed and one of his front teeth missing.

INTERLUDE IV
Solving the "Jewish Problem"

Prior to Hitler's ascent to power, anti-Semitism in Germany ranged from mildly xenophobic to (seldom) outright hatred. It was part of a largely religion-based European anti-Semitism that, in the past, had produced such radical measures as the expulsion of Jews from England and Spain, and Russia's violent and recurrent pogroms. In 1812 new laws ended the social, political, and economic ghettoization of the Jews in Prussia. During the latter half of the nineteenth century, as liberalism gained a foothold in German states, many Jews established a strong presence within the middle and upper classes.

There were wide differences in the way Jews themselves adapted to the Christian majority. Some steadfastly refused any concessions to their orthodoxy, while others chose baptism or changed their family names in the hope of eliminating all outward distinctions. Driven by a desire to blend in, parents celebrated Christmas and ignored the Sabbath. In World War I, many Jewish men served voluntarily, making the ultimate sacrifice for the country they loved. Those promoted to officer ranks, or cited for bravery, were proud of their honors, which many later believed would save them from Nazi persecution.

Until 1933, mixed marriages were frequent, although I doubt anybody has the precise numbers. Historically, German Jews possessed a profound cultural affinity to their homeland, which found expression not only in the closely related Yiddish language, but also in the large number of famous Jewish writers, poets, composers and actors, as well as outstanding scientists, who drew their creativity from the strength of their deeply felt Germaness.

During and after World War I, many Jewish bankers and merchants acquired considerable fortunes, which allowed them to do better in the Great Depression than their non-Jewish fellow citizens. From its earliest days, the vicious propaganda of the fledgling Nazi party pilloried Jewish *Kriegsgewinnler und Schieber* (war profiteers and racketeers), who allegedly, by not participating in the war, had been able to amass great fortunes. People were peppered with the image of Jews as usurers who, over the centuries, had driven hard-working peasants from their heavily mortgaged family farms.

To Germany's educated middle class, such unvarnished anti-Semitic agitation sounded vulgar and extreme, but was widely expected to calm down, along with other propaganda excesses, once the upstart National Socialists had consolidated their power. It didn't happen, though for a while the issue became somewhat muted while other programs—some popular, some less so—seized the public's attention.

It is my contention that until the late 1930s, with *Kristallnacht* on November 9, 1938, being the pivotal date, anti-Semitic sentiment among ordinary Germans—those outside the Party, the SS, or SA—manifested itself more in condescension or social contempt toward the minority than by verbal, let alone physical, attacks. No doubt, there was widespread derision for the perceived Jewish obsession with money, an attitude which dated back to the ghettos when moneylending had been the only permitted business contact for Jews with the non-Jewish world. Yet, personal feelings of hatred almost certainly fell far short of what existed in Poland, Russia, and countries that had once belonged to the Austro-Hungarian Empire, including Austria itself. (According to Paul Johnson writing in the *Washington Post*, a third of the SS extermination units were manned by Austrians, who also commanded four of the six most notorious death camps, where nearly half of the six million Jewish victims were killed.)[2]

Before the emergence of National Socialism, Germany seemed a rather unlikely country to stage the worst Jewish genocide in history. With only 500,000 Jews, or 0.7 percent of the German population, the Jewish minority, for business reasons, preferred to settle in large cities, such as Berlin (four percent) or Hamburg (three percent). Nowhere, however, was the Jewish population even close to that of Vienna (eight to ten percent *Glaubensjuden*[3]), a multicultural city, where Hitler had first received his vicious anti-Semitic indoctrination. Many Germans, living in smaller cities or in the country, never met a Jew in their lives. The closest my parents ever came to a Jewish acquaintance was the half-Jewish wife of our "Aryan" family doctor; despite repeated harassments by the SS, the brave man succeeded in keeping his wife safe and his practice open.

To flesh out the picture of how middle-class Germans generally felt about the Jewish business class, I will relate a few personal memories: *Man kauft nicht beim Juden* ("one doesn't shop at the Jew's") was probably one of the best-known maxims, usually referring to the low-end character of many Jewish stores. Another derogatory reference to the Jewish business world was the *Judenpreis*, meant to point out the misleading nature of prices ending in .99 instead of round figures. That this attitude had more to do with bourgeois snobbery than anti-Semitism was borne out by the fact that high-end Jewish stores—furriers and jewellers, in particular—enjoyed great prestige and were highly favored. The middle ground, meanwhile, was held by large department stores, or *Warenhäuser*, a category of enterprise dominated by Jewish proprietors. If anti-Semitism came up in any significant way between German customers and Jewish store owners, it was here. *Warenhäuser*, though much patronized, were considered un-German, Jewish-American inventions that exploited size and convenience to feed on people's greed, while discounting traditional German shopkeepers out of the market.

Social outclassing of the Jews further expressed itself in coarse jokes alluding to Jewish noses, gestures, ostentation, or their preference for strong spices, especially garlic (seldom used in German households). Most people at the time—if they had paused to think about it—probably saw these jokes as an expression of some mild xenophobia rather than in any way connected to the Nazis' vulgar anti-Semitism out in the streets. It is the aspect of ostentation that brings up the memory of my first encounter with Jews.

It happened in the summer of 1936 on the Danish island of Fanø, where we spent our holidays at a modest hotel-pension at the edge of the North Sea. Among the other guests at the nightly dinner table were a middle-aged couple with two daughters close to my own age of eleven. Both girls had beautiful black curly hair and were dressed in floor-length pink and light blue taffeta dresses with ruffles around their necks, sleeves, and hems. I had never seen such wonders. Clad in my simple hand-me-down cotton frock, I felt envious and embarrassed, and bitterly resentful of my family's parsimonious life style. The scene might have been long forgotten, had it not been for my father's terse remark: "Jews from Germany—typical." How could he tell? And why had he, a gentle man, come down on people who were clearly so much more attractive and elegant than we were? I didn't ask, and he never explained.

Names could be a heavy burden for Jews. In the eighteenth century, when German surnames became mandatory in the ghettos, malicious bureaucrats deliberately chose names for the Jews that were easily recognizable and frequently open to ridicule. Many referred to valuables like *Geld* (money), *Silber* (silver), and *Gold*; to animals such as *Katz* (cat), *Hirsch* (deer) or *Wolf*; to trees like *Mandelbaum* (almond tree) and *Tannenbaum* (spruce tree); to character traits like *Süss* (sweet) and *Reich* (rich), or simply to cities (*Frankfurter*), regions (*Elsässer*), and countries of origin (*Deutsch*). Later laws permitted Jews to modify their names in ways that would ease some of the embarrassment, but not alter their meaning. My mother liked to tell the story of a neighbor who, during the Kaiserreich, succeeded in improving his name from *Kuheuter* (cow udder) to *Milchsack* (milk bag). Of course, the privilege of such an "adjustment" required the outlay of large sums of money and was no longer available when the Nazis came to power. But, she had yet another, more personal story to tell: Born in 1895, she entered school shortly after the turn of the century. On her first day, she was approached by another little girl. Pointing at my mother's long, thick, pitch-black hair, the new school-mate contemptuously remarked: *"Du siehst genau aus wie ein Israelit"* (You look exactly like an Israelite). I have always thought the incident interesting for two reasons: First, anti-Semitism was sufficiently widespread that it could be picked up in families by very young children, and second, the word *Israelit*—as strange to me in the forties as it must have been that day to the little girl with the extraordinary hair—disappeared entirely from the language between her generation and mine. This idiomatic change may well signify the transition from the (relatively harmless) religious anti-Judaism in the *Kaiserreich* to the fanatically racial anti-Semitism of the Third Reich.

While clearly discriminatory and hurtful, such manifestations of anti-Judaism were usually not motivated by a consuming racial hatred. Provided a Jewish family was well-established, it could live comfortably enough in spite of a silly name. Indeed, Jewish lawyers and physicians enjoyed such fine reputations that the very Jewishness of their names could serve as advertisement for their talents. All such fame and comfort, however, became targets for Hitler's vitriolic and militant brand of anti-Semitic ideology the instant his party took over the government in January 1933. For years the Nazis had left no doubt about their anti-Semitic feelings and the real threat they would become to Germany's half-million Jews the moment they came to power. Up to that point, their worst shenanigans and harassments had still been checked by the police, though many policemen secretly or openly sympathized with the raucous Party. My future father-in-law had been Police President in Freiburg, a dignified university city of about 120,000 people at the edge of the Black Forest. Like all high-ranking administrative positions, his had been a civilian career appointment based on two law degrees and twenty years in the government's service. For years he had openly fought Nazi rowdyism in his city, a reputation that, in 1933, led to his prompt dismissal. He was later reassigned to a somewhat lower, small-town position (*Landrat*, or district administrator) without any executive powers, where his every move was watched and often overridden by Party officials.

After 1933, anti-Semitism among Germany's middle class, previously restrained by the dictates of good manners and the liberalism of the professionals, was openly encouraged. Still, many non-Jewish landlords, employers, or customers of Jewish enterprises initially tried to skirt the new laws, or applied them with reluctance and shame. It should be mentioned, however, that throughout the Kaiser Reich and the Weimar Republic, upper-class institutions and societies such as the military leadership, universities and student fraternities, the aristocracy and both Christian churches had never disguised their anti-Jewish sentiments.

While European anti-Semitism was traditionally rooted in the dogmas of Christian religion, the secular twentieth-century variety, based on the theories of social Darwinism and eugenics, created the new pseudo-scientific concept of the "Jewish race." Determined to expel Jews from the community of the "Aryan race," the Nazi ideologues carried their secular anti-Semitism to irrational, and finally murderous, lengths: Contamination of the "genetically superior Aryan master race" by Jewish blood was declared a racial disgrace (*Rassenschande*), punishable by the severest measures, including death. According to the infamous Nuremberg Laws of September 1935, it was on the basis of bloodlines rather than religion that a person was legally declared a Jew. Throughout the 1930s, Jews were subjected to ever more restrictive rules and regulations aimed at isolating them from all social and economic contact with the *judenreine* (free from Jewish blood) majority. Their civil rights withdrawn and their financial means confiscated, they became socially ghettoized and depersonalized long before the deportations began.

By the mid- to late-1930s, though still emphatically rejecting the vulgar label of "anti-Semites," most Germans were probably sufficiently indoctrinated by the relentless Nazi propaganda to accept the exodus of wealthy Jews as a somewhat embarrassing, if not entirely unwelcome, development. Evidently, they thought, Germany *did* have a "Jewish problem"—those people *were* strangers who had enriched themselves far beyond the norm. Later, people watched with more satisfaction than pity as the abandoned villas and enterprises of their Jewish fellow citizens were taken over by "Aryans" at ruinous prices. As Jews with money and connections fled Germany in growing numbers, the Party's war chest swelled with the fortunes they were forced to leave behind. Of 500,000 Jews, about one-third found sanctuary abroad.

In 1941, families for whom escape had not been an option—either for lack of money or foreign sponsors, or because they refused to believe that Germans would do to them what Nazi propaganda incessantly promised they would—were forced to sew the *Judenstern*, the yellow Star of David, to their outerwear. The *Judenstern* invited harassment by every lout in the street (as it was intended to do), while stores, restaurants, movie theatres, and other public and private institutions came under strong pressure to refuse service altogether. With husbands thrown out of work and children dismissed from schools, dignities were shattered and Jewish lives reduced to the most furtive existence.

The moment of truth, however—the crucial event that would forever define the new Nazi-ordained relationship between Germans and Jews—had already occurred three years earlier: On November 9, 1938, the SA and SS, in a concerted nationwide action, burned down synagogues and brutally and senselessly destroyed Jewish stores and properties. "You must never forget this," my father said soberly as we waded through broken glass, past looted shelves gaping from vandalized stores, and precious furs floating in the brown waters of the Alster canals. This had been Hamburg's most exquisite shopping area. Could anybody ever forget? Something evil had happened, something vicious, like the furious outbreak of a deadly plague that would infect us all, carriers of its lethal germ; we were no longer innocent; we had *seen* and now we were *involved*, silently drawn into the knowledge of some dreadful scourge.

The costs for the clean-up of what was mockingly called *Kristallnacht* (Crystal Night, because of the masses of broken windows) were charged to the Jews. Officially, ninety-one Jews were murdered and about 30,000 taken into *Schutzhaft* (protective custody), allegedly to shield them from the *Volkszorn* (people's wrath). They were sent to Dachau and other concentration camps, many never to return.

Such acts of barbarism against a defenceless people created shock waves far greater than the Party had anticipated. It was the second and last time (the first having been on April 1, 1933, when the SA had called for a general boycott of Jewish businesses that was largely ignored by the population) that the Nazis would go about their odious business so openly and brazenly. To establish the concept of "collective guilt," one has to pin one's argument to November 9, 1938, when the first big step in an evolving genocide was taken with the full awareness of every ordinary German. Though most of them stayed away from the rampage, after *Kristallnacht*, no German could ever claim ignorance about the Nazi government's deadly serious intent to make Germany *judenrein* just as the Führer had promised. Neither could hundred thousands of policemen, neighbors, and friends later deny that they had turned their heads and walked away.

The mere fact that *Kristallnacht* was instigated so openly suggests that at that point, the SS state considered itself safely established. Though few people possessed concrete knowledge of its true size and power, most knew enough to carefully avoid antagonizing its institutions. The majority may have sensed the odd twitch of conscience, but thought it best to leave the whole nasty problem with those who had the competence and authority to deal with it. They knew, of course, who those "with competence" were, and many surely had at least a general idea about their government's plans, even if these had not yet reached the level of outright genocide. But the traditional German deference to authority quickly stilled whatever secret misgivings people might have harbored.

Kristallnacht took place only six weeks after the Munich Agreement, when England, France and Italy, in the name of appeasement ("Peace in our time!"), gave in to Hitler's peremptory demand for the Sudetenland, to be followed in March 1939 by the treacherous partition and occupation of Czechoslovakia. During those portentous months, while food rationing and air-raid precautions were energetically pursued, Germans became fully aware that war was just around the corner. From then on, until the Reich's collapse six years later, survival became the number-one exigency. As those poorly dressed people with their furtive looks gradually vanished from public sight and consciousness, "the Jewish problem" sank to the very bottom of the average German's personal priorities. Surely, somebody somewhere was taking care of the matter.

*   *   *

In the early 1940s, in response to pervasive rumors about the terrible conditions in the concentration camps, Nazi propaganda produced a movie of "Life in a Concentration Camp." Theresienstadt in the Sudetenland, a concentration camp originally meant for higher-class Jews or those with connections to the SS hierarchy,[4] was upgraded to a model camp. With great fanfare, a delegation from the International Red Cross was then invited to inspect the site.[5] The film was shown on German newsreels to persuade the population that their former fellow citizens had merely been relocated to some pleasant and well-maintained "garden city," where healthy workouts and cultural entertainment were provided for their physical and mental welfare. In spite of its crass tendentiousness, the trick largely succeeded. People believed what they wanted to believe. After all, if the Red Cross was satisfied, and if no European country raised any objections, why should one stick one's neck out for people one didn't even know? "Theresienstadt" soon became shorthand for "things are not really that bad," a soothing balm for the occasional twinge of doubt.

Probably more people survived in Theresienstadt than in any other concentration camp. But over time, even the Nazis' "model camp" (its reality far removed from the euphemized film version) became overcrowded, and surplus prisoners were routinely shipped off to Auschwitz. In his novel *War and Remembrance*, Herman Wouk provides an unforgettable, if fictional, account of life at Theresienstadt.

*   *   *

For the SS fanatics deeply imbued with the mission of making Germany and Europe *judenrein*, the ultimate challenge arose in June 1941, when, with the invasion of the Soviet Union, the "master race" was confronted with an overwhelming number of people of "inferior races"—Jews, Slavs, and gypsies—a fact that could hardly have surprised the Führer. Indeed, two equally firm, yet entirely unrelated convictions had occupied Hitler's mind as far back as the 1920s. Arising from quite different lines of thought, one politico-economic, the other ideological, together they had shaped his belief that, in order to survive, Germany had to destroy

Poland and ultimately the Soviet Union. The first axiom demanded Germany's acquisition, peacefully if possible, by force if necessary, of *Lebensraum,* or living space, in Eastern Europe as an indispensable requirement for the prosperity of the fatherland. Though dangerous and clearly out of step with international sentiment in the post-World War I era, the conquest of foreign territories had been part and parcel of European nation-building for centuries. The huge economic benefits were well understood by Germany's elites, the visions of glory enthusiastically supported by her indoctrinated youth.

In contrast, Hitler's second obsession, concerning the "Jewish–Bolshevik conspiracy," probably had few supporters outside his clique of fiercely loyal lieutenants. Alleging a disproportionately high number of Jews in the Communist Party, Hitler again and again lashed out at the putative conspiratorial link between world Jewry and international Communism. Nazi propaganda, from its earliest days, ranted against *Weltjudentum,* which, it was claimed, wielded enormous power and was bent on destroying Germany. Only the harshest measures could protect the imperiled homeland. Any sympathy the German people might feel for their disenfranchised brethren would be misplaced, because of the Jews' "devilish traits and deceitful nature." (Some kind of proof of the alleged Jewish–Bolshevik conspiracy came after 1941, when—entirely as a consequence of Hitler's own wildly irresponsible diplomacy—"Jewish Wall Street" began to finance shipments of American weaponry and materiel for Stalin's Red Army.)

Of these two war aims, *Lebensraum* almost certainly had priority on Hitler's mind when he attacked the Soviet Union. Expecting to defeat Russia before the winter, he was convinced that England—deprived of its last major ally—would then be forced to agree to a peace settlement that would give Germany dominance over Europe, leaving Great Britain with its overseas empire. But things didn't turn out as Hitler had anticipated. According to Sebastian Haffner, it was the Red Army's huge counteroffensive on December 6, 1941, taking Hitler completely by surprise, that convinced him Germany no longer had a chance to win the war, even if a separate peace with England could be arranged. Becoming entirely reckless, he declared war on America on December 11, just four days after Pearl Harbor, hoping that, as quid pro quo, Japan would open a second front in the far East, along the Manchurian border. Switching his priorities, he now concentrated his energies on Plan B, to be accomplished as long as there was still time: the elimination of European Jewry. Says Haffner: "The politician Hitler permanently resigned in December 1941, in favor of the mass murderer Hitler."[6] Plans for the Final Solution were presented on January 20, 1942, only six weeks after the beginning of Stalin's counteroffensive against an unprepared German army that was stuck without winter supplies outside Moscow and desperately clinging to Russia's frozen soil.

Goldhagen arrives at a less emotional and more political explanation for the timing of the Final Solution: Citing Hitler's obsession with the "Jewish–Bolshevik conspiracy," he argues that between the conquest of Poland in September 1939, and the invasion of the Soviet Union in June 1941, nothing too serious or permanent could have been done to Poland's ten percent Jewish population, because Russia, while still observing its non-aggression pact with the Reich, occupied Poland's eastern half. Trying to interpret Hitler's mind, he argues that mass killings of Poland's Jewish population might have provoked the Jewish–Bolshevik leadership in Moscow into attacking Germany, before Germany herself was ready to strike first.[7]

Thus, Nazi Germany's efforts to solve the "Jewish problem" ran in three escalating stages. Between 1933 and 1939 and even into the early years of the war, emigration was the preferred measure of getting rid of Germany's half-million Jews. Unfortunately, only about one-third found acceptance abroad. Between the invasion of Poland and the German attack on the Soviet Union, ghettoization became the method of choice. It served as a holding measure either in specially appointed areas of larger Polish cities (Warsaw, Bialystok, and Vilnius among others, where major uprisings later occurred), or in Polish concentration camps, until the time when the Nazis finally felt safe enough to dispense with all considerations and improvisations. Hitler's dream of two decades stood at the threshold of realization: Europe, dominated by German troops from the Arctic to the Mediterranean, from the Atlantic to the Volga, was going to become *judenrein*.

For the ideologues in the *Reichssicherheitshauptamt* in Berlin and the murderous *Einsatzgruppen* (special task forces) of the SS and SD, there now existed a clear directive: Find a way to destroy the Jews, or the Jews will destroy the fatherland. In the mind of every SS leader, that directive was nothing less than a *Führerbefehl*, a command from Hitler himself, and therefore of the highest priority. No such document, signed by the

Führer, has ever been found, although he undoubtedly knew all about it and feverishly desired its outcome. Between 1941 and 1944, this desire— supported by the entire Nazi brass—led to the step-by-step escalation from earlier killings by such "inefficient" methods as machine-gun bullets or carbon monoxide, to the infamous *Endlösung*, or Final Solution.

Plans for the *Endlösung* were revealed during the Wannsee Conference (named after a Berlin suburb) on January 20, 1942, only a few weeks after the Russian counterattack which, according to Haffner, had greatly spooked Hitler. To understand the direct and early involvement of Germany's highest civilian bureaucracy, it is important to know that the conference was called by top SD leader Reinhard Heydrich (in the presence of Adolf Eichmann) for the benefit of nineteen deputy ministers representing all major government departments. There were no recorded objections to the SS's horrifying plans. Instead, the conference took place in the congenial and relaxed atmosphere of a high-level cocktail party.

Meanwhile, the bombardment of the population with the most heinous anti-Semitic propaganda—now based on the image of the impoverished, orthodox East European Jew, rather than the prosperous, integrated, and educated German variety—went on relentlessly through cinema, party newspapers, and even the schools. By comparing the East European Jewish underclass with germs and vermin, Goebbels's Ministry for People's Enlightenment and Propaganda lowered its anti-Semitic rhetoric from the pseudo-scientific racial level to an aesthetically repulsive one designed to provoke powerful feelings of disgust against those *Volksschädlinge* (parasites of the people). Goebbels's "crowning achievement" was the movie "Jud Süss," made in 1940 by famous director Veit Harlan[8] with the co-operation of some of Germany's greatest actors. There were few people who did not see the film, and most of those who did, were deeply ashamed for having done so.

There have, of course, been genocides before and after the Holocaust: Armenians, Kurds, Cambodians, Bosnians, Hutus, Tutsis. What distinguished them all from the Nazis' Holocaust were not only the numbers of people killed, but the clockwork precision with which the killings were carried out. If the Nazis could coordinate huge battles under blitzkrieg conditions, the mechanical perfection of the Jewish genocide was just another challenge: doable, and doable German-style—not just better than anybody else, but better than anybody could *imagine*. Paradoxically, the best cover-up for what Sebastian Haffner called, without overstating, a *Zivilisationskatastrophe* (a catastrophe for all civilization) was its unbelievable inhuman efficiency. It defied all imagination; it still does.

It was in that smooth, cold, businesslike way that the gigantic plan was designed and executed, from the roundup, transportation, incarceration, and extermination of millions of European Jews, to the "processing"of their bodies and worldly possessions, including the melting down and banking of 2.6 tons of gold from teeth and jewellery.[9] But, once one acknowledges the existence of such a vast operation, whose exigencies often interfered with, and even took precedence over, those of the Wehrmacht, one has to conclude that it could not possibly have escaped the attention and co-operation of tens of thousands of civilian and military administrators at all levels of government.

That assertion lies at the heart of the unresolved problem of quantifying the guilty and the guilt. To get an idea of the numbers, one has to know that all echelons of civilian administration were paralleled by a corresponding Nazi hierarchy. Relationships between the two were frequently strained, if not downright hostile, with the Nazi structure ultimately being invested with superior powers. Above and between this dual system existed the tightly woven mesh of the SD and the SS, controlling every move, watching every mood within the populace for the earliest signs of protest or—God forbid—revolt. It was this carefully constructed network of hundreds of thousands of *Bonzen* (party hacks) and members of the SS, SD, the Gestapo, and the police that was ultimately responsible for the roundup, deportation and extermination of the Jews inside, and later outside, Germany.

Many civilian administrators may have tried to keep their heads down and their hands clean. That said, it is impossible to believe that any of them, regardless of position, could have remained ignorant of what went on in their area of jurisdiction. Knowing something about German bureaucratic efficiency, it is much more likely that for every arrest and every deportation by Nazi strongmen, a detailed list was handed over to their civilian "colleagues." These administrators would then be obliged to have the local police provide an inconspicuous and undisturbed environment for the forced measures, followed by the bureaucratic erasure of every name on the list together with a reallocation of housing and the termination of ration cards.

Whether a local mayor or regional administrator could have done anything meaningful to influence this coldly efficient process is a moot point. He could not. He may have saved a few people through some personal intervention; and many, particularly in smaller communities, probably did. But in the end, the vast majority co-operated because, apart from themselves and their careers, they had their families to protect. After all, these people were "ordinary" Germans, and to acquiesce rather than take a lonely stand is the ordinary person's very ordinary way to act in the face of unlimited power. Those who argue differently tend to ignore the pervasive might of the SS state, or the fact that to be ordinary means to follow the strongest instinct in all living things: the wish for survival. It also means to behave cowardly rather than heroically, to know the right thing, but to do otherwise—to become guilty not for what one does, but fails to do. It is the fundamental truth behind the collective guilt argument. The "Jewish problem" was "solved" by tens of thousands of perpetrators, supported by hundreds of thousands of collaborators, and by millions of ordinary people who knew that something horrible was going on, but averted their eyes and closed their mouths. No court of justice could find them guilty. "Collective guilt" does not exist in man's book of law. It exists in the consciences of ordinary people, and in the collective silence of the post-Nazi era. But mostly it exists in the terrible question—forever unresolved by the grace of God, or the wheel of time—of how many ordinary Germans did indeed, fully or partly, support their government's deadly anti-Semitic ideology.

Where there are generalizations, there are also exceptions and they lie on both sides of the human equation: the good Samaritan, the soft-hearted tyrant. Among the many mixed marriages, for instance, there were thousands of "Aryans" who stubbornly refused to divorce, but held on to their marriages to protect their Jewish spouses. How many half-Jews, or even Jews, were thus saved from deportation, nobody knows. Thousands more provided secret shelters for Jewish relatives or friends. Whether, proportionately, there were as many in Germany as there were in Holland, or in Munich as there were in Berlin, again, nobody knows.

No one who did not live through the terror of the Gestapo can possibly appreciate the daily heroism and the unimaginable strain demanded of those who chose to help. Apart from such hardships as daily air raids, worries about loved ones at the front, and meager rations that had to be split even further, there was the constant threat of being betrayed, subjected to a humiliating show trial, and sent to concentration camp or death. How many people had the strength to expose not only themselves, but their entire families to *Sippenhaft*, the barbaric way of Nazi revenge and punishment?

Examples of private initiatives against the ideology-driven campaigns of the SS were few and far between. In order to succeed, they invariably depended on some open-minded Nazi official. As is in any large organization, there was corruption, which could be exploited for beneficial ends, as illustrated in the Steven Spielberg docudrama *Schindler's List*. But the inference from such heartwarming, though isolated, cases that the SS might have been deterred from its genocidal mission, had only enough ordinary Germans tried really hard, is naive and ill-informed.

Though the Holocaust is probably the single most widely known aspect of the Nazi era today, things were entirely different at the time it occurred. While the war absorbed all energies, the "Jewish problem" sank ever deeper into the shadows of a lengthening list of subjects which were better left alone. Although the existence of concentration camps was never disguised, there was a deliberate information blackout surrounding the death camps. The regime went to remarkable lengths to keep the extent of the genocide from public knowledge, something that, because of the size of the operation, was not entirely successful. People knew about the ongoing persecution of the Jews, they knew about camps "in the East," and they knew and used the word *vergasen* (to kill by gassing), albeit in the form of black humor. In short, people knew that many of the deported Jews were killed by gas in concentration camps somewhere in occupied eastern Europe. But exactly where? And how many? Very few Germans cared. Besides, it was safer not to know, an attitude that mirrored the ambiguity of their government: While Hitler continually promised to save the German people from the conspiracy of world Jewry, the genocide itself remained a closely guarded secret. Therefore, if after the war people claimed not to have known about the extermination of millions of Jews in death camps in Poland, they were largely right. Whether such knowledge would have altered their conduct, whether they would have risen in protest or held on to their self-protective indifference, nobody will ever be able to guess.

There can be no doubt that the only way to stop the Holocaust was to defeat the SS state. That said, a few things might have had a deterrent or crippling effect prior to Germany's final surrender: bombing the rail tracks and SS quarters of the concentration camps, for instance. Eugen

Kogon describes the devastating effect on SS morale achieved by the Allied bombing of the armament industries near the concentration camps Buchenwald, Dachau, Sachsenhausen, and Auschwitz, with their thousands of inmate workers.[10] One wonders what would have happened to the morale of the SS had the extermination camps themselves been bombed, had several hundred, perhaps thousands of prisoners been killed, but a hundred thousand escaped?

All this, of course, is simply musing; it is also passing the buck. The Jewish genocide was a uniquely German affair, masterminded and executed by Germans. No other pogrom in history has ever come close to the mechanized horrors of the Nazi death camps. This was no religious fanaticism of a medieval mob, no desperate peasant uprising against extortionate landlords. It was a perverse ideology elevated to the level of sanctified dogma that demanded the elimination of a minority of less than one percent to assure the survival of the majority. No matter how grotesque, it was cold reasoning that stoked the fires of Auschwitz. Hitler's and Himmler's killing machine did not need the raging passions of millions; on the contrary, what it needed was the indifference and noninterference of the masses.

* * *

Half a century later, an embarrassing and senseless event highlighted the precarious state of Germany's *Vergangenheitsbewältigung*, the government's ongoing effort to come to terms with the German past.

On November 10, 1988, the Bonn government invited Germany's Jewish and political elites to a solemn fiftieth-year commemoration of *Kristallnacht*. The president of the *Bundestag* (federal parliament), Philipp Jenninger, born in 1932, gave a speech, which he had insisted on writing himself and to which, over the course of many weeks, he was said to have given much thought. Not surprising then was his deep shock when, midway through his talk, people began leaving the hall. The ruckus that embroiled him afterwards forced him to resign from the second-highest office in Bonn.

Among the media responses I obtained from the *Bundestag* press office, I counted eighteen condemnations, two solid endorsements by columnists of *Die Zeit* (which editorially castigated the speaker), and three articles somewhere in-between. In one of the last-mentioned, Ekkehard Kohrs of the *General-Anzeiger* wrote: "It is because of this [sensitive] subject that the audience was not prepared to acknowledge historical reality in such a speech. The president of the *Bundestag* was ruthlessly explicit when talking about uncomfortable truths, but he also did so without any sensitivity for the subject and the place."[11] (My translation.) What dreadful things had Jenninger said or done?

Among his major faults: the woodenness of his speech; his appalling failure to emphasize the quotation marks in his manuscript, causing the cited Nazi defamations of Jews to sound like his own; his talk of five years of Hitler's "accomplishments" (authoritatively described by Sebastian Haffner[12]) given as explanations for Germany's idolatry of its Führer. In sum, he was denounced for his naive decision to speak about the reality of the Third Reich, rather than to issue conventional words of sorrow and distress.

Poor Jenninger, he meant so well, but only succeeded in upsetting a precariously laden apple cart. Still, according to the Bonn publication *Aktuell*, 10,000 ordinary Germans wrote letters thanking him for his honesty.

Notes to Chapter 4

1   According to Coesfeld City officials, the most likely place where I spent my prison days was the huge *Wehrbezirkskommando* or Regional Military HQ, where the Wehrmacht had kept a number of prison cells. While ninety percent of Coesfeld had been destroyed, this was one of the few buildings that survived the war. It was taken over first by the Americans, then by the British, and used for administrative purposes, although it may well have housed political prisoners as well.

2   Johnson, Paul, *Eine Epidemie des Hasses*. In: Schoeps, Julius H., ed.: *Ein Volk von Mördern? Die Dokumentation zur Goldhagen-Kontroverse um die Rolle der Deutschen im Holocaust* (Hamburg: Hoffmann & Campe, 1996), 30.

3   Jews practicing their belief. By "racial standards," the number was much larger.

4   Similarly, Bergen-Belsen in Germany was originally earmarked for Jewish "celebrities" to be held for later exchange against German POWs or other prisoners in Allied camps. When British troops liberated the camp in 1945, they had to put bulldozers to work to bury the dead.

5 According to Michael Ignatieff (*The Warrior's Honour* [Toronto: Viking, 1998], 136), the International Committee of the Red Cross refused to visit the German concentration camps, because their mandate did not include civilian camps; they also feared political reprisals for Switzerland. It may therefore be assumed that the famous visit to Theresienstadt took place by the *national* German Red Cross, whose leader was Dr. Ernst Gravitz, an SS officer who conducted human experiments and killed himself in the spring of 1945.

6 Haffner, Sebastian, *Anmerkungen zu Hitler* (Munich: Kindler, 1978), 180.

7 Goldhagen, Daniel J., *Hitler's Willing Executioners: Ordinary Germans and the Holocaust* (New York: Alfred Knopf, 1996), 144.

8 Veit Harlan (1899–1964), who enjoyed the full patronage of Goebbels's Ministry, continued to make Nazi propaganda films until 1945. His last color production, *Kolberg*, about the Prussian fortress that bravely resisted Napoleon's troops, was released when few movie theaters were left standing in Germany. After the war, he was restricted from working. Though that order was soon lifted, he had no further successes.

9 Böhm, Kleine-Brockhoff, Willeke: "*Das deutsche Bankgeheimnis*" (The German Bank Secret), *Die Zeit*, No. 34, 1998.

10 Kogon, Eugen, *Der SS-Staat: Das System der deutschen Konzentrationslager* (Munich: Kindler, 1974), 299.

11 Kohrs, Ekkehard, *Eine falsche Rede* (A faulty speech), *General-Anzeiger*, November 11, 1988.

12 Haffner, Sebastian, op. cit., 37.

5

RECKLINGHAUSEN

Recklinghausen is one of the major cities of the *Kohlenpott* (coal pot), once the most densely industrialized and urbanized part of Germany, and possibly of all of Europe. Distanced in space and spirit from the Hanseatic cities to the north and the picturesque Bavarian villages to the south, this region is where high-grade coal has been mined since the dawn of the Industrial Age. Brought to the surface through ever-deeper networks of shafts crisscrossing the areas along the Rhine and Ruhr rivers, much of the black gold is immediately fed into the rapacious blast furnaces dotting the area like monstrous mushrooms. For generations, they have been the cradle of much of the world's finest steel, while their owners amassed immense fortunes. As the Kaiser's, and later Hitler's, beloved *Waffenschmiede* (weapons smiths), the Ruhr barons were major collaborators in Germany's role of aggressor in two world wars.

Not surprisingly, Recklinghausen and its neighboring cities were prime targets of Allied bombing. After the war, whatever had survived destruction became attractive bounty for reparations payments. (In the American and British zones of occupation, the dismantling of the country's remaining infrastructure was halted after the first two or three years.) In recent decades, many of the *Kohlenpott* mines have been closed for economic reasons, followed by huge clean-up operations of air and ground that have turned the nearby cities into jewels of urban renewal. I grew up, however, with images of soot-smeared men going deep into the belly of the earth in clanking crates, while outside the ubiquitous dust darkened the sun and penetrated the lungs, enveloping all in a suffocating shroud of dirt and disease.

Coming from Coesfeld prison in mid-November 1945, the arrival of our truck at British internment camp Recklinghausen was remarkable only for the total lack of interest it aroused. There was a perfunctory registration at a small office near the entrance, where our military driver delivered Müller and me along with our transfer papers. Our IDs were carefully copied and politely returned. There were no questions, no explanations. At the end of the process, Müller was led away. I was met by a sturdy, middle-aged woman, who introduced herself as the supervisor of the women's compound (*Lagerälteste*). She accepted me with neither smile nor frown, then strode ahead in that self-assured manner born of undisputed authority.

The women's compound, enclosed by high fences and barbed wire, consisted of a number of Nissen huts—large structures of corrugated metal measuring roughly 60 by 120 feet and accessible only by a small anteroom. I am uncertain about the number of inmates, but somewhere around sixty to eighty per hut would be a fair guess.

By the time I arrived at the camp, most of the women had been interned for almost a year. They had been living in the war-torn areas sandwiched between the Rhine's left bank and the Dutch and Belgian borders. Originally captured by the Americans eager to spot and arrest every Nazi, big or small, they had been held at the huge and ill-reputed Wuppertal penitentiary. When the Potsdam Conference in the summer of 1945 carved up defeated Germany into four military zones of occupation, granting Wuppertal and the Rhineland to the British, the erratic and intensely disliked U.S. prison masters were replaced by the ever-so-correct *Engländer*. As soon as some order was installed into the rather arbitrary system of taking and holding political prisoners, the women were moved to a camp near the city of Recklinghausen, an immense improvement in their circumstances. They were positively ecstatic to be where they were, and continued to recount the most ghastly tales about their former wardens. Though none of them claimed personal molestation by the American guards, the male prisoners were widely rumored to have been sadistically abused.

Not having been there, I don't feel free to add any details. But I am still bothered by the fact that it never occurred to me to ask Müller who had beaten him up. When I saw him in the back of the truck in the Coesfeld prison yard, I simply assumed that his swollen mouth and missing tooth were the work of his British interrogators. Looking back, however, I am not so sure. Just as likely, it had been those dubious German guys who picked me up.

As I try to recall the fellow inmates I met at Camp Recklinghausen, a composite picture emerges in my mind of a clean-looking, housewifey, full-bosomed type with light hair that has outgrown much of its dye and turned brown or grey along the part; middle-sized, middle-class, middle-everything. Nice solid German women between the ages of twenty-five and forty-five, some younger, some married, who had occupied positions of leadership within one of the three female Nazi organizations: The *Jungmädelschaft*, or JM, for girls between ten and fourteen; the *Bund deutscher Mädel*, or BDM, for fourteen- to eighteen-year-olds; and the *Frauenschaft*, for women of all ages. Some had held very low ranks before being rounded up during the fervent early weeks of the conquest. Others had worked in salaried positions, defending the ideological line and exercising powers which, though only loosely defined, were seldom challenged by the thousands under their command. At Recklinghausen, the same as in all other camps, they were collectively categorized as *automatische Verhaftungen*, or automatic internees, comprising the vast majority of all female prisoners, possibly as many as ninety percent.

At the time of my lonely arrival—there had been no newcomer in months—there were rumors about their pending release. As they patiently waited for their long-delayed freedom, the women—or so it seemed to this mystified newcomer—displayed a surprising lack of indignation or nervousness about their fate. Bound together by their old camaraderie, even friendships, they seemed well-adjusted, neither particularly happy nor unhappy, as though their present sojourn in a detention camp was not all that much different from the many Hitler Youth camps they had organized and attended during their earlier days of glory.

As I came face-to-face with them now on supposedly equal footing and a proximity unfamiliar and not altogether reassuring, they all seemed cut from the same cloth, their collective rectitude unsullied, their chumminess reminiscent of happier days when they had proudly carried the swastika banner ahead of their marching maidens.

If I had any doubts about the accuracy of these impressions five decades later, I felt reassured by the memoirs of Ursula Fischer,[1] a former JM leader, born in 1925. Her account of four years of hardship in a number of political internment camps in the Soviet zone (later East Germany) positively oozes collectivity and comradeship. No doubt in a far worse situation than her *Kameradinnen* in the West, she and her colleagues were sustained by their firmly closed ranks, their old loyalties, the Great Faith they once had shared

* * *

In 1936, when membership in the National Socialist youth movement became mandatory for all youngsters over the age of ten, I ignored my parents' mild, if vague, reservations and eagerly joined the *Jungmädelschaft*. I was extremely proud of my new uniform and of belonging to the biggest in-thing for every boy and girl. However, my enthusiasm for their action-driven fanaticism flagged surprisingly fast, perhaps after a year or two, a fact I made every effort to conceal from even my closest friends. Why such caution at such a tender age? I don't recall anybody actually telling or warning me to be careful. Children simply *knew*— then, as now—about things others try to keep from them. Without intentionally watching or listening, they invariably know what their parents think, sense the hypocrisy of their teachers, the double-talk of their religious leaders, the phony rectitude of every adult—friend or foe. Accordingly, most children during the Hitler years simply *knew* where their schoolmates stood, their parents, teachers, ministers, or priests. I knew that my parents hated Goebbels's tirades against their social class, despised those raucous marchers in their brown SA uniforms, and were suspicious of the SS. But I also knew that for me to voice even the slightest reservation or hint of disapproval would have promptly triggered such calamities as isolation from my peers, questions from teachers, and an escalating pressure from the *Hitlerjugend* leadership.

Despite my growing distaste, for four years I attended, more or less regularly, compulsory Hitler Youth events such as sports and field trips on Saturdays, and small gatherings, called *Heimabende*, where we sang songs and had ideological pep talks every Wednesday afternoon. I was fifteen when I quit, just half a year into my new status as *Schaftführerin*, the lowest rank in the leadership hierarchy and a promotion almost automatically bestowed on every reasonably intelligent girl. In the end, I simply dropped out. I don't know why on that particular day and why so precipitously, but that is precisely how it happened. I confronted one of my highest-ranking leaders just as she was in the middle of organizing a big rally.

"I don't want to be *Schaftführerin* any longer," I declared, interrupting and perplexing her at a most inopportune time. As I remember the incident, I had been on my way to the great event, when certain thoughts which, until then, I had only vaguely entertained, suddenly hit me with the force of truth: that the *Hitlerjugend* with its prescribed enthusiasm, its endless and often mindless activities, and its obsession with health and sports was not only a dreadful bore, but increasingly became a conflict with things I considered more important and certainly more pleasurable—theater and opera, reading and school studies, or the need to simply be left alone.

Right then and there, the mythical semi-Wagnerian, semi-Nietzschean Nazi *Weltanschauung* and I parted company. Not through any profound philosophical or ideological insight (I had none), but as a small step in the process of growing up. Once I had discovered the priorities of my own (slightly inflated) persona, I was no longer willing to waste my time on behalf of an organization I considered a nuisance rather than a value in my personal life.

Perhaps the leader was too stunned or preoccupied; or perhaps she simply forgot. In the end nothing happened; no reprisals, no consequences. An insignificant incident altogether—rash, youthful, impolite, perhaps a bit silly, and without so much as a pretense of deep conviction. And yet, it supports an assertion frequently made years later, when Hitler and the Third Reich and National Socialism were all gone: that when confronted by a determined position, Nazi officials tended to pull back. Not always, of course, and frequently not without repercussions for prosperity and profession, but the possibility clearly existed.

How compulsory was the Hitler Youth? How much real power did its leadership have? Were there laws, or merely rules and regulations? My guess is that membership was urgently desired and strongly promoted, but ultimately unenforceable. The fact is, my best friend stayed out of the organization altogether, because her parents didn't want her to join. Her family was from old money and nothing happened to any of the four children. In the end, she and I joined *Glaube und Schönheit*, the innocuous organization described in the prologue. Our attendance at their once-a-week reading sessions for prescribed National Socialist literature permitted us to finish high school without further interference by the Hitler Youth. Three months later, we graduated at the top of the class.

(It would be nice to leave the story there—so ennobling, so politically correct. For the sake of truth, however, I have to add a prosaic ending: A few years ago, the two of us—both grandmothers now and wise in the ways of life—reminisced about those long-ago times. It was then that my friend, somewhat ruefully, admitted that rather than having felt relieved of the whole dreadful bother—as I had always enviously and admiringly assumed—she had actually resented the parental dictum that prevented her from being one of the gang. *Pueri pueri sunt*—whatever the ideological flavor of the time.)

Taken singly, most of these Nazi women leaders were harmless and well-meaning, becoming obnoxious only by virtue of the mass organizations they represented, and the ominous power that stood behind them. After the collapse of the Hitler regime, and a period of detention for a relatively small number of *Führerinnen*, all youth organizations were exempted from further war crimes prosecutions, their leaders—male and female—freed and sent home. After their release, most of them promptly forgot everything they had once so fanatically believed. Without further ado, they simply slipped into the faceless masses of their defeated people. As years went by, they would increasingly distance themselves from their former positions. When reminded by others, a tale of convenience would readily come to their lips belittling their erstwhile involvement with Nazism as an amusing but inconsequential affair. Such creative reinterpretation of former loyalties and convictions, of course, did not differ significantly from the "reformed" recollections of tens of millions of other Germans (and Austrians), reborn Nazi opponents one and all.

* * *

Having sketched a composite picture of the "automatic detainees" making up the vast majority of women at Camp Recklinghausen and every other camp, I must now report on my own situation which was, alas, entirely different.

Physically, I was younger, taller, and darker than most. I came from Hamburg, a large and elegant Hanseatic metropolis 400 kilometers north of the *Kohlenpott,* and from a family that was politically conservative and socially traditional to the point of snobbery. Ethnically, linguistically, and socially, I was far removed from my fellow inmates. I had a stiff north German accent with lots of sibilant "S's" and the sharp Anglo-Saxon "Sp" and "St," whereas everybody else spoke the soft Rhenish dialect, with its abundant "Sh's" turning every sentence into a confidentiality.

These, however, were only the outward distinctions, noticeable but of little consequence when measured against my truly disastrous abnormality: I was a *Sonderfall*, a special case, a person who belonged into a category of one. In an environment where codes of acceptance were rigidly observed, this was indeed an extraordinary misfortune. Defined in the most general way, a *Sonderfall* was a political prisoner detained for reasons other than membership in a Nazi organization, which, theoretically, left almost limitless possibilities. Practically speaking, however—meaning in the eyes of the *Automatischen* who set all the rules and regulations—a *Sonderfall* had almost certainly been a member of some secret organization, a spy who wouldn't think twice about reporting on her fellow prisoners in exchange for some personal gain.

In retrospect, I agree entirely with this assessment and the majority's instinct for self-preservation by isolating the dubious party. I hasten to add, though, that of the small number of female "special cases" I met, none was under the shadow of such general mistrust. They had either been able to establish their bona fide harmlessness, or their strong personalities had fended off the offensive attitudes of others. I failed on both counts. I did manage, however, to overcome their prejudices. It took many months, and there were other factors involved. But, by the time I bid farewell to the remaining *Automatischen,* I had gained a good deal of respect and even friendship, which satisfied me immensely, as it had been a tough thing to accomplish.

I don't believe that I met more than a half dozen "special cases" during the entire period of my captivity. Though most of them were inmates of the Sennelager, where I didn't get to know them until many weeks later, I will describe some of them now, in order to highlight their colourful "specialness" amid the rather depressing uniformity of the automatically detained.

The most impressive was a tiny dynamo by the name of Frau Dr. Wirth (no first-name familiarity permitted here), who had been director of the women's penitentiary in Cologne. She was a sharp-tongued, highly intelligent woman who demanded respect and got it, along with a good deal of affection. In early 1946, she was unexpectedly released because of her severe state of malnutrition. Personally I had never been close to Dr. Wirth. I was therefore surprised when the night before her departure I received covert word that she would be willing to smuggle a note to my parents in Hamburg. Leaping at the chance, I wrote a message using indelible ink on a tiny shred of wet cloth, advice and material kindly supplied by some old-timers more eager to please Frau Dr. Wirth than me. The incriminating piece was carefully dried, then sewn into the gusset of the formidable little prison director's underpants. It was a high-risk venture, as everybody was well aware. When there were no repercussions during the next twenty-four hours, I knew that the missive had passed safely through the controls. I never did learn, however, why the tiny lady lawyer, as gruff as she was emaciated, was so generous to me, or, for that matter, why she had been interned in the first place. Whatever the explanation, I remember her as a truly remarkable person. To connect her with something as vulgar as spying would have been utterly absurd.

The same held for Marlies, who otherwise had as much in common with Frau Dr. Wirth as an eggplant with a string bean. A bottle-blond, fair-skinned, curvy woman in her mid-twenties, with a quick wit and good-natured chumminess, Marlies looked and acted like the archetypal Rhenish character. From what I recall of her case, she had been employed by somebody high up in the Nazi government, the exact details of her services remaining undisclosed. Like Dr. Wirth, I met her at the Sennelager, my fourth and final station, where I was to spend almost half a year. Marlies' hostile reaction to my arrival was as prompt as it was undisguised. When the supervisor of the women's compound assigned me to the bunk above hers, she sullenly turned her back, refusing all further personal contact then, and for months thereafter.

I might have found it easier to accept her rejection had Marlies not been the most popular woman in the barracks and the toast of the do-it-yourself entertainment scene. Every night after lights out, a stream of off-color jokes would flow from her cherubic lips, her ribaldry touching off waves of laughter that cleansed away homesickness, fear, and despair. Sadly, most of the jokes passed me by because of their local accent and content, and my remarkably uninformed state of sexual enlightenment. By day, Marlies' aggressive wit and open contempt for her bunk mate further enhanced her popularity, while effectively diminishing mine.

There were more than three months of this—and then the unimaginable happened: On April 1, the day I turned twenty-one and expected no one to notice, Marlies handed me a present. She still looked sullen, or tried very hard to. Yet, there was a twinkle in her blue eyes as she watched me unfold the little item: A bra! A perfectly fitted bra stitched by her own hands from a very fine cotton obtained by some mysterious and extraordinary means. I was overwhelmed, moved to tears. The humble garment had a surprisingly pleasing fit. Much more important, though, it signaled the start of a warm and precious friendship that had been withheld for so long, for reasons I was never allowed to learn. Surely, nobody suspected the popularity queen of having been a spy, deviously planted as a snitch in our little community.

The same couldn't be said of Shirley, an Englishwoman and agent who had worked for the Germans. Short and scrawny, Shirley looked remarkably out of place among the lot of wholesome German women. Probably no more than thirty-five, her face was deeply lined and pallid, a condition that she masked with a lavish coat of makeup. Being British, she alone had the fortitude to disdain the popular convention: *Eine deutsche Frau schminkt sich nicht* (A German woman doesn't use makeup), suggesting that a healthy complexion derives from good genes rather than good chemistry.

Like Dr. Wirth and Marlies, I met Shirley at the Sennelager, where she had been for more than half a year. Since there was no secrecy about her former activity, I presumed that she had never tried to hide it. By talking about it freely, she may have hoped to undercut the suspicion and ostracism she must have foreseen to be her lot. Certainly, in her heavily accented German, Shirley sounded agreeably honest, almost tragically so, provided one took her openness as entirely her own idea, rather than the suggestion of her superiors. The fact is, she and she alone was called up for interrogations, which may have dealt with her own situation, or that of others, or both. I cannot remember how often these happened, but they provided her with a running supply of cigarettes she couldn't do without in an environment totally devoid of tobacco. When she received her orders for departure—not for freedom, as she well understood, but for transferral to England—Shirley accepted them in her usual stoic manner. We all shook her hand and tried to say something encouraging. To each of us she replied with a shrug and a smile and a few words in English that nobody understood. We never learned what became of her on the other side of the Channel, but it can hardly have been a bed of roses.

By writing about some of the *Sonderfälle* I was to meet over time, I have allowed myself to get far ahead of my story. I now return to Day One of my life in an internment camp.

*   *   *

The low-arched Nissen hut, to which the women's supervisor had led me, was a kind of housing I had never seen in my life. (As I was to learn many years later, this strange contraption was a triumph of the inventiveness of Canadian army engineers, and the source of much national pride. In the early fifties, on my medical rounds through the outskirts of Hamburg, I visited patients, refugees from East European countries, who still lived in those huts seven years after the war.)

Ignorant of the things to come, I felt nothing but relief for being out of jail. Whatever lay ahead, I told myself, I wouldn't be alone anymore; the shame and anxiety of imprisonment, now shared by hundreds, would be mitigated. Unfortunately, the elation was short-lived, quickly replaced by feelings of oppression and apprehension. Nothing I had ever experienced came close to the low-ceilinged, poorly lit interior of a Nissen hut filled with women, bunks, smoke, noise, and a sustained level of mild chaos. If there was any purpose behind the clattering activity, it was not immediately evident. (There was none, as I was soon to discover, save for the desire to kill time during the endless waits for never enough food.)

The supervisor dropped me off at my new living quarters, a narrow cot without straw or blanket, crudely fashioned from a two-and-a-half by six-foot board with low edges that could hardly prevent a tumble during a bad dream. I was to reside on the top bunk of three, shakily balanced against another identical stack. There was a space of about two meters separating each six-pack from the next, where experienced veterans, enjoying the proprietary advantages of old-timers, had stashed their belongings in all sorts of contraptions. Bedposts stood in shallow metal cans filled with petroleum to discourage the ascent of bed bugs. Still, vast armies of them persisted, though by happy fluke they passed me by. Other prisoners were less fortunate, the ugly proof of their nocturnal torturers all over their bodies.

My arrival, though barely acknowledged by most, did prompt a few questions among my immediate neighbors. Where did I come from, and why, and why so much later than everybody else? Looking back, I am amazed at my early instinct for self-preservation. I didn't confide. I answered willingly, but gave nothing away. Still, they must have recognized my circumstances in minutes. Since I couldn't cite any group of organized females that had been under my charge, I had to be a "special case." Having no knowledge about the finer points of the camp's political infrastructure, I was not worried. That first informal interrogation, which was to be followed by many others, both formal and informal, went something like this:

"Where are you from?"

"Hamburg."

"How come you're here? Don't they have camps up there?"

"I was picked up in Dülmen. On a farm."

"Dülmen? Why Dülmen?"

"I was visiting a friend. We had been together in Marburg."

"But that's in the American zone."

"It's a long story ..."

"Tell us." My inquisitors sounded friendly and genuinely interested.

"My friend—she is much older than I am, married and all that. She already had a little boy and in August she had a second baby. So her father came down to Marburg on his truck to take her and the children with him to Dülmen. He has a big farm. No hunger there!" They responded by laughing at my little joke, which everybody understood: starving people in the cities, fat cats in the country.

"And her husband? Is he a prisoner of war? In Russia or what?"

It was a dangerous question and I skidded around it: "I don't know. She hasn't heard from him yet."

"Probably in Russia ..." They nodded sympathetically.

"Anyway, her father loaded up all her belongings and mine, too. Or what was left of them. You see, I'd been bombed in March, and after that I moved in with my friend."

"And that's how you got to Dülmen—of all places. And you from Hamburg."

"No, no. In July I'd left for Hamburg to find out whether my folks were still alive. I hadn't heard from them in ages—" The familiar guilt about abandoning Josephine crept up again. Worse, even to my own ears my tale sounded terribly complicated and totally irrelevant, invented mainly to confuse. I could see it in their eyes. Some shrugged and drifted away.

Others persisted: "But you've said you were picked up in Dülmen—"

"Yes, yes, I'm coming to that. You see, my friend had sent me a letter that she had arrived there from Marburg with all our things. And that I should come and decide what to do with my stuff. So I came down—a long trip in an empty coal wagon, not very comfortable, as you can imagine. But I did get there and we had a very happy reunion—"

"And did you find your things?"

"We never got around to looking for them. They were probably stored in the attic or somewhere. Those first hours we just talked and played with the kids. And then, just as we were sitting down for lunch, there was a huge commotion." I paused for dramatic effect. "Army trucks full of British soldiers converging on the farm. Tons of soldiers, all with their rifles and machine guns, running around, blocking off the entire place."

I had their attention now. The whole thing must have sounded a lot more exciting than what they had been through.

"What did they want? Had they discovered a black market hub in good old Catholic Dülmen or something?" They laughed at the preposterous suggestion.

"They were looking for some SS men who had been hiding there. From what I've heard, they'd been working as farmhands. Somebody must have given them away."

"What SS men? And how come they were in Dülmen? Did you know them?" The questions rained down fast and hard.

I suddenly remembered that I had promised Josephine I wouldn't talk about this. I hastily back-pedalled: "I really know very little about the whole thing. They kept my friend and me isolated under house arrest, with a guard at the door."

"Sounds scary."

"It sure was. Well, there were rumors that some of the guys hiding out at the farm had been members of an *SS-Studentenkompanie* in Marburg. Since I had been in Marburg, and my friend too—" I shrugged. "Somebody must have made a connection."

"But did you know them?"

"One I did. Sort of. He'd been *Hauptsturmführer* and the boss of the student outfit. He was also the boss of my fiancé, who was a member of that company. That's how I met him."

"And where is he now? I mean—where's your fiancé? Is he in Dülmen, too?"

"No—thank God. Actually, I have no idea." Which was true. "It's all very complicated. And a stupid coincidence that they had to raid the place just on the day I arrived."

That was my story. And it remained my story throughout. Everything in it was true, insofar as it contained no lies. But, as Oscar Wilde put it so wisely, truth is rarely pure and never simple, which left my fellow prisoners—and later my interrogators—with the angry suspicion of somehow having been had.

Still, looking back on those first days at Recklinghausen, I don't remember any open hostility of the kind I would later encounter at the Sennelager. There was a certain coolness, no doubt, but no outright ostracism. Perhaps I was too ignorant to notice, too overwhelmed by the many unfamiliar things that demanded my immediate attention. After all, I was a newcomer among a large group of people who had known each other for months; under the circumstances, a certain initial aloofness should not have struck me as unreasonable or unfair. Besides, there must have been at least one kindly soul, who quietly supplied me with eating utensils, since I don't remember digging for empty tins from the camp's rubbish dump.

Perhaps it was the same person I had met during the first minutes of my arrival, a thin and dejected-looking girl who, during my short stay at Camp Recklinghausen, would become more attached to me than I might have wished, given the choice. She was a friendly, simple-minded creature of seventeen or eighteen who, within the first hour of our acquaintance, entrusted me with the extraordinary (and highly unlikely) secret that she had been a member of the dreaded Werewolf, a rumored band of former SS men determined to carry on their struggle against the Allies from the underground. Whether I had heard about this mysterious organization before, or whether this was the first time, I don't recall. But it surely wouldn't be the last, as this nebulous outfit would soon loom large in my own personal predicament. Naturally, her professed past had instantly turned her into a *Sonderfall* par excellence, the most special of special cases. Not that any of her fellow prisoners truly believed her tale; indeed, one wonders how she managed to get herself arrested in the first place—what kind of sleuth had fallen for her story.

The girl happened to occupy the top bunk adjacent to mine. Since I had the small blanket I had brought from Josephine's, and she had a coat, we learned to pool our meager resources while hugging each other tightly between the flimsy covers and drafty boards.

I don't remember her name, so I will call her Elli, because somehow that was the way she looked—like a working-class girl who had left school at fourteen to work in the local rubber factory. I have no idea whether this picture comes anywhere close to reality; I'm just trying to describe her type: She had black, unruly hair gathered carelessly into a single braid. Her face was small and pale, with brown eyes under heavy brows, and the hooked nose of a gypsy. Her figure looked undernourished rather than slim; her clothes poor rather than worn. Even after all these years, I can still picture her—dark, different, and vulnerable. At times, Elli was as talkative as a child, at others, strangely remote. Her mood swings perplexed and discomfited me, until the day I suddenly understood her predicament, which was tremendous and unsolvable at the time. As it happened, that day would turn out to be my last at Camp Recklinghausen, with more excitement and better-remembered than all the previous ones put together.

During my second week, I had begun to attend lectures at the "camp university." It was a pleasant distraction for academics, who, by special fiat, were allowed to visit classes taught by former professors, now inmates. Lectures in anatomy, biology, history, and German literature were held in a barracks in one of the men's compounds, with chairs for about forty and a primitive lectern. There were no special rules; once a prisoner was permitted to "enrol," he could choose whatever courses he pleased. It seemed everyone chose the lot, since attending lectures was incomparably better than sitting around doing nothing.

That day, returning from camp university in a happy and relaxed mood, I came face to face with Elli's problem. We had just received our one ladle of turnip soup when the girl asked me to sit next to her on the bench. We slowly sipped the disagreeable slop while chewing on a chunk of dark, heavy bread, our ration for the day.

"I am going to have an attack," Elli said suddenly. She had shoved aside her bowl, which was barely touched. Her head was bent down, and I wasn't sure whether I had understood her.

"You are going to have what—?"

She looked up, searching my face. "The others haven't told you?" It was less a question than a statement.

"Told me what?" I was irritated by the suggestion that I might not be part of anybody's confidences but hers. I looked around and realized, as I might vaguely have done before, that we were indeed isolated. I felt resentment, as though it was all her fault; that to be seen associating with this peculiar girl had somehow made me her equal. "I have no idea what you're talking about."

"I'm going to have an attack," she repeated, speaking very clearly now, albeit in a low voice. "I'm an epileptic, you know." Her dark brown eyes anxiously tried to connect with mine.

I did not know what to say. With two semesters of medical studies, and seven or more months of nursing experience under my belt, I felt I should know what she was talking about, and embarrassed because I did not. I had never seen an epileptic seizure and hadn't a clue how to handle it. "What do you want me to do?"

"It would be nice if you could be around. Just in case."

"Sure—when?"

She shrugged. "I don't really know. Soon anyway."

When, less than an hour later, her seizure began, I was still sitting beside her. But preoccupied with some other distraction, I had all but forgotten about my promise. She emitted a strange strangling noise, then sprawled across my lap, her head and limbs jerking violently. I fought desperately to regain my balance, so as not to be thrown off the bench by the force of her wildly flailing arms. Somebody with more experience wedged something between her teeth to prevent her from biting her tongue, while gentle hands lowered her to the floor, an arm cushioning her head against its convulsive hammering.

When it was over, Elli slept for a long time, while I reflected on the only other case of epilepsy I had heard of. It had been in the winter of 1943 to 1944 and my first year at university. During the day, while I was away at classes, my mother was alone in the house. She had a new maid then, a dull but friendly girl of about eighteen. Two weeks into her employ, the girl suffered a seizure; she fell on the heavy iron door of the open furnace, and severely damaged her skull. My mother did her best to protect her, and later cleaned her up while she slept. But it had happened so fast, so unexpectedly, and the girl had been heavy, heavier still for her wild lashing. When I came home that night, my mother was angry at the maid for not having told or warned her of her condition. The girl's labour report card showed a long list of former employers. But my mother hadn't asked about it, and the labour office hadn't explained. In 1943 a prospective employer needed a doctor's certificate for the privilege of domestic help, and had to be grateful if some was supplied. My mother was faced with an unpleasant decision: Should she keep the girl? What if she hurt herself badly, perhaps had a seizure during an air raid? She clearly couldn't keep her, she absolutely could not. It all sounded completely rational. I remember wondering why my mother made such a fuss about it. She had been duped, hadn't she? Put deliberately into an impossible situation by the labour office. Of course, I knew nothing then about the Nazis' euthanasia program. Did my mother know? The next day, she told us about her visit to the employment office to ask for a replacement.

"Your reasons?"

"The girl doesn't have enough experience."

The woman across the desk glanced at the girl's record with its long list of short-term positions.

"Perhaps you should send her someplace in the country?" my mother suggested. "She may have an easier time there."

The official looked at her, then back at the record. "Does she steal?"

"No, no, of course not. Just as I said—perhaps a bit slow."

"We get all kinds nowadays," the woman sighed. "We have to do something with them. If we don't—" Her voice trailed off.

Euthanasia killings had stopped in 1941 after protests by the Catholic Church, but forced sterilization and other wilful acts against "unworthy lives" continued. Perhaps my mother really hadn't known about the rumors. But then—why did she avoid telling the truth? Did she want to protect the girl out of some dark sense of danger? Or, more prosaically, was she unwilling to forgo the help she felt was her due, while being embarrassed by her lack of compassion? If the latter sounds unbelievably selfish today, it did not then. After all, housework meant carrying heavy pails of coal to fire the furnace, hours of waiting in shopping lines, no cars for easy transport, no hot water, no washing machine, no refrigerator—and certainly no willing husband to lend a helping hand.

My mother soon got another maid. She was my age and she liked my things, which she stole brazenly and continually. We couldn't get rid of her, because we couldn't catch her in the act.

God knows how Elli had escaped the SS's draconian measures against people with mental conditions. Or had she? She might have been sterilized; she never said. Indeed, I never talked to her again. By the time she woke up, I was surrounded by half the barrack's population, my obscure persona suddenly famous (or infamous, depending on one's perspective) by the monumental news that the next station in my checkered career as a "special case" would be Iserlohn, home of the British Secret Service.

* * *

Altogether, I spent only a little over two weeks at Recklinghausen, certainly not enough time to acquire an accurate picture of the British, let alone Allied, internment system. In order to give a fairly authentic account—strictly from memory, because requests for information from British agencies have not proven very successful—I have to mix in later experiences from another, much larger camp, the Sennelager near the city of Paderborn.

Actually, there is reason to suspect that many of the rules of the camps' operations—even within the same zone of occupation—were enforced differently by different commanders at different times. Starting in early 1946, there were large roundups of former German administrators, bureaucrats, teachers, and other officials, including a good number of relatives and acquaintances of my parents' generation. Their tales drew a picture of much less oppressive conditions than I had encountered, with visits, letters, books, and packages they were allowed to receive. All of those uncles and friends had been civilian administrators, and had therefore belonged to the comforting majority of the *Automatischen* rather than to the small group of "special cases" with their uncertain fates. When they later talked about their experiences, they spoke of the stupidity of it all, the annoyances and inconveniences they had been forced to endure, the lost time and broken careers. None mentioned fear for liberty or life, isolation, despair. All of this must have happened on another planet. At no point do my own experiences reflect those of all the others. But of course, these men were of another generation, they had held positions of power and influence. Remembering Dr. Wirth, whose earlier "status" had quite naturally followed her into the barracks, I strongly suspect that throughout their detainment, those worthy department chiefs, mayors, directors, and principals carried themselves as though these positions were still theirs.

At the peak of Allied internment policy, there were about half a dozen major camps in the British zone of occupation, holding 5,000 to 10,000 inmates each, plus a string of smaller ones, mostly at the site of some former German concentration camp or military installation: Eselheide, Fallingbostel, Neuengamme, Recklinghausen, Sennelager, to name the most famous. The camps were generally divided into five or more compounds, each holding a thousand or more internees. In addition, there were administrative buildings, soldiers' barracks, kitchens, and a hospital. The last was reserved for the most severely ill, while less serious cases were treated at sick bays. Each compound was surrounded by sturdy mesh fencing topped by barbed wire and separated from the next by asphalt-covered passageways. For prisoners, movement between compounds was allowed only in the presence of armed military police.

The women's compound was guarded by female police, called Red Caps for self-evident reasons. They were a sullen lot, studiously aloof, who appeared only for *Appell*, the twice-daily roll call. Red Caps didn't carry weapons and handed over their charges to armed male colleagues whenever a woman prisoner had to leave the female compound. I don't recall any incidents involving the female guards, nor open breaches of the no-fraternization rules. Whatever went on in the way of bartering or bribery must have been done with the utmost discretion.

To my recollection, no woman was ever reported missing at Camp Recklinghausen, although escapes from the men's quarters were frequent. This was the end of November, with heavy clouds covering the sky, and a constant drizzle transforming the grounds into a sticky mud. Spotlights grazed slowly over the low roofs at night as Elli and I, anxiously huddled together beneath our sparse covers, listened to the bursts of rifle fire from guards trying to stop yet another fugitive heading for the safety of the nearby city.

Nobody was permitted outdoors after dark. For those who could not make it through the night, an old fuel drum, cut down to an appropriate height, was set up in the dark anteroom of the Nissen hut. What this "toilet" lacked in comfort, it made up for in discreetness, in stark contrast to the official facilities outside.

Indeed, next to my nightly communion-in-fear with Elli, my most vivid memories of Camp Recklinghausen were its sanitary installations, or lack thereof. When I was first led to the eight or ten doorless stalls (only later did I discover one with a door), I was so overwhelmed with shame that nature's urgent call instantly evaporated. The sight of those neat and orderly women openly pursuing their most private business while joking and chatting like a bunch of *Kaffeeklatsch* ladies, shocked me in a way few things had ever done.

There were other things I learned to cope with, or do without. Paper, for instance. There was none: no newspapers, books, magazines—not a shred. Instead of toilet paper, one was advised to use a small washcloth, wetted before and washed out after. More awkward was the menstrual bleeding, for which a couple of sanitary napkins were handed out, if supplies were available. Fortunately, in times of profound stress or undernourishment, nature frequently closes down the regular flows to spare the body's diminishing energies.

I still didn't have a single piece of clothing beyond what I had been wearing when imprisoned. Washing an item meant joining the line for the communal bowl, an enamelled basin little larger than a British army helmet and as shallow, then waiting for one's turn at the one-foot-square oven plate to heat the icy well water. Soap, even the coarse, non-foaming variety of wartime economy, represented an irreplaceable luxury not to be wasted on laundry. A similarly arduous procedure was followed on the extraordinary occasion of having one's hair washed and set by a fellow inmate blessed with a dozen rollers and some talent, in exchange for a predetermined quantity of bread. Outside the camp's barter economy—limited to those with articles to barter—bread was the only currency. Considering my short stay at Recklinghausen, however, there was clearly not enough time to fathom the intricacies of the bread currency, let alone win the privilege of joining the shampoo line.

*   *   *

As I assemble this composite picture of camp life from the odds and ends stored in my memory, I am struck by one glaring omission: I cannot remember a single discussion of any of the momentous subjects which, at precisely the same time, were causing heated arguments among politicians, historians, intellectuals, the military, media, judiciaries, and clergy in every part of the world. As we were busily chasing boredom with idle chatter, a strange silence blanketed such urgent topics as Germany's war and defeat, Hitler, the Nazis, the concentration camps, or the dreadful reports about mass killings by the SS. What did inmates think about these revelations and accusations that had not only destroyed their ideals and livelihoods, but had, by no matter what reasoning, provided the very justification for their present predicament? Did they protest their innocence, claim ignorance of everything that had happened? There were no discussions—none; a fact which only mirrored the collective indifference and staunch forgetfulness among the population at large. Looking back, I am certain that I was neither surprised nor upset by what for every non-German observer must have seemed a baffling discrepancy between the world's terrible accusations and the strange aloofness of the people immediately affected. Indeed, I don't believe that I gave it a single thought during the entire time of my internment. But then again, there had been little in the way of debates before. Only those desperate emotional outbreaks in Josephine's small kitchen during the early days of occupation, the angry demands for answers from people who were no longer there, who could not, or would not, shoulder the responsibility we were convinced was theirs. I cannot recall any thoughtful conversation later in Hamburg, either with my parents or my friends. By then, three months had passed since the demise of the Hitler Reich, while the hectic struggle for survival under a fast-crumbling economy had dissociated people from any hopeful plans for the future, or serious contemplation of the past. Terms and issues like "crimes against the peace," "war crimes," and "crimes against humanity," would not be on the public agenda for more than half a year and the start of the Nuremberg Trials. During those early postwar months, they were not only unknown, they were literally *unthinkable*.

And not for any lack of information either; quite the contrary. As American and British armies advanced ever deeper into Germany, liberating concentration camps and disclosing their horrors, an avalanche of revelations and accusations descended upon a shell-shocked population still struggling to come to terms with the immediate consequences of their own personal disasters: the loss of a husband and provider, a son and heir, a home or livelihood; bombed, expelled, without money or refuge—without hope or future. In 1945 millions of Germans felt that things could only get worse, that nothing really mattered, or would ever matter again. Apathy and cynicism were prevalent within a population that was emotionally and physically exhausted, too beaten down to direct its feelings outwards, to feel pity for others, responsibility for what had happened, even remorse. If it is true that every person is closest to himself (*Jeder ist sich selbst der Nächste*), Germans were never closer to themselves than during that first postwar year. We all carried a festering wound deep inside our hearts, that might never completely heal, but needed to be left alone.

Was that it then? Were we too numbed, too fatigued to absorb any more calamities? I am sure that was part of it. Yet, physical and mental depletion were not the only reasons for the collective catatonia. There was also the almost total rejection of all politicians and media as a consequence of the Nazis' extraordinarily skilful propaganda. Goebbels's lies and distortions had succeeded in fooling the nation until the very end, leaving people feeling humiliated, bitter and cynical. "Once burnt, twice shy"—the quick and widespread denial of most of the Allied reports on Nazi crimes was to a large extent the instinctive reaction of a population whose trust had been exploited for too long.

Were there any feelings of guilt among my fellow inmates? That question is, of course, impossible to answer. But, following my remarks about the mood of the time I feel strongly inclined to reject that entire notion. As for myself, I believe I can honestly say that whatever my thoughts or emotions about the twelve-year Nazi era, personal guilt was not among them. I had never hurt anybody, never done anything distressing to another person, never been in a position that would have allowed me to do so. Remorse? Certainly, I felt remorse for not having listened to my father's gentle warning to stay away from Müller. But what about fear? In the six months since that last appalling night at the *Dienststelle*, I had talked myself out of it completely. In fact, the more I learned about Hitler's insidious Reich, the more I felt out of the loop, judging (quite correctly) my humble assignment as a medical student to a subdivisional SD office in small-town Marburg to be of infinitesimal significance. But then came prison and those frightful fantasies that tormented me during the long hours of nightly solitude. With my transfer to camp and the new company of hundreds of fellow prisoners, my mood had changed again. It would experience yet another wild swing only two weeks later, on that last day at Recklinghausen, when reality would catch up with me in no uncertain terms.

*   *   *

Elli was still in her comatose sleep when I received word that the following morning I was to be transferred to Iserlohn. To be sure, the ominous name had come up before, but always in a hush-hush way that allowed myths and rumors to take the place of hard facts. Nevertheless, there was no uncertainty about the fact that in that charming Westphalian city, nestled among wooded hills about forty kilometers southeast of Recklinghausen, the intelligence headquarters of the British Army of the Rhine were located. Very few women had ever been sent there from the camp; none had ever returned to tell her story. Hence the assumption that, after a stay at Iserlohn, a prisoner would either be turned over for special prosecution elsewhere, or released and sent home. Put another way, a transfer to Iserlohn "for special interrogation" was half the ticket;

whether it was the winning or losing half would be for others to decide.

During the previous two weeks, I had become vaguely aware of the "special status" that placed my case outside routine procedure. Ironically, I had found that fact rather consoling, as it could only be a matter of time until the authorities recognized their unfortunate mistake and hastened to correct it. Comforted by these expectations, the order for transfer to be interrogated by British intelligence hit me like a rock. I don't remember who told me, or where I was when I received the news, or what I said or did afterwards, which suggests that my mind was frozen from shock. Memory picks up again the next morning, when, surrounded by an almost reverential crowd, I walked from the barracks to the gate of the compound and the waiting Jeep.

In the pecking order of a political internment camp I, the latecomer of questionable credentials, had within hours become a heroine of mystifying circumstance. As I boarded the Jeep, I left behind a sea of faces, chattering mouths, and waving hands—and the safety of the collective of which I was no longer a part.

INTERLUDE V
Collective Guilt — The Controversy

The issue of collective guilt in the Third Reich, almost completely discarded in contemporary Germany, comes up repeatedly in these pages. Was there in fact such a thing and how could it be determined? And if it did exist, would it apply to all adult citizens at the time, myself included? What are the quantifying or qualifying rules by which to judge? Universal standards, laws of statistics by which to measure? There are none. There are only opinions; philosophical, political, emotional, and juridical ones. And every opinion carries its own bias. My bias is based on the fact that my youth was marked by the entire period of the Nazi dictatorship, followed by another twelve years (until emigration) of the country's scant efforts to come to terms with its past (*Vergangenheitsbewältigung*). I witnessed, and shared in, the Third Reich's final collapse and the people's desperate struggle to handle their total defeat. In short, I was one of the ordinary Germans who *were* the Third Reich, the same people who, when it was all over, turned around and built the successful New Germany. Based upon that complex experience, I will examine the deeper questions of the German people's guilt, their postwar silence and the consequences it brought about.

National Socialism, the ideological framework of the Third Reich, was instrumental in one of the three daring attempts at social engineering that marked the twentieth century. Unlike its contemporary cousins Marxist-Leninism and Maoism, however, its utopian program did not grow out of a proletarian revolution, but found its enthusiastic support among the broad, well-educated middle class, and the patriotic aristocracy. Opinions may differ on whether the ordinary Germans should have foreseen, and effectively resisted, the fanatical course that National Socialism would take to create the hegemonic "Aryan master race." The fact is, not only did ordinary Germans not foresee or resist a course that would lead to the extermination of millions of people of "inferior races"; they ridiculed the "Aryan ideal" as ideological claptrap, pointing to the many members of government who looked nothing like the Aryan prototype. The human, or rather inhuman, possibilities of the new *Rassenhygiene* (eugenics), the scientific premise of the crude anti-Semitism out on the streets, were probably never thought through to their logical end by anybody but the SS leadership in the *Reichssicherheitshauptamt*. Taken in by the more popular endeavours of Nazism (order and cleanliness, good health, sports, optimism, camaraderie, full employment and, later, the long line of military victories), people enthusiastically supported the regime—and, by extension, its experiment in the mental, physical, and even spiritual masterminding of the New German.

While the SS men were bound to the Führer[2] by their personal oath of allegiance, Hitler based his dictatorship on the faith and support of the mesmerized people. Thus, the Third Reich was a highly complex web of personal loyalties and nationalist emotions that went far beyond devotion to one's country, sense of duty, or whatever else may move a people to stand by its leadership. Surrounded and protected by the fanaticism of the SS and endorsed by the millionfold "love for the Führer", Hitler, the political evangelist, made each member of the "Aryan" population feel included in the great *Volksgemeinschaft* (community of the people). When, in the end, this web of trust and belonging was ripped into millions of disconsolate shreds, not so much by the loss of the war as by Hitler's ignominious exit by suicide, people felt betrayed and adrift.

Through decades after the fall of the Third Reich, the Hitler era has been presented as a political tyranny forced upon the German people by a small clique of Nazi madmen. It was nothing of the kind. It was a powerful totalitarian *Führerstaat* that was enthusiastically endorsed by the collective will of the people. As historians continue to "discover" the close collaboration between Nazis and ever more groups and individuals,[3] certain facts become indisputable: that the regime was built on, and actively supported by, huge popular approval; that Hitler's warmongering made a great many people rich; that the "solving of the Jewish problem" (if not the Final Solution) was widely accepted as "necessary, if regrettable" and, that National Socialism was the political culture of the time.

Like every mainstream ideology, it quickly created a formidable bandwagon: bankers and industrialists, insurance managers, judges, professors, generals, historians, actors, writers and poets hastened to join the circle of sycophants and dedicate their talents to National Socialism's hegemonic goals. That these goals demanded certain disagreeable measures such as cleansing the German people of all inferior blood, the enslavement of millions of foreign laborers to replenish a workforce diminished by the war effort, and the brutal suppression of every kind of resistance inside and outside the country, was well-understood by the nation's elite, and shrugged off by the ordinary people as something those "up there" had the competence to decide. It is a fact that the Nazis did nothing against the *expressed* will of the majority of the people—although the public's indifference and fear of asking questions were certainly exploited. (Thus, the euthanasia program was not stopped by ordinary folks, such as the relatives of the victims, and not even by doctors or clerics, but by one outraged Catholic bishop.) Except for the Final Solution, most of the state's criminal activities were not even carried out in great secrecy. It wasn't necessary. The German people had thrown in their lot with the Führer—and he would always decide what was the best course.

That these statements contain some generalizations and simplifications cannot distract from their basic truth. Yet, over the decades, a comforting misconception has been quietly allowed to grow out of the initial collective denial; it is the suggestion that the majority of the German people had been forced under the yoke of a handful of Nazi criminals who had done their evil deeds without the knowledge, condonation, or participation of the population. Only during the last fifteen years has this comforting veneer shown signs of cracking, with the true extent of National Socialism's power and influence on every transaction and every individual life in Germany slowly beginning to sink in.

Even so, the issue is not about to become popular overnight. After half a century of collective repression, the subject of collective guilt is so deeply buried under wordy equivocations that, before the ethical aspects of the phrase can be evaluated, the definition of "collective" has to be clarified: What exactly does it mean? Everybody? The vast majority? Is "most" still a valid quantity? The ambiguity of the term has, of course, not remained unrecognized. If it could be shown that not *all* Germans followed the Führer, the collective guilt argument, many felt, would collapse on its own tenets. After Hitler's rise to power, tens of thousands of citizens with strong political, philosophical, or humanitarian convictions, continued to fight against the new totalitarian government. Communists and Social Democrats, including a great number of intellectuals and artists on the political left, resisted the National Socialists' ruthless measures. Many left the country, while others vanished into the underground or were rounded up and sent to concentration camps. According to Bernt Engelmann, between 1933 and 1939 more than 225,000 men and women were convicted for political reasons.[4] The non-communist world has largely ignored them in favor of the group to be discussed next, but this should not take away from their remarkable courage and early insight.

In 1944, near the end of the clearly doomed Third Reich, a group of Wehrmacht officers and civilians staged an assault on Hitler's life in order to force an end to the war. They failed, and many of the conspirators were subjected to the most brutal reprisals. As brave as these people were, in total they numbered at most in the (tens of) thousands—a tiny fraction of the eighty million who continued to support the Führer.

It is a sad fact that what little there was in the way of resistance against the Nazi regime emerged from either the left or the right. Not only were the actions of the two sides separated by more than a decade, their political aspirations were clearly incompatible. Among those who on July 20, 1944, undertook the attempt on Hitler's life were high-ranking officers and members of the aristocracy, some of whom could look back on personal histories of great patriotism and Führer loyalty. In the 1930s, they almost certainly had welcomed the purge of the German left for its real or supposed connection with international Communism. Ironically, the respective political philosophies of both groups placed them outside the political mainstream of their time: In the thirties, following the turbulence of the Weimar Republic, there was an overwhelming trend to the right; in the summer of 1944, the majority of the people still believed in Germany's victory. Had either group achieved its goal, the country would likely have witnessed a revolution resulting in an aristocratic-military oligarchy (with little interest in liberal democracy)[5] or a socialist republic not unlike the future East German state. Yet, beginning soon after the war, the names and deeds of the resistance fighters were venerated like national treasures—in capitalist West Germany the conspirators on the right, in Communist East Germany the ones on the left. Since reunification in 1989, it is the former who enjoy continued idolization, while the latter receive only a scant fraction of their former glorification.

Nobody would begrudge the martyrs of July 20 their posthumous honors: They risked their lives and the freedom of their families, and suffered unspeakably for their failure. But fail they did, and history offers rare examples of immortalized failure. Why, then, are they worshipped in a manner so disproportionate to their unrealized hopes? It would be hard to deny that those few who so bravely fought the regime were later used by the new German elites in both East and West for their own political purposes: Didn't their actions prove that not all Germans had been enthusiastic supporters of National Socialism, who allowed Hitler and his minions to commit ever more heinous crimes? Here, for all to see, were the noble examples of true German liberalism and decency, men and women prepared to die so that others could live in a better land. All true, and all highly serviceable arguments against the irritating issue of collective guilt.[6] It honored the deserving few with the admiration and gratitude of the undeserving many—including those who, truth be told, harbored some lasting resentment against what they thought had been either an act of high treason or a bungled effort.

*　　*　　*

As the glamor of the resistance movements is slowly fading (partly because of their small size, partly because stopping the Holocaust was not part of their political agenda), the true extent of National Socialist collaboration becomes ever more difficult to ignore. Over the years, as I have written and rewritten these pages, the circle of the accused has continued to widen. In 1996, Goldhagen's sensational best-seller, *Hitler's Willing Executioners*,[7] hit the market and perforated the German public's complacency. Since then, whole categories of "collaborators" have been unearthed at an alarming rate. There are also those embarrassing files in the Berlin Document Center, listing fifteen million men and women, who as members of the Party, the SA or SS, or as doctors, teachers and artists, had supported the Nazi system. Had they all been secret antifascists and forced into membership, as many would later claim?

Of course not. Neither had all, or even most, been participants in the regime's murder machine. Clearly, the collective guilt argument is a political or attitudinal rather than a judicial one, and cannot be detached from the pervasive political and social culture of the time. Guided by my twelve-year experience with National Socialism's mass-seducing ideology, I base my reasoning on the following points: First, had there been any polls at the time, it is a fair guess that until late 1944, Hitler's personal approval ratings would never have dipped much below eighty percent, and may have been as high as ninety percent after Victory in France.

Second, neither Hitler's totalitarian Third Reich nor Himmler's SS state—if such a distinction were possible—could have been created and continually strengthened without that significant popular support for the Führer; and third, many of the regime's most egregious programs were fully or partly known—the concentration camps, the "solving of the Jewish problem" (without the Final Solution), euthanasia (as the fight against "worthless life"), the maltreatment of Russian POWs ("a subhuman species"), the shooting of Soviet commissars, and the murder of downed enemy pilots. It is an undeniable fact that *everybody* knew something that contravened the Geneva Convention, the Bible, or one's own conscience as physician, lawyer, soldier, or simply as human being.

Therefore, whether by timid acquiescence or enthusiastic endorsement, the population's support for the regime—and, by extension, its crimes— was millionfold. The moral guilt resulting from the people's failure to resist their government's obscene deeds (*Unterlassungsschuld* or guilt by omission) had been vaguely felt, perhaps even recognized, for a number of years. Why else after the war the collective mental and verbal denial, if there never had been a collective bad conscience in the first place?

Eminent German philosopher Karl Jaspers (1883–1969) was an early proponent of Germany's collective political guilt. Only by acknowledging their national responsibility for the crimes committed by the Nazi state would the German people be able to transform their society from its state of collapse into a responsible democracy, he argued. In his early work *Die Schuldfrage* (the question of guilt), he insisted that political responsibility belonged even to those who, for fear of becoming victims themselves, tolerated the NS state—in short: everybody who survived. Not surprisingly, his ideas found little response in postwar Germany. In 1966, in his angry book *Wohin treibt die Bundesrepublik* (Whither drifts the Federal Republic), Jaspers reiterated his thoughts for a readership less inclined than ever to listen to the existentialist philosopher's dictum.[8]

*   *   *

So far, my argument has turned on the moral issue of complicity through inaction. The really difficult questions—How many murders or other severe crimes were committed by how many perpetrators?—have suffered from statistical uncertainty or downright obfuscation. I begin with the murders.

There cannot be a literate soul alive who has not heard the figure of six million and wouldn't instantly connect it with the Holocaust, or *Sho'ah*, the genocide of European Jewry. Many may know little else about Germany, its history or its people, but that terrible number sticks in their minds. Where did it come from and when? Did it slowly percolate down from dozens of sources? So-and-so many Jews alive before the war, so-and-so many after? In whatever way the six-million number was gathered, it appeared quite early. G. M. Gilbert, the prison psychologist at the Nuremberg Trials, notes that American Justice Robert Jackson, in his opening speech for the prosecution on November 21, 1945, stated that sixty percent of the Jews in Nazi-dominated Europe—or about 5.7 million—were murdered.[9] Indeed, the highly imperilled situation of European Jewry was obvious to the concerned observer long before Hitler's killing machine shifted into high gear. In his book *My People*, first published in 1968, Israeli diplomat Abba Eban quotes Chaim Weizman, the Zionist leader and Israel's first president, making this dark prophesy as early as November 25, 1936: 'There are six million people doomed to be pent up where they are not wanted, and for whom the world is divided into places where they cannot live, and places which they may not enter. Six million.' Eban continues: "In eight years' time the problem presented by these six million Jews was to be solved. In 1945, these six million were dead."[10]

Since the Auschwitz trial from 1963 to 1965, that place has entered the Western vocabulary as history's most horrifying example of human inventiveness, a hell on earth, where an estimated 1.2 to 1.5 million people were killed with industrial precision. Other major extermination camps in Poland, such as Majdanek, Treblinka, Chelmno, Sobibor, and Belzec contribute their own numbers of victims. So do the liquidations in East European rural and urban centres, not to mention the rounding up of other groups deemed "undesirable" by Nazi ideologues: political prisoners, homosexuals, and a loosely estimated half-million gypsies. To what number do they all add up? Many of the records, meticulously kept by SS bureaucrats and confirmed and reconfirmed during the interminable twice-a-day *Appells* (roll calls) in the camps, were destroyed by the SS prior to liberation by the Allies, or may have been hidden somewhere and never found.

Eugen Kogon has arrived at an estimate of 6,680,650 deaths in the concentration camps. The actual figure, he writes, may be "considerably higher."[11] Not included in this number, one may assume, are the million or more non-Jewish Poles, professionals and intellectuals who, according to Sebastian Haffner, died at the hands of the Germans to extinguish the Polish elite;[12] or the untold numbers of Jews and Russians shot on the spot. Raul Hilberg states that Jews alone accounted for 1.3 million people murdered outside the death camps,[13] while an estimated 2.8 to three million Russian prisoners of war did not survive their German captivity.[14] If, as is generally accepted, the Holocaust took the lives of six million Jews, these vague estimates suggest that the total number of victims of all the German extermination programs, including euthanasia with its 100,000 dead, must have been much higher—higher by millions.

In his recent book, *The Holocaust in American Life*, University of Chicago historian Peter Novick states that the most frequently used figure today is eleven million victims: six million Jews and five million "others."[15] While he considers five million much too low for all non-Jewish civilians killed by the Nazis, or much too high for non-Jewish *groups* that were targeted, like Jews, for extermination (gypsies, homosexuals, criminals, politicians, intellectuals), he explains that the number of "eleven million, including six million Jews" was simply "invented" by Simon Wiesenthal, a Mauthausen concentration-camp survivor turned famous Nazi-hunter, who, in 1948, wished to make the Holocaust an inclusive, rather than a specifically Jewish, tragedy. The number became widely accepted in 1961 with the opening of the Simon Wiesenthal Center, dedicated to "six million Jews and to five million of other faiths." There were many who disagreed with this version, most notably Auschwitz survivor and American novelist Elie Wiesel,[16] who, in 1979, was appointed chairman of President Carter's commission for the creation of a United States Holocaust Memorial Museum in Washington. After a long and bitter fight between the White House and Wiesel, the museum was finally dedicated, against Wiesel's wishes, to "eleven million." But Carter's victory was a pyrrhic one; the inclusive concept, aimed at avoiding "second-class victims," was never realized; in content and emphasis, the museum became Elie Wiesel's memorial to the murder of six million Jews in the Holocaust.

The distinction between " eleven million" and "six million Jews plus five million others" may seem academic. For many Jews, however, the issue is of the highest political and ethical importance, meant to guard and protect "the specifity" of the Jewish Holocaust up to, and including, its sacralization by American "folk Judaism" (Novick). Granted, the six-plus-five argument is foremost a Jewish concern. But one may well bear in mind that the five million *non*-Jewish number is based on one man's rather arbitrary guesswork, and, according to Novick, is still far too low. Such gaps and contradictions in our knowledge about the true extent of the Nazi genocide are among the most disturbing consequences, not only of postwar Germany's wilful neglect of its odious past, but also of the early breakup of the wartime alliance that led to the Cold War—all of which put an end to investigations and prosecutions at a time when people's memories were still fresh, and witnesses and documents might still have been available.

The same historic obstacles have effectively shaped our ignorance about another question: Who were the people who committed the bloody deeds, and how many of them were there?

In the absence of any certainty about the names and numbers of the perpetrators, it has long been customary to refer to them simply by the generic term "Nazis." Used mindlessly and ubiquitously, that term could refer to Hitler and his entourage, or the Party, the SS, Gestapo, the guards in the concentration camps, or all of the above. It could mean thousands or millions, or the entire population. This semantic tangle, carelessly echoed by respected writers and journalists, is by no means of negligible importance. In fact, it lies at the heart of the understanding of the Third Reich.

Apart from the physical difficulty of supplying witnesses and documents, there were complicated ethical and juridical problems with respect to the legal responsibility for the crimes of the Hitler regime: At what level of the political or military hierarchy had an order become a crime? At the top? All the way down, soiling every hand that passed it on? Or only at the final link, making the ultimate executor of the order the sole de facto criminal? The defence of SS *Obersturmbannführer* (lieutenant colonel) Adolf Eichmann, kidnaped by the Israelis, and tried, convicted and hanged in Jerusalem in 1962, failed in its argument that Eichmann, the organizer of the Jewish deportations and of the Final Solution, had merely been a cog in a huge wheel, receiving and executing orders. In contrast, Federal German judges in 1965 convicted the "last links" in the chain of command, the primitive killers and torturers in the Auschwitz concentration camp. Their superior officers, meanwhile, received minor sentences for "aiding and abetting murder;" they were freed three years later under a new statute of limitations for aiding and abetting, made retroactive to 1960.[17] (The unfortunate practice of turning on the "little guy" was repeated in the 1990s, when, after reunification, German courts tried and convicted the *Mauerschützen*, former East German soldiers who had followed their government's criminal orders to shoot on the spot anybody trying to cross the Berlin Wall.) Other questions were equally puzzling: On whose terms of law were the prosecutors to proceed? On those of the victors, to be applied retroactively? Or on those of the former Nazi government? For the first scenario, no legal precedent existed; for the second, the case could be made (and was made in vain by the German defence lawyers at Nuremberg) that in a dictatorial state where all orders originated from one person—Adolf Hitler, deceased—nobody could be held accountable merely for carrying out a command.

Who, then, was guilty?

The predicament has never found a satisfactory solution. Once the Cold War broke out, with the Western powers' urgent demand for German rearmament—met by the German government's counter-demand for American leniency towards Germany's former military brass, including the SS—the pardoning of clearly identified perpetrators, the early release of others, and the final scrapping of the whole unhappy affair by the Americans, became politically inevitable.

While the Allies' hunt for tens (or possibly hundreds) of thousands of Nazi criminals "with blood on their hands" was quietly laid to rest during the early fifties (only reluctantly to be taken up again by German courts in the sixties), the West German people gladly accepted their own collective exculpation from their highly respected first president, Theodor Heuss. Guided by one of the fundamental principles of Enlightenment liberalism, which holds that guilt can only be personal and individual, and that collective guilt therefore does not exist, Heuss retired Germany's vexing problem of *Gesamtschuld* by replacing it with some ersatz repentance called *Gesamtscham* (collective shame), a moral discomfort that everybody could live with happily ever after. (The fact that shame is equally personal and individual, even if not indictable, did not spoil the collective relief.) Since then, it has been axiomatic that there was no collective guilt in Nazi Germany, and few serious writers have allowed themselves to be trapped into defending that soundly rejected concept.

However, in his 1996 book *Hitler's Willing Executioners: Ordinary Germans and the Holocaust*, Daniel Jonah Goldhagen, the thirty-eight-year-old assistant professor at Harvard University, puts on the table the very facts the argument is based on, and which, for five decades, everybody had been busily denying: that the vast majority of Germans had supported the Nazi government; that there had been widespread knowledge about the deportations of the Jews (if not about the measures and the true extent of the Holocaust); and that through fear, indifference, or downright approval the majority had failed to act. But Goldhagen goes much further. Claiming the existence of a deeply rooted and pervasive anti-Semitism in Germany that long predated Hitler, he insists that a large majority of Germans fully supported the Nazis' "eliminationist" anti-Semitism as it progressed from the policies of emigration, to ghettoization, to the Final Solution by extermination.

Goldhagen's thesis, that the German people (collectively) accepted the "elimination" of the "Jewish race" as the unpleasant, yet ultimately inescapable burden of the superior Aryan race, is of course impossible to substantiate. He is on even thinner ice when he claims that the majority of Germans would have acted as "Hitler's willing executioners," had that summons come their way. After all, regardless of how many people were involved in the extermination programs, their number remains a fraction of a population of eighty million. It becomes still smaller when one considers the thousands of *Hilfswillige* — Lithuanians, Latvians, Ukrainians, and others—who eagerly volunteered to rid their countries of Jewish minorities. The trouble is, if Goldhagen's claims cannot be proved, neither can they be disproved.

No single book has ever caused such widespread controversy in postwar Germany. Thousands turned out at the author's speaking tour. As Volker Ullrich later wrote in the respected weekly *Die Zeit,* the audiences seemed to accept that long-standing taboos were finally being overturned, "that the distinction between 'criminal Nazis' and 'normal Germans' is wrong; that the readiness to kill millions of Jews came from the centre of German society; that Hitler and Himmler found hundreds of thousands of willing executioners, *and that this crime became possible only through the moral indifference of the vast majority of the population, even if they did not actively participate.*"[18] (Emphasis and translation mine.)

With new evidence emerging steadily about the German people's overwhelming acquiescence to, and association with, the Nazi state, the old and bitter debate about a colossal, collective, moral failure during the Hitler regime is no longer a question of historical truth, but merely one of semantics. If the term "collective guilt" has been discredited once and for all, perhaps somebody will come up with another concept to capture the moral and political failure resulting from that fatal combination of Führer idolatry, political naïveté, personal cowardice, deference to authority, and—most pertinent of all—societal distrust of non-German blood, culture, and tradition.

*　　*　　*

Recently I found some unexpected support for my iconoclastic views on the subject of collective guilt. It came from a highly experienced person, who is eminently qualified to give her considered judgment on the half-century-old argument. In an interview with Canadian writer and journalist Erna Paris, Louise Arbour, the chief prosecutor of the International Criminal Tribunal for the Former Yugoslavia (ICTY), offered the most thoughtful analysis yet of the moral and juridical problem that continues to vex jurists, theologians, philosophers, and politicians. Since, according to Arbour, the ICTY is only authorized to look at "personal criminal responsibility in a very tightly defined, narrow way," that means "[w]e do not have a mandate to establish the moral responsibility of those who saw things happen and did nothing, including people who might have had the capacity to stop the process and did nothing. But we have to be careful in thinking that just because we focus on individual criminal guilt we therefore absolve the community. The old distinctions are too simplistic when we move up the chain of command and witness the merging of the collectivity into the personae of these charismatic political and military leaders."

Paris thinks Louise Arbour, now Justice for the Supreme Court of Canada, "is brave and outspoken." So do I, and I am immensely grateful for her definition, which sounds so simple, yet catches the heart of the problem: that the line that separates individual guilt (so dear to our Western civilization and jurisprudence) from the supposedly non-existent collective guilt, is the same one that separates the criminal leadership from the people. Where the latter line dissolves through the merging of purpose, identification and support, the former dissolves also.

Erna Paris' comments are equally impressive, and I quote them here in their entirety:

> I think the parallels with Germany are striking. The Nuremberg trials allowed Germans to distance themselves from the Nazis,

even though there unquestionably was what Arbour has just called "the merging of the collectivity" into the persona of Adolf Hitler. The process of distancing permitted people to recover their pre-Nazi moral roots and move on, but it had also led to a distorted historiography that pinpointed a tiny number of major perpetrators and ignored the rest, including the bystanders. The shifts that took place in Germany over the decades—from the accusations of the young against "the fathers," starting around 1968, to the conflicted, diffused guilt of the 1980s and 1990s, to the collective indictment of Daniel Goldhagen's *Hitler's Willing Executioners* in 1996—were, perhaps, one result of a too narrowly focused [Nuremberg] trial process. Germans cried "Enough!" from time to time, but the problem of the perpetrators and the collectivity was still present in German culture.[19]

As Erna Paris will probably agree, it still is.

Notes to Chapter 5

1 Fischer, Ursula, *Zum Schweigen verurteilt: Denunziert – verhaftet – interniert (1945–1948)* (Berlin: Dietz, 1992).
2 One month before the war, Hitler operationally integrated the Waffen-SS into the Wehrmacht. But that unifying move did not change the SS's loyalty to the Führer, which overrode all other soldierly obligations.
3 In his book *Deutsche Medizin im Dritten Reich* (Frankfurt: S. Fischer, 2001), author Ernst Klee alleges that many German scientists, including Nobel Prize winner Adolf Butenandt (1903–1995), collaborated in medical experiments with Auschwitz physician Dr. Josef Mengele, and other SS physicians. Klee's investigations were particularly directed at human experiments conducted by "Rassenhygieniker" (specialist in eugenics) Otmar von Verschuer and others, funded by the *Deutsche Forschungsgemeinschaft*, the primary research support organization in Germany. (*Die Zeit*, No. 44, 2001.)
4 Engelmann, Bernt, *Einig gegen Recht und Freiheit* (Gütersloh: C. Bertelsmann, 1975), 342.

5 According to the memoirs of former German federal president Richard von Weizsäcker, the British government, though well-informed about the resistance movement, chose not to support it, but rather to wait for Germany's unconditional surrender. When the assault on Hitler's life failed, one member of the British Foreign Office wrote: "…we are better off with things as they are today, than if the plot of July 20 had succeeded … The Gestapo and the SS have done us an appreciable service in removing a selection of those who would undoubtedly have posed as 'good' Germans after the war…" (Weizsäcker, Richard von, *Vier Zeiten* [Berlin: Siedler, 1999], 131).

6 In a bitter commentary on the postwar German government's handling of the guilt question, philosopher Karl Jaspers writes: "…the dependents of the victims of July 20 … remained for years without help, the widows without a pension … The men of the assault (on Hitler) were taken out of mothballs, when the politics of the federal government considered it opportune in light of the emptiness of its ethical foundation. (My translation.) Jaspers, Karl, *Wohin treibt die Bundesrepublik?* (Munich: Piper, 1988), 68.

7 Goldhagen, Daniel, Jonah: *Hitler's Willing Executioners: Ordinary Germans and the Holocaust* (New York: Knopf, 1996).

8 Jaspers, Karl, op. cit., ref. 6, 69.

9 Gilbert, G. M., *Nuremberg Diary* (New York: Signet Book, The New American Library of World Literature, 1947), 40.

10 Eban, Abba, *My People* (New York: Random House, 1984), 397.

11 Kogon, Eugen: *Der SS-Staat: Das System der deutschen Konzentrationslager* (Munich: Kindler, 1974), 177.

12 Haffner, Sebastian, *Anmerkungen zu Hitler* (Munich: Kindler, 1978), 168.

13 Hilberg, Raul, *The Destruction of the European Jews: New Viewpoints* (New York, 1973). Quoted by Jäckel, Eberhard in Schoeps, Julius H., ed., *Ein Volk von Mördern? Die Dokumentation zur Goldhagen-Kontroverse um die Rolle der Deutschen im Holocaust* (Hamburg: Hoffmann und Campe, 1996), 189.

14 Numbers from Militärgeschichtliches Forschungsamt, Potsdam, Germany.

15 Novick, Peter, *The Holocaust in American Life* (New York: Houghton Mifflin, 1999), 215ff.

16 In 1986, Elie Wiesel won the Nobel Peace Prize for his extensive literary work on the Holocaust.

17 Wesel, Uwe: *Geschichte des Rechts* (History of Law), Munich: C.H. Beck, 1997), 518. See also Postscript fn 17.

18 Ullrich, Volker, Goldhagen und die Deutschen, *Die Zeit*, No. 38, 1996.

19 Paris, Erna, *Long Shadows* (Toronto: Knopf, 2000), 419–420.

6

ISERLOHN

No doubt, without my transfer to Iserlohn, a major intelligence center of the British Army of the Rhine, this book would never have been written. My case as a political internee would have remained one of an estimated 240,000, shrugged off as an unpleasant experience not much different from, and a lot less horrible than, many others during the six years of a brutal war. By singling me out in such a special manner, however, my *Sonderfall* status, more quixotic than threatening before, suddenly acquired shades of a much larger, more ominous scheme, far beyond the experience or responsibility of a twenty-year-old medical student.

Surely, I told myself, there had to be a misunderstanding, a mix-up of sorts, which would be resolved as soon as somebody took a closer look. After all, what could they possibly charge me with? Since I knew for a fact that I had never been party to a criminal act, nobody in the world could prove otherwise. Even in the worst-case scenario—whatever that might be—I could not possibly be considered as anything but the puniest player in somebody else's fanciful game of conspiracy. Did I actually reason along such reassuring lines? Did I succeed in calming my fears, which must have been substantial, even if partly repressed? I doubt it. The sheer magnitude of the calamity must have weighed heavily on me. Besides, there is a famous German saying which almost certainly went through my mind: *"Mitgefangen, mitgehangen"*—if you are caught near somebody's wrongful action, you share the consequences. Put differently: You don't find yourself in bad company without a reason. Therefore, whatever Joseph Müller and his clique of SS and SD officers had done, I was involved by the undeniable truth of having been attached to their organization for a period of three to four months. Sooner or later I would have to face their accusers and could possibly share their punishment. The fact that I had been imprisoned only a day after the *Hauptsturmführer* was caught clearly proved that a connection had been made. What connection and how it had come into the open was the real riddle.

Actually, there had been one brief moment when I had the chance to confront Müller. It happened in the Coesfeld prison courtyard just prior to our transfer to Camp Recklinghausen. There was a lot of activity around us, with soldiers readying the pickup truck for transport. Nobody was watching as I climbed into the vehicle and placed myself next to my former boss. (As I would soon learn, there were strict orders to keep us separated during transports; I sitting in the front with the driver and a guard, Müller in the back with any other prisoners.) He appeared shrunken and dispirited, his whispering voice hard to understand through swollen lips and the gap from his missing tooth. He had no answers to my urgent questions about how it had all come about, what had brought the British military to the Dülmen farm, and why old Herr Hilltrupp was still being detained in Coesfeld. Müller insisted he hadn't seen him, but felt awful about having involved him at all. He claimed not to know what lay behind the whole kerfuffle which, after my first uneventful interrogation, I had firmly believed would soon be over for me. We kept our heads low and shielded from the guards' eyes.

On the basis of our shared humiliation, one might assume that I would have felt more relaxed in the presence of the former *Hauptsturmführer*, perhaps even somewhat condescending, considering the magnitude of his fall from grace. Though these were partly my feelings, I knew that I could not afford to show them. Under the circumstances, it was his sense of fairness—still unproven, as far as I could tell—that was invested with absolute control over my security. In the end, it would be his word confirming mine; or it would be something quite different—mischief for instance, the wish to have somebody come along on his way to judgment. Naturally, I was worried about my complete dependence on a man who was so obviously broken, physically as well as spiritually, and no longer the self-assured SS officer I had known in Marburg. Clad in his shiny boots and dark green leather coat, he had been an intimidating figure. His frequent absences from the office had created the impression of someone besieged by affairs of great importance. His grand finale prior to joining Germany's victory-or-death struggle—something he probably forgot the moment he left the building—was deeply etched in my mind. At that nerve-racking moment, I had been truly afraid. As I discovered now, I still was.

"Why didn't you keep me out of it?" It was the all-important question, and even today I remember the dread I felt waiting for his reply. Because I suddenly knew that he had lied and would lie again to his interrogators, if it suited his cause. I also knew that he would lie to me out of weakness. And I feared the proof of that knowledge more than I feared the man.

"I tried. I really did."

"What did you say? Did you explain that my working relationship with the *Dienststelle* was by special arrangement to spare me from factory work?"

"Sure—"

"Did you tell them that I never contributed anything and never received any pay?"

"Sure—"

"What did they say? Did they believe you?"

"I guess so. They must have …" A beaten and frightened man. The PhD graduate, ex–high school teacher, ex–*SS Hauptsturmführer*, ex–*SS Studentenkompanie* leader, ex–SD officer and snoop, demolished after a dozen days in captivity.

With twelve of my twenty years spent under the heroic banner of National Socialist ideology, the suddenness of Müller's moral collapse was a devastating mental assault, and second only to the news that Hitler, after killing his dog and his mistress, had shot himself in the head thirty feet below ground in the bunker of the *Reichskanzlei* in Berlin, just a stone's throw from the encircling Russian lines. Granted, the proportions were different, and so were the circumstances. Yet, as far as they concerned me personally, those two acts were really quite similar: Both men had promised to die with their soldiers, yet Hitler absolved himself from all responsibility for the destruction of Germany and the deaths of fifty million people, while Müller abandoned all considerations for those who had been in his personal charge and who had trusted him.

In the end, *der grösste Feldherr aller Zeiten* ("the greatest military leader of all time," a bombastic Nazi slogan contracted to *Gröfaz* in embittered postwar parlance) had revealed himself to be no different from his lowly underling—ordinary cowards both, unable to face history or justice or truth, failing their people when the bells tolled.

After that brief encounter in the prison yard, I felt increasingly pessimistic about Müller's sense of responsibility towards me, and doubted whether he would protect me in future interrogations. I reasoned that he must have been asked about me prior to my own incarceration. The fact that I had still not been released clearly suggested that his assertions about my harmlessness had been less than convincing to his interrogators.

Though I only learned about this many years later, a possible clue to the riddle of my internment did, indeed, exist. It related back to that fateful day of my arrival at the farm. As we were sitting down to lunch, Karl mentioned that Müller would be a minute late, as he was just finishing a letter to his wife in Marburg. With no postal service between the zones of occupation, Müller had found somebody willing to take it into the American zone. I later learned that before he closed the letter, he added a postscript: *Gerade ist Fräulein Mackprang aus Hamburg angekommen* (Miss Mackprang has just arrived from Hamburg).

For anybody investigating the former *Hauptsturmführer* on suspicion of conspiracy and sedition, that letter, still in his pocket when he was taken into custody, must have looked pretty incriminating. Whatever other fugitives were on the farm, here at least were two—Müller and Karl, both from Müller's old *SS Studentenkompanie* in Marburg. In addition, there was a "messenger" who had just arrived from faraway Hamburg—a messenger who herself had been a member of the *SD Dienststelle*—which made it all amount to something big enough to warrant further investigation at a time when the spectre of hidden underground resistance networks (Werewolf) haunted every Allied security officer in occupied Germany.

I don't recall whether I had heard of the *Werwolf* prior to my captivity. Elli's bizarre tale about that mysterious outfit, which allegedly had brought her to Camp Recklinghausen, had probably been the first time. Nevertheless, there is evidence that during the last desperate months of the war, *Reichsführer SS* Heinrich Himmler ordered the drawing up of plans for an underground resistance, code-named *Werwolf* after the peasant guerillas of the Thirty Years' War. Divided into small bands, these SS units were to operate from their hideouts in the German and Austrian alps. There is no proof that any such groups ever materialized, let alone that their operational planning ever came to fruition. But all of this was not to be established until much later, and could not have been of any benefit to me at the time.

I may have been ignorant of the postscript in Müller's letter and the rumoured existence of an underground resistance; but I certainly was not unaware of my perilous lack of knowledge concerning the Allies' handling of their political internees, or of my total impotence as a member of a prisoner category of one. I had no lawyers fighting for me outside, no friends inside, no network of cronies like the automatically interned, who enjoyed protection by the sheer weight of their numbers.

I met the *Hauptsturmführer* one more time before he permanently disappeared from my sight, if not from my odious surroundings. It happened on my first day at "university" at Camp Recklinghausen. He was sitting in the left section of chairs as I rushed in and grabbed a last-minute seat on the right. He seemed quite relaxed, even boisterous, an entirely different man from the one I had talked—or whispered—to on the truck just a few days earlier. He had apparently visited classes regularly, while I had waited a full week for the permission to attend. He acknowledged me with a short nod, then ignored me for the rest of the morning. As he left, he joined a group of his new buddies. He seemed quite at home, his face healed despite the missing tooth. I wasn't sure what to make of his snub. My instinctive reaction was annoyance at what I saw as his familiar arrogance. Or was there a reason? Was he trying to put distance between us? Follow non-communication orders? Did he try to protect me? Himself? I never found out. Though I was the only woman attending the lectures and was usually surrounded by a group of men, Müller was never among them.

I have no recollection about our transport to the Center of Intelligence at Iserlohn, but I am certain there were no further communications between Müller and myself, which, considering the sudden high profile of our case, seemed like a sensible precaution on the part of our keepers.

*   *   *

After Coesfeld prison and Camp Recklinghausen, life at Iserlohn was positively cozy. Good food, woollen blankets, and heated rooms afforded a degree of comfort exceeding that of most German homes at the time. Since this was a major intelligence installation, spying and eavesdropping were probably going on at all times. But there were no whispering men in trench coats and fedoras exchanging money (or bread, as it were) for secrets in dark corners, no cloaks and daggers, no corpses.

Needless to say, things were not quite as innocuous as they appeared. Underneath the detached correctness of the British, and the sullen submission of the Germans, one could sense a high degree of suppressed tension, which flared up at the slightest provocation. As for my personal reaction to that phony calm, I can only describe it—with a good deal of embarrassment—as juvenile. Never before or since have I experienced such a sustained mood of reckless hilarity.

Instead of being meek, or at least cautious, I was insolent and brazen, cheeky to the guards and arrogant towards the male prisoners. Perhaps it was simply a nervous reaction, a defence of sorts, however silly and ill-conceived, against my degrading incarceration and barely concealed fear. But it is also true that despite my surroundings, on a deeper, subconscious level, I was still completely "soul deaf" to the monstrous crimes that had necessitated the network of internment camps in the first place. As far as I was concerned, there was no side of the angels; it was simply a case of winners and losers, *them* against *us*—or, having only contempt for most of my fellow prisoners, them against *me*.

It surprises me how much I actually remember of Iserlohn, its person-nel, prisoners, rooms, and routines. Apart from a weekly rotation of guards, whose contact with the inmates was strictly limited to watch duties, there were the commanding officer, three or four interrogating officers, a staff sergeant (*Stabsfeldwebel*), and a handful of house and kitchen staff. On the other side of the fence, so to speak, were some twenty-five to thirty prisoners, three of us female. Altogether it was a surprisingly small, almost intimate, group; British and German, well-educated, well-mannered, cohabiting in a park-like setting: the British in a villa built by a late-nineteenth-century industrialist,[1] the Germans in barracks formerly owned by the Hitler Youth. Of these people, six merit further description because of the way they defined my life at Iserlohn.

A young woman I will name Karla, and a grey-haired lady we called Mami, shared my room. Major Brown held the lofty position of commanding officer, and Staff Sergeant Morris Salmon was in charge of the day-to-day routine, including inspections, meal times, yard exercise, and punishments, such as single-cell and dark-cell confinement. And finally, there was Kurt Gerdsmeyer, privileged prisoner, fire stoker— and my uncle, whom I met by dint of a fantastic coincidence.

Arriving on one of the last days of November 1945, I was received by a stocky man in his late twenties dressed in British army woollens, with laced boots beneath gathered trouser legs, who introduced himself as *Stabsfeldwebel* Salmon. In contrast to the immortal image of a Prussian staff sergeant, Salmon's military comportment was unimpressive, to say the least. Heavy-set and folksy, he pined for recognition, a conflict that, as I was soon to find out, made him alternately jovial and dangerous. He was German by birth, a misfortune he tried to overcome by looking every bit the plucky British soldier who won the war with blood, sweat, and tears. His strawberry-blond hair was cut military-style; like every other British soldier, he wore a beret. He had watery blue eyes, framed by pale lashes and enlarged by steel-rimmed glasses, and a broad nose and soft lips that he kept pressed together to demonstrate determination.

Salmon's welcome was friendly enough. As we marched side by side across the yard towards the far edge of the property, my eyes were level with his cap. Short legs worked against his height; they also turned a crisp military gait into a curious waddle. Together we entered a large barracks with a half-dozen doors leading off the long central hall. Salmon stopped at the first to the right. His brisk knock and twist of the handle were masterfully synchronized; the door flew open without a second's delay: "*Ach-tung!*"

Two women rose in slow motion. In a clipped tone, Salmon introduced us and pointed out my bed. He advised me of the house rules, and warned me not to talk to other prisoners outside this room, then marched back to the door. Grasping the handle, he stretched to his maximum height. "*Auf Wiedersehen!*" he shouted, looking straight at nobody.

"*Auf Wiedersehen, Herr Stabsfeldwebel,*" echoed the two, their voices bored. The door was closed, but not locked, leaving me stunned and momentarily silenced.

I looked around. The room was furnished with a square white table, some straight-backed chairs and three beds with sturdy frames, thick mattresses, and a couple of grey army blankets. It was clean and bright with light from two windows. The women gave a derisive chuckle in the direction of the door.

"His real name is Salomon, Moritz Salomon," explained Karla, a cheerful woman with a narrow face and pale skin blotched with large freckles. She had thick hair, which she kept tied in a single braid. Having grown out most of its blonde, it had returned to its former shade of dusty hay. "They say he changed his name to Morris Salmon when he went off to England."

"Who says?"

"Rumors," she shrugged. "Like everything in this place."

"Jewish, of course," added the other woman, who liked to be called

"Mami." She must have been in her late forties, older than any of the women I had yet met at camp. She had grey hair neatly gathered in a bun, a full figure, and the gentle authority of someone long accustomed to power. Mami had been a high-ranking leader in the *Frauenschaft*, the National Socialist women's organization. What hot political secrets that job had entailed, deserving of special attention by British intelligence, she never disclosed. "He's from Franconia, from a small village near Würzburg."

"Everyone calls him 'Bimbo,'" Karla added. "Behind his back, of course."

"Bimbo? Why?"

She shrugged. "Maybe the way he looks. Or walks—"

"—or waddles," Mami said with a twinkle.

I was impressed by the women's knowledge and the nonchalant attitude with which it was shared.

"What's he like? Do you like him?"

"He's mean—mostly," replied Karla. "You'd better watch out."

"They say he likes women," said Mami. "'Bimbo' means *Schürzenjäger* (skirt chaser). That's what the guards say."

I pointed to the soldiers across the yard who guarded the entrance to the villa, knowing there were others at the main gate and two more near the barracks. "Not very likely that he's going to rape us," I laughed. The image of that pompous little sergeant making sexual advances towards a female prisoner seemed utterly absurd.

"Who knows—there are ways." They looked at each other as though sharing a secret.

Then came the familiar inquiries: Why was I imprisoned and why had they sent me to Iserlohn? I answered in the usual evasive way. Here at intelligence headquarters, the tale of the young medical student caught in a military roundup while visiting her friend's farm sounded even more far-fetched. I could see it in their eyes, as I had seen it in others' before. They didn't press me. By some unwritten code of conduct, "special cases" were not expected to reveal too much—or to be believed when they did. In return, I accepted Karla's tale about her work as a nurse at the Volkswagen factory; at least I said I did.

According to her, there had been a maternity ward set up especially for Ukrainian slave laborers working at the auto plant, with Karla as the midwife. (In Germany, all normal deliveries were handled by midwives. Doctors were in attendance, but intervened only in surgical cases.) "We worked day and night, went all-out to help these women, who had never been used to anything civilized in their lives. You know how it was with those constant air raids and all. Now they claim we had too many dead babies on the ward, that we didn't look after them, simply let them die." She sniffed contemptuously. "These women bred like rabbits—God, did they ever. And too lazy to nurse their own brats." She stared out of the window, her eyes dry, hands clenched.

We never talked about it again. Two weeks later, she was sent somewhere else, presumably for trial. But I have often wondered: What kind of midwife had she really been? What were the conditions under which the mothers delivered their babies? How soon were they forced back to the assembly line, and who had looked after the children then? On the other hand: How many losses had been due to real and widespread shortages? I remember soldiers arriving from the southeastern front after days on the road, the advanced putrefaction of their wounds dressed with bandages of soaked-through crepe paper. That was in late 1944, in an army hospital, and those were *our* soldiers. If severely wounded German soldiers were bandaged with paper instead of cotton, what did a factory hospital have in the way of diapers? Where was the line between circumstance and deliberate neglect? Perhaps the mothers had been too malnourished to breastfeed their newborns, as had happened with so many women at the time. And the infants themselves had been too weak to tolerate the diluted cow's milk, the only alternative available then. Had the babies been intentionally murdered? Was I sharing a room with a murderess?[2]

I have nothing else to say about Mami, a woman of natural dignity, if a bit plain and parochial. She was friendly and helpful, while exerting gentle authority over Karla and me when we lost sight of the dangers around us and the trouble we might cause by our excessive childishness. It was mostly Salmon who was the butt of our jokes; in other cases it was the *Herr Major* whose daily visits had the phony solemnity of a mock funeral.

Major Brown was of average size with clean, almost classical features framed by straight dark-brown hair, cut short and smartly topped by a beret. His dark eyes and pale complexion made him look vulnerable and romantically attractive. For his position he seemed surprisingly young, not more than thirty-five, perhaps less. Clearly, there was more to Brown than his slender frame suggested. Behind his immaculately tailored uniform, presented to maximum effect by a parade-ground bearing, I sensed a complex personality. I don't remember whether I was afraid of him; if not, I probably should have been. Contact with his prisoners was prescribed and formal and in fastidious observance of protocol.

Every morning between nine and ten, he would leave the villa and cross the square, followed closely by Salmon and two guards. Upon arriving at the barracks, Salmon would step forward, knock sharply, and fling open the door in one single, precise movement. "Attention—*Ach-tung!*" The three of us would rise smartly, much in contrast to Salmon's welcome, which was relaxed, at times almost friendly. Then a cool "Good morning" from the major, very erect, very unsmiling, tipping his beret with his swagger stick. Our chorus in reply: "*Guten Morgen, Herr Major.*"

Brown: "Any wishes or complaints?"

Salmon translating: "*Irgendwelche Wünsche oder Beschwerden?*"

Chorus: "*Danke, Herr Major.*"

Salmon: "Thank you, Sir."

Brown, raising his swagger stick: "Goodbye."

Chorus: "*Auf Wiedersehen, Herr Major.*"

Salmon, holding the door: "Attention—*Ach-tung!* " The major exits; Salmon, at his heels, closes the door behind them. We sit down, restraining our laughter lest it penetrate the walls, while the procession continues down the corridor, repeating the ritual at every room.

If Brown possessed a sense of humor, his prisoners were certainly not the company in which to display it. What he did have was a sense of fair play and gentlemanly behavior, most likely acquired in private and military schools. He also had an instinct for the same in others. That these others happened to be his prisoners, on account of their former political or military ranks, he chose to ignore when promoting them to "privileged status."

The prisoner barracks at Iserlohn had two rooms that remained unlocked during the day: one for the women, the other for six or eight men whom the major considered worthy of his trust. The men in the Privilege Room were allowed to work in the kitchen or elsewhere on the grounds. Those long hours of absence, along with the strictly enforced rule of non-communication between prisoners, explain why I don't remember any of these men. Except one.

It happened in the women's washroom at the far end of the hallway on the second or third day after my arrival. Not expecting any disturbance, I failed at first to notice the gentle tap on the wall. When I recognized it for what it was, my initial reaction was fear: Somebody was out to harass me, to draw me into trouble with his stupid approach. Then I heard a whisper: "*Sind Sie Fräulein Mackprang aus Hamburg?*" (Are you Miss Mackprang from Hamburg?)

I was stunned. My heart beat wildly. After more than a month of total abandonment, here finally was somebody I knew, or who knew me, who perhaps could help me—God knows what thoughts rushed through my mind. "Yes. Who are you?" It couldn't be Müller. He would never have had the courage to contact me. Besides, I had not seen him arrive and he had not surfaced from whatever confinement Salmon had chosen for him. (He never made it to the Privilege Room, despite his PhD and good breeding, a fact which, in retrospect, greatly enhances my admiration for the major.)

"I'm your uncle, Kurt Gerdsmeyer," he whispered urgently. "You wouldn't remember me. The last time we saw each other, you were riding on my knee. I saw you outside when you arrived. I recognized you immediately from your likeness to your mother." I was dumbfounded by the incredible coincidence. I still hadn't seen his face, but I remembered that he was the younger brother of my godmother, the one I had intended to visit that night in Osnabrück when curfew had forced me off the street. She was not a real aunt, but my mother's dearest friend. Neither, of course, was he a real uncle, but someone I had known about all my life. I wanted to ask dozens of questions, but he cut me short:

"We cannot risk knowing each other and talking to each other without telling the major. Bimbo is bound to find out and that will be the end of it. Telling the major is our best chance." Uncle Kurt was clearly in charge, knowing exactly how to handle this delicate situation. I tried to protest: "But what if he locks us up, punishes us?"

"It's a risk we have to take, but it's the lesser one. Believe me." Gerdsmeyer continued: "My door here is open. I work as a stoker. I look after the ladies' hot water." He chuckled. "When you go out, turn around so that we can see each other, but don't say anything. Okay?"

"Okay." Despite his reassurances I felt uneasy. Yet, as I left, I did as I was told, smiling at this uncle I didn't recognize, a tall and broad-shouldered man in his mid-forties.

It was later that day, when Salmon's characteristic knock and stormy entrance interrupted the tedium of an early darkness. This being an unscheduled appearance, we were immediately on our guard: "*Guten Abend.*" Good evening.

"Guten Abend, Herr Stabsfeldwebel." In slow staccato.

"Mackprang, by special order of Major Brown you are not to talk to your Uncle Gerdsmeyer again ."

Silence. There was nothing to say.

"All future communications with Gerdsmeyer are to be made through me." He paused, then continued in a somewhat more conciliatory tone: *"Herr Major* has appreciated Gerdsmeyer's voluntary information about your family relationship and has waived punishment for your breaking the rules of non-communication among prisoners."

"Danke, Herr Stabsfeldwebel."

"You have to thank the major. He is a very generous man." There was no doubt about Salmon's own feelings in the matter.

Thereafter, despite the major's gag order, my situation improved in a way that is hard to describe and impossible to measure. The mere knowledge that there was somebody strong and experienced who knew about me, perhaps even kept an eye out for me, gave me confidence and renewed hope. It may also have raised my status among the British. Alhough Uncle Kurt could not really do much for me in practical terms, he did one extraordinary thing: From his own supplies he gave me a pair of red-and-white-striped pyjamas, size XL, the most wonderful piece of nightwear I would ever possess. Now, for the first time in many weeks, I could change before going to bed, even wash my underwear, letting it dry overnight.

Kurt Gerdsmeyer, with a doctorate in economics, had been a senior provincial administrator in the Ministry of Trade and Industry. A heavy man standing over six feet tall, with dark hair and a ruddy complexion, Kurt radiated good-natured self-confidence and easy authority. I liked him for his kindness and joie de vivre, about which I had heard throughout my childhood. The major must have appreciated his understated intelligence (so very British) as well as his strong and honest character. After his release from Iserlohn, I never saw Kurt again. (Childless, he drew strength from the deep love he shared with his wife, whom he called Ping, a woman I never met. He died in the late 1950s after a long battle with hepatitis. Ping, unable to face life without her beloved husband, joined him voluntarily shortly after.)

The gift of Uncle Kurt's pyjamas—dutifully submitted to Salmon, who then handed them over to me—had an entirely unexpected consequence: Three or four days after the happy event, Bimbo burst into our room. "Mackprang," he barked, "this is for you." Without looking me in the face, he presented me with something off-white and shapeless, while adding gruffly: "We can't have people getting sick."

What I held in my hands was some kind of unisex undershirt, coarsely knitted with plain straps, tube-shaped and long enough to reach down to my knees. There were no darts to signify front or back, nothing to mitigate the severity of a garment that might have warmed some nineteenth-century Mennonite, maiden or man. Was Salmon trying to make fun of me? How was I supposed to react? Was I to laugh at his joke or grovel with gratitude? To win time, I held the monstrous item against my body as though modeling a piece of sexy lingerie.

"*Danke, danke vielmals, Herr Stabsfeldwebel,*" I said coquettishly, suddenly close to tears and feeling like giving that awful sergeant a great big hug. Salmon himself appeared uncharacteristically self-conscious. He beat a hasty retreat, mumbling something like "*schon gut, schon gut*" (okay, okay), momentarily overwhelmed by his own generosity. It may have been the closest he ever came to feeling moved by anybody in his charge; it was not, however, the last time that I would become the cause of his profound embarrassment.

(I never learned how he got hold of what we girls promptly dubbed the *Bimbo-Hemd* [Bimbo shirt]; perhaps through some local charity that he may have approached after hearing about my appalling poverty from Uncle Kurt. Whatever the story, the *Bimbo-Hemd* stayed with me for several years until rationing was finally lifted in an improving German economy. Through several harsh winters, with temperatures in the classrooms dipping below ten degrees Celsius, I sat cosily wrapped in my Bimbo shirt. While it did nothing to enhance my figure, it faithfully insolated me from Hamburg's notoriously inclement weather.)

There were other incidents involving Salmon and me, some ridiculous, some unpleasant. I begin with the ridiculous, and an event too silly to recount here had it not been for what it revealed about the high level of secrecy and security pervading the installation.

Every morning before the Major's inspection, all rooms had to be swept and the wooden floors washed. Doors were unlocked, water fetched and pails emptied. For the men not in the Privilege Room, it was a rare chance to enjoy a few minutes of free movement, the water-run a pleasurable duty rotated among them. One morning, a small box of pink dental paste was swept under our door. Scratched into the compacted square was the message: *Ich liebe Sie*, I love you. We all laughed. Though confined to our room during the cleaning process, Karla and I opened the door a crack to discover the amorous sender, a Wehrmacht lieutenant with one empty sleeve pinned up to his uniform, while his other arm struggled awkwardly with the long handle of a broom. He was tall and slender and had a pinched face, possibly due to his wounds. He also had a nice smile that conveyed an apology for his boldness. After checking the hall to make sure nobody was listening, he made it clear that I was the target of his aroused feelings. We laughed and winked, then quickly retreated to our room.

Sadly, the budding romance came to a noisy end as soon as the major had completed his rounds. We watched Salmon, having first followed his superior back to the villa, storm across the yard and back into the barracks. Further down the hall, we heard him banging doors and yelling at the top of his voice before crashing into our room.

"Mackprang!" His little eyes brimmed with fury, and while an outside observer might have thought him a rather comical sight, I felt genuine fear. "The lieutenant may thank his amputated arm for having been spared from dark confinement (*Dunkelhaft*)," he screamed. "You have both acted against strict regulations. If I catch you again, I shall report you to the Major." With a menacing gesture of his fist, he ran out, locking the door from the outside. It stayed locked until the next morning, when the guards opened it as usual, leaving it unlocked for the rest of the day.

Several lessons were to be learned from that outburst, which we discussed in a frightened whisper: First, there were informers everywhere, perhaps microphones, even cameras. We immediately went on a search of our room, but were unable to find anything more suspicious than the blind end of an old wire, which we had inspected before and judged harmless. Another lesson suggested that there were certain things only Salmon knew, and others that he allowed Major Brown to know, and that there was a gap between the two which he controlled. It was my reckless breach of that gap which, some days later, sparked a string of incidents and an entirely new level of danger.

It began the morning after a new detachment of guards had arrived in Iserlohn, a routine event that usually went unnoticed by the prisoners. In general, the soldiers seemed harmless enough; no hint of sleuthing, just ordinary young men in pea-soup uniforms with matching berets over short hair and ruddy cheeks. Our association was limited to the evening lock-up (whose time I can't remember) and a six a.m. wake-up call. Just before lights-out, final visits to the women's washroom were scheduled, but unescorted. None of the soldiers stayed inside the barracks after lock-up; what provisions were made for an unscheduled call of nature I do not remember. Fortunately, I was young and slept through the night like a baby—which leads me back to my story.

Even before my arrival, it had been customary for my two roommates to simply ignore the wake-up call by turning over for another half-hour of sleep. As long as we were ready for breakfast at seven, nobody complained. At that time a large tray of porridge, bread, and ersatz coffee would arrive at our room. We would then duly apportion the food to the other prisoners as they passed our door in single file. Despite tight security, this was the one opportunity for a quick exchange of words. It was a dangerous game, however—dangerous enough that some of the prisoners would even avoid eye contact. Still, news was transmitted, warnings conveyed, accusations made.

On that particular morning there was, as always, a sharp rap at the door, the turning of the key, then silence. This day, however, the soldiers returned after a few minutes, loudly demanding that we get up. When nobody stirred, they barged into the room and started to throw us out of bed. Most of the physical attention was directed at me, who lay wrapped like a mummy in a blanket, skilfully sewn up into a long cozy bag by some previous occupant of the bunk. The comfortable shell had served me well during my pyjama-less days, and still did. Covered with a second blanket carefully tucked in on all sides, it demanded an exercise in cocoon-shedding to emerge to the challenges of the day. On this morning, surrounded by a bunch of cheering and ogling soldiers, there was simply no discreet way to perform the act.

Not surprisingly, the ribald scene soon turned ugly as the soldiers believed their authority was being mocked. With their rough hands pulling and tearing, they tried to force me out of my bag. By the time somebody ordered the men out of the room, I lay on the floor arms flailing, legs straining, yet still trussed up like a burglary victim.

First I had laughed, then yelled; after it was over, I cried. Not because somebody had hurt me (there was never the slightest danger of assault), but because of the outrage of these young men, who had rudely exploited their gender and numbers, not to mention their status as victors and members of the occupying forces.

Of course, a good part of the blame had to be apportioned to us. Had we followed orders instead of taking advantage of a certain relaxation of the rules, the incident would never have taken place. But that's written in hindsight, aided by the wisdom of age and a sober recognition of the hatred and contempt felt for Germans all over the world, feelings that were almost certainly shared by every officer and soldier at Iserlohn. At the time, however, I sadly lacked the humility or objectivity to judge myself or my country in such scathing terms . Instead, despite whatever fears I may have had about the ultimate outcome of my detention, there was no doubt in my mind that I had to present a stiff upper lip towards my "enemy-conquerors." I had to be aloof at all times, obstreperous if possible, and unequivocally hostile where my personal honor was at stake. Wasn't that how the proud heroes in all the books on war and captivity had behaved? After all, I was a young woman with a good background, not a common criminal.

Perhaps Mami or Karla tried to persuade me to let it go, to relax and forget the whole thing. If they did, their words fell on deaf ears. Later that morning, when the major arrived for his daily tour of inspection, I was still hot under the collar. Instead of being guided by caution, I felt propelled by the angry righteousness of my youth.

The tour began routinely enough with Bimbo barking *"Ach-tung!"* and the major stepping in with a calm "Good morning," answered by our trio's solemn *"Guten Morgen, Herr Major."* Again, Major Brown, politely bored: "Any wishes or complaints?" and Salmon's routine translation: *"Irgendwelche Wünsche oder Beschwerden?"*

It was at this point that I interrupted the daily farce of a civilized exchange. With my head held high I stepped forward: *"Jawohl, Herr Major, ich habe eine Beschwerde."* (Yes, Sir, I have a complaint.) Once I had begun, I rattled on, pouring out the whole incident and leaving Salmon no chance to translate.

The major listened, stone-faced. When I finished, the staff sergeant tried to break in, waving his arms, his whole body contorted in a mixture of beseeching and despair. Brown cut him short. Raising his swagger stick to his cap, he spun on his heel and exited without a word. Instead of continuing on his tour, he marched across the yard and back to the villa, Salmon's short legs straining to keep up.

What, if anything, had Brown understood? How had a prisoner's audacity offended his pride, tarnished his style? What would his reaction be? A deadly silence descended like fog on the barracks. As in all places of confinement, every prisoner was instantly aware of what had transpired. Now that it was too late, I was mortified by my senseless act of bravado, and terrified of the consequences it would bring for myself and others.

It didn't take long for Salmon to come rushing back to deliver his furious dressing-down, most likely having received similar treatment at the hands of the major. Ironically, it was precisely the reaction I needed to restore my own pluck and defiance: "What's the purpose of the major asking the same question every day, if all hell breaks loose as soon as somebody does come forward with a complaint?"

"You are supposed to tell me first. I'm the one who then informs the major." He had a good point, of course. As always, that day he had made his rounds ahead of his boss. Why was it, then, that he had not been informed of the early morning ruckus? Because everybody despised him and gleefully hoped for exactly the sort of thing that had just occurred? I cannot remember. He reached the pinnacle of his long tirade by threatening me with his special dark-cell treatment. After that, he pointed out the generosity and great patience—entirely undeserved on my part—displayed by both the major and himself.

The next morning, all three of us shot out of bed the moment we heard the guards' timid knock. There was no need, however; none of the soldiers showed his face. Later that day, Uncle Kurt found a chance to whisper that, during the night, the whole crew had been sent back to their garrison, and another had been rotated in. It was the end of the matter. Or so it seemed. Whether what happened the following day had anything to do with the incident, I never found out.

It was shortly after lunch when Bimbo charged into the room. "*Mackprang, Sie werden in Einzelhaft verlegt.*" I was to be put in solitary confinement.

To say that I was shocked would badly understate my emotional turmoil; I was horrified. All my old fears about Müller, the SD, and some dark conspiracy instantly came back and raced through my brain. Why me? Why now? Was it revenge for my outrageous complaint, or was I to be softened up for an interrogation still to take place? Salmon didn't explain. He issued the order while keeping his eyes averted.

"You go across the hall. There is to be absolutely no contact with other prisoners, including the women. If you have to go to the bathroom, call the guard." With that, he set out to heave the heavy straw mattress off my bed, through the door, and into the narrow room across the hall. I followed meekly with the blankets. When all my meager belongings were assembled, Salmon locked the door and marched off.

It was a small room, barely big enough to hold a bed. Its single window was set in the narrow side of the building next to the entrance. I could see the back section of the yard, which contained a shed surrounded by weeds and shrubs. It was a grey day with a drizzle that had the guards finding shelter somewhere out of my line of vision. There was nothing to do but sit on the bed and stare at the wall, while trying to keep the most frightful imaginings at bay. Suddenly, late in the afternoon, somebody stopped in front of my door. I stared at the lock, waiting for the key to turn. Instead, a barely audible whisper slipped through the keyhole:

"Are you all right?"

Uncle Kurt! I leaped up and pressed my ear to the door, realizing the enormous risk he was taking.

"Yes, I'm okay."

"Listen—the men here think Bimbo has certain intentions. That he has done this sort of thing before. They want me to warn you to barricade your door during the night."

"What do you mean? How am I supposed to do that?"

There was no answer. He had quietly moved on, leaving me confused and frightened.

Outside, the feeble December daylight had given way to early darkness. By now, I had spent five or six hours in solitary confinement, but it already seemed like an eternity. Granted, my present conditions, though cramped, were vastly better than jail. I had a soft bed with warm blankets, I could see a bit of the outside world through a large window, and the voices and activities of many people around me allowed for a measure of reassurance. Though locked up, there was not the sense of abandonment that had tormented me in my basement prison cell at Coesfeld. On the other hand, there was the complete inexplicability of the situation, which was worrisome. Who was behind it, and why? And could Uncle Kurt's warning really be true? Was there the slightest possibility of such lawless conduct within that tight military security? I thought of my two dozen countrymen separated from me by thin wooden planks; for all the protection they could afford me, those planks might have been the walls of a bunker.

At eight o'clock I had my last escorted trip to the bathroom.

Thereafter, the room was locked and the light turned off. I quickly got up. By now I had convinced myself that Uncle Kurt's warning lacked any shred of credibility, and that, likely as not, it was the product of some fellow prisoner's overactive imagination. Nevertheless, I tried to devise some kind of defence against any unwanted intrusion. There wasn't much to work with. Apart from the bed, a rough-hewn bench was the only piece of furniture. As quietly as possible, I wrestled it from behind the foot of the cot and placed it across the door. It was an old beat-up thing, narrow and shaky, but long enough to span the width of the frame—an alarm bell rather than a barricade, primed to go off the moment somebody tried to enter. I knew that I had to remove it before the guards came back in the morning.

Once my eyes adjusted to the dark, I noticed that the room benefited from some powerful lights out in the yard. The one nearest the entrance shone right into my face, and gave me the confidence to stay awake all night. I was deeply worried, my mind bringing up, sorting out, and discarding ever more exotic reasons for my present predicament. When the bench toppled over with a loud bang, I was convinced I had not slept a wink.

The crash woke the barracks, which shook from the uproar as every inmate began to hammer his fists against the walls. I tried desperately to come up to some level of rational thinking, as my eyes blinked in the glare of the ceiling light. Salmon stood in the door, barred and dumbfounded, and deperately trying to make himself heard above the furious racket. "*Sie müssen in Ihr Zimmer zurückgehen.*" He repeated his words several times. I tried to understand, but my ears were plugged by sleep and deafened by noise. "You have to go back to your room. We need this one for somebody else."

It wasn't so easy. The bench, knocked over on its side, blocked the narrow space between the door and the cot, limiting the staff sergeant's approach to just a few inches. As I reached out to push the obstacle away, I found myself confined in a by now familiar manner. Salmon pointed out the obvious: "You are sewn in." He gestured with his hands, uncertain whether to help me out of my cocoon or to discreetly withdraw. In the end, we managed together to manoeuvre the bench out of the way. Dragging a trail of grey army blankets behind me, I tiptoed across the hall, followed by the staff sergeant straining under the mattress he had lugged in the opposite direction a mere twelve hours earlier. I climbed back into bed and Salmon turned off the light and locked the door. After that, silence descended on the barracks as everybody tried to get back to sleep. Just as I was about to drift off, the staff sergeant returned.

"Everything okay, Mackprang?" he whispered outside.

"Thank you, yes, fine." I secretly smiled, savouring my salvation from—or was it my triumph over?—that mean little ex-German.

After that, I found it difficult to settle down again. Sure, I was swamped with relief, but mostly I was plagued by questions: What were the real circumstances behind the mystifying affair? Perhaps Salmon was telling the truth, that he had suddenly received orders for the use of the room. A plausible explanation, but it didn't account for my presence there in the first place.

About an hour later, we were woken up by yet another commotion. A car stopped outside, doors opened and slammed; there were voices, orders, running steps. Several people entered the barracks, somebody was hustled into the room I had just vacated, and then all was quiet. This time it remained quiet.

There were no explanations, of course. But by the next day, everybody knew that the new man across the hall had been one of Hitler's adjutants. I don't recall how we learned about it. Did Salmon drop the big news in order to boast, or to explain the kerfuffle that preceded the man's arrival?

I only saw the new prisoner once, a well-built man in his early thirties with short blond hair and fair skin, whose vaguely familiar face could fit thousands among Germany's officer class. Today, when everything, however loosely connected to the Führer, appears to be worthy of documentation, I regret that I cannot remember the adjutant's name, if, indeed, Salmon ever mentioned it. No notes were allowed, no writing materials issued. But, there were other reasons too, why I never got a real grasp on the things that happened around me, why I drifted—my mind preoccupied by the rules and exigencies of confinement—through places and circumstances that, in hindsight, might bear some considerable historical import.

Never for a moment did I consider my bizarre adventure as a part, however minuscule, of the great moral epilogue to one of the most extraordinary chapters in human history, a *Crime and Punishment* footnote to something so horrid that it will forever defy comprehension. I was no Albert Speer, eager to chronicle every detail of his detention, a Nazi star whose *post factum* insights and moral restitution would fascinate the world for decades to come. All I could feel about my situation was anger and embarrassment, sometimes heightened by almost irrational fear. I was one prisoner among hundreds of thousands, with just a bit more bad luck than others; a victim of circumstance and coincidence, to be sure, but mostly a victim of my own folly. Why, for God's sake, had I ever joined Müller's outfit? Voluntarily and against my father's sage counsel? That's what really rankled. It was mortifying to think of the dreadful lies others would spread about me, as I, myself, would *never* be able to tell the story, which was far too embarrassing to be lived down in a lifetime.

Finding myself among former Nazi celebrities—that is exactly how I saw them: as *former*—I felt contempt and more than a touch of satisfaction about their misfortune. But mostly I was preoccupied by the here and now, and intent on coping as skilfully as my wits would allow. Ahead lay an uncertain and worrisome future; behind, a past of which the less said, the safer.

While the good-looking Führer-adjutant in his solitary confinement may have enjoyed a certain measure of notoriety among his fellow officers, there were other "guests" at Iserlohn whose celebrity status was worldwide. Not for the people they knew, but for the people they were.

Through our windows facing the yard, we watched their arrival. It was a grey day in December, when a convoy of black limousines slowly drew up to the front of the administration building. Doors were opened and assistance rendered, courtesy of the British Army of the Rhine. Slowly a group of dignified gentlemen alighted from their private Mercedes-Benzes. Their suits and manners grandly defying prevailing circumstances, they looked remarkably like the CEOs of mighty conglomerates, which indeed is what they were. Assembled there, on the dusty yard of Major Brown's SIS station, were some of Germany's industrial elite. These were the men who, in the early 1930s, had showered the new Führer with their admiration. Their pledges of co-operation had been decisive in shaping Hitler's ambitious plans for Germany's rearmament and return to world-power status. Without their support, Hitler might well have remained just another loud-mouthed politician, peddling some grand design for saving the nation. As it happened, their votes of confidence not only assured him of a firm economic base on which to erect his Third Reich, they also provided him with the social acceptance necessary to win over millions of middle-class Germans who had contemptuously dismissed the fanatical Austrian upstart.

I only caught a glimpse of the small number of sombrely dressed gentlemen who, through generations, had built their empires on steel and armaments. *"Da kommen die Ruhrbarone"* (There come the Ruhr Barons), Mami said, as the men peeled themselves out of their plaids. Strangely, it is the detail of those red-checkered blankets, which the chauffeurs carefully folded and reverently placed back into the majestic cars, that looms large as I recollect the scene. In years I had not seen a luxury item like that. Surely, any mother fortunate enough to possess such a treasure had long since converted it into some desperately needed item, a skirt or a jacket, a baby blanket, a cozy wrap for an unheated bedroom. It struck me how that opulent comfort, demanded and granted for a mere hour's ride, epitomized just how good the war had been for the few who had wanted it most—and how dehumanizing it had turned out for everyone else.

There was no haste, no embarrassment on the part of the newcomers, just the dignified arrival at a villa which, though presently neglected, still displayed the architectural splendor of some bygone industrialist's residence. Steps behind their uniformed captors, the gentlemen slowly ascended the stairs to the stately entrance and disappeared. I never saw them again. Salmon later hinted at solitary confinement. Whether there were some comforts, he didn't say, but knowing a few things about the major, I quickly rejected the image of a dark cell and a bowl of gruel. On the other hand, no Flick or Krupp showed up in the major's Privilege Room. Whether in Brown's estimation they ranked too high or too low will never be known.[3]

Somebody else, however, made the upgrade from dark-cell confinement in the villa's basement to the barracks' Privilege Room in one giant leap. The way I remember him, he was a slim, medium-sized man in his early twenties, with dark hair and a shy, narrow face that would be easily overlooked in a crowd. His uniform bore the stripes of an NCO. It had been Germany's unconditional surrender, followed by the Allies' eager quest for their enemy's military secrets, that had turned this humble radio operator in Field Marshal Erwin Rommel's headquarters into a prized catch for British military intelligence. Whatever he had to disclose about the fabled Desert Fox, he was rewarded for it with the relative comfort of Major Brown's Privilege Room.

*   *   *

I have often reflected on the relationship between Brown and Salmon. Was the major's reserved attitude towards his staff sergeant simply a case of a superior's arrogance, or another version of the old good-cop bad-cop game, used to elicit information otherwise not easily obtained? Granted, this rather Machiavellian aspect of Brown never occurred to me at the time. But it might explain the very different ways in which the commanding officer and his sergeant treated that strange assortment of prisoners, each with a story to tell and all with the will to resist. At the same time, unavoidably, another question arises: Was Salmon-Salomon, the Jew from Franconia, a vengeful man, somebody who saw a chance to get even with his former countrymen, and used it? Political correctness demands immediate rejection of such a question on the grounds that it would be racist to suspect Salmon of racism. And yet, the staff sergeant was clearly vindictive (as he had every reason to be), dangerous in fact because of his unpredictable moods, which may or may not have been caused by feelings of inferiority: A German emigrant turned British subject, who had come back as a member of the victorious enemy army, he was clearly despised by the prisoners, no matter how valid his reasons. (Non-Jewish Willy Brandt, German federal chancellor from 1969 to 1974, could never completely shake off the distrust of the opposition for having spent the Nazi years with the resistance movement in Norway and Sweden.) Worse for Salmon, he may not have found much affection among his comrades-in-arms either, partly perhaps because of his rank—too high for the troops and too low for the officer class—and partly because his strong German accent was apt to invite taunts.

Salmon was the first Jew I ever met. Had I stayed in Germany, where Jews still number fewer than 50,000, chances are I would never have met another. Instead, I lived in the United States and later in Canada, where I have come to know a good number. Over the years, I have accepted the fact that no Jewish individual of my generation can learn of my German background without a certain reaction. Most of the time, this reaction is well-controlled by the person's education and good manners. But I know it is there, because I can sense it. I can also see it in their eyes. In a split second, a volume of emotional communications passes between us, usually resulting in a gracious "Nice to meet you" extended from the other side. But the knowledge remains like an immovable rock, forever marking the path of our common heritage.

Only once was my company rejected. It happened in 1959 in Washington, where I had joined the Welcome to Washington Club for the wives of congressmen, diplomats, visiting professors, and other members of the capital's transient society. For each meeting, I was responsible for a carload of non-driving women, whose far-flung residences kept me going for an extra hour at either end of the event. Returning late one night, I invited the last of my passengers, a young woman about my age, to move up from the back seat of the car. She did so, but remained unresponsive to my efforts to draw her into conversation. Suddenly, she blurted out in a voice that barely repressed her emotions: She had recognized my accent, she explained. To find herself so physically close to a German caused her anxiety and pain. She simply couldn't talk to me. After that, there was nothing for either of us to say. I let her off at her house; a few days later, I dropped my membership with the club. I never saw the woman again. Forty years later, the experience is still with me, still troubling.

How carefully chosen should my words be, when talking about Morris Salmon? Would it be inappropriate to mention his personal "hippodrome," the dusty yard where, his stumpy legs firmly planted on the ground, he kept his prisoners running around in circles until total exhaustion? Not all were young or militarily fit. We watched the punitive act from the window. How often did it happen during my four-week stay? Three times? Five? More? I don't remember. When he was done, he sent his captive into dark-room confinement. There were no beatings, no blood, never an ambulance for a failing heart.

All things considered, Salmon's treatment of his prisoners was probably not worse, and possibly better, than the standard for political internment camps. Nowhere—and I say that with confidence for all camps in the Western zones—were conditions even remotely comparable to what had gone on in German concentration camps during a dozen years of Nazi tyranny. I am reminded of the bulldozed mass burials at Bergen-Belsen after its liberation by the British, scenes now familiar to people all over the world. If, indeed, any of the officers at Iserlohn had been among the witnesses to that gruesome event, a special tribute, even if belated by half a century, seems appropriate for their extraordinary restraint in the treatment of their own political prisoners, many among them top leaders.

*　　*　　*

The Allies' internment camps warehoused huge numbers of former Nazis, either as a measure of punishment, or to prevent them from going underground, or perhaps for lack of a better method to handle the mass of Nazi functionaries nobody had really planned for. For the interrogating officers at Iserlohn, however, the foremost task was the careful selection for future trial of prisoners suspected of, or having important knowledge about, war crimes or crimes against humanity. Years later, I sometimes wondered how Uncle Kurt, a high-ranking civilian economist, had gotten himself into that company. Perhaps as an expert adviser on the coal and steel empires of Krupp and Thyssen located in his former administrative realm? I never asked. At Iserlohn, it would have been impossible to do so. But the truth is, the question never occurred to me. People had long grown accustomed to the postwar social upheaval that turned everybody into something different, something disreputable and completely incongruous with their former selves—prisoners, fugitives, black-marketeers, beggars, thieves, informers—so that nothing could really surprise anymore. If this was true across Germany, it was even truer inside the camps. Hence, while I never wondered about Kurt's presence at Iserlohn, neither did it occur to me that he might wonder about mine. Like guests at a masked ball, we played our parts in an absurd game of shifting identities, behind which we still were who we always had been—or thought we were. Or pretended to think we were.

There were three, possibly four, interrogators for the twenty-five to thirty inmates scheduled to be "processed" within a month's period. By now, more than three weeks had passed since my arrival. Karla, Uncle Kurt and a dozen others had left, while I continued to wait. Whether Mami was still there, I can't remember. I do know, however, that no other woman joined us during the rest of my stay. As days went by without anybody calling me up, my anxiety grew. Yet, the morning I was finally summoned by a guard, I was numb with shock. Suddenly, there wasn't a second to lose, no time to comb my hair or do whatever one considers important prior to a momentous occasion.

I followed the soldier across the yard and up the stairs of the villa, as I had so often watched others do. Seen up close, the building's stucco looked dark and grimy, like the walls of a railway station. Inside were wooden boards laid across the hall to protect the floor from scratches. We climbed a wide, poorly lit central staircase, which led up to the first floor and to a double door blocking our progress. The door was painted a simple white that looked incongruous and offensive against the panelled walls. Obviously, after the villa's requisition for Allied purposes, a number of offices had been crammed into a large, high-ceilinged hall that still displayed signs of its earlier splendor.

The soldier knocked, then opened the door and stepped aside. At the far end of the room, his face shadowy in the light from the window, an officer rose as I entered. He shook my hand and introduced himself, then quickly settled back into his chair, one foot resting on the opposite knee. He pointed his pipe at the chair across the desk. In his late twenties or early thirties, he was of medium height with wavy chestnut hair and the healthy look of an athlete. There was no hint of belligerence, urgency, or even curiosity; only the relaxed bearing of somebody who had seen and heard it all, and expected no surprises, good or bad. Not knowing anything about the British military, I didn't take note of his rank which, in any case, seemed immaterial to his present assignment. There was a Belgian army badge on his sleeve, a detail I would hardly have noticed, had I not been told about it beforehand. (Irrelevant little things like this were the only bits of information volunteered by other prisoners after their interrogations.)

I don't know how many Belgians served with the Allied armies, or even how many were at Iserlohn. All three of us women could have had the same interrogator, or there could have been more Belgians around; there was no way of telling. Clearly, this man was superbly suited for His Majesty's Intelligence Services. He spoke an impeccable German, probably in addition to English, French and Flemish, and he seemed well-educated, with the easy demeanor to prove it. He looked at ease and confident, more like a don in a private school than an investigator bent on flushing out the weaknesses in a suspect's tale. He offered tea and when I replied "*Ja, danke*," he dispatched a soldier to fetch it.

At this point I have to admit to an embarrassing truth: Of all the spellbinding things that must have happened during the next hour, the humble tea is what pressed itself most clearly on my memory. It was served in two large flowery cups with saucers (mugs not being part of the German culture) and generously laced with cream, something extraordinary I had never encountered before. Born with a strong aversion to milk, I was immediately repulsed by the caramel-colored mixture. I stared at the revolting brew and seriously considered rejecting it. But when the officer calmly started to sip his tea, I quickly chose manners

"Villa Elizabeth," site of the British Intelligence Service in 1945/1946. The stairs and main entrance were located where the 1923 photograph shows a large balcony. The prisoners' barracks were at the site from where the picture was taken. The large pile of rubble suggests that major reconstructions were going on at the time.

over idiosyncrasy and followed suit. To my surprise, the tea tasted sweet and delicious. Indeed, after years of ersatz everything, I suddenly experienced an incredible sense of comfort, completely incongruous with the precarious nature of my circumstances.

To hint at bribery would be gauche. The tea was simply part of a courteous routine that had proven useful in softening an atmosphere adversarial by definition. Of course, with little choice in the matter and even less experience, I performed precisely as expected, by allowing the little ceremony to soothe my nerves, and make me feel relaxed and important. In reply to the Belgian's casual inquiries, I expounded in chatty detail on my family background, education, Hitler Youth association, even my relationship with Müller and the *Dienststelle*. I was optimistic and cooperative. The interrogator didn't really interrogate, at least not that I noticed. Mostly he just sat there, making trivial inquiries and listening patiently to my elaborate answers, drawing little question marks on his foolscap.

Actually, I noticed his doodling only during the next day's session. This time, the Belgian asked a string of questions about things and people. Again, he was low-key and casual. Did I know this SS officer or that one? Had I ever met this person at Müller's office, heard that name? At each negative reply, he nodded earnestly. All the while, the question of what exactly I *did* do at the *Dienststelle* never came up.

My eyes followed his pencil as it traced the same curved lines. He seemed pensive. Did he believe me? Mostly yes, sometimes no, judging by the question marks. Why do I remember something as trivial as question marks, when all the names he asked me about I have forgotten? Partly because I had never heard of any of these people, and partly because I was embarrassed. The Belgian's thoughts were all too painfully clear: How in the world had this clueless girl managed to end up in Iserlohn? Which idiot had been responsible for this colossal foul-up?

I should have felt relief. Instead, I was crushed. Such was the power of the environment that I suddenly began seeing myself through the eyes of the Belgian: As a pretentious brat lusting for notoriety, stealing hours of everyone's precious time; a cheat, a fraud, who by her very presence had made a mockery of the system.

The officer pushed his writing pad aside, signaling the conclusion of the interrogation. With deliberate casualness he slipped in an oblique offer of some undefined co-operation with the services he represented. I shook my head and he didn't press the point which had likely come up merely as a matter of routine. He rose. Walking me towards the door, he threw in one more name: SS Führer so-and-so, Gestapo—did I happen to know him? It was at this point, with the interrogation behind me, that my old cheekiness shot up. My head held high, I declared defiantly: "There are two categories of people I never encountered before coming to Iserlohn: Gestapo officers and British staff sergeants."

There! Take that, Bimbo—

He smiled, but didn't respond. He may have heard worse. Or he may simply have been too well-bred to take offence from an ill-mannered German.

*   *   *

My interrogation was over and so was my stay at Iserlohn. Salmon was in a jovial mood the next morning as he accompanied me to the camp's exit. I would be shipped back to internment camp, he explained, just as I was about to get into the Jeep. "It is their job to release you—the bureaucratic route, so sorry." I was shocked. Hadn't the women at Recklinghausen insisted that no one ever returned from Iserlohn? Where had all the others gone? Had the rules been changed? Salmon didn't explain. He pressed my hand. "Cheer up, Mackprang—you will be home for Christmas." He waved as the Jeep took off. I was the only passenger.

Still numbed by the new and entirely unexpected course my way into freedom was taking, I tried to concentrate on the officer's interrogation. Had I spoken the truth? Had he been satisfied? What *did* I do during those three-and-a-half months at Müller's *Dienststelle* that the Belgian had not considered sufficiently important to ask about? (He might have heard enough from Müller. More likely, the small SD branch in Marburg had never been of interest to the big-time sleuths at Iserlohn. Rather, it had been the scent of some clandestine conspiracy that had set the hounds on Müller's trail, snaring the unforeseen "messenger" as a bonus.)

So, what exactly did I do at the *Dienststelle*?

To be truthful, with the outcome of the war no longer in doubt (though nobody dared say so out loud), we tried to kill time without looking too obvious about it—extended lunch hours, some trumped-up errands, sitting in air-raid shelters, engaging in what might pass for serious discussions. These were expressions of the slow mental and physical disengagement from a workplace that was clearly doomed and would disappear within the foreseeable future. I had never experienced office work; yet even the most casual observer could not fail to notice that things were not quite as they were supposed to be. As discipline slowly disintegrated, zeal and precision, so highly cherished at every German place of work, were ever more openly dispensed with. Still, the pretension of normalcy had to be maintained at an acceptable level to avoid retributions from some overly ambitious superior in an atmosphere that was highly charged and thick with fear.

When I showed up at the *Dienststelle* in early December 1944, Müller assigned me my task, which was to write about things going on in the city: What people were thinking, how they were coping, everyday stuff. His orders referred specifically to students, though there were few students left, and none that I knew. Personally, I did not have to talk to people my own age, however, to know exactly what Germans were thinking; apart from fanatics, ideologues, and high functionaries, they all thought the same. It was an assignment for which twelve years of schooling afforded ample training. All I needed was an open mind, untroubled by propaganda and political slogans.

So I wrote my reports. To be precise, I dictated them freely and without a moment's hesitation to that gentle secretary whose husband was a Wehrmacht officer wounded somewhere at the Eastern front. Her incredible dexterity at the keyboard allowed her to keep up, rarely stopping for typos. What were those reports about? What were the issues Müller considered of interest? Or more to the point, what could I, a naïve young student, possibly have known that he or his superiors did not?

I am sure that aspect didn't bother me one bit. It may have amused me, though, since I considered the whole activity to be nothing but a pretentious sham. My two or three reports—certainly not more, as they couldn't be anything but repetitious—dealt with the daily concerns of ordinary people; or of students, if that was the required version: Their fear of air strikes and anger over the growing shortages; their mistrust of the Nazi leadership (always exempting Hitler), and their weariness of the war in general. To me, the experience was nothing less than liberating: Here I could vent my personal resentments by simply extrapolating to the silent masses; better yet, I could bring them to the attention of one of the most feared Nazi organizations. If I wrote "one says" or "they think" in place of the first person singular, anything seemed acceptable.

But how could anyone at the *Dienststelle* or elsewhere accept as useful information the commonly known facts that I simply dictated off the top of my head? The people at the office faced the same hardships as the rest of the population. Could it be that I, the young ignoramus in that organization, was allowed the *Narrenfreiheit* (fool's licence) to write about things they all knew to be true, yet dared not report themselves? Was my boss quietly passing on my "intelligence" to others so high up that they actually might not know how the people felt?

There is, of course, another explanation. In totalitarian Germany, where opinion polls were unknown and everybody was expected to cheer regardless of true feelings or opinions, reports like mine were the only way to gauge the mood of the population. It was a data-gathering process that was bureaucratic and cumbersome and yielded results that were only as close to reality as the thousands of SD writers and their superiors would allow them to be. Even as late as February or March of 1945, many fanatics might still have felt it their patriotic duty to conceal the truth of Germany's impending collapse behind the rosy colors of ideological hype. But all that is mere speculation. In fact, I never learned what happened to my reports: whether they were passed on, filed, or simply thrown out the moment they landed on Müller's desk.

As for the work of the others, I am sure it was never discussed in my presence. Looking back, I think of the staff as a rather harmless bunch of small-town people playing spy games among the unwitting citizenry of a university town. Nobody will ever know. But one thing is certain: such parochial amateurism—if that, indeed, was all it was—was not the way the SD was supposed to work, or in fact did work in larger centers. There were aspects about the organization I happened to pick up at the *Dienststelle*, despite efforts to keep me outside their real work; others I learned about later.

It was during one of those dull afternoons, whiled away with empty chatter, that an offhand remark alerted me to the true purposes of the SD. Rolf, the young fanatic in the office, casually observed how regrettable it was that the inland arm of the *Sicherheitsdienst* possessed no "executive powers." Never having heard the word *Exekutivgewalt* before, the comment caught my attention. I immediately and instinctively knew what it meant. "Executive power" sounds harmless enough in English, usually referring to the decision-making authority of a company CEO. In Germany, the expression refers first and foremost to the legitimate powers of the state and its executive institutions and therefore has much stronger connotations. But Rolf was not talking about any legitimate powers of the Reich government. What he had in mind was the power of the SD to break, enter and shoot, rather than merely sniff out subversive activities. Unfortunately, as he explained it, that kind of decisive action was the sole prerogative of the *Geheime Staatspolizei*, better known as the Gestapo or Secret State Police, to whom the rather sissy *Inlands SD* had to turn for help if "executive powers" were required. How often that happened, and whether it ever happened on Müller's watch, he didn't say.

The implication of Rolf's remark, of course, was that the *Auslands SD*, operating outside German borders, was not bound by such restrictions. As became clear after the war, their activities had indeed been among the most heinous and murderous in every country of German occupation. In charge of the dreaded *Einsatzgruppen* (special-task commandos), which followed the advance of the Wehrmacht in Poland and the Soviet Union, the *Auslands SD* was responsible for more roundups and killings of Jews than any other organization.

In fact, inside Germany the SD was anything but a harmless organization invented to merely gauge the mood of the population. Indeed, it was one of the most insidious institutions of the Third Reich. Its network of officers and collaborators penetrated every administrative body and agency within the government, as well as all public and private institutions—listening, observing, reporting on everything and everybody.

Eugen Kogon, a leading authority on the complex structures of the SS, suggests there were 100,000 to 120,000 members of the Inland SD in 1939; twice as many during the war. (See also Chapter 2, n. 10.)

Whatever their numbers, few of them showed up at the *Dienststelle*. Therefore, when I told the Belgian officer that I knew nobody within the Nazi establishment, I spoke the truth. Müller was the only SS officer with whom I ever exchanged more than a few words.

Even less than a few words were exchanged during the two single encounters I had with Nazi big shots. Unrelated though these encounters were, they nevertheless illustrate the arbitrary powers of the vain and omnipotent—and later frightened—Nazi establishment.

I have only the vaguest recollection of the first event. It consisted of little more than a handshake with a certain Dr. August Hirt, professor of anatomy at the *Reichsuniversität Strassburg* (Reich University Strasbourg), and one of the most notorious figures in the medical profession during the Third Reich. One morning, I was called to Müller's office, where the *Hauptsturmführer* presented his distinguished guest to the young medical student. He beamed with pride as he explained Hirt's exceptional work and outstanding reputation: Through mass measurements of Jewish skulls, the professor had endeavored to prove scientifically what Nazi teachings had claimed all along—the "racial inferiority" of Jews. (According to Eugen Kogon, Himmler once ordered the *Wirtschafts-Verwaltungs-Hauptamt* [Economic and Administration Main Office]—one of a dozen innocuous-sounding "main offices" of the *Reichssicherheitshauptamt*, responsible for the administration of the concentration camps—to supply Hirt with the bodies of 115 specially selected Jewish prisoners from Auschwitz to facilitate the professor's research. Later, as the Russian army approached, Hirt ordered the murdered and preserved bodies to be dismembered and incinerated.)[4]

I don't recall much about Hirt, except that he was slim, of average size, and wore the uniform of the Waffen SS. He was polite but cool, and as arrogant as could be expected for a man of his power and status. Fifteen years later, I was fascinated to read in Rolf Hochhuth's notes to his famous play *Der Stellvertreter* (*The Deputy*), that Hirt looked like a vulture because of a gun wound to his jaw. For the play, using Hirt's real name, Hochhuth transforms the rather tight-lipped professor into a jovial bon vivant, whose cynical disregard for life is masked by a rotund figure and Swabian chumminess.[5] Hochhuth further claims that Hirt was never found by the Allies. In fact, he was sentenced to death by a French military court, but committed suicide in June of 1945.

If my encounter with Hirt was brief, another one I had with a Nazi VIP was even briefer. Though I never learned the man's name, the event is deeply etched in my mind because of the fear and outrage it provoked.

It must have been during the final weeks of the war, when tensions in the tottering Reich were escalating by the day. I had been chatting with one of the secretaries, when suddenly the door to the inner sanctum flew open and Müller stormed into the room. In a sharp tone, quite different from his usual civility, he ordered me to pick up a letter from the main post office and hand-deliver it to some high-ranking party official. *Sofort*—at once. Peeved by his pompous display of power, I mumbled behind his back: "I'm not his errand boy." Granted, this was a highly injudicious remark, one which I regretted the moment I realized it might have slipped through the closing door.

I bit my lip as I put on my coat, and set off at a little above normal speed. Further down the Bahnhofsstrasse I entered the post office, where I found a long line of people nervously waiting to be served. (By this time, nobody ventured too far from home without first ascertaining the distance to the nearest bomb shelter.) Upset by the unexpected delay, I elbowed my way through the crowd to impress the urgency of my mission upon the female clerk behind the wicket. Alas, my demands for immediate service were curtly rejected. I was told to wait like everybody else, while a stream of foul invective about *Bonzen* (party brass) and privileges rewarded me for my trouble.

Some forty-five minutes later, letter in hand, I arrived at the nearby address of a very fat official in a brown uniform, who accepted the envelope without so much as a nod. Ignoring his bad manners, I returned to the office, refreshed by the walk and in generally good spirits since, for once, no air raid had forced me to duck. At the door, I was stopped by Rolf.

"The boss is expecting you. You are going to get a *ganz dicke Zigarre*." And a huge dressing-down was exactly what I got when I entered Müller's office. Fat Man was outraged, having phoned twice to complain that he had still not received the letter, and why was it that it took Müller's messenger so long. *Where had I been?* I wanted to explain, but never got the chance. For ten minutes, Müller ranted about insubordination and subversion, hinting darkly at the consequences of Fat Man's wrath.

Writing this down today, the whole scene sounds preposterous. Had there, in fact, been some danger? Could either of those paranoid bigwigs have done me real harm? Of course they could. People vanished for far lesser offences than my alleged sabotage or obstruction, whatever. What crucial message or vital order did that letter contain that merited its utmost protection? Had I met somebody, talked to somebody on the way? Clearly, with enemy troops less than one hundred kilometers away, high-ranking Nazi officials were on the brink of hysteria and eager to drag along, on their way to hell, as many bystanders as they were able to snatch.

After that, Müller kept his distance. It was only a few days later that both the office and my apartment were bombed. There were no more orders, at least not until that spooky night when the files of the Marburg SD were incinerated in the *Dienststelle*'s final clandestine operation.

* * *

Though it would be tempting to do so, I cannot, in good conscience, close this chapter without mentioning the one incident that has stuck in my mind with a clarity befitting the passage of five, rather than fifty years. It concerned an assignment given to me by Müller with the suggestion that I take Rita along, the other student at the *Dienststelle*.

I don't know how she got conscripted. Like me, she had started in early December. At the time, I assumed Müller had asked for another student in order to justify my own somewhat questionable employment, an explanation I still consider valid. As it was, her attachment to the work-place was casual from the start, her appearances irregular and increasingly random. The staff simply ignored her; so did Müller. It was I, therefore, to whom he turned:

"Fräulein Mackprang, are you Catholic or Protestant?"

"Protestant."

"What are your feelings about the Church?"

Nazi Germany was a state with an avowed anti-religious attitude. So I shrugged to indicate my indifference, which I didn't have to pretend: Apart from being baptized and confirmed, I had never attended a church service, nor had anybody else in my family—Nazi state or no Nazi state. "I'm not religious."

"Then you may be surprised to hear that while everyone in Germany puts his shoulder to the wheel, there's still teaching going on at the theological faculty. I want you to find out what they're saying in their lectures."

Instinct told me that this was precisely the sort of thing I should stay away from. It came perilously close to what my father had warned me about: spying on other people. "I have no idea how," I stalled. "I don't know anybody outside the medical faculty. And I know nothing about theology."

"High time you learned something about it then," Müller snapped. "Take the other girl along. Together, the two of you should be brave enough to enter their sanctum sanctorum."

And so we did. Keeping our voices down to a whisper, Rita and I tiptoed past dark columns and empty rooms the size of monks' chapels. These were the vaulted halls of Marburg's *Alte Universität*, dating back more than 400 years and oozing that special mix of wax, incense, and piety produced by centuries of Christian veneration. We checked the numbers on the doors against the notes obtained from the dean's office. The lecture on early religious history was already underway when we made our entrance. We tried to be inconspicuous. It didn't work. Nobody can inconspicuously enter a room that size, occupied only by a professor and four male listeners awkwardly cramped into old prayer pews.

Everybody was polite and discreet. Nobody stared, though the professor did pause for a second before going on. We squeezed into the last bench, placed paper and pen in front of us, and tried to listen to the lecturer's description of what I took to be a primitive stone altar at a site of ancient sacrifice. Perhaps we had caused the professor some discomfiture after all: Over and over, he repeated the same simple features, walking up and down a narrow space between blackboard and front pew. Later, he approached us to ask in a friendly tone what had brought us to his class. Interest, we replied. He beamed and invited us to come again. And we did—once more. After that, memory fails.

I never wrote a report on the visits, because more urgent events—the bombing, and two weeks later the arrival of the American army—intervened. Besides, numbed by the professor's dullness and baffled by the theological jargon, I hadn't really understood a whole lot. Still, there couldn't be any doubt that what Rita and I had attended was a class in ancient religious history.

In fairness to Müller, I have to admit that I am surprised that such an arcane subject could still have been taught at a time when even the medical faculty, despite mounting war casualties, had been forced to close its doors to all but fourth- and fifth-year students. On a more cynical note, I am fascinated by the bizarre paradox of that mild-mannered professor in his monastic room instructing a class on Western civilization's most ancient roots, just as that civilization was about to reveal the depth of its barbarity.

Chances are that nothing would have happened to the professor, no matter what I might have reported. Time had run out for the SS state. Within a month, Müller's world would collapse, and the former SD boss would be a fugitive headed for the Swiss border. But even if there had been no such urgency, the worst that might have occurred was the cancellation of the course and the dispatch of the young students to the front. Any more serious meddling by the state would have prompted a fierce argument with the synod which, at this precarious point, was something the Nazis would almost certainly have wanted to avoid.

Why then, if there never was any real danger for these men, have those lectures stuck like a fishbone in my craw? The operative word is shame. I felt, and still feel, profoundly ashamed for having spied on innocent people. The fact that, in those final tumultuous weeks of the country's collapse, nobody had asked for that wretched report, does not make me feel any better. Under different circumstances—say, a year or two earlier—I almost certainly would have obeyed orders to assure my own safety. Out of fear, I would have acted the way everybody else did: I would have complied. From whatever I had been able to glean from the lectures, I would have produced my report.

There, but for the grace of God—

INTERLUDE VI
National Socialism and the Christian Churches

Measured against the extraordinary and continuous media interest in the history of the Jewish genocide, the strained relationship between National Socialism and the Christian Churches has received rather scant scrutiny. The reasons have at least partly to do with the Churches themselves, which were as eager as the rest of the population to bury their often ambiguous relationship with the Nazi system as fast and as deeply as possible. Another explanation may be the lack of esteem accorded to religious institutions in general, and the public's dwindling interest in the Churches' role in society. Also, there are the close financial and cultural ties that, by law, bind the Churches in Germany to the state, and the benevolent hand that all federal chancellors have held over their welfare and reputation.

Squeezed between the new Hitler government's openly anti-religious stance and the hopes of hundreds of thousands of imperilled Jews for the Churches' aid and intercession, Germany's Christian institutions found themselves in one of the most intractable political and ethical conflicts. Aggravating their moral dilemma was their own age-old anti-Judaism, rationalized with the words of the New Testament. Though much less pernicious in twentieth-century Germany than during medieval times, it was still widely upheld throughout the Christian establishment as well as by large parts of the population. In this highly delicate situation, both Catholic and Protestant Churches tried for a neutral position, while quietly feeling not unsupportive of the increasingly blatant measures against the Jews

Caution was certainly advised in the face of the overt religious antagonism displayed by the newly empowered Nazi thugs, who were harassing tens of thousands of clergymen, sending many to concentration camps, and not shying away from murdering them. In his book *The Catholic Church and Nazi Germany*, which first appeared in 1964, Günther Lewy quotes the number of 326 priests liberated at Dachau, with more having been killed or dying from starvation.[6] To protect the spiritual work, even the lives, of his imperilled clergy, Pope Pius XI, on May 7, 1933—just three months after Hitler's ascent to power—signed the famous Reich Concordat, the treaty between the Vatican and the Berlin government that bound both sides to a policy of non-interference. (It would prove to be one of the few treaties that Hitler did not break, although infringements were made and protests became regular events.)

For the Nazis, the pact was a remarkable achievement, as it seemed to signal to the world that the new National Socialist leader was not a vulgar upstart and loudmouth like so many of his underlings, but a respectable diplomat, someone with whom even the Vatican could do business. In practical terms, the Hitler government demanded—and got—the assurance that the Catholic Church would limit itself to spiritual matters only, while observing a neutral position vis-à-vis the new political order—including, by implication, the Nazis' plans to "solve the Jewish problem." Denying the possibility that the Vatican could have been ignorant about the German government's intentions, British historian John Cornwell, writes: "The potential in the Reich Concordat for sanctioning the destruction of the Jews was acknowledged by Hitler himself in his cabinet meeting on July 14, 1933."[7]

Hitler's interest in the treaty, however, went much further: Well aware of the potential danger of the powerful Catholic hierarchy to rival his own dictatorship, he was determined to avoid another *Kulturkampf*, that disastrous struggle fifty years earlier, when the predominantly Protestant Bismarck government had tried—and famously failed—to curb the Catholic Church's political and cultural influence. No competitive political, social, or religious institution was permitted to muddy the waters in Hitler's New Germany.

Most Germans, including a large number of bishops, hailed the Concordat as an extraordinary diplomatic achievement; however, aided by newly released documents, judgments have become much more critical of the Vatican—close to the point of condemnation. Indeed, from today's vantage point, it seems difficult to understand an agreement that appeared to hand over all the advantages to the Nazi government, while the Catholic Church withdrew into its own spiritual fortress. On July 5, 1933, only two months after the signing of the Concordat and five months after Hitler's coming to power, Germany's large Catholic Center

Party (*Zentrumspartei*),[8] the last political opposition to Hitler's NSDAP in the *Reichstag*, "voluntarily" dissolved itself under strong pressure from the Vatican. Similarly, all Catholic youth organizations in Germany were disbanded and integrated into the *Hitlerjugend*. Thanks to the Church's extraordinarily accommodating attitude, Hitler gained a huge amount of political space in which to expand practically unopposed. Writes Cornwell: "... [t]he Concordat ... became the supreme act of two authoritarians, while the supposed beneficiaries were correspondingly weakened, undermined, and neutralized."[9] Further he states: "Nothing could have been better designed [than the Concordat] to deliver the powerful institution of the Catholic Church in Germany into the hands of Hitler."[10]

Why did the Vatican put its signature to a document that ended the strong political and cultural presence of the Catholic Church in a country where it had historically been such an important part of the political and social fabric? How could there be such a lopsided treaty, binding together the radical ambitions of a tyrannical government with the spiritual aspirations of an increasingly introverted and transcendental Papacy? The answer lies in the Vatican's early twentieth-century history: Ever since Pope Pius X (1903–14), a strong anti-modernistic, anti-democratic movement within the Roman Curia had aimed at centralizing all hierarchical and spiritual powers of the Church in the Holy See. Complete obedience in all religious matters went along with the curtailment of regional (national) influence and interference, be it with the appointment of bishops or the instructions in Catholic schools and in the military.

Reading Cornwell's lengthy biography of Pope Pius XII, there can be little doubt that the true *spiritus rector* of the Concordat was Eugenio Pacelli, then the Vatican's State Secretary (Foreign Minister) and former Papal Nuncio (Ambassador) to Berlin. After years of frustrating negotiations with the various governments of the Weimar Republic, Pacelli was determined to reach a formal treaty between the Vatican and Hitler's new Nazi government, similar to the 1929 Lateran Treaty with Italy's Fascist leader Benito Mussolini. Pacelli, who in 1939 became Pope Pius XII, was perhaps one of the most controversial figures of the entire Hitler era. Deeply religious—pious, angelic, mystic in the eyes of his admirers—he directed his extraordinary intelligence and ambition towards the spiritual purity and hierarchical order of a strongly centralized Church, often overriding or ignoring the prudent advice of his German bishops and cardinals. Like an absolute ruler, he jealously guarded his own sphere of influence—from the Catholic schools in Germany to the strictly devotional work of the Churches; from the international prestige of the Vatican to its unique artistic possessions. Yet, in spite of his spiritual demeanor, personal isolation, and asceticism, he was a thoroughly modern man who perfectly understood the symbols of power and knew how to use them. He was well-informed about Nazi atrocities, including the Holocaust, yet he refused to raise his voice in protest.

Pius XII's non-interference with the Jewish genocide remained largely unobserved and undisputed among non-Jews until 1963, when, five years after the Pope's death in 1958, Rolf Hochhuth's play *The Deputy*[11] hit the world stage. After eighteen years of collective indifference or frequent denial, the deportations, the death camps, the cynicism of the Nazi establishment and—the central issue of the play—papal silence, were presented to a German and international public with brutal clarity. Not only did the Pope stand accused of appeasement and non-interference, not to mention failure in his Christian duties, but the entire subject of the Jewish genocide was newly revived.[12] While it would take another fifteen years and another cultural event—NBC's 1978 televised series *The Holocaust*—to finally turn the extermination of Europe's Jewry into an accepted fact, Pacelli's name, deeply revered before, had become irrevocably tarnished. In *The Catholic Church and Nazi Germany*, Lewy says about Pacelli's papacy: "The policy of accommodation ... provides but the most recent striking example of the Church's inability to transcend her institutional interests and to be a guardian of human morality... [By retaining a friendly relationship with the Nazis, rather than making a strong statement against the genocide, the Church] compromised its absolute spiritual essence." And he concludes, "... in the face of an upsurge of monstrous barbarism it was wrong to be guided by "reasons of state or *raison d'église*."[13] Cornwell's judgment thirty-five years later is even more devastating: "That failure to utter a candid word about the Final Solution in progress proclaimed to the world that the Vicar of Christ was not moved to pity and anger. From this point of view he was the ideal Pope for Hitler's unspeakable plan. He was Hitler's pawn. He was Hitler's Pope."[14] But when Pope John Paul II, on the occasion of the Holy Year 2000, spoke his long-awaited words of repentance for centuries of errors in matters of faith by the Catholic clergy (rather than the Holy Church), he never mentioned his controversial predecessor, Pius XII.

How could Pacelli act and interact with the Berlin government, the way he did? What political climate, which ideological beliefs made the interests of the German dictator and the highest priest in Christendom run on such closely related tracks? Who was Pacelli, the man and the pontiff? Was he the pious Deputy of Christ, as those who now work toward his beatification and canonization maintain? Or did he, the germanophilic pontiff, keep silent about the greatest mass crime in history in order to protect his clergy from an anti-religious regime—*ad maiora mala vitanda*, to prevent worse? Was he the ambitious diplomat, who upheld his strict neutrality in hopes of later being chosen by an international tribunal as a peace negotiator? Was he the conscientious preserver, who appeased the Germans so that they might not bomb St. Peter's glorious basilica and thousands of other irreplaceable Roman treasures? States Cornwell: "From 1917 ... Pacelli and the office for which he was responsible betrayed an antagonistic policy towards the Jews, based on the conviction that there was a link between Judaism and the Bolshevik plot to destroy Christendom."[15] Among all the possible reasons for the pontiff's inaction in the face of the Nazi genocide, this explanation seems the most plausible, as it reflects the widely accepted ideology of the time. Substituting "Christendom" for "Western civilization," notably German civilization, it entirely corresponds with Hitler's convictions.

There are those, of course, who are eagerly pushing for Pacelli's beatification. Apart from his deep spirituality, even saintliness, they stress the fearlessness that allowed him to stay in Rome during the German occupation (unlike the Italian King Victor Emmanuel III). They also praise him for hiding 4,000 of Rome's 8,000 Jews in monasteries and even in Vatican City, and for permitting diplomats of the Holy See to provide fake birth certificates to save Jews from the Holocaust.[16] How many Jews were rescued, directly or indirectly, by the protecting hand of Pius XII, nobody will ever know.[17] Between those who want to canonize him for his pious life, and those who criticize him for his failure to act in the face of the Holocaust, the latter seem to be holding the lead in popular support, particularly in Germany where, since the 1960s, *The Deputy* has been a hallmark in an increasingly iconoclastic culture.

*   *   *

The Concordat offered the German Catholic clergy a state of cohabitation with National Socialism; it was never intended to ring in a love fest.

Hitler's priority was peace in his backyard while he pursued his ultimate goal: Germany's supremacy over a Europe of non-Jewish, Aryan peoples. Still, it was an uneasy truce with untold cases of martyrdom: Thousands of priests and ministers who dared resist the Nazis' anti-religious (though not necessarily their anti-Semitic) ideology were persecuted. Some were shot on the spot; others were sent to concentration camps where many of them perished. The majority of their brethren, however, following the example of the Holy See, quietly complied with National Socialist policies in order to secure the daily execution of their clerical tasks. They also took care to keep themselves out of the way of the Holocaust. They may have despised the Nazi state and the brutality of its minions. On the "Jewish question," however, their collective conscience could rarely be stirred into protest. The pogroms of religious anti-Semitism belonged to the Dark Ages. Their poisonous beliefs, however, after centuries of Christian indoctrination, were far from dead: The Jews, who had crucified Christ, and who for 2,000 years had refused to atone for their sin through the holy sacrament of baptism, were hardly the people on whose behalf to jeopardize the sacred Church. Notes Cornwell, formerly an admirer of Pius XII who turned sharply critical of the pontiff as his research progressed: "Pacelli failed to sanction protest by the German Catholic episcopate against anti-Semitism. Nor did he attempt to intervene in the process by which Catholic clergy collaborated in racial certification to identify Jews, providing the essential information that aided Nazi persecution."[18] In short, Catholic priests (and Protestant clergymen) opened their *Kirchenbücher* (church registers) to expose those Jews who had chosen the Christian baptism in order to integrate with the majority. The Protestant clergy may have behaved even worse. In close cooperation with the SS Reich Center for Genealogy, the Church Register Office for Old Berlin, under the direction of a Protestant minister and strong Nazi sympathizer, searched the city's church books back to 1800 to record "all Jewish blood" among baptized Christians. When Jewish deportations began in 1941, the SS had the results of those meticulous investigations done in Berlin and elsewhere already on hand.[19] I have often wondered how the SS was able to identify so many Jews in Germany, where integration had gone further than in any other European country. The fact that there were a great number of denunciations from neighbors, colleagues, and so-called friends cannot take away from those shocking revelations regarding the conduct of both Christian churches during the time of the Third Reich. In his extensive bibliography *The Hitler of History*, John Lukacs tries to be slightly more conciliatory about the Catholic clergy: "Among all of the institutions, including the Churches ... the record of the Catholic Church—of some of the bishops and priests as well as some of the Catholic population—was, relatively speaking, the least compromised and was sometimes even inspiring."[20]

There is one issue on which probably everybody agrees: In Pacelli's eyes, Nazi Germany was the last bulwark against Bolshevism's deadly threat to Christianity, even to the survival of the Church itself. Could his silence in the face of the Holocaust therefore be seen as a case of papal *realpolitik*, the wish to avoid at all costs the antagonism, or defeat, of the only power that stood between the hordes of Satan and the Holy See? Or was he entirely wrong even on that issue, choosing appeasement where strong language might have offered the only hope?

Few would claim that the Pope could have stopped the Holocaust by the moral force of his office. After all, in Stalin's immortal words: How many divisions has the Pope? But there can be no doubt that Pius XII's silence made Hitler and his entourage even more arrogant as they carried out their murderous plans; worse yet, it lightened the consciences of the ordinary people. If even the Pope didn't see fit to interfere, surely things could not be all that bad. Without trying to pass the buck, it seems impossible not to speculate: What if Pacelli had risked his German clerics' collective martyrdom at the hands of the SS by tearing up the Concordat? What if he had gone public about the Nazi murder machine in Catholic Poland? Official Church policy at the time (and still reiterated today) rejected any public intervention by the Pope because it could only worsen the situation. But would that have been true? Nobody will ever know. Lewy argues that a flaming papal protest would have run up against the "indifference of the German population toward the fate of the Jews, and the highly ambivalent attitude of the German (Catholic) hierarchy toward Nazi anti-Semitism ... (It) might well have led to a large-scale desertion from the Church."[21] Lewy may be right. But the fact is that Hitler and Goebbels were anxiously watching the Vatican's every move. It may also be interesting to know that, according to "common knowledge"—meaning information not contradicted by Goebbels's Ministry of Propaganda—Hitler never gave up his membership in the Catholic Church. He and Goebbels must have been well aware of the soothing effect on the country's Catholic population of the Führer privately distancing himself from the atheist ideology of his minions.

* * *

Until the end of the Hitler era and the terrible revelations of the Nazis' Jewish genocide, religious anti-Semitism, or anti-Judaism, was a widespread phenomenon in the Western world. But it was German xenophobia that traditionally rejected anything foreign, non-Germanic, together with German feelings of superiority over almost all other peoples and cultures, that allowed such ideological concepts as "master race" or "Jewish race" to find their popular acceptance.

Therefore, if it was religious anti-Semitism, overlaid with National Socialist racial ideology and nationalist paranoia, that facilitated the Holocaust, one could argue that the Roman Catholic Church with its supranational structure takes the place of a secondary, albeit powerful, player, whose primary commitment was non-German and non-nationalist. Conversely, the German Protestant episcopate, whose clergy frequently subscribed to religious anti-Semitism as well as a strong German nationalism, may well deserve some greater public scrutiny than it has generally received. As Goldhagen observes:

> ... even such knowledge [about the mass killings in the East] did not temper much of the [Protestant] Church leadership's hostility towards Jews and its support for the regime's policies ... On December 17, 1941, Protestant Evangelical Church leaders of Mecklenburg, Thuringia, Saxony, Nassau-Hesse (sic), Schleswig-Holstein, Anhalt, and Lübeck collectively issued an official proclamation which declared the Jews to be incapable of being saved by baptism, owing to their racial constitution, to be responsible for the war, and to be "born enemies of the world and Germany" (*geborene Welt- und Reichsfeinde*). They therefore urged that the "severest measures against the Jews be adopted and that they be banished from German lands"... With these words, the Protestant Church leadership of a good part of Germany ... on their own initiative, implicitly endorsed the mass slaughter of Jews.[22] (Quotation marks and italics by Goldhagen.)

Goldhagen, in his eagerness to demonstrate the German people's collective murderous instincts may have given an interpretation to the Church leaders' proclamation that goes way too far. After all, the notorious Wannsee Conference, which put the finishing touches on the Final Solution, took place on January 20, 1942, more than a month after the proclamation. Even so, the open endorsement of the abrogation of all civil rights and of the mass deportations of Jews to places outside Germany—clearly meaning concentration camps in Poland—strike me as being viciously anti-Semitic and dreadfully un-Christian. Moreover, those pious men, while serving God and Christ, not only suffered from a lack of compassion, but also from an all-too-ready sense of remorse: On October 18, 1945, in their famous Stuttgart Declaration, the German Protestant clergy stated "... that we not only feel united with our people in a great community of suffering, but also in a solidarity of guilt ... We accuse ourselves in that we did not confess more courageously, pray more faithfully, believe more cheerfully, and love more fervently." (My translation.) While the declaration was widely applauded as a great spiritual catharsis, I remember my own reaction, which was quite different. At such an early time, when each of us still had to cope, physically and emotionally, day and night, with the catastrophic consequences of the war, eager confessions of a monumental Christian failure struck me as sanctimonious. Also, the proclaimed community of suffering with "our people" sounded rather ingratiating, since most people who were bombed or expelled, who had lost their homes or providers, had suffered—and were still suffering—immeasurably more than the state-supported clergy. As for the solidarity of guilt, I felt that a lot more of it should be apportioned to God's professional servants than to the average person. How many ordinary Germans shared my heretical views is impossible to say. There can be no doubt, however, that the Stuttgart Declaration brilliantly succeeded in allowing the entire German Protestant clergy to rise above the bitter controversies about responsibility and guilt that were still to come and that would tear the country apart.

Looking back, it seems only fair to say that it was not intended that way. Rather than creating an instrument of instant absolution, the Declaration's principal author, Martin Niemöller, had clearly wanted to write a heartfelt and honest confession of guilt. A U-boat commander from Word War I, and later a pastor in Berlin, whom eight years of suffering in concentration camps had convinced of the collective guilt of all

Germans, he strove for an integrating community of guilt and faith. A proclaimed pacifist, Niemöller stood up against the politics of the Cold War, specifically West Germany's strong Western orientation, its re-armament, and its membership in NATO. He soon became a highly visible and controversial figure, who maintained contacts with East Bloc countries throughout the years of East–West confrontation. During the early 1930s, Pastor Niemöller had kept up a courageous fight against the Nazi government's efforts to bring the German Protestant Churches in line with National Socialist politics and ideology. As the founder of the Pastors' Emergency League (*Pfarrernotbund*) and the leading founder of the Confessing Church (*Bekennende Kirche*)—the only organized reli-gious resistance movement in the Third Reich[23]—Niemöller was arrested in 1937, and spent the rest of the Nazi years in the Sachsen-hausen and Dachau concentration camps. It was inevitable that the post-war German government would be eager to recruit this blue-ribbon resistance fighter into their midst. Unfortunately, Niemöller refused to play along. Instead, his unshakable belief in Germany's collective guilt, together with his socialist tendencies, made him a painful thorn in the side of German Chancellor Adenauer's *realpolitik*.[24]

History's judgment of the Churches' conduct during the Hitler era is controversial and dependant on whether one evaluates their resistance against National Socialism's anti-religious, or anti-Semitic ideology. There is also more personal bias on the side of historians than on almost any other aspect of the Nazi period. Take, for instance, the statement by Gerhard Ritter, a respected historian during the Nazi era, who was close to the resistance movement of the "Martyrs of July 20," and continued teaching long into the postwar years: "There can be no stronger proof of the popu-larity of the Churches' resistance in Germany than the fact that the tyrants never dared raise a hand against the bishops ..."(My translation)[25] Written in 1955, Ritter's uncritical enthusiasm for the Churches' alleged opposition to the Nazi government would probably raise a few eyebrows today.[26] In *Hitler's Pope*, John Cornwell distinguishes between Pacelli's appeasement faction within the Catholic hierarchy and its opponents, mostly simple priests who refused to hand over German political Catholicism to the Nazi government.[27] Goldhagen, true to form, considers only the anti-Semitic attitudes of the Church leaders: "... the eminent Protestant theologian Dietrich Bonhoeffer ... despaired at the flood tide of antisemitism that even his colleagues were then expressing. Shortly after Hitler came to power, Bonhoeffer wrote to a theologian friend that regarding the Jews 'the most sensible people have lost their heads and their entire Bible.' "[28] (Bonhoeffer was murdered in the Flossenbrück concentration camp on April 9, 1945, one month before the end of the war.)

To what degree did Nazi politics benefit from Pacelli's pressure on the German Catholic establishment to voluntary disengage from all political activities? Or differently asked: Had there ever been the realistic alternative of two rival authoritarian systems living side by side under a dictatorship? On the other hand: How politically important and spiritually influential was the Confessing Church? How nationalist, even National Socialist, were many of Germany's Protestant bishops and clergy? And the most important question for both Churches: How instrumental was the traditional anti-Judaism of the Christian establishment in ensuring compliance with Nazi policies by a great number of clergymen, even their silent acceptance of the mass deportations of the Jews? It is unlikely that anybody could come up with truly objective answers; too many personal and institutional hindrances and prejudices obstruct every reflection. Yet, it can hardly be denied that, faced with the people's surprisingly quick surrender to the massive onslaught of National Socialist ideology, neither Church stood firm on its Christian premises and principles.

Discussions of the Holocaust today center almost entirely on the racial anti-Semitism prevalent in pre-war German society, while religious anti-Judaism and widespread Nazi collaboration by both major Churches have largely been dropped from public scrutiny. It is only Pacelli's appeasement and his silence in the face of the Jewish genocide that maintains its presence in the German psyche. Five decades after the demise of the Hitler era, it is not the German Protestant clergy, publicly exculpated by their Stuttgart Declaration in 1945 (and greatly honored for their contribution to German reunification during the late 1980s), but ascetic, saintly Pius XII, the misguided diplomat and zealous Pope, who alone remains burdened with the Catholic Church's irredeemable failure during the years of the Third Reich.

Notes to Chapter 6

1 Thanks to the research of the Iserlohn *Stadtarchiv* (city archive), it seems almost certain that the place in question was the huge "Villa Elisabeth," originally owned by manufacturer Carl Ludwig Herbers at 53 Gartenstrasse. The house was built in 1876. After being sold in 1914, it had a number of users, including the municipality, a school, police, Wehrmacht, British SIS, and refugees. Along with the barracks in the park, it was demolished in 1966.

2 "Polish and Russian babies were separated from their mothers immediately after birth. The nursing staff was overworked and for the most part poorly trained. Until the end of the war, 365 children died from neglect and undernourishment. The supervising factory physician, Dr. Hans Körbel, who wrote *angeborene Schwäche* (congenital weakness) on the death certificates, was executed by a British military court on March 7, 1947." *Erinnerungsstätte zur Geschichte der Zwangsarbeit im Volkswagenwerk*, Editors: *Volkswagenkommunikation*, *Unternehmensarchiv*, Wolfsburg, p. 52.

Volkswagen's communications office further informed me that nurse Ella Schmidt, born in 1905, and with twelve years' experience in nursing, was also condemned to death, while nurse Liesl Bacher received a five-year prison sentence. Ella Schmidt's death sentence was later commuted to an unspecified prison term. It may be assumed that either Ella Schmidt or Liesl Bacher were identical with "Karla."

3 I have described the scene as it appeared to me at the time. The biographies of the most important *Ruhrbarone* (Encyclopaedia Britannica, *Enzyklopädie des Nationalsozialismus*) allow the following assumptions:

One of the arriving persons was almost certainly Gustav Krupp von Bohlen und Halbach (1870–1950), accompanied by his director(s), physician, and valet. As an enthusiastic Hitler follower and president of the *Reichsverband der Deutsche Industrie* (German Industrial Association), Krupp spent huge amounts of money (and urged others to do likewise) for the Nazi government. At the Nuremberg Trials of 1945/46, he was indicted as "Major Offender" (*Hauptschuldiger*) for "preparing a war of aggression." When it became clear that

Gustav would be unable to stand trial because of senility, his son Alfried (1907–67), during the following Krupp Trial, was indicted for mass looting in the occupied territories and exploitation of slave labour. He was sentenced to twelve years' imprisonment and confiscation of his possessions. On May 31, 1951, U.S. High Commissioner John McCloy pardoned Alfried (America needed his company's production for fighting the Korean War) and returned to him all his possessions. If the then thirty-eight-year-old Alfried was in Iserlohn in December 1945, he would certainly not have arrived in a Mercedes-Benz, since I had already met him two weeks earlier "through the fence" as a prisoner at Camp Recklinghausen, where he gave upbeat speeches before his adoring fellow Rhinelanders.

Friedrich Flick (1883–1972), Germany's richest man and Hitler's biggest financial backer (7.65 million *Reichsmark*), was arrested on June 13, 1945. He was convicted on Dec. 12, 1947 and sentenced to seven years' imprisonment and seizure of 75% of his wealth (estimated at one billion RM) for the use of slave labor. He was pardoned in August 1950. It is not clear where the sixty-two-year-old Flick spent the two years prior to his conviction. It is possible, though not very likely, that he took part in the "procession" which I watched.

Fritz Thyssen (1873–1951) supported Hitler's ascent to power with three million RM. He later distanced himself from the Führer and fled abroad. In 1941 he was captured in France and sent to concentration camps Dachau and Buchenwald, where his wife joined him voluntarily. Eighty-eight million RM were confiscated by the Nazis. In 1948 a German denazification court declared Thyssen a "Minor Offender" and garnisheed 15% of his fortune. An embittered Thyssen left Germany in 1950 for Argentina, where he soon died at age seventy-seven. There is no hint that Thyssen ever had anything to do with the Allied intelligence services.

4 Kogon, Eugen, *Der SS-Staat: Das System der deutschen Konzentrationslager* (Munich: Kindler, 1974), 208.

5 Hochhuth, Rolf, *Der Stellvertreter (The Deputy)* (Reinbek bei Hamburg: Rowohlt, 1963), 28.

6 Lewy, Günther, *The Catholic Church and Nazi Germany* (Da Capo Press, copyright 1964, First Da Capo Press Edition 2000), 309.

7 Cornwell, John, *Hitler's Pope: The Secret History of Pius XII* (London: Viking, Penguin Group, 1999), 296.

8 The party's president was Ludwig Kaas, a priest and close confidant of Eugenio Pacelli, (the future Pope Pius XII), whom he later served in the Vatican.

9 Cornwell, John, op. cit., ref. 7, 84.

10 ibid., 85.

11 Hochhuth, Rolf, op. cit., ref. 5.

12 Using his private funds, Rolf Hochhuth recently acquired a Berlin theatre, where he stages his own "reality plays" that have gone out of favour with younger impresarios, though probably not with the public.

13 Lewy, Guenther, op. cit., ref. 6, 337–341.

14 Cornwell, John, op. cit., ref. 7, 296.

15 Cornwell, John, ibid.

16 Numbers by Guenther Lewy, op. cit., ref. 6, 301. According to Lewy, a further 3,000 were hidden by Roman friends and neighbors, leaving 1,000 victims of the SS roundups.

17 Equally unknown is the exact number of Nazi war criminals who were saved from postwar prosecution by the Allies or their native countries through the "charitable work" of Bishop Alois Hudal, the head of the German church in Rome. Hudal came from Graz in Austria. Through false documents, he organized the escape of "thousands" of leading Nazis from Germany, Poland, Ukraine, Croatia, and other countries, to South America. Becoming an embarrassment for the Vatican, Hudal, in 1952, was forced to resign his office. (Lewy, Guenther, ibid, xxivff.)

18 Cornwell, John, op. cit., ref. 7, 296.

19 Gailus, Manfred, *Für Gott, Volk, Blut und Rasse* (For God, folk, blood and race), *Die Zeit*, No. 44, 2001.

20 Lukacs, John, *The Hitler of History* (New York: Vintage Books, 1998), 217.

21 Lewy, Guenther, op. cit., ref. 6, 303.

22 Goldhagen, Daniel J., *Hitler's Willing Executioners: Ordinary Germans and the Holocaust*, (New York: Alfred Knopf, 1996), 112.

23 The Confessing Church (*Bekennende Kirche*) was created in protest to the German Christians, a Nazi-supported "Aryanized" German Evangelical Church, led by Reich Bishop Ludwig Müller. While the German Christians remained at the religious fringe, the Confessing Church gained considerable support among the population, and hostility from the government. From the mid-1930s on, it suffered from internal confessional and political strife. Nazi pressure and the arrest of Niemöller and others in 1937 forced the weakened *Bekennende Kirche* underground.

24 Between 1961–1968, Niemöller was a president of the World Council of Churches. He received the Lenin Peace Prize in 1967 and West Germany's highest order, the Grand Cross of Merit (*Grosses Bundesverdienstkreuz*), in 1971.

25 Ritter, Gerhard, *Carl Goerdeler und die deutsche Widerstandsbewegung* (Stuttgart: Deutsche Verlags-Anstalt, 1955, 116).

26 During the early postwar years, the "leading and influential conservative histo-
    rian Gerhard Ritter [put forward] the thesis that the Third Reich had been a
    'technical accident' (*Betriebsunfall*) of history." Wickert, Ulrich, *Deutschland auf*
    Bewährung (Munich: Heyne, 1999), 219, 221.

27 Cornwell, John, op. cit., ref. 7, 144ff.

28 Goldhagen, Daniel J., op. cit., ref. 22, 109.

7

SENNELAGER

A clear winter night, snow blanketing the land, and the sky brilliantly lit by a myriad of glittering stars—a Canadian scene, experienced hundreds of times at my cottage near the shore of a river angrily growling against the shackles of its icy cover; always new, always wondrous, the untamed power of nature frozen into a glance that humbles the human observer. The smell of burning wood, sweet and acrid, rises from the chimney, white smoke bearing the warmth and hominess of my living room out into the frigid night.

Then, suddenly, the image transforms. It is not my cottage anymore, not the forbidding, yet strangely alluring, cold of a Canadian winter night. I am back at the Sennelager; after so many years, the memory still returns, unbidden, unmellowed by time.

The bright night, the dome of brilliant stars are delusions, of course; they must be. How many nights are there on the plains of northern Germany when the heavens are not shrouded by rain or fog? Furtively stolen moments they must have been, when the clean, cold air penetrated the lungs and the heart felt young and gloriously free and far from the squalor and misery of reality. Short glances of a starry sky, snatched during the early mid-winter darkness, the hour before lock-up, the pale moon rising over the dying day. Huddled figures dart among the shadows, fetching water from the outside taps. Thin curls of smoke drift over the long, orderly rows of barracks.

Then, the couplet begins its maddening tour, round and round in my head: *Gott, der Herr, in seinem Zorn / schuf die Senne bei Paderborn.* (God, our Lord, in His wrath / created the Senne near Paderborn.) *Boom-baboom-baboom-baboom / boom-baboom-baboom-baboom . . .*

Die Senne, short for Sennelager, or Camp Senne, extends over some fifty square miles northwest of the city of Paderborn, a bishopric and as "black" (Catholic) a city as Rome itself. A vast, flat and treeless terrain, the Senne used to be one of Germany's largest, and certainly its most detested, military training ground. Every soldier sent there spent weeks crawling on his belly through a three-inch layer of sand, eating dust, breathing dust, eyes red and itching, holding his precious rifle a foot above ground. The last to use the camp before Germany's surrender were Waffen SS units. There was no indication that they had enjoyed the Senne's amenities any more than the thousands of soldiers who preceded them. In any case, none of their officers insisted on the erasure of that blatantly subversive rhyme, scratched into every lavatory door. So close to the end of the war, they may have run out of time, or energy, or simply conviction. *Gott der Herr in seinem Zorn / schuf die Senne bei Paderborn.* Heavy boots stomping the desolate ground. *Boom-baboom-baboom-baboom / boom-baboom-baboom-baboom.*

Around and around...

I arrived at the Sennelager in a Jeep. There were no other prisoners in the vehicle. As I left the park-like grounds at Iserlohn, Bimbo had assured me that my return to camp would be a mere formality. Christmas was only days away, and my release would not come a day too soon. That I was not on my way back to Camp Recklinghausen, but to an entirely different camp, was a minor change that nobody had remembered to tell me.

"Don't you worry," the driver assured me, as he let me off at my new destination, "you'll be out before Christmas." A smile and a friendly wave, and off he went.

It didn't take long for me to realize that things were different at the women's compound of the Sennelager—not much different, but enough to cross the line between uncomfortable and unpleasant. While I was at Iserlohn, the Sennelager had increased its own substantial inmate population with transferees from Camp Recklinghausen; having spent only two weeks there, I didn't recognize anybody. During my absence, the groups from the two different camps had worked out some arrangement for amicable co-existence. If there was no universal love among the inmates, I saw no serious disagreements, either. Everybody seemed able to live within the established rules officially overseen by the *Frauenälteste*, the leader of the women's compound who, in turn, reported to a group of mostly absent and entirely indifferent Redcaps.

I don't remember anybody welcoming me at the gate. Maybe nobody did.

The barracks were much larger than the Nissen huts in Recklinghausen, with wider aisles between the beds. Bunks were stacked in two's instead of three's, their legs on the floor rather than in cans of petroleum. The Sennelager was bug-free, guaranteed by decades of German orderliness.

As I described in an earlier chapter, I was assigned the bunk above Marlies, the blonde Rhenish woman and one-person entertainment wonder. Her hostility towards me, the newcomer, was unprovoked but intense. Like toxic gas, it penetrated the wooden boards and the palliasse between us. The straw mattress, though thin, was a huge improvement over Recklinghausen, where there had been none. Over time, I would observe others stuffing their bags with straw appropriated from the sacks of released prisoners; access to the straw line, however, required seniority, which took months to acquire.

If my *Sonderfall* status had caused a certain coolness at Recklinghausen, Marlies' hostility, picked up by others, was in an entirely different league. It took me a while to figure things out; when I finally did, I was crushed by the realization that there was absolutely nothing I could do about my situation. The mere fact that I had spent weeks at mysterious Iserlohn created plenty of notoriety; being returned to camp rather than being released for home, as was still considered the rule, turned ugly suspicions into certainty. The British had gotten to me; I was an informer, for sure, a spy, planted among my fellow Germans.

To make matters worse, there was my wretched singularity—no pattern to fit into, no group to absorb me now that every woman had found her personal niche within the established order. It didn't take long for the hostility to become obvious. When, on my first night, somebody began ladling out the turnip soup, the only warm meal of the day, I found myself without utensils again. This time, however, there was no offer of help. Instead, I got plenty of gratuitous advice about where to find the necessary items to start up my own domesticity.

I found the place, all right. I don't know what I had expected from the gleeful instructions, but I could hardly have imagined that mix of sand and trash in a far corner of the compound.

This, then, was the measure of my new life—literally and metaphorically speaking. What lay beneath my feet, scattered, partly or entirely buried, were the pathetic remnants of some earlier existence, a soldierly existence, with things to use and things to discard. The discards had been turned over and picked over, and discarded again many times. I tried not to step on the disgusting debris, as I was looking in vain for anything useful. The grey afternoon light began to fade, and there was a drizzle. Cold, frightened, and desperately lonely, I knelt down and forced my fingers into the ground. The sand was wet and surprisingly firm. There was no way of knowing what lay beneath it, what my hands would touch, would come up with. Was there a smell? I don't recall. And I don't remember how long it took; but in the end I found it.

From that repugnant expanse of waste and sand I unearthed an honest-to-goodness ten-ounce can, which I would show to the others, who had clearly bet on failure. The can had a sharp edge and was brown from rust. I didn't care. Under the outside tap, I scrubbed it with fine-grained Senne sand. I even managed to dull its rim on the hard cement of the basin without bending the vessel out of shape. I was tremendously proud. I had created something using my own hands and wits, something vitally important and urgently needed. Over time, I would find more things, discover different uses for different discards. That day, unfortunately, my triumph was short-lived.

On my arrival in the morning, I had unwisely proclaimed that my stay would be temporary; that I had been released from Iserlohn and would be released from the Sennelager within days. After all, I was only repeating what I had been told by Salmon. Perhaps I felt provoked by Marlies' hostility and wanted to show off my "special status," which, after the personal attention and relative comfort experienced at headquarters, I had begun to consider as a privilege rather than a disaster. I was dreadfully naive and I had said about the worst thing I could have said, stupid and tactless. Looking back, I find it difficult to understand how I could have misjudged my situation so completely; how, finding myself back at camp and among the faceless thousands, I could still have believed in the *Dienstweg*, the bureaucratic process necessary to bring about my release. If the detour through the camp was a requirement, why hadn't they simply stamped my papers at arrival, then shipped me off to the nearest station? The question never occurred to me. And of course there would have been no answers, not then, and not today.

Marlies simply shrugged at my announcement; others laughed uproariously as word of my "preferred treatment" got around. After all, as veterans they recognized an informer when they saw one. And just so that there wouldn't be any further misunderstanding about my place within the community, the *Frauenälteste* advised me that I had been detailed for work at the wood-chopping site.

Granted, I was young and healthy, and I was new. There was no particular reason not to choose me for the hardest labor in the compound. Still—the German language has an expression which in the eyes of non-Germans is typical of the German character and therefore untranslatable. The offensive word is *Schadenfreude*, the nasty glee that a person's misfortune evokes in others. My assignment may have been routine, but it certainly generated a great deal of *Schadenfreude*. Not only had I boasted about some kind of special arrangement that would whisk me through the camp in no time at all, but I had completely overlooked the plight of others who had been imprisoned for close to a year. I had behaved like a fool, and the comeuppance for my hubris was swift.

Naturally, I didn't see it that way. I was furious over what I considered some mean and unjust treatment; I was unhappy, homesick, and desolate—but mostly I was cold.

I had never cut anything thicker than a piece of cardboard, never handled a saw, never lifted a six-inch trunk onto a sawhorse. The saws were dull, the wood green, and the drizzle unrelenting. And it was Christmas; the days before and the days after, the whole week I spent on the wood site. The other women, all of sturdy build and accustomed to hard work, took obvious pleasure in chopping and splitting the logs, assigning me to the lighter job of manning one end of a two-handled saw.

Most of them were ten or fifteen years older than I. God knows what political misdemeanors or outright crimes had brought them here. They could have come from a regular *Arbeitsdienst* camp, or from some Nazi minister's private kitchen, or a concentration camp. None of them talked with me much, just the minimum necessary to get the job done. To them I was just a spoiled youngster who had never seen an honest day's work, which of course was true. They may have felt contempt for my poorly developed skills, but they were not vicious or vindictive. And they genuinely felt sorry for my lack of outdoor clothing, for which they had no cure. I still wore what I had worn when first imprisoned: a tailored jacket over a tweed skirt.

In the end, this was what saved me from a prolonged stay at the wood site in the middle of winter. There was nothing the authorities feared more than an epidemic, and my skimpy outfit must have looked like a welcome mat for every flu virus adrift. So I was permitted to stay "home," but that privilege soon turned out to be utterly boring. There was nothing to do but wait for food, parcel it into minuscule portions to be rationed over the day, and listen to others talk incessantly about dishes and recipes from a glorious pre-war past that lacked for nothing in haute-cuisine detail except a measure of probability.

Food was everything, because there was so little. It was constantly in one's dreams, the ones at night and the ones the mind makes up by day to torture itself. For the next five months, my daily diet consisted of a two-inch chunk of dark, heavy bread, with tiny portions of jam and margarine, and a bowl of turnip soup at lunch. I don't know what nutritional ingredients went into the soup besides turnips; my guess is, a few scoops of cereal starch on good days, less on others—there was no visible evidence of meat. Twice, however, there were exceptions.

The first occurred at Christmas, when each female prisoner received five medium-sized potatoes boiled in their skin, courtesy of the pious city of Paderborn. I don't know how many potatoes, if any, the men got. All I know is that the largesse, preceded by days of joyous anticipation, never recurred throughout my stay.

The second diversion from the staple menu took place sometime in February, when the awful turnips were unexpectedly supplanted by a fine-looking carrot soup, its sweet taste creating the illusion of a high-calorie diet. Unfortunately, after a few days of this delicacy, the carrots proved themselves a highly effective laxative, causing varying degrees of diarrhea among the inmates, and a profound aversion to the sweetish slop. It took much longer, however, for the kitchen staff to exhaust its ample supplies, and to restock with tons of trusty—though equally despised—turnips.

But if everybody hated the humble root, there was also another side to it, a bright and shiny side, even if only I was caught in its glitter. Indeed, it was that ugly clod, maligned by thousands, that was destined to shift my life into a new and entirely unexpected direction.

The *Frauenälteste*, having observed my growing listlessness, came up with the inspired suggestion: "Why don't you volunteer for one of the *Arbeitskommandos* (work details) at the hospital?" Her tone was friendly, though tinged with doubt about my basic suitability for any kind of physical work.

"Can I?" My unfeigned enthusiasm must have surprised her. "But how do I get in?" I had not failed to observe the daily comings and goings of a good number of women who, through channels I knew nothing about, were licensed to leave the compound for undisclosed purposes.

"You have to wait for a vacancy. I've heard you're a medical student. Maybe you can start in the hospital kitchen, and when they need somebody on the wards, you would be right there to move up."

It sounded simple, wondrously simple. I thanked her profusely. And, in my eagerness to embrace even the slightest expression of kindness, I promptly revised my earlier judgment of her as an aloof and unapproachable woman who found herself in an ambivalent position; she was not one of *them*, but not quite one of us either. Maybe she wasn't bad at all, just someone trying to make unpleasant circumstances tolerable for a mixed and crowded community. I was proud that she had noticed me, knew who I was and what I did. She had cared, the first person to do so. Better yet, she was true to her word: Within a week, I was told to be ready in the morning to leave for work in the hospital kitchen.

As I left with the other workers, the rest of the camp still asleep, I felt a warm glow of pride, gratitude, and accomplishment. Things were finally going my way. It was January, a new year. I had been in Camp Senne for almost three weeks—my discharge papers would be ready any day now. Meanwhile, I was relieved of the stupefying monotony, the mean jealousies and pinprick hostilities, the tall tales of amorous conquests, and the pretentious evocations of gourmet cooking.

Soldiers unlocked the gate of the women's camp, then led us along asphalt-covered paths bordered by high double fences which separated each compound from its neighbors. I felt elated, as though I had made an important step forward. The rain-soaked light of winter morning, the treeless sandscape subdued by acres of wire, corralling men and women like cattle, the inhumanity, the despair—nothing could touch me. I was optimistic, excited—and suddenly I could picture the day when I would leave this dreadful place for good; when I would finally be allowed to go home.

It was an illusion, of course, a silly dream. And it didn't last. Nothing had really changed. A dozen women had left that morning and would return at night—an escape from the boredom, perhaps some modest profiteering from the spoils of the workplace, but not one inch closer to freedom.

And yet, things would no longer be quite the same. My physical circumstances would improve, slowly at first, then faster, until a certain level of comfort would be attained. But as my captivity lengthened, as weeks rolled off the calendar, then months, and time became as meaningless as waves running up the shore of the ocean, hope would gradually fade, its space replaced by gloom. And from gloom would grow frustration and finally anger, as suspicion turned into certitude that in some mysterious and inexplicable way, my physical existence had been "misplaced;" that somehow, somewhere, a bizarre administrative foul-up had occurred that had transformed the spirited young student into a Kafkaesque character: The prisoner without a file.

*   *   *

The Senne camp's hospital was a large, solid building of yellow brick with a red-tiled roof and a broad staircase leading up to the main entrance. It was surrounded by a wide yard covered with asphalt and bordered by a perimeter of the ubiquitous fine-packed sand. If there had once been trees or shrubs to soften the landscape, they had long been replaced by army vehicles and strolling guards. Built to serve generations of German soldiers, the hospital was well-equipped with surgical and clinical facilities, and had spacious hallways and whitewashed rooms. Now, in the winter of 1945 to 1946, it was staffed and operated by imprisoned personnel, doctors and nurses, for the benefit of other inmates, whose cases were too serious to be treated at the sick bays attached to each compound.

On that first day of my new job, I was led to a large, somewhat dank area in a basement with a concrete floor and poor lighting and no hint of the fine equipment upstairs. There were a couple of long tables with heavy wood tops, on which stood huge tin vessels; long-handled cleavers and knives of various shapes were neatly arranged at each workstation. There was running water, but it was cold and came through a black hose, or from a brass tap serving a large basin—either way, ill-suited for personal hygiene. The targets of all this heavy-duty cleaning lay in a corner of the room beneath a delivery chute. Instead of a mound of coal which, in happier times, might have passed through that opening, there was now an enormous pile of turnips, in much the same condition as when they were dug up from their winter pits.

The turnips were heavy and slippery from dampness and rot. I was assigned the lowly job of runner. For the next few days, I ran from turnip heap to table and back, keeping the cleavers supplied. Although I managed only one turnip per trip, where others might easily have handled two, I did make some progress: Piling up a half-hour's supplies near their feet, I was temporarily allowed to join the women at the chopping table.

True, I had never cut up a turnip in my life, but there didn't seem to be all that much to it. After all, I was a real pro in potato-peeling, the proud legacy of seven months of labour service. But, as I would quickly find out, nothing in the artistry of potato-peeling prepares a person for the intricacies of turnip-slicing. The knives were dull and the turnip wedges produced by the cleavers too large to grip firmly with fingers stiff from cold. Yet others could do it and did it quickly, without letting a piece slither away, skip across the table, and plop lustily onto the messy floor. I don't remember whether I cut my fingers; I probably did. But somehow I stuck it out. I even got better, though not by much. And the women were kind, kinder than at the woodyard. They showed me how to slice and slice again, how to push the slices into neat little stacks, and to carve these up once more so that in the end there was a trim little pile of golden bricks, glistening from their sweet juices and smelling fresh and agreeable.

We ate all day. We chopped and sliced and talked, while chewing the crunchy vegetable—so different from its soupy reincarnation at lunch. From the day I joined the turnip gang, hunger had lost its sting. But mostly I gained the feeling of companionship, of being included in other women's banter, their coarse jokes and barking laughs. I was still considered an outsider—how else could I be perceived by those formidable housewives, Rhenish in figure and temperament, and bonded together by happy memories of a shared National Socialist past? Each woman's defining characteristic was her status as an automatically arrested member of this or that Nazi outfit. They had been "organized," they still were; I was not. But, away from the barracks and its web of old loyalties, they were nice enough in a hands-on, can-do sort of way, making good-natured fun of me rather than cutting me down. When, a little after a week, word came down from Internal Medicine that a nurse was needed on the ward, and that I had been chosen for the position, they all cheered me on. As I took my leave, I was more nervous than I cared to admit, and somewhat saddened to part so soon from those who had just become willing to adopt me into their circle.

I don't remember much about the days I spent clad in a striped dress with a white apron and cap, what I did or how I got along with the other nurses. The work was largely routine. Though the hours were long, I had no trouble performing my duties, thanks to varied experiences gained as a nurse during semester breaks and at the army hospital in Austria.

With thousands of prisoners to draw from, the hospital's 300 beds were never sufficient to fill the most urgent needs. Even so, when a priest from the local diocese expressed a desire to share the reality of an internment camp, the British commander was quick to comply. The priest was given a nice room on the hospital's ground floor, with a wash basin inside and shower stalls and flush toilets down the hall. It wasn't exactly "reality," of course; neither were the clean sheets and warm blankets, the towels and toilet paper that came with it. Reality was two thousand feet away, beyond the high fences, barbed wire, and armed guards; a reality that starved, shivered, and feared, but did not impinge on the missionary work of the pious man.

With a group of other nurses, I watched from an upstairs window as the hospital's administration took steps to accommodate, with military precision, the priest's wishes: An army truck arrived, and four patients were returned on stretchers to their compounds, two at a time. Orderlies then removed three beds which were no longer needed. Later in the day, a Jeep brought the priest from the nearby town, and the young driver helped the man in the black frock with his luggage. I worked on the second floor and had not known any of the four patients, but I thought it might be difficult to forget that little incident—and I never did.

Just as I never forgot seeing a man die. I knew he was dying, and I sat there with him and waited until he was dead. It was the first time I witnessed a death. Afterwards, I was saddened because of the terrible waste. The man may have been in his late twenties. He was tall, and had once been strong and won an Olympic medal. I don't know what kind of medal, they just said he had won it. When he died, he was terribly emaciated. His face was pointy with a long nose and protruding cheekbones over hollow stretches that ran into deep lines around his mouth. He never opened his eyes. But it was the hair that really told about his state of privation. A faded blond, it receded into thin, dried-out wisps, which seemed to belong to a man thirty years older. How and where he had gotten into that condition, I never learned; neither did I know the reason for his presence in the camp. When I was assigned to his care, he was already beyond talking. In the end, his kidneys failed, allowing him to pass away in the insensate grace of a deep sleep.

There was a simple chapel in the building and I went there for the *Totenmesse* (mass for the dead). Two or three patients were there, Catholics, like the deceased. I felt strange among them, mystified and excluded by the ritual. Uncertain how to behave, I sat quietly on my chair, hands folded and eyes fixed on the narrow coffin crudely fashioned from unstained boards. There were no flowers, of course, no ribbons or candles to console the survivors, if not the erstwhile Olympian. Later, I learned that the casket was regular army issue, to be returned after use. A sheet was provided for the body, though, or so they said.

*   *   *

I was told about my promotion to clinical lab work by the *Chefarzt* (head physician), whom I will call Dr. Hoffmann, since I don't remember his name. He was a tall man who held himself slightly stooped, as though his daily examination of dozens of bedridden patients had made him reject a straight-backed posture as an effort no longer worth his while. His blond hair had greyed at the temples and was kept short, military style. A quiet man in his early forties, he emanated competence rather than authority. He maintained a friendly distance, which he occasionally bridged with self-deprecating humor. Like his colleagues, Dr. Hoffmann had been an officer in the Waffen SS, whose uniform he still wore. Whether they had been transferred from a POW camp to a political internment camp as a matter of routine, or whether there had been other, more serious reasons, I never knew.

The doctors, regardless of their political pasts, automatically enjoyed the status of demigods, whose high medical calibre nobody doubted. Like every female on staff, I glowed in their benevolence towards lesser mortals, going, as time would show, to extraordinary lengths to seek not only their professional approval, but some ever-so-modest degree of personal attention.

"You simply have to help us out," Dr. Hoffmann declared as he stopped me in the second-floor hallway. Although he had never talked to me before, he confronted me with my transfer to the hospital's clinical laboratory as something already decided. He didn't invite me to sit down or allow me time to think things over. He was in charge, and the request was an order.

"One of the girls in the lab is no longer here. She did something stupid, a letter or something. Anyway, the *Kommandant* has ordered her privileges withdrawn. She is back at the camp." He shrugged. As I would later learn, the woman had been an experienced clinical technician and well-liked. She had tried to smuggle a note out of the camp, and the person entrusted with it had been caught. It was one of the more serious transgressions, and despite his friendly relations with the CO, Dr. Hoffmann was unable to save the woman. He was clearly frustrated. As an internist, a smoothly functioning lab was his lifeline. Without it, his medical expertise would be little better than shamanism.

Impatiently, he continued: "We'll teach you. There's another girl here who's quite good. Her name is Inge. She's no professional *Laborantin*, but she has learned on the job. So will you." He smiled. "You study medicine—that sort of thing shouldn't be beyond you." He turned to leave. "Are you coming?"

"Now?" I was full of doubt. I was elated by the promotion, certainly, but instinct told me that things couldn't possibly be that easy. I remembered a girl from high school who, after graduation, entered a two-year course to become a lab technician. What skills had she acquired over twenty-four months, and what was I expected to do with no training at all? "I'd better tell the head nurse," I stalled.

"She already knows."

The decision that had been made entirely without my participation would lead to a number of results, all positive: By providing me with paper, towels, soap and the use of a clean shower and toilet, my new job immediately eliminated the worst hardships of prison camp. Over time, it would yield valuable dividends for my medical career, as it helped me gain considerable proficiency in lab work, as well as a good understanding of its value and limitations for clinical diagnostics. But, most importantly, in a circuitous way, it would bring about an end to my inexplicable situation. It would take time, but eventually my work would connect me with people willing and able to reactivate my file—and my life.

That morning, however, I felt mostly nervous and less than enthusiastic about my startling career change—emotions that would soon enough prove to be justified as events went from difficult to bad to outrageous, like the script of a modern farce.

Inge was a sweet-looking girl, pretty in a way that all my cousins were and I was not, because of the genes brought into the family by my black-haired mother. With her straight, blond hair, blue eyes and athletic figure, Inge epitomized the nordic race and rosy German womanhood.

Whenever I picture a model youth leader, a strapping *Jungmädelführerin*, I remember Inge. Complementing her healthy looks was a keen intelligence. In short, Inge was a born leader. Had I been a follower, things might have been different. But I was not.

During most of the twelve years of Nazi *Volksgemeinschaft* (community of the people), I had at first been too shy and later too bored to bother with *Führerschaft* (leadership), or any other "ship or "*schaft*" that entailed forcing fun and discipline on a gang of unenthusiastic youngsters. Every high school student had felt the pressure to sign up for *Führerschaft*, and to dedicate time and effort to the ideological, mental, and physical improvement of others less privileged or less interested. I didn't want to lead, but I most certainly didn't want to be led. That need for personal independence (to put a positive spin on a rather selfish attitude) had complicated my life in the Hitler Youth as well as in the Labor Service. In Inge I had met my match. Under the circumstances, she was in charge, and she knew it. As things turned out, she also used it.

The recognition of our basic incompatibility was mutual and instantaneous. To begin with, she was smaller and younger than I was, if by only a few months. Considering her age, she had reached an unusually high rank within the Nazi girls' organization, a fact that filled her with pride. Inge oozed *Jungmädelschaft*. It was easy to imagine that she had been good at sports, singing, marching, recorder playing, or setting up camp. If punishment was the intent, whoever had sent her to the Sennelager had failed dismally. Inge was perfectly organized and right at home. That she had been chosen for some complicated job, which she had never done before, was simply in the nature of things: For anyone looking for somebody competent, Inge had to be the choice.

Dr. Hoffmann introduced us and told her to teach me everything she knew as quickly as possible. His tone was amiable, even warm. He clearly liked and trusted her. When he was gone, Inge embarked on a three-hour crash course entirely for my benefit. She was friendly, efficient, and perfectly focused. I watched her as she handled glass tubes and bottles, microscope, centrifuge, acetic acid, sodium hydroxide, ether, alcohol and Fehling solution, her hands working with speed and dexterity. She showed me how to test a sample of urine and to prick an earlobe for a blood specimen. We measured hemoglobin, counted cells, and studied their shapes. As I stood beside her, it all looked very smooth and relatively easy.

Measured against a civilian lab, let alone a modern one, our facilities were limited, even primitive. They nevertheless gave the physicians most of the essential data for their clinical diagnoses. As long as our little outfit did not overlook an abnormal blood smear, a high sedimentation rate, or substances in the urine that didn't belong there, the doctors could probably take it from there.

Naturally, I didn't understand all that much of what Inge had taught me; and by the next morning I realized that almost nothing had stuck through the night. But not to worry—Inge would handle the lab until I was properly trained. She would show me again, and, if necessary, again. After all, there were patients at stake, not to mention the orders from Dr. Hoffmann to instruct me.

Unfortunately, this is where our incompatibility got in the way. Inge was too clever to blatantly withhold her help and risk angering Dr. Hoffmann; his disappointment would have mortified her, as she had a poorly veiled crush on the great man. Instead, she allowed herself to fall ill.

As the rest of the hospital workers assembled at the gate, someone from her barracks reported her sick. To say I was shocked badly understates my emotional response. I felt paralyzed, stiff with dread over the situation I suddenly faced. The night before, Inge had looked perfectly healthy. Was there possibly some connection between her sudden malaise and my being parachuted into the lab? Had wholesome, honest Inge, that paragon of young German womanhood, resorted to such cheap and transparent subterfuge? There was no further information to be had. The women I asked just shrugged, then trudged silently into the dismal dawn.

Later, however, as word of Inge's surprising illness worked its way through the barracks, condemnation was swift and unanimous. I, on the other hand, received a great deal of sympathy on my return from the hospital, something which touched me, even if it failed to console me.

That morning, on arrival, I was welcomed by a group of men patiently waiting in one corner of the room. Since the lab had no separate waiting area, they would stand or sit there until their names were called. On a large table in another corner, also waiting for my ministrations, were a dozen tin cans of various shapes and sizes, pressed into service as urine containers by the sickroom attendants of outlying compounds. Alongside there, the proper glass receptacles for in-house patients were arranged.

Ignoring the urine collection, I boldly set out to attend to the waiting men. For the next two hours, my recollections are blurred. There are snapshots trapped in my memory of punctured veins and a mutilated ear, the long, whitish lobe of a very anaemic man I cut so badly that he later needed a stitch. Surrounding each bravely smiling victim was a chorus of soldierly encouragements—"Hold still, man, or the Miss will hit your carotid."; "Watch it buddy, you're all pale."; "Don't worry, Miss, he's been through worse than a couple of cuts from the tender hand of a beautiful lady."—cheerful inspirations to alleviate their fright as much as mine. It didn't do any good, of course. The blood I managed to draw into sedimentation tubes promptly leaked out; smears from blood drops were far too thick and entirely useless. So were all the other data.

Looking back, I wonder where I got the nerve to even consider handling those instruments, the counting chamber, the microscope. What had I hoped to accomplish? The only explanation that comes to mind is habit—the habit of following orders, no matter how ill-conceived or downright asinine. Obstacles, we were taught, were only there to be overcome. In the Nazi educational system, there was no contingency for failure. Wherever the Party, the military, the war put you, you coped or you tried your hardest. Over the last two years, I had tried to cope with a catheter pulled out from an old man's prostatic bladder; I had handled putrefied wounds wrapped in crepe-paper bandages; I had dealt with being bombed, imprisoned, interrogated—always squeezed between the unexpected event and the blocked retreat. To run for help was simply not an option. Perhaps that morning, trying to cope, no matter what, was all I could think about.

Meanwhile, word got around that Inge had absented herself from the lab and that, under the sole attendance of the new technician, the situation there had deteriorated to crisis conditions. When Dr. Hoffmann arrived at the scene, he found a group of wildly cheering patients surrounding one flushed and flustered bungler.

The doctor had a young man in tow whom he introduced as Dr. Clausen,[1] an internist like himself who, Hoffmann explained, might profit from a refresher course in lab practices. Then, in a quiet and efficient way, he began to demonstrate techniques. He didn't comment on the bloodied cotton and discarded tubes testifying to two hours of struggle; nor did he disgrace me in front of the patients. He acted swiftly and naturally, and suddenly the various tasks didn't seem quite so forbidding. When he was done with the patients, he turned to the disgusting collection of urine containers. Over the Bunsen burner, he tested a few specimens for sugar and albumin, then centrifuged two pointed tubes in a little machine attached to the table top. After turning the crank for a couple of minutes, he poured off the urine in a quick movement and put a drop of the sediment under the microscope. The demonstration completed in a little over an hour, Hoffmann departed, leaving us awed and determined not to fail the great man again.

We started by taking turns at the crank of the centrifuge, a primitive gadget meant for a country doctor's office, and hopelessly slow at processing five dozen samples a day. But, it was all we had, and neither of us had heard of labor-saving devices.

(Most of my memories are focused on one little knife, a poorly sharpened, narrow steel blade which served to puncture a patient's lobe. Not until a couple of years later, while doing clinical work at a civilian hospital, did I come across the miraculous snappers that could pierce an ear to the proper depth in a split second, ten times out of ten. I clearly remember my delight. I don't recall any sterilization or exchange of blades, however, other than for reasons of bluntness, since the risk of hepatitis B transmission by doctors and technicians didn't become widely recognized in Germany until the early 1950s.)

Over the next few days, Dr. Clausen and I honed our skills, while bringing the lab back to near-normal conditions. Thanks to my partner's clinical knowledge, the technical data quickly fell into logical patterns that I found easy to understand and remember. I loved the work. I even became reasonably good at it. Demands from the wards to repeat a test because of some highly unlikely results stopped after a few days. Dr. Clausen showed me how to draw blood from a vein without creating a bruise. In most cases it was easy, because the patients were so emaciated that their vessels stood out like river systems.

Inge returned after a week or two. If she was surprised by my newly acquired dexterity, she didn't show it. Instead, she graciously complimented me for having held the fort, at first with Dr. Clausen, and then on my own after he was recalled to his ward. She displayed all the pleasantness and warmth that her talented persona had to offer, and we became good friends who trusted and helped each other during those endless grey winter months.

*　　*　　*

We worked seven days a week. I might have mistrusted my memory on this particular point, had there not been one outstanding aspect: Our Sunday afternoon "social hour." Not that we used that expression, or any other. We didn't have to. Those hours were simply the uncontested highlight of the week, the centrepiece of a cheerful covenant.

In hindsight, it all looks terribly trite. But, at the time, it had the effect of a wonderful drug that could make us forget the misery of the rest of the week: the cobwebs of fog and drizzle that hung in the fences, the monotonous twice-a-day march, the bored young guards with their ruddy faces and dull eyes, the drab evenings in the crowded barracks; a week that had passed only because it had been in the way of another week, equally empty and without purpose. Our Sundays were like tiny beacons stuck in the sand of a timeless void.

I secretly suspected these gatherings had been regular events long before my arrival at the lab, making me more of an interloper than a co-founder. Inge never spoke about it, but the authority with which she organized the preparations clearly relegated me to second place. Either she possessed some long-standing experience, or her on-the-spot inventions were unbelievably clever. I didn't ask; I didn't want to know. But this is how it worked.

We started on Mondays by saving a small section of bread from our daily rations. That section was then consumed on Tuesday, and a slice of twice the thickness reserved for Wednesday, by which time the spared portion had tripled. And so on until Sunday, when both of us had collected a seventh of our weekly allowance, which we cut up into very fine slices. Using the Bunsen burner and some steel netting, the bread was then carefully toasted to some stone-age version of today's factory-perfect Graham crackers. There were tiny quantities of jam and margarine, also saved from our rations and neatly arranged on watch glass dishes. And there was tea. Where and how it was obtained, I never learned. Black-marketing with the guards was a perilous business, and whoever had established such contacts obviously didn't reveal the details.

The preparations completed, Inge would knock on a door, through which Drs. Hoffmann and Clausen would enter. (None of the other doctors ever participated, though they all maintained an amiable and helpful relationship with us.) We greeted our guests politely, even respectfully, and they responded in a friendly and somewhat fatherly manner. After all, they were both family men. The subject of their children came up frequently, and old snapshots were circulated and amusing stories shared. There was never any departure from the most proper conduct; everybody behaved even a touch more formally than during working hours. The doctors usually had a couple of cigarettes to add to the bounty, and these were ceremoniously passed from hand to hand in an equitable and companionable manner. In black market currency, they were worth a fortune and practically unobtainable by lesser captives.

What did we get out of these occasions? Why did we make such sacrifices at a time when food was at a premium? To enjoy a measure of dignity, mostly. Given the care we took in setting the table, in trying to recreate a world accessible only in our dreams, we must have experienced something of the excitement and pride our mothers felt as they got out their best china for a kaffeeklatsch. Did we flirt? Sure, that too, a bit; anything else would have been quite unnatural. We both worshipped Dr. Hoffmann, though looking back, he didn't seem unusually handsome or witty, let alone a ladies' man. Still, he was the man in power, a strong aphrodisiac under any circumstances—even if that power didn't extend beyond the walls of the hospital. To him we may have been just a couple of silly girls, nice to look at and quite amusing. He never made a pass. Perhaps I should modify that statement: If he had a relationship with Inge, I was too naive to discover it.

*   *   *

As weeks dragged into months, an increasing number of women prisoners were released, steadily improving conditions for those of us left behind. As soon as a cot was vacated, its boards were smashed up and burned in the happily glowing wood stove. Initially, the wilful destruction of military property was anxiously watched by everybody in the barracks. But, when reprimands from the Red Caps failed to materialize, it became clear that internment rules were becoming more relaxed, giving way to wild hopes that the whole scheme was slowly dissolving. (It wasn't, at least not yet.)

Over time, my own life, divided between barracks and hospital, reached a level of physical comfort that probably was not all that different from conditions outside, which I knew were badly crowded and at poverty level for anybody not connected to the black market. With bunks no longer stacked and the remaining ones spread out, I had moved to the far corner of the room with a window on the side. I had two mattresses, two blankets and whatever I needed for storage or dishes, all inherited from lucky dischargees. From hospital supplies, I had appropriated soap, shampoo, toilet paper, and menstrual pads. I even had a new skirt, cut from the coarse denim of a straw mattress, and sewn together by my own hand. I was immensely proud of my handiwork, which I planned to wear beneath my frayed old skirt on the day of my release. I would have to pray the guards didn't find it and send me back on charges of theft.

As the number of releases increased, the atmosphere in the barracks became more relaxed, at times even cheerful. Gradually, the sting of suspicion that had isolated me from the crowd during earlier months was replaced by friendly acceptance, a gratifying development that was aided by my long absences during the day and a general and generous respect for my work. It was a slow process, drawn out over weeks. Preoccupied as I was at the lab, I didn't particularly notice my improving popularity, nor did I really care any longer. And yet, when my turn to leave finally came, and one of the women stepped into my path to present me, in the name of the others, with a farewell gift, the gesture completely bowled me over. Just as when, many weeks earlier, Marlies's gift of a bra had turned my twenty-first birthday into one of the most memorable ever, I was deeply moved by my farewell gift: a large and beautifully decorated carrying bag, patiently crafted by one or more women from thousands of fine threads pulled from a paillasse. It was a most thoughtful gift, meant to replace my old bag which, as the women had quietly noticed, had long lost its handles and much of its fabric.

*   *   *

As it happened, there were two Dr. Hermanns working at the hospital. To distinguish one from the other, people referred to their epithets: Dr. Hermann-*blutig* did the "bloody" work of a surgeon, while Dr. Hermann-*unblutig* held the "bloodless" job of interpreter assigned to the camp commander. It was Hermann-*unblutig* who came to my rescue in the end, though I never found out exactly what he did or how it all worked. But, once the connection was made, things started to roll.

It all began during one of our Sunday social hours with Hoffmann and Clausen. I don't remember how the subject came up. Perhaps anger and frustration had reached a point that started me off talking about my own case, something one rarely did. I mentioned my *Sonderfall* status, which clearly surprised the good doctors, who had simply taken for granted that I had been a Hitler Youth leader like Inge. Encouraged by their interest, I spoke of my stay at Iserlohn (which surprised them even more) and my suspicion that somehow, somewhere, my file had been lost, gone astray, or fallen through the cracks.

It was the end of April. There were many fine days now, when Inge and I would spend the lunch hour outdoors. With our backs against the warming bricks of the wall, our faces caressed by the spring sun, every part of our young bodies sensed the new life trying to reawaken this barren stretch of abused land. For the first time in months, we spoke of dreams all but forgotten, about things we had lost, and of things we hoped would still be waiting for us when we went home.

When we went home ... The cocoon-like numbness in which I had wrapped myself suddenly lifted. I was overcome with anger at the prospect of more empty months piling up on the heaps of time already wasted, with no end to my captivity in sight. I had been imprisoned since late October, and held in the Sennelager since Christmas. As far as I could tell, nobody had yet established any reason for arresting me in the first place, let alone for keeping me detained for an indefinite period.

During a long and unusually cold winter, I had occupied my mind with the work I loved and looked forward to every new morning. I had learned to keep my senses dulled to the fact of being a prisoner. Surely, camp life was abnormal, but not that much worse than outside, where hunger and shortages were the order of the day. Or so I had told myself whenever reality had threatened to smash the cocoon. But now that spring and sunshine had returned, the dismal reality of being incarcerated, of not being free, of not being able to do what I wanted, when or where I wanted it, suddenly became intolerable. (That kind of freedom didn't exist anywhere in Germany, of course, but, seen from the inside, the outside looked rather rosy.) The mud now turning into dust and sand, the fences and barbed wire, the guards, rifles, and watchtowers inflamed my sense of justice. I couldn't, I wouldn't sit still any longer; things had to change, I had to get out. Now. Somebody had to listen. Four months after having been checked and double-checked by Britain's security brass, there wasn't a reason in the world to keep me one more day.

I worked myself into a fine steam, which I vented on Dr. Hoffmann, who accepted it all with a patient smile. Trying to keep me from going over the top, he insisted that his own limited powers were strictly clinical and definitely not along such political lines. But he did come up with a suggestion, one which surprised me because it was so obvious. I should talk to Dr. Hermann-*unblutig*, he said, who, as the interpreter, had the commander's ear and might be persuaded to bring up my case. Hoffmann promised to make the connection. But when he saw my excitement, he warned me not to expect too much. After all, there were ethics involved, a code of conduct inherent in an interpreter's position, that sort of thing. I hardly listened. I knew Dr. Hermann by sight. On occasion, I had seen him walk down the corridor accompanying the commander, but had never spoken to him. Intercepting the steps of the CO must have seemed as outrageous an idea as blocking the path of God.

Hoffmann made good on his promise. After a couple of days, I received word that I was to meet the interpreter at such and such a time. Alone. Well, if the meeting turned out to be not exactly private—taking place, as it did, in a corner of the hallway—it didn't seem to generate any particular interest among other staff either. Still, I was terribly nervous.

Hermann was a bespectacled man my father's age, of above-average height with slightly stooped shoulders and a worried expression. His hair, a dull mix of brown and grey, was thin and stringy. Given his military environment, Dr. Hermann-*unblutig* looked decidedly unheroic. Like the commander and the priest, he didn't wear a white coat; unlike these two, he was in baggy, ill-fitting, civilian clothes. He listened politely to my long and convoluted story, giving no indication whether he believed it. Neither did he let on whether he would allow himself to become my highly irregular conduit of protest.

I didn't particularly like him. He seemed cold and distant and more like one of them than one of us. He had the reserved demeanor of a high school headmaster.

That night, I was overcome by a depression bordering on despair. I knew that I had explained myself poorly to the interpreter. I had been disorganized and defensive rather than cool and detached. Worse, the moment I began, I recognized the enormity of my imposition. By then it was too late to stop. Now, because of my impudence, I was convinced, I would never get out. There had to be a reason for my continued detention, a plan, a conspiracy in which I had an unwitting part to play.

During the days that followed, I became listless and uncommunicative. But, when a whole week passed, and another, and a third, I slowly managed to put distance between myself and an initiative which, in hindsight, seemed brazen and bizarre. How could I have dared? A girl, and one of the youngest people among thousands? I concluded that I had gone too far, that it had been completely counterproductive—probably causing vexation in high circles—and I forced myself not to think about it any longer. Instead, I tried to concentrate on my work, which in any case continued to demand all of my attention.

*   *   *

There are eight stamps on the two sides of a document entitled RELEASE FROM CIVILIAN INTERNMENT CAMP. The paper is of wartime quality, yellowed and frayed, the words barely legible. Yet the stamps are still clear, making it possible to reconstruct the time and process it took to bring about my release.

Assuming that my conversation with Dr. Hermann took place during the last week of April, and that he had—despite my gloomy expectations—promptly approached the commander, the response to the good doctor's intervention must have been swift indeed. The earliest date on the document is "26 Apr 1946," when somebody filled in the details on the dotted line: "To Allied Military Personnel: This is to certify that Mackprang Gertrud Hilde, a German citizen resident of Hamburg–Harburg, was on 2 May 1946 released from No 5 Civilian Internment Camp unconditionally."

Never mind the convoluted syntax and the dates on the document: On May 2, I was still a full-time prisoner without a clue about my lucky prospects already confirmed on 29 April 1946 by GENERAL STAFF, INT. I CORPS (signature) COL GS, HEAD, RUHR INTELLIGENCE LIAISON STAFF. Wherever the head of Ruhr Intelligence Liaison Staff resided, it surely was nowhere near the Sennelager, a.k.a. No. 5 Civilian Internment Camp, as it took eighteen more days for the certificate to thread its way through bureaucratic channels. It was on May 17 that the almost no-longer-expected event finally occurred, as documented by a stamp confirming that on that particular day, I received *Warmverpflegung*, a warm meal, at Hannover railway station, halfway between Hamburg and Paderborn.

Nobody else was freed that day. The *Lagerälteste* accompanied me to the gate. She had been there when I first arrived, and she was still a prisoner when I left. She was friendly and solicitous in a motherly way, and wished me the best of luck. Then she handed me over to the guard, who accompanied me to an office near the gate, where I received my release

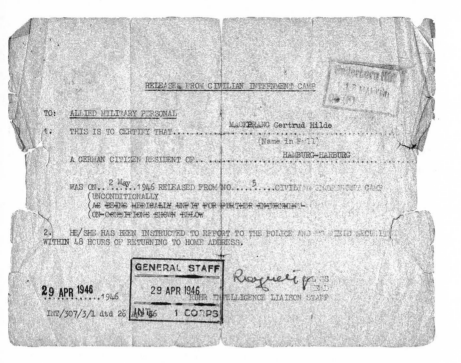

papers along with a string of admonitions. Numbed by excitement, my ears clogged by a crazy buzz, I was unable to follow the officer's instructions, instantly forgetting all of them with the exception of the one that was written down: Within the next three days, I was to report at an address at Harvestehuder Weg in Hamburg. I agreed to everything, signed whatever I had to sign and, still in a daze, climbed into a British military vehicle for the last time in my life. Half an hour later, the driver dropped me off at the Paderborn railroad station, where I waited till early afternoon for a train to pass through. I reached Hamburg the next morning, after a trip that lasted three times its normal length.

It was a dismal ride that testified at every stop to the desperate state of the country's economy. The bombed-out cities looked exactly the same as they had the previous October, at the start of my ill-fated trip to the Hilltrupp farm. The rail system, which had been seventy-five-percent destroyed, was still operating at an improvised level at best. There was some improvement, however. No longer in total chaos, the trains were now running on some kind of schedule, though it was vastly insufficient for the masses of people who were in desperate need of a service that was just barely functional.

In May 1946, one year after the country's surrender, millions of refugees, displaced persons, ex-POWs, expatriates, and other voluntary or involuntary migrants of more than a dozen nationalities were traversing Europe during mankind's greatest migration ever. Railroad stations were crammed with people waiting for trains that were often late and recklessly overloaded. There were no services to speak of at the stations, which mostly consisted of a couple of open platforms, with all other structures burned out or blasted away. Wherever the trains stopped, they were immediately surrounded by military police controlling papers, packages, and people—sorting out German civilians from refugees, soldiers, Nazi functionaries, black-marketeers, or travellers without papers. The last-mentioned, a large group, had nothing in common with one another but a lack of documented identity. Mostly from East European countries, they were people whose homes had been overrun by the war, burned or expropriated by the Red Army. Many were *Volksdeutsche,* German by blood and language, expelled by their adopted countries and *staatenlos* (stateless) with no place in the world to call home. Others, East European nationals mostly—but also Western members of the various foreign legions of the SS—couldn't go back to wherever they had come from, because as soldiers or civilians they had collaborated with the Nazi system. Most had prudently rid themselves of their German-issued uniforms and papers and now tried to lie their way out of trouble. How many there were, how many were caught, detained, released, and eventually given refuge somewhere, perhaps Canada, nobody will ever know, nobody can even guess. One of them had crossed my path the previous summer, while I was still staying with Josephine in Marburg.

One evening, shortly before dark and the onset of curfew, a tall, slim, soft-spoken young man in civilian clothes knocked at the door, asking for overnight shelter. He turned out to be an acquaintance of Karl, Josephine's husband. Formerly one of the 25,000 Waffen SS men Holland had contributed to Hitler's Russian campaign, he was now hiding from Allied military police while trying to reach Spain or Portugal. He vanished the next morning before we were up. On the kitchen table was a note. He thanked Josephine warmly for her hospitality (not an easy thing to give at the time, and certainly not without risk). Later, we discovered that he had availed himself of my bicycle, which he found in the basement.

I bristled with anger at the theft of this priceless and irreplaceable possession. Josephine, always inclined towards generosity, refused to acknowledge my dismay; in fact, she seemed to think me rather mean-spirited and
selfish. To keep the peace—and without any choice in the matter—I
swallowed my anger and tried for a bit of Christian compassion.

Amid the frantic and frightened masses that mobbed the trains wherever they stopped, there was charity too. Day and night, groups of
women in striped dresses and white aprons waited patiently at the edge
of the platforms. When a train arrived, they would pour coffee into the
hundreds of cups held out from the windows. For passengers with travel
permits, there were sandwiches and warm meals. I waved my "Release
from Civilian Internment Camp" at one of the women, hoping she
would stamp it for *Warmverpflegung*, a cup of hot pea soup or whatever
might be the menu of the day. She examined the paper, then asked in
surprise from which camp I had come. She clearly hadn't seen a document like this before, let alone in the hands of a young woman headed for
Hamburg. She called out to the others, and a group of women gathered
at my window, each of them apparently knowing someone who had been
interned. They asked for names and all sorts of things I didn't really want
to talk about. I didn't remember whether my release had carried a gag
order. But instinct told me that those who had just handed me back my
freedom, by the very character of their job, might not care for too much
publicity. I told the women that I had been at the Sennelager, but that I
had not become really close with anybody, and besides, I hadn't been
there all that long. They nodded and smiled; they understood my
dilemma. I received a hefty sandwich along with a cup of hot soup, my
first turnip-free meal in months.

My parents were glad to see me, and there were hugs. But there were
no tears. Throughout the months of captivity, whenever I had dreamed
up the scene of my homecoming, I had imagined some replay of the way
things had gone when I had returned from Marburg the first time after
the war. Then, we had all cried in a magnificent paroxysm of joy, which
washed away years of terror and grief. It was also an experience of great
bonding, inclusive as it was cleansing. For once, my parents and I had
been on precisely the same wavelength. Their tears mingled with mine,
as together we put the grim past behind us to face a future that would be
free of fear and quite wonderful.

Well, things hadn't turned out all that great, certainly not for me. And now that I had returned a second time in the role of lost daughter, there was no repeat performance of that cathartic scene. Everybody was much too busy, and there simply was no time or taste for such outbursts. My older sister had a new boyfriend who, at that point, had not yet made his intentions clear. As he was to arrive later that morning, bread had to be baked, sandwiches made, and the laundry he had left behind on his previous visit folded and packed. As we were introduced, he welcomed me, the naughty little sister, with a spirited intimacy that lacked only the smack on the butt. He knew where I had come from, he declared, winking, but I looked much too healthy for any hard-luck story. Everybody laughed at his amusing ways. Wasn't it charming how he accepted the return of the family's black sheep?

Worse than the sudden requirements for additional food and accommodation was the embarrassment that my sudden return brought for my family. For months, they had been pestered by all sorts of solicitous inquiries by neighbours and relatives about my disappearance. How long had they been able to stick to the story that I was visiting a friend? Was I pregnant and in hiding? What could they do but grin and bear it? But now that I was back, uncomfortable questions would have to be dealt with. Just when their economic hardships had eased a bit—by learning about the intricacies of the black market—I had brought the worst kind of trouble upon the family: I had been *politically involved*.

By now, however, I had learned it was wiser to keep my mouth shut rather than to attempt to explain. Besides, nobody wanted to listen. Thankfully, as happens with all things, big and small, people soon lost interest. Whatever suspicions they may have harbored they tactfully kept to themselves. After all, hadn't my parents suffered enough already?

They had also paid heavily in financial terms: The extraordinary sum of 2,000 Reichsmark, more than three months' salary, had gone to lawyers hired to track down my whereabouts. This human species had never before intruded upon our prudent lives; worse, their efforts brought no results whatsoever.

When, after a couple of weeks, I had neither returned nor written from the Hilltrupp farm, my mother sent a letter to Josephine, who promptly replied. Since that note never arrived, Josephine later suggested that it must have been removed from her neighborhood mailbox by secret hands, German or British. Such a violation of privacy would have been unthinkable in any respectable country, but this was occupied Germany, still in terrible disorder just months after the demise of the Nazi regime. With husband Karl somewhere in hiding, British agents did nothing to conceal their surveillance of Josephine and everybody else on the farm. Watching her post a letter to the parents of one of their captives certainly must have aroused their interest.

Weeks of intensive pressure on his wife—including her temporary detention in the same Coesfeld prison cell that I had occupied—forced Karl finally to give himself up to the British, who promptly sent him to internment camp. It must have been a short while later, when something unimaginably tragic happened, something that would dwarf everything else that occurred during that terrible winter of 1945 to 1946. To write about it, I have to digress one last time before I finish my story.

With her husband interned and the family's future uncertain, Josephine enrolled for a high school teacher's diploma at the University of Münster, some fifteen kilometers from the farm. Though she held a master's degree in the humanities, she realized she had no choice but to channel her education into a marketable skill. Commuting was impossible, so she took a room in the city, while people at home looked after her children.

I don't know when they got sick, where they picked up the deadly diphtheria infection, or how Josephine learned about the disaster: When she got home, both of her boys were dreadfully ill, baby Manfred worse than his older brother. She bundled the baby up and, without waiting for one of the overcrowded und unreliable trains, she drove him in a hitched wagon to the pediatric clinic in Münster.

It was too late. Little Manfred died within hours.

Even now, I cannot rid myself of the image: The flat, wintry landscape, the straight rural road. Was it night? I don't know. But there it is, the horse-drawn wagon with the raw board hammered down in front, a seat for a farm boy. But today there is no farm boy. Instead, a small, white coffin with a tiny body inside is tightly held by the hand of the mother, her other guiding the horse on their lonely way back to the farm.

And then the picture dissolves into a new image, a triangle, where God has entered the scene of mother and child, an angry God who has taken swift revenge for one of His children's spiteful act. Through His local servant, who has known every member of the farming community since childhood, He refuses to grant the baby a Christian burial in the sacred soil of His garden. After long and bitter pleadings by the mother and grandfather, the priest finally relents. Baby Manfred, the child that had been baptized in the heretical faith of Protestantism only half a year earlier, is granted permission to return to the bosom of the Holy Church. His stricken mother, however, remains unforgiven and is ordered to stay home while the sacred act is performed. Only the grandparents are admitted.

The priest drove a hard bargain, and in the end he won. Her soul shattered into a million fragments, Josephine accepted the harsh judgment that God had dealt her. Her later children—like the eldest who, thankfully, survived—were dutifully baptized in the true faith, to which she, unreservedly repentant, gave herself throughout her future years.

As I have said, when several weeks went by without the arrival of a letter from either me or Josephine, my parents turned to a lawyer to pick up my tracks. By that time they must have been sick with worry, or they never would have taken such an outlandish step. Knowing their shy ways that always tended towards concession rather than confrontation, I admire the effort it must have cost them to venture that far outside their nature. Prevailing circumstances may explain why they turned to a private lawyer rather than the police: Always an institution in Germany a respectable citizen would rather avoid than seek out for help, the police had been closely linked with political rioting during the Weimar Republic and with the Gestapo during the Nazi regime. Now their reputation was further sullied by having been infiltrated, or taken over, by Communists or professional criminals, recently released from the concentration camps. Besides, there must have been restrictions on their jurisdictional territory, something that also held true for the Hamburg lawyer, who fortunately had a colleague in Essen, a large city not far from Dülmen. That man set off on my trail with zeal. After visiting the Hilltrupp farm, he moved on to Coesfeld prison, where he was informed that I had been transferred to an internment camp near Recklinghausen. Off he went in hot pursuit. There were delays, however, deliberate or otherwise, in processing the German lawyer's request for information about a young female from Hamburg who had vanished under British military jurisdiction without notifying her family.

I have always thought highly of the genteel ways of the British, who usually prefer some polite abstention to a nasty kerfuffle. In reply to the lawyer's queries, however, it seems they became rather direct. There were no apologies, no indication that a mistake had been made, or that the girl in question would soon be released. Instead, they curtly informed the good man that the subject of his research had been transferred to military security headquarters for reasons not to be disclosed. And would he please refrain from further inquiries, lest his credentials be withdrawn and he himself shipped off to the other side of the fence.

The lawyer did as he was told, and then informed his Hamburg colleague who, in turn, advised my parents that all legal avenues had been exhausted. My parents accepted the verdict, by now thoroughly convinced that I had been involved in something really terrible. It may be hard to understand today, when everyone is well-informed of his or her basic rights. But there were no rights for Germans then; just the rough justice of the military occupiers. Young people today may argue that parents should stick with their children, regardless of circumstances. And this was certainly what I had expected. In fact, during all those months in captivity, it never occurred to me that they might doubt my innocence, not once. It didn't take long, however, to realize just how wrong I had been.

Fifty years later, I still find this hard to accept, though I am able to look upon it with more charity. People of my parents' generation had never questioned authority. In this particular case, authority—as represented by the British military, the occupiers, the victors—was as intangible as it was absolute. Should they themselves have ventured to Dülmen to talk to Josephine and try to pick up my trail, regardless of the lawyer's failure? Again, it is easy to say they should have. But then I think of the risks and uncertainties of my trip on the open freight train. And I remember how old they looked when I got home, worn down by the most horrid bombings, the loss of their savings, property, and whatever insurances they once held against an unforeseeable future. Only in their fifties, they were defeated. There was nothing left, no spirit, no fire. Others recovered; they never did.

My parents claimed to have sent me parcels of warm clothes, but nothing ever arrived. Once, in January or February, I was allowed to write ten words on a Red Cross–sponsored postcard; and there was the illegal missive that the formidable little lawyer smuggled out of the Sennelager in her underpants. Apart from that, there were no communications, in or out.

*   *   *

Two days after my return, I went to the address on Harvestehuder Weg, where I presented my "Release from Civilian Internment Camp"

264 IN THE SHADOW OF SILENCE

document. A file was opened, papers were stamped, and I was instructed to report back whenever I planned to leave Hamburg for more than three days. As I was about to leave, a young British civilian who had been standing in the back of the office, stepped up and asked in impeccable German: "Are you the daughter of Paul or Walther Mackprang?"

"Of Walther Mackprang," I replied, puzzled.

"I was a *Volontär* with your uncle before the war, but I met your father too," he explained. "How are they?"

"Fine."

"Well, give them my best," he said, dismissing me with a friendly wave of his hand.

Volontäre were the sons and heirs of wealthy merchants who volunteered to learn their professions in the firms of their father's friendly, often foreign, business partners or competitors on some kind of privately organized exchange program. There was little pay; the young scions being expected to be financed by their families. But, experiences were gained and valuable connections made within the guilds, which had their own centuries-old codes of conduct, untouched by national politics and international wars. When I came home I told my father about the encounter. I described the young man and mentioned his name, but he had no recollection of him after so many years.

There were other offices to visit, signatures to obtain, ration cards to procure. But, after a few weeks, I settled back into the routine of family life. *Organisieren*, or organizing, was the operative word. It was all about finding ways—legal (rarely), semi-legal, or illegal (mostly)—to obtain food, fuel, shelter, clothing, shoes, or any other necessities of life after six years of getting by with little or doing without. These precious supplies, once obtained by barter, trade or outright theft, were then either used directly or exchanged on the black market. After what I had been through, I felt little desire to get into another scrap with some stern-faced military police officer, so I stayed out of that game, allowing my sister and father to provide for the family.

Towards the end of July, my family decided on a trip to the North Sea island of Sylt. In spite of poor transportation, we were determined to get there. We all felt the need for a holiday, our first since the early forties. Thus, a second trip to Harvestehuder Weg became necessary to declare my intent to leave the city. On entering the building, I immediately asked for my friendly *Volontär*. The polite young man at reception shrugged:

"He was called back to England a couple of weeks ago. I'm sorry. Is there anything I can help you with?"

I gave him my release certificate. "I'm going to leave town for more than three days. I understand I need special permission."

The official studied the document. "Excuse me a moment." He disappeared to get my file. When he returned, he looked puzzled: "We have no file by that name," he said, handing me back my paper with a mixture of surprise and apology, like a grocer who has suddenly found himself out of an essential stock.

"That's fine with me, don't worry," I assured him, rewarding him with a warm smile.

Does God hold a special place in heaven marked "Volontäre?"

INTERLUDE VII
Victors' Justice

History offers few examples of charity extended to the government of a country that loses a war. Either the defeated people themselves take revenge for their wasted sacrifices by toppling their erstwhile rulers, with or without staging a bloody revolution; or, the victors take the initiative by removing the dangerous warmonger from the international scene. For the first scenario, Germany's Kaiser Wilhelm II comes to mind, forced into lifelong exile after World War I; for the second, there is probably no example more famous than Napoleon's banishment to the Mediterranean island of Elba, later the remote island of St. Helena in the South Atlantic. Both leaders failed in their efforts to build new empires; both were responsible for huge European wars causing terrible bloodshed. Neither, however, was considered a common criminal, deserving execution at the hands of their own people or after a trial by their former enemies. In contrast, the Nazi leadership after World War II was never in danger of being hanged or exiled by the Germans, with or without a revolution; Germans never had the chance. Instead, in 1945 both the Nazi government and—at least initially—the German people were considered guilty, all their civil, political, and military institutions dissolved, controlled or superseded by those of the victors.

This approach was certainly a novel one, causing huge legal difficulties that, even today, despite the best judicial and philosophical arguments, have not been unequivocally resolved.

This is not meant to sound critical of the victors' handling of the German guilt question. After all, the Nazi government, by trying to forge a new world order under the supremacy of the Reich, had been responsible for the deaths of fifty million people. Granted, vast empires had been won and lost before in history, but this had happened centuries ago in a sparsely populated and largely tribal Europe and Asia. To impose the Reich's hegemony on twentieth-century Europe, including Russia, was a preposterous and megalomaniac undertaking. The victors, after six years of bloody fighting, rightly decided that the Nazi state had to be purged down to its roots, lest it ever shoot up again. Its roots, of course, were the German people, in the eyes of the world a fickle breed whose collective soul was inherently and dangerously torn between romantic Weltschmerz, Wagnerian bombast, and maniacal fervor.

During the Yalta Conference of January 1945, four months before the end of the war, the Allied leaders Roosevelt, Churchill, and Stalin agreed to eradicate all traces of National Socialism through a cleansing process called "denazification." The punitive effort was to be accompanied by mass programs of political re-education, differing between East and West according to the victors' ideological credo.

In the American, British, and French zones of occupation, Germans took to a democratic form of government like ducks take to water. Though most people firmly rejected any further personal political involvement, they nevertheless obediently and willingly accepted the new democratic rules imposed by the Allied Control Council. During the following years, as Nazism and right-wing ideologies were renounced by the people with the zeal of the truly converted, the new West German state, founded in 1949, quickly recovered, its economy fired up by generous American credits (Marshall Plan) and large supply orders for the faraway Korean War. During the next four decades, the young country's own socio-economic brand, the so-called *soziale Marktwirtschaft*, a mix of free enterprise and statism, became one of the world's most successful economic models.

Alas, while the re-educational part of the two-pronged treatment of the defeated Germans worked like a charm, the punitive one proved to be a costly legal and moral quagmire.

To begin with, there were the forbidding dimensions of Germany's social and economic calamity. Faced with the collapse of the country's entire infrastructure, the occupying authorities had to turn their immediate attention to the feeding, housing, policing, employment, education, and relocation of forty million people within the three Western zones of occupation. In May 1945, most German communities were cut off from regular supplies of food, electricity, water, gas, and coal. Over the next few years, up to ten million men returned from POW camps and had to be reintegrated into civilian life. Another eleven to twelve million refugees and displaced persons from ethnically cleansed areas in Eastern Europe, as well as from Soviet-occupied East Germany, streamed into the West, eventually bringing the total number of West Germans to sixty million. To confront the chaos and begin rebuilding the country required tens of thousands of administrators, engineers, architects, teachers, and other professionals untainted by the Nazi brush.

But where was one to find such worthy people? How did one determine who had been a Nazi and who had not? Coming up with an answer to this apparently simple question soon proved to be incredibly difficult.

Consider, for instance, the 10.7 million men and women who had been members of the NSDAP. Were they all guilty of Nazi crimes? As it happened, most of the civil servants who were urgently needed to get the country restarted had been party members; for them, as they would claim, party membership had simply come with the job. And what of the dozens of professional associations sporting the prefix NS-, National Socialist, or Reichs- in order to demonstrate their loyalty to Third Reich ideology? Had their members—490,000 teachers, 72,000 doctors, and countless lawyers, architects, professors, economists, bankers, and merchants—all been Nazis who should now be barred from employment? How did one distinguish between those who had openly supported the Nazi system, and those who had silently paid their dues, hoping to be left alone? Was one to follow up on every hateful denunciation by former colleagues, neighbors, friends? And were all those who now claimed to have opposed the Hitler regime from the beginning— suddenly an overwhelming number of Germans—to be believed?

Furthermore, there was the large and influential cultural establishment. During the preceding twelve years, many visual and performing artists and writers had offered their loyalty to the Nazis in exchange for career security. The best were heavily courted by the government, most notably by Joseph Goebbels, the powerful Minister for People's Enlightenment and Propaganda. How better to enlighten the people than through the creative work of their own artists? Thus, an astounding 185,000 writers, actors, singers, film and theater directors, painters and sculptors had become members of Goebbels's *Reichskulturkammer*, the eminent patronage body that dispensed money and prestige. Were they all ideologically contaminated, their talents to be permanently scorned?

While big show trials in Nuremberg were being prepared to deal with the most notorious leaders of the Hitler regime, Allied internment camps warehoused tens of thousands of public servants, members and functionaries of the various Nazi organizations, as well as a diverse assortment of people whose former positions and responsibilities made them prima facie suspects of some yet-to-be-adjudged Nazi crime. It has been estimated that, by the end of 1946, the occupying forces had interned 240,000 people. Many prisoners were released within six to eight months, while others waited a year or more for their "cases" to come up for investigation. Very few did. Whatever the reasons for setting up the detention camps— apart from taking a great number of small functionaries, civil servants, and state employees temporarily off the scene—determining Nazi crimes and meting out justice were not among them. Most of the political detainees, freed after months of idle waiting, joined the ranks of those who fought their way through the tedious process of denazification. It was a colossal bureaucratic effort aimed at ferreting out tens of thousands of unidentified Nazis. Every person seeking to retrieve his old job, or apply for a new one, faced a 131-part questionnaire about his exact position in, and relationship to, the various organizations of the former Reich.[2] After completion, one or more witnesses had to be found who were willing to testify to the veracity of the applicant's answers. Weeks of anxiety would pass until a tribunal (soon taken over by German *Spruchkammern*) rendered a verdict that ranked the person in one of five categories: *hauptschuldig* (major offender), *belastet* (offender), *minderbelastet* (minor offender), *Mitläufer* (follower), or *entlastet* (exonerated). Those in the "major offender" or "offender" categories were automatically handed over for prosecution. According to A.J. Ryder, there were 545 such tribunals in the American zone alone, employing a staff of 22,000.[3]

Ryder also notes that there were substantial differences in the way the Allies handled denazification. In the American zone, between May 1945 and September 1946, more than thirteen million questionnaires were completed, 3.6 million Germans charged, and 800,000 penalties—usually in the form of a dismissal from work—meted out. Despite a larger population in the British zone, only 2.1 million Germans were charged in that jurisdiction, and 156,000 temporarily removed from office.

Nowhere were the occupiers more easygoing than in Hamburg, a city of nearly two million inhabitants. Perception on the street was that to have Germany's biggest and richest port within their zone of occupation filled the British with extraordinary satisfaction, which they had no desire to spoil with anything but the most restrained search for Nazi perpetrators. (According to personal inquiries, none of the Hitler Youth leadership was interned.) Meanwhile, as fraternization between occupiers and occupied spread, the historical friendship between the two large merchant classes of England and the "Free and Hanseatic City of Hamburg" was quickly re-established. Less than three months after my return from camp, I joined an English-German friendship club, where I improved my language skills and enjoyed a relaxed atmosphere of hospitality and companionship.

The denazification procedures, which lasted until the early 1950s, must have been one of the strangest bureaucratic boondoggles ever invented. Amazingly, the combined efforts of tens of thousands of personnel and millions of pages of documents turned up only a handful of real Nazis in Nazi Germany—all others having been "followers" or "minor offenders," allegedly pressed into party membership to secure their jobs. Equally baffling: Nobody had ever known anything reprehensible, let alone been involved in any criminal activity.

A ludicrous farce? A travesty of truth and justice? Did the cynicism it bred among Germans turn a deeply exhausted, demoralized, and sorrowful people into today's nation of self-assured, success-oriented people?

*   *   *

While denazification processed millions of "ordinary" Germans, the Nuremberg War Crimes Tribunal concerned itself with the uppermost political and military echelon of the Hitler regime. As the first such juridical institution in history, the trial was conducted according to the articles of a charter signed by the Allies in London on August 8, 1945. These articles included the rules for Anglo-Saxon court procedures and laid down the main "principles" for the prosecution: crimes against the peace, wars of aggression, war crimes, and crimes against humanity. According to Uwe Wesel,[4] professor of law at the Free University of Berlin, discussions between the British and the Americans on how to prosecute the crimes of the Third Reich—where and by whom, and on which legal principles—had been going on for years. The British had deep reservations about a judicial solution on the basis of international law, because it could easily be turned against their own country. Such misgivings also existed in the United States, until Justice Robert Jackson, later the American Chief Prosecutor in Nuremberg, won the argument: "To free [the prisoners] without a trial would mock the dead and make cynics of the living."[5] The Nuremberg Trials were essentially his work. In his magnificent opening speech he spoke of the morality of a justice system based on the principles of law rather than on the arbitrary exercise of power, as had been the case under the Nazi regime: "That four great nations flushed with victory and stung with injury stay the hand of vengeance and voluntarily submit their captive enemies to the judgment of the law is one of the most significant tributes that power has ever paid to reason."[6]

The defendants' reactions to the Nazi horrors described in the indictments ranged from shock to cynicism to quick denials of all personal involvement, mirroring the predominant feelings within the German population. Göring's commentary, as documented by the prison psychiatrist G.M. Gilbert, was perhaps the most typical: "The victor will always be the judge, and the vanquished the accused."[7]

The Nuremberg Trials began on November 20, 1945, against twenty-four indicted Nazi war criminals who represented—after the deaths of Adolf Hitler, Heinrich Himmler, and Joseph Goebbels—the highest level of the political and military leadership of the Third Reich. All accused were tried at the same time by one-hundred prosecutors aided by a full-time staff of 2,000. After 284 days of sessions, the judges spoke their verdicts: three discharges, twelve death sentences by hanging, prison terms from ten years to life for the rest of the indicted. In contrast to later trials, many Germans, perhaps even the majority, felt a good deal of satisfaction about most of the sentences, including the death sentences against Frank, Frick, Kaltenbrunner, Rosenberg, Sauckel, Seyss-Inquart, Streicher and Bormann.[8] With their ideological hubris, undisguised cruelty and vulgarity, these men had offended the German people for many years. Granted, this was "victors' justice"—what else could it be? At that point in time, no German court had the moral or juridical authority to rid the country of the Nazi evil.

There may have been mixed feelings about the hanging (rather than shooting) of Field Marshal Keitel and General Jodl. There cannot be the slightest doubt, however, about the extraordinary glee, which greeted the news that popular "Hermann" (Göring) had cheated the judges by poisoning himself the night before his hanging. According to unlikely rumors, a note beside Göring's body carried the words of his last hurrah: *Hätt' ihr mich am — geleckt, hätt' ihr auch das Gift entdeckt.* (If you had kissed my —, you would have discovered the poison.) True or false, the vulgar message had revealed a glimpse of true German feelings.[9]

After the first and most famous Nuremberg Trial, staged by the combined efforts of the United States, Britain, the Soviet Union, and France, each of the wartime Allies conducted further trials in their own zone of occupation. Nuremberg, which was located in the American zone, was the site of twelve more trials against 184 defendants, resulting in twenty-four death sentences, half of them commuted. The defendants included ministers and state secretaries, field marshals and generals, members of the SS and Gestapo, physicians involved in the Reich's euthanasia program, high judges and prosecutors, the CEOs of large industries that conscripted thousands of slave laborers, and members of the foreign service. (The trial against some of Hitler's judges, who "in the name of the people" had meted out more than 30,000 death sentences, became immortalized in 1961 by the extraordinary movie *Judgment in Nuremberg,* with its defining words on the corruption of all moral and legal standards in the Third Reich.) On the territory of the former concentration camp Dachau, near Munich, the Americans conducted 489 trials against 1,672 defendants. Many of the accused had been guards and functionaries at concentration camps, members of the murderous *SS Einsatzgruppen* and the *Reichssicherheitshauptamt* (Himmler's SS head-quarters). A death sentence was received by 426 defendants, while others were convicted to long prison terms.[10] The total number of convictions in the three Western zones of occupation was 5,025 with 806 death penalties, of which 486 were carried out.[11]

I fully agree with Ulrich Wickert's assessment that most Germans saw the later trials as *"Siegerjustiz"* (victors' justice), as something "that would never have happened if they had not lost the war." Wickert is also right when he considers this attitude as proof that the majority of Germans never welcomed the Allies as "liberators,"[12] as claimed by the former German Federal President, Richard von Weizsäcker, in his famous speech of May 8, 1985. According to my own recollections during the early postwar years, the Allies were seen as victors and occupiers— benevolent in some cases, ruthless in others. As the trials went on, and more and more people were convicted to death or lengthy prison terms, sympathy with the defendants grew, either because people refused to believe the horrors presented by the prosecution, or, because by rejecting victors' justice on principle, they hoped to recover a modicum of their shattered national pride.

Over the next few years, many sentences were commuted, and, in 1950, responsibility for the further prosecution of Nazi criminals in the Western zones of occupation was handed over to the government of the newly founded Federal Republic of Germany (West Germany). By then, the Cold War was the central political issue, and strong German sentiment demanded the cessation of all prosecutions by the former enemies and the commuting of earlier sentences in return for the country's participation in Western Europe's rearmament effort. As the erstwhile victors scrambled to secure their share of experienced German intelligence officers and military strategists, the vexing problem of finding, and prosecuting, former Nazi criminals was relegated to the back burner.

Thus, sometime between the late 1940s and early 1950s, the internment camps were dismantled and the prisoners sent home or turned over to German authorities. Of the six million cases that had been charged with some kind of infraction during the denazification process, only a paltry one-half of one percent were ultimately classified as "major offenders" or "offenders" (mostly SS, Gestapo and SD), and handed over for prosecution. Few had to suffer for long. As the American administration leaned heavily on their judges and prosecutors to ease up on an estimated 30,000 former Nazi criminals still facing justice, many among the American military were horrified by the course history was taking before their very eyes. After years of battle and millions of dead, "what had the war been all about?"[13]

On January 31, 1951, American High Commissioner John McCloy ordered a general amnesty for all convictions carrying a sentence of less than fifteen years. During the following eighteen months, most prisoners were released. By 1952, only 1,017 were still being detained. Even so, on June 7, 1951, five members of the *Einsatzgruppen* and the *Reichssicherheitshauptamt* were executed. Although another five death sentences were commuted to life in prison (none of them served to completion), the final executions engendered strong protests from the German government, opposition, military, and churches.[14] This was America's last attempt to deal with the crimes of the vanquished Nazi state. From then on, the defence of Western Europe became the United States' paramount concern, making their former enemy their most prized military ally.

*   *   *

Over the past five decades, the moral, legal, and political aspects of the Nuremberg Trials have been scrutinized by generations of lawyers, politicians, historians, and writers from all over the world. With the benefit of hindsight, a majority of people, including Germans, would probably agree that the judges succeeded in most major aspects. "[B]y stressing universally understood moral law that transcended the jurisdiction of the individual state, the tribunal helped to revive social commitments that had been distorted by war," writes Erna Paris.[15] And, in a similar vein: "[L]aws passed by sovereign nations that are contrary to the precepts of universal rights and morality are not to be obeyed and that to do so is no defence."[16] To place universal human rights above national laws was a concept that had certainly not existed before.

Still, as Paris admits, "[t]here were [also] blatant hypocrisies and major mistakes ... Victors' justice entailed serious shortcomings [and] *realpolitik* was never absent from the scene."[17] The legacy of the Nuremberg Trials rests on the legal, human and political messages they imparted at the time, and the long-term consequences they brought about. What objections there were centered mostly on the juristic aspects of the trials: The so-called International Tribunal was international only in name; it was the court of the victors who had unlimited access to witnesses and documents, who controlled the procedures and set the rules. There was also the *tu-quoque* (you too [are guilty]) issue that must have been obvious to every observer, and certainly to the participants at either side of the bar.[18] It suggested that some of the countries whose judges presided over the procedures were also vulnerable to charges under the London Charter: Stalin's attack on Finland in 1939, his annexation of half of Poland earlier that year, and the Soviet murder of 15,000 Polish officers in Katyn fell clearly under the principles of the London Agreement. Yet, Stalin was not the only one facing the *tu-quoque* problem: The carpet bombing of German civilian populations, the dropping of the atomic bombs on Hiroshima and Nagasaki, and the postwar expulsions of eleven to twelve million Germans from all areas east of the Oder and Neisse Rivers were almost certainly offenses under the new Charter. Then there was the venerable legal principle *nulla poena sine lege* (no punishment without a [previously existing] law). Since, as the defence maintained, the accused had acted under the laws of the Nazi system, they could not be punished under retroactively introduced new laws. In contrast to later German courts, the Nuremberg judges, much to their credit, ignored the defence's arguments. According to Uwe Wesel, those arguments were correct only inasmuch as they applied to "crimes against the peace", or "wars of aggression," while crimes against humanity ([mass] murder, deportation), as well as war crimes, had been indictable by German law since 1871 and 1907, respectively. Besides, Wesel concludes, in view of the unspeakable crimes of the Third Reich, the historic influence of the trials remains untouched by legal arguments and petty criticisms.[19]

Few would dispute his point. However, if one of the objectives of the trials was the re-education of the morally wayward Germans, the psychological consequences of disregarding other wartime atrocities cannot be ignored. For years, Germans, exposed to the most extensive Allied bombing, had considered themselves the victims of deliberate terror. After VE Day they had to absorb the fact that others had been the victims, and that they, the Germans, had been the perpetrators of unspeakable crimes. The sudden adjustment to such an inverted perspective of guilt and innocence demanded a mental somersault that the exhausted and demoralized population had no strength to perform. Hence the split feelings about the trials: On the one hand there was satisfaction that the Reich leaders, who had brought so much suffering, guilt and shame upon the people, had been given their just dues; on the other hand, there was frustration and disbelief at the judges' rejection of any reference to the carpet bombings of German cities, the estimated 600,000 civilian casualties, and the wanton destruction of a unique cultural heritage. As the trials, with their aspiration for the highest legal and moral standards, proceeded, a conviction grew among the people that— regardless of all the high-minded arguments—the odds had been stacked against them from the beginning.

While the population in the Western parts of postwar Germany struggled to get on with their lives, flight and expulsions from Eastern Europe continued to drive people west. As thousands of families in overloaded wagons, and waves of destitute people on foot arrived, asking for shelter and food from the bombed-out and overcrowded communities in the West, there was little Christian compassion to welcome them. Allied and German administrations and charitable organizations did their best to get the people off the road and into emergency shelters. But the hostility from the local populations was intense and it lasted for years, perhaps as long as a generation. It was cruel and unpardonable—yet it was the all too human failure of a people thrown back to its narrowest tribal loyalties: men, women, and children clinging to life among the ruins, each family jealously guarding its tiny space, its meagre rations, the small measure of security they had staked out for themselves. Stealing, dealing, bartering—everyone for himself; and God nowhere. Many of the newcomers were forced out of the cities and into the countryside, where they were even more isolated, and where the chances of finding work to rebuild their lives and their former careers were almost zero. An article in *Die Zeit* from November 22, 1951—more than six years after the war and two-and-a-half years after the founding of the Federal Republic— tells a story of desperation and rejection:

> [Five years ago, the refugees] arrived on the *Reichsstrasse* 201. On the *Bundesstrasse* 201 they want to move on.[20] They came because Red Army soldiers had driven them from their farms, destroyed their fields, and raped their women. They want to move on, because without work, without home, without possessions or hope they must perish ... [Here at Süderbrarup] things are not worse than anywhere else in the state of Schleswig-Holstein ... 2,000 locals are confronted with 2,400 refugees. Half the population lives on public funds ... This is how it was yesterday, how it is today, and how it will be tomorrow. (My translation.)

Many of the expelled Germans had been living for generations as *Reichsdeutsche* (citizens of the German Reich) in East Prussia, Silesia, and Pomerania; or as *Volksdeutsche* (German minorities in non-German states) in the Baltic countries, on both sides of the Vistula River, in Czechoslovakia and in the Balkans. Under the banner of Nazi expansionism, an estimated one million Germans (farmers, functionaries, administrators, entrepreneurs) had been settled on formerly Polish territory after that country was conquered in 1939. In Poland and later in the Ukraine, a brutal twentieth-century colonization program had treated the Slavic peoples as a subhuman species destined to serve their German masters. To that end, there were large-scale expropriations, mass expulsions, and the notorious roundups by the SS of whole communities for deportation into slave labor. According to Sebastian Haffner, between one million and three million non-Jewish Poles, mostly from the intelligentsia, were murdered in the attempt to subjugate the Polish people.[21] All this on top of the ghettoization and later extermination of six million Jews—three million from Poland alone. It was in Poland and the Western Ukraine where Germans perpetrated most of their heinous crimes.

Six years later, the tables were turned. The radical eviction of *Reichs-*

deutsche, Volksdeutsche, Nazi settlers, functionaries, and tens of thousands of foreign collaborators by the advancing Red Army and the newly liberated nations prompted the greatest migration in human history. It also caused immeasurable grief, loss of life and livelihood, of health and home. The postwar expulsions from Eastern Europe have frequently been described as crimes against humanity. If one follows Hannah Arendt's reasoning, this is incorrect.[22] The mass evictions may have been new in scope, but they were neither unprecedented, nor had they anything of the calculated precision of the Holocaust. The Jewish genocide was a new phenomenon. It happened under the cover of war, but independently of the war. It served no military purpose, the extinction of an entire human group being nothing more than an ideological obsession. In contrast, the expulsions, in time and place, were clearly connected with the war: they were war crimes; they were not crimes against humanity. If one finds fault with the omissions of the Nuremberg Trials, this distinction seems important.

It is to the great credit of successive, notably Social Democratic, Federal German governments to have spent money and used diplomacy to arrive at a peaceful settlement with neighbouring Poland. For decades, efforts at reconciliation with the country that suffered so terribly in World War II went hand in hand with government pressure on the *Vertriebenenverbände* (associations of expellees) to let up on their claims to the old German Reich territories Pomerania, Silesia, and East Prussia,[23] now settled by Poles, and a small enclave of Russians. Despite large sums of money to compensate them for their permanently lost homelands, the *Vertriebenenverbände* frequently undercut the government's efforts through their large and clamorous gatherings that increasingly estranged them from West Germany's political mainstream. Since German reunification and the end of the Cold War, things have calmed down in East Central Europe, with a unified and extended Euroland now the next milestone to be reached together.

The Nuremberg Trials were the most important part of the victors' well-intended and thoughtfully applied justice. They produced new and lasting concepts of personal guilt and universal justice, whose fruits, after fifty years, are about to be reaped, as prosecutors in The Hague are bringing national leaders and their henchmen—their crimes no longer protected by national immunity—before the International Court of Justice. Only six months after the greatest killings in history, legal order and open proceedings set an impressive example of justice, in sharp contrast to twelve years of arbitrary power in Germany. Nuremberg was not the place to bring up the omissions or correct the hypocrisies of the victors. There probably never was such a place. Human nature can only go so far in its eternal endeavour to make amends for its frailties and imperfections. Today, younger generations in Germany see the fire-bombings of Hamburg and Dresden as just punishment for the earlier German bombings of London, Coventry, and Rotterdam.[24] And the expulsions, most politicians agree, eventually turned out a blessing as they eliminated many of the vexing ethnic instabilities that followed the break-up of the Austro-Hungarian Empire after World War I.

A legacy of crime and retribution is about to be settled by the passage of time—and the determination of the German people to put an end to the legacy of their past. Germany's cities have been rebuilt, and millions of refugees have been integrated and become valued contributors to the country's economy. Apart from some yellowed, surreal-looking old photographs, and the self-pitying tales of a dying generation, there is little left to stir up old arguments.

Notes to Chapter 7

1   The names of both Dr. Hoffmann and Dr. Clausen are invented.

2   The laborious process was ridiculed by Ernst von Salomon in his bestseller *Der Fragebogen* (The Questionnaire) (Reinbek bei Hamburg: Rowohlt, 1951) which, by 1999, had sold almost 100,000 copies.

3   Ryder, A.J., *Twentieth-Century Germany: From Bismarck to Brandt* (London: MacMillan, 1973), 469–470.

4   Wesel, Uwe, *Geschichte des Rechts* (History of Law) (Munich: C.H. Beck, 1997), 515.

5   Quoted by Paris, Erna: *Long Shadows* (Toronto: Knopf, 2000), 405.

6   ibid.

7   Gilbert, G. M., *Nuremberg Diary* (New York: Signet Book, The New American Library of World Literature, 1947), 10ff.

8   Martin Bormann, "Secretary to the Führer" and a racial fanatic, was convicted to

death in absentia. His body was identified in 1972 and his death officially dated to May 2, 1945, in Berlin. (*Enzyklopädie des Nationalsozialismus* [Stuttgart: Klett-Cotta, 1997], 824.) After Himmler, the shadowy Bormann, who was closest to Hitler in the Reich Chancellery, was the most feared man in Nazi Germany.

9   How the cyanide was smuggled into Göring's cell, or how he kept it hidden, has never been ascertained. A cylindrical container was later found, which suggests that, at least temporarily, he kept it in his rectum, as the note suggests.

10 Wesel, Uwe, op. cit., ref. 4, 517.

11 *Enzyklopädie des Nationalsozialismus*, op. cit., ref. 8, 593.

12 Wickert, Ulrich, *Deutschland auf Bewährung* (Germany on Probation) (Munich: Heyne, 1999), 237.

13 A line spoken by the American prosecutor in the movie *Judgment in Nuremberg*.

14 Giordano, Ralph, *Die zweite Schuld oder Von der Last, Deutscher zu sein* (The second guilt or about the burden of being a German) (Hamburg: Drömer, 1987), 119.

15 Paris, Erna, op. cit., ref. 5, 409.

16 ibid. 411.

17 ibid. 408.

18 Arendt, Hanna, *Eichmann in Jerusalem: A Report on the Banality of Evil* (Harmondsworth, England: Penguin Press, 1977), 255.

19 Wesel, Uwe, op. cit., ref. 4, 516.

20 *Bundesstrasse* (Federal Road) is the postwar designation of *Reichsstrasse*.

21 Haffner, Sebastian, *Anmerkungen zu Hitler* (Munich: Kindler, 1978), 68.

22 Arendt, Hannah, op. cit., ref. 18, 275.

23 In contrast to the Nazi-occupied territories in Poland and the Ukraine, Pomerania, Silesia, and East Prussia had been Prussian provinces, later Reich territories (*Reichsgebiete*), for at least two hundred years. Their populations had little to do with the Nazis' "crimes against humanity" in Eastern Europe. They were expelled when the Allies granted their land to Poland to compensate for that country's loss of its eastern half, annexed by the Soviet Union.

24 German raids on Britain during the whole war killed about 50,000. (Greenhous, Harris, Johnston and Rawling, *The Crucible of War, 1939–1945: The Official History of the Royal Canadian Air Force*, Volume III. [Toronto: University of Toronto Press, 1994], 697 fn.)

THE LEGACY
OF POSTWAR GERMANY

Since the early 1990s, Germans have been examining their *past* in an almost obsessive manner. The *past*, as should be explained, is distinct from the *history*, which is, in turn, of particular interest inasmuch as it precedes, and is consequential for, the *past*. The latter began on January 30, 1933, when Hitler attained power, and it ended on May 8, 1945, with Germany's unconditional surrender after World War II. The *past*, therefore, is simply a euphemism for the Third Reich. Selected pieces of *history* include Prussia's victory over France in 1871, followed by Prussian prime minister Otto von Bismarck's founding of the Second Reich by persuading his reluctant King Wilhelm I to accept the German Emperor's Crown. Wilhelm's grandson, Kaiser Wilhelm II, whose arrogance provoked friend and foe, militarized the country, and abdicated in 1918, after losing World War I to France, England, the United States, and a host of other nations. After the devastation of World War I, the Treaty of Versailles separated Germany from a good part of its territory and forced it to pay huge reparations that threatened to ruin its economy.

Between Bismarck's Second Reich (1871–1918) and Hitler's Third Reich (1933–1945), there was the Weimar Republic (1919–1933), so named because its constitution was proclaimed in the peaceful little Thuringian city of Weimar, rather than in revolutionary Berlin. Visiting Weimar today means rendezvousing with Germany's greatest poets, Goethe (1749–1832) and Schiller (1759–1805), walking through beautiful parks, and driving out to the Buchenwald concentration camp, a mere eight kilometers from the pristine city. In Weimar, Germany's illustrious cultural past meets the *past*. Of the republic that carried the city's name, there remains little. After its birth, the government moved to Berlin, where it survived—under frequent changes—the Great Inflation of 1923 and the Roaring Twenties, but succumbed to the turmoil of the Great Depression. In early 1933, Germany's elderly but highly respected president, Field Marshal Hindenburg, hoping to save the country from further political disorder, reluctantly agreed to appoint the leader of the right-wing Nazi Party, Adolf Hitler—"the Bohemian corporal," as he famously called him—as Reich Chancellor of the Republic. At that point Germany's *history* ends, and its *past* begins. How postwar Germany handled that *past* (*Vergangenheitsbewältigung*) has come up in this book before, and will now fill its last pages.

A good starting point is what Germans refer to as *die Stunde Null*, or Zero Hour, when World War II ended with the Wehrmacht's surrender, and a new Germany rose from the ashes. In fact, though, it did not rise at all, but rather sank ever deeper into chaos. Others have chosen different dates for Zero Hour. Wickert, for instance, points to June 20, 1948, when the Western Allies introduced the new Deutschmark that triggered West Germany's "economic miracle."[1] Historians would probably assign the term Zero Hour to May 23, 1949, when the three Western zones of occupation formed a new country, the Federal Republic of Germany. This date has logic on its side, although the most auspicious event of the day, the proclamation of the Republic's new democratic constitution, was barely noticed by a population fed up with politics and determined never to get involved again.

Ignoring logic and taking one's cue from the cataclysmic collapse of the Third Reich, one is compelled to choose May 8, 1945, as the only date that truly lives up to the emotional and physical image of Zero Hour. On that day, Hitler's Third Reich vanished instantly and completely, as though it had never been. Whatever was to come would be harsh, humiliating, and fearsome; it would bring starvation, poverty, and homelessness on a mass scale. But the killing had stopped. And possibly—just possibly—over the years, Germans might yet be able to better their circumstances. A total end marking a beginning of sorts—Zero Hour.

As things turned out, circumstances improved much faster than people had reason to expect; or—as many foreign observers thought—than they deserved. Over the next four years, the initial confusion and physical and mental dislocation were overcome, and, under the watchful eyes of the Western occupying forces, new democratic structures were slowly introduced. In 1949 the Federal Republic of (West) Germany was born, quickly followed by the (East) German Democratic Republic under the tight control of the Soviet Union. In 1989, after forty years of forced separation and Cold War hostility, the erstwhile victors of World War II—the United States, Great Britain, the Soviet Union, and France—would grant the two Germanies permission to reunite. Now eighty million strong, much of the Germany of old has been restored, minus one-quarter of the Reich's territory and all hegemonic ambitions.

If Germans loved the image of Zero Hour, so did the politicians. The determined emotional and mental break with the Hitler Reich, followed by the total political remake of the country, became a tremendous success. By liberating people from the burden of shame and guilt, and allowing them to concentrate on the future rather than the past, the energies necessary to bring about the hectic economic recovery of the 1950s and 1960s were released. While West Germany reached an unprecedented level of prosperity, the young country's peaceful integration into NATO, the UN, and the European Community signified more than thirty years of unparalleled political achievement. Granted, a good deal of cynicism was mixed in with the politics of West Germany's first chancellor, Konrad Adenauer: the quick retirement of the guilt issue for example, not to mention the near-total abandonment of the East Germans living under much harsher economic conditions, in spite of pious protestations to the contrary. According to historian Jeffrey Herf at Ohio University, West Germany's government was faced with a clear alternative: "democracy" or "memory and justice," a choice between winning the votes of an electorate eager to relinquish its *past*, or keeping that past alive through the continued prosecution of its crimes. "(Adenauer) believed that the best way to overcome Nazism was to avoid a direct confrontation with it while transferring ever more authority to German political leaders. Economic recovery and political legitimacy, not additional purges, were the proper medicine. Democratic renewal went hand in hand with silence and the forgetting of a dark past."[2] Meanwhile, the chancellor's opponent, Social Democrat Kurt Schumacher, who strongly opted for "memory and justice," lost the election. This was *realpolitik* most "real"; it was also the time when this euphemism for an old way of doing politics was coined.

In its new constitution, the Federal Republic of Germany declared itself the legal successor to the German Reich (*Rechtsnachfolgerin*). Accepting the enormous financial obligations of the Hitler state, the country wasted no time in paying vast sums of money, quietly and efficiently, to people inside and outside Germany. An equalization tax helped compensate millions of Germans whose families had been killed or displaced, or whose property had been damaged or expropriated by the National Socialists, the war, or its aftermath. In 1952, a reparation agreement with Israel, totaling $3.4 billion, did much to improve West Germany's relationship with that country. In 1953, the London Agreement settled West Germany's entire foreign debts for $7.5 billion.[3] Unable to undo what had been done by a former German government, the successor state conducted itself honorably and generously. No fair-minded person would argue the contrary. To date, Germany has shelled out more than $54 billion to Holocaust victims. A final payment of $10 billion to the survivors of Nazi Germany's estimated ten million slave laborers is being negotiated against the promise of no further financial demands. By and large, these huge expenditures, facilitated by the country's rapid economic recovery, were willingly accepted by a population eager to pay off its terrible debts.

Even more popular was the government's quiet retiring of the vexing guilt problem by measures still to be explained in these pages. Meanwhile, the challenging task of exploring and trying to understand the Third Reich, its disastrous ideology and bizarre Führer cult, was seized by others, mostly British and American writers and historians "unrestrained by the taboo of touch" (*Berührungstabu*).[4] To the ordinary German, who had long since decided he had heard enough of the ghastly subject to last a lifetime, the "externalization" of the historical interpretation of his nation's past was of little interest. Also, since there was hardly a chance of ever personally meeting one of the surviving thirty to forty thousand Jews still (or again) residing in Germany, the postwar relationship between Germans and Jews—a veritable hot potato for the government and an emotional minefield for every German living abroad—remained a non-issue for the ordinary German in Germany.

What else then could the government have done? With the benefit of hindsight, I would argue that, had the Federal Republic accepted not only the political and financial successorship to the Deutsche Reich, but also burdened itself with the moral legacy of the crimes committed by the Reich, the exercise might have turned out to be a bold and ultimately therapeutic one. It would have put the Adenauer government on the side of the angels (instead of in the good book of the Americans),[5] winning it a lot of moral ground at a time when moral ground was at a premium. To be sure, acknowledging collective responsibility for the Reich's million-fold atrocities would have proved highly unpopular. But, as with many bitter medicines, benefits might ultimately have accrued—among them the gratifying sense that, having conducted their own expurgation, Germans could then have begun to concentrate on the serious task of establishing a durable and honest relationship with the *past*, a moral equilibrium between truth and sorrow with which they and their children and grandchildren could be able, and would be willing, to live. (The political and moral implications of the South African Truth and Reconciliation Commission, the only comparable effort in recent history, will not be known for many years.)

A nice thought, but it did not happen. Hitler's contemporaries dodged the challenge. Today, as the European Union becomes rapidly a political, economic, and social reality, Germany's uncompromising Western orientation and integration (*Westeinbindung*)—started by Adenauer and resolutely pursued by all West German federal chancellors—receive unequivocal praise from the country's growing circle of allies. Meanwhile, the *past*, still restless, still haunting, is more than ever alive. Whether this is in consequence of the first chancellor's early rejection of "memory and justice" (Herf), is no longer a subject of the country's official discourse.

After the main Nuremberg trial in 1945 to 1946, Allied military courts convicted 5,025 perpetrators, most of them high-ranking SS and Party officials. Of the 806 defendants sentenced to death, 486 were executed, the rest imprisoned.[6] (See also the American numbers cited by Uwe Wesel, Chapter Seven, n. 10.) With the rapid escalation of the Cold War, however, the Americans needed a strong and experienced military force to stave off the Russians. By the early 1950s, the demand for German rearmament, in a quid pro quo, brought about the cessation of Allied prosecutions of Nazi war criminals and the large-scale granting of amnesty for those already convicted. Meanwhile, in 1950, the judicial system of the new Federal Republic of Germany became operational for crimes committed in Germany. Following its self-ascribed legal successorship to the German Reich, the country retained—with certain amendments and deletions—the Reich's criminal and civil codes (*Strafgesetzbuch* and *Bürgerliches Gesetzbuch* [BGB]) of 1871 and 1900, respectively. Thus, even today, Germany's legal system is based on the codified instruments of justice used during the *Kaiserreich*, the Weimar Republic, and the Third

Reich. Among many other traditional provisions, the BGB retained Germany's ancient citizenship laws, based on bloodlines and culture rather than birthplace and residence. The concept of national borders surrounding—and protecting—a people of ethnic purity and cultural homogeneity had, of course, been at the heart of Nazi ideology. It also was—and possibly still is for many—at the heart of "Germanness" and the reason why the country's conservative parties, for years, staunchly rejected the legal integration of Germany's seven million foreigners, mostly Turks, many of whom were born and educated in Germany. It took until the year 2000 and a new Social Democratic government under Chancellor Gerhard Schröder to adjust Germany's immigration laws to the modern ideas of globalization and multicultural integration.

During the late 1940s and early 1950s, still fully preoccupied with the ongoing challenges of daily life, few Germans took more than a passing interest in the governance of their recently constituted and quasi-independent country. (There were still large Allied military contingents on German soil to prevent the Cold War from turning hot.) Even fewer felt sufficiently informed or interested to take issue with the continued use of the traditional criminal and civil codes. Thus, Article 103, Section 2, of the new Basic Law (*Grundgesetz*) retained the crucial legal principle *Nulla poena sine lege*—no punishment without a law, meaning no crime could be punished that had not been punishable at the time of the offence (*Rückwirkungsverbot*). By upholding this venerable and widely recognized statute—which the Allied judges in Nuremberg regretfully but unanimously overruled, thereby sending many of the former Nazi brass to the gallows—German judges dismissed the vast majority of cases against officers and functionaries of the Hitler state.[7] There was no public outcry. Not about the mass pardoning of perpetrators whose actions, though clearly criminal, had not been indictable during the Third Reich; and certainly not about the observance of yet another cherished article of the Basic Law.

Article 131 guaranteed the continued financial welfare of any civil servant fired by the federal government. Thus, the young *Bundesrepublik* suddenly faced ruinous pension payments to tens of thousands of former employees who had been members of the Party, the SA or the SS, should they, through some comprehensive cleansing operation, be denied re-employment by the new German state. In the end, these drastic measures never materialized.[8] Far from biting such a costly and vastly unpopular bullet, the government reinstalled virtually the entire National Socialist bureaucracy into the services of the Federal Republic of Germany. As Wickert observes: "By the early 1950s, ninety-eight percent of the civil servants previously dismissed because of their Nazi connections were back in office."[9] Looking at the early decades of the postwar era, it is easy to agree with Herf that "[t]he Nuremberg interregnum of 1945–1947 was the golden era of judicial confrontation with the Nazi past."[10]

Quite within the spirit of *realpolitik*, Federal Chancellor Konrad Adenauer chose as his State Secretary, Head of Chancellery, and closest adviser one Dr. Hans Globke, who in 1935 had been instrumental in writing the 300-page commentary on the Nazis' infamous Nuremberg race laws. That appointment, which scandalized the political left, became the new political and social charter from which thousands of high-ranking appointments took their cue. Needless to say, what amounted to "political restoration" in the eyes of the opposition, proved highly popular among the majority of the people.

The New Germans were on the roll: According to A.J. Ryder, living standards in 1953 had surpassed those of 1938,[11] the last of the pre-war "good years." The Nazi past lay far behind. Almost everybody was reinstalled in his former position or had found gainful employment elsewhere. Many who for years had held powerful offices in a state that had deprived millions of innocent people of their human rights could now vote, occupy influential posts, or obtain passports to travel as successful businessmen favored and supported by a network of former fellow officers or functionaries. *Da samma wida!*, the cheeky Bavarian slogan "there we are again!" which in standard German may have sounded too frivolous even for German ears, became the defining epigraph of the frantic 1950s and 1960s. Another popular term that cropped up in the late 1950s was "junior victors," which cynically referred to West Germany's eager adoption of American lifestyles and values. The Third Reich was long forgotten, so was everything else that had gone along with it. We hadn't really done too badly for ourselves by losing the war, or had we?[12] We were America's best friends, well on our way to prosperity, and ready to fight another war against the evil Bolsheviks we knew so well. As West Germany's collective energies rebuilt the country with unprecedented speed and efficiency, the Hitler era became something mentioned only flippantly, if mentioned at all. During the student revolt of the late 1960s, however, the sleeping monster of an unresolved past finally began to stir, though it needed another generation to fully reveal itself. By then, the mental link between what *happened* and those *who must have been there to make it happen* could no longer be made. The Nazis, the "bad guys" that Germany's postwar generations talk about, bear no relation to their still-living, still-remembered parents and grandparents. They are an abstract collective without faces and families, clichés, cartoons, already a myth—a grey and nameless people far removed from anybody's reality.

* * *

Following the collapse of the Nazi dictatorship, one of the most urgent undertakings was the reform of the country's educational system. Under the watchful eyes of the Allied Control Council, all schools had to face the immediate task of coming to terms with Germany's guilty past and their own considerable share in it. Having indoctrinated a whole generation with the perverted Nazi ideology, they were now under extreme pressure to adjust to new democratic principles. Within months, they had to hire or rehire reasonably "clean" staff and rewrite much of the curriculum, notably in German history, literature, and culture. Not surprisingly, a great number of teachers were emotionally unable to touch, let alone teach, the subject of their country's legacy. Many had been teaching during the Weimar Republic and, after 1933, were either pressured into joining the Nazi Party, or did so voluntarily.

The teachers' reluctance to discuss the Third Reich, together with most parents' evasive accounts of their own roles and experiences, had predictable results: Young people born in the 1940s and 1950s appeared remarkably uninformed about the Nazi period, including World War II. In 1964, during my first visit to Germany after emigrating in 1957, I overheard my thirteen-year-old nephew, while working on some school project, ask his father: "Dad, who lost at Stalingrad, the Germans or the Russians?" With 100,000 German soldiers dead and 90,000 captured (of whom only 5,000 survived), the battle of Stalingrad was Germany's greatest military disaster of World War II. The boy's ignorance saddened me. It also opened my eyes to how far removed the *past*, including the war, had already become.

Recently I was reminded of that small incident when, as I was leaving the beautiful Italian city of Bologna on the way to medieval Ferrara, I found myself driving along a wide boulevard incongruously named *Via Stalingrad*. I later asked a group of German baby boomers whether they had a Stalingrad *Strasse* in their cities. They all shook their heads, puzzled by my inquiry. Had I embarrassed them or myself? I don't know. Neither do I know what role Hitler's Axis partner had played in the dreadful battle. But, on that sunny Italian road, I was unexpectedly reminded of those 100,000 frozen bodies, young men who once had caused—and endured—such unspeakable suffering in order to "save the fatherland from the Bolshevik onslaught." They didn't save it, of course. Instead, they and the other twenty million who followed orders in "Hitler's criminal army" became a troubling subject to their contemporaries, and a belated target for today's scornful baby boomers.

By rejecting the concept of collective guilt—criminal, political, or moral—right from the beginning, the new German government gave up much righteous ground.[13] Thus, in the late 1950s, it lacked the nerve to remove the judges who had meted out "justice" in conformance with the laws of the SS state. According to Uwe Wesel, many jurists in the British zone of occupation returned to their former offices on the "piggyback principle:" Every judge cleared by the authorities was entitled to sponsor one former colleague.[14] Belated efforts to cleanse the young West German state of a judiciary that had condemned up to 50,000 people (Wesel) to death and untold thousands to long prison terms, often for the most trivial offences, were defeated by yet another hallowed principle dating back to the Bismarck Reich: *Recht ist was Gesetz ist*, or "justice is what is law," was the defining argument in the successful defence of the Nazi judges whose own harsh justice had been applied in accordance with the laws of the Third Reich.[15] What had clearly amounted to state-sanctioned murder became legally defensible in the highest court of the successor state to the Deutsche Reich. Totally blind to the role they had played in a corrupted justice system, Hitler's state attorneys and judges, unrepentant and unreformed, almost unanimously rejected the government's generous offer of fully pensioned retirement. When, in 1961, the American movie *Judgment at Nuremberg*—arguably the best film on the issue of ethics among Nazi Germany's legal elites—was premiered in West Berlin, the audience felt piqued.

In the early 1960s, it was the single-minded determination of the attorney general of the state of Hesse, Fritz Bauer, that eventually defeated the delaying tactics of the courts reluctant to prosecute old Nazi crimes. Acting on documents received from a journalist in 1958,[16] Bauer took five years to carefully prepare his great Auschwitz trial. Beginning in 1963 and lasting until 1965, the trial revealed for the first time the gruesome facts—either never fully believed or already half-forgotten—about the worst of the extermination camps. Cruelly exploiting the witnesses' bewilderment and weakened memories, however, defence counsels succeeded in securing light sentences for most of the twenty-two defendants. Only six perpetrators received life sentences, while three were released. But even those who were convicted did not have to suffer long: In 1968, while the Bonn parliament haggled over the statute of limitations for Nazi murders (not removed from the books until 1979), a statute of limitations for *aiding and abetting* murder, retroactive to 1960, was quietly written into law. Since the actual murderers at Auschwitz and elsewhere had usually been lower ranks, many SS officers, including leaders of the *Einsatzgruppen*, became retroactively classified as "aiders and abetters" and were subsequently released. Cases where "racial hatred" had motivated the murders, which would have legally invalidated the statute of limitations, were practically impossible to prove after a twenty-year interval.[17]

Today, "Auschwitz" epitomizes the Nazi state and the Final Solution. Until the trial, however, the name had remained largely unknown among non-Jews. To be sure, like so many other death camps "somewhere in Poland"—Majdanek, Treblinka, Chelmno, Sobibor, Belzec—Auschwitz had been mentioned. But these places were all located far beyond the Iron Curtain, and few people took the trouble to find them on a map. Looking back, it should not surprise then that even the very public trial of the 1960s did not elevate Auschwitz from near-obscurity to the most widely known site of the Jewish genocide. Indeed, it would take another decade to break up the public's indifference, and still more years to turn Auschwitz into the most important symbol of Nazi terror that it is today. The revelations brought out during the two-year procedure were certainly shocking. But, the delaying tactics of the articulate, well-dressed defence lawyers, their cruel sarcasm and superior attitudes towards the elderly, impoverished and poorly educated victims, achieved their desired effect on the public. The spectators "had heard it all before" and were loathe to connect any of the gruesome courtroom tales with "real people"—meaning the successful and prosperous Germans in the New Germany. As instances of justice, both the Auschwitz trial and the ensuing Majdanek trial were hallmarks in postwar Germany's juridical efforts to come to terms with the Nazi crimes. To what extent they succeeded in permanently influencing the people's emotional and moral attitudes towards the *past*, remains much less clear.

The fact that the entire Auschwitz trial never registered in my own mind has puzzled me; it has also embarrassed me. Granted, the early 1960s were a rather difficult time for my family. After a few easygoing years in San Francisco and Washington, we moved to Canada, where a lower income and higher cost of living meant forcing roots into tougher soil. There was no money for German newspapers, let alone for trips to Germany. Our home was our castle; to keep it going, even to put a few dollars aside, demanded frugality and quite a bit of energy. Germany seemed very far away, forever in turmoil about the divided city of Berlin, the Cold War, the East German enemy-brothers. Besides, as letters and visits proved, nobody, apart from a handful of writers and filmmakers, displayed the slightest interest in the *past*.

Meanwhile, our new television revealed an insatiable North American appetite for World War II stories. Most evenings, the brutish German Wehrmacht (or the sneaky Japanese) lost yet another skirmish, while British and Canadian navies sank a seemingly unending supply of enemy vessels.[18] I have no recollection, though, of films about the war in the East, the twenty million losses and terrible sacrifices of the Soviet Union, America's former ally and later Cold War enemy; and, until *The Holocaust* series in 1976, I cannot remember any television program on the Jewish deportations, the death camps in Poland, or the SS *Einsatzgruppen*. Did I notice these omissions? I am certain I did not. But, even if I had, I would hardly have been surprised. After all, the Western Allies' theatre of war had been the Atlantic and the area between the Normandy beaches and the Elbe River. How Nazi Germany solved its "Jewish problem" had not been part of their strategic concerns. I was surprised, therefore, to read the observations by Jewish-American historian Peter Novick concerning the mood in the United States during the late 1940s, 1950s and early 1960s, which seem to make these "omissions" somewhat less accidental than I had previously assumed. He argues that, with its unprecedented postwar optimism and its economic and military superpower status, America might have cast a rather jaundiced eye on thousands of Jewish immigrants bringing nothing to the New World but their old laments. Of greater importance, however, was the rapidly escalating Cold War, America's number-one priority. Forthcoming German military support was essential and not to be jeopardized by stories about

Nazi death camps in Poland. In spite of the American Jewish leaders' strong anti-German sentiments, "there was their special obligation to safeguard the reputation and position of Jews in American society ... [which meant] that Jews were not perceived as out of step with other Americans. In addition, there were particular constraints on publicly grounding their opposition to Germany's rehabilitation on the Holocaust."[19] Add to this Senator McCarthy's witch hunt for Communist sympathizers among American artists and intellectuals, a good number of them Jews, placing the senator's paranoia in the neighborhood of Hitler's "Jewish-Bolshevik" obsession. Hence the Great Silence,[20] even in America, even among Jewish-American survivors. Novick's explanation for something very few non-Jews had probably ever noticed, let alone questioned, has the logic of *realpolitik* on its side. Yet, it is also disconcerting, not least because it puts Germany's postwar opportunism in the unexpected company of Jewish-American imperatives. Victim and perpetrator, cloaked in the same silence; so devastating for the one, so beneficial for the other.

Not even Germany's baby-boomer generation, in retrospect, rates the Auschwitz trial as the decisive event that finally forced the world's spotlight on the Nazi crimes. "Nobody is talking about the Hitler era," the letter of a friend curtly dismissed the subject in the mid-1960s. But, just as the bothersome period was about to slip from people's memories, Alexander and Margarete Mitscherlich's erudite work, *Die Unfähigkeit zu trauern* (The Inability to Mourn), shattered the complacency of the late 1960s. Their theories about the Germans' "libidinous relationship" with their Führer was the first attempt to psychoanalyze the baffling phenomenon of an entire people's voluntary enslavement, from which it had been unable, or unwilling, to free itself.[21] For some time, the psychoanalysts were widely quoted among like-minded intellectuals. But, though the book became a huge success, it had little influence on the nation's collective amnesia. Over time, its popular title degenerated into a catchy phrase stripped of much of its scholarly meaning.

* * *

With the benefit of hindsight, one can build a catalogue of events, which, over an extended period, eroded the collective repression of the *past* and finally forced the crimes of the Hitler era, notably the Jewish genocide, onto everybody's mind. Depending on age, political agenda or personal bias, different people have different catalogues. Living abroad since the late Fifties, I expect my perspective to be different from that of a German living in Germany. It should also be informed by age, meaning I witnessed the entire Third Reich.

My catalogue has a very clear beginning: In 1963 Rolf Hochhuth's *Der Stellvertreter (The Deputy)*[22] had an extraordinary impact, as described in Chapter Six. The play permanently changed the image of Pope Pius XII. But it did more. Though some critics argue that all attempts to depict "the hell of Auschwitz" are bound to fail, Hochhuth went ahead and bestowed on the Jewish deportations and the human selections at Auschwitz the three-dimensional "reality" of live theater. Whether the decision was theatrically sound seems irrelevant in view of the general power of the play.[23] (The true identity of the *Doctor*—also called the Beautiful Devil [in the play], the Angel of Death, or the Angel of Auschwitz for his deceptively charming manners and good looks—who performed the selections at Auschwitz, and performs them in the play, was probably unknown to the author. In his extensive notes accompanying the play, Hochhuth writes: "A figure so exaggerated as the Doctor, who does not carry a civilian name ... shows that imitation of reality was not desired."[24]) *The Deputy's* long-term impact may have been mostly on the reputation of the Holy See. But, for anybody truly interested in the crimes and cynicism of the Third Reich, Hochhuth's reality play— concurring with the beginning of the Auschwitz trial—was an extraordinary breakthrough.

While *The Deputy* is my choice for number one, the catalogues of most baby boomers begin with the 1968 student revolt in West Germany. Compared to the widely supported 1968 rebellion in France that led to a general strike, not to mention the 1960s' social revolution in the United States fired by racial conflict and the war in Vietnam, the West German "revolt" was largely a narrowly based attack on the authoritarian structures of an archaic university system. It had little support among the middle class, and none among workers. Partly inspired by Maoist ideology with more than a hint of a cultural revolution, it was loud, destructive and often extremely personal, even vindictive. Whatever the role of the student revolt in breaking up the universities' hierarchies—even exposing some Nazi professors still in office—it was not a serious confrontation with the *past*. As Wickert, himself a student at the time, writes: "In the 1960s, students in West Germany argued intensely about the professors' National Socialist past ... But the Third Reich, the Jewish genocide, the Second World War were considered ancient matter [*Aktenkunde*]. Small wonder, because the victims were either dead or lived abroad, (and) the perpetrators had seemingly vanished from the face of the earth." (My translation.)[25] Denouncing the German federal government as lackeys of the fascist United States and its brutal imperialism in Vietnam, Iran and elsewhere, the increasingly radicalized student revolt adopted the slogans of revolutionaries such as Che Guevera, Mao and Ho Chi Minh. The movement was fatally damaged when some of its members crossed the line from social protest to urban guerilla and political terrorism, leading to tumultuous trials, isolation cells and multiple suicides. In the end, however, the revolt was not without its merits: By refusing to be provoked into applying police state methods, the young German republic experienced a strong push towards democratization.[26]

Number two in my catalogue is probably found on everyone's list. In 1979 the German version of the American four-part television series *The Holocaust* had a difficult launch. Rejected by Germany's two state-financed television companies, it was finally aired by the one existing private station to a small late-night audience. In a scathing article, one German commentator called the story of the destruction of a Jewish physician and his family a *Schmalzsäule*, loosely translated a "maudlin pile of schmaltz." With typical intellectual superiority, Germany's media zeroed in on the melodramatic elements rather than the devastating effect of this first reconstruction of Nazi Germany's horrific crimes produced for a mass audience. After much infighting and reluctance by major television managers, the series was finally aired in prime time to twenty million deeply moved German viewers. The country's media, however, had overlooked something much more important than the series itself: the birth of an epithet. "The Holocaust," simply meaning "widespread destruction by fire," was first used to translate *Sho'ah* from Hebrew into English in the 1948 Israeli Declaration of Independence.[27] Elie Wiesel mentions the term in his book *Night* (1960) and Raul Hilberg in his seminal *The Destruction of the European Jews* (1961),[28] as did American journalists covering the Eichmann trial, also beginning in 1961.[29] For the next fifteen years, however, the term remained rather academic until television suddenly gave it worldwide recognition. More than one-hundred million Americans watched the series, thirty-three countries acquired the film.

Many like to equate the effect of *The Holocaust* series with another Hollywood production: Steven Spielberg's 1993 film *Schindler's List.* The story of a small-time German industrialist who rescued 1,200 Jews from the gas chambers by claiming their indispensability for the war effort was loved by German viewers. In spite of its horror scenes, this was finally a feel-good story about a German who had ruined himself for the sake of "his Jews." It was also a docudrama, meaning it probably contained a number of half-truths. Schindler, his ninety-year-old embittered widow said in an interview in 1997, was a great womanizer and scoundrel, who not only profited enormously from his cheap Jewish laborers, but dodged military service. "There never was a Schindler's List ... It was drawn up by a man called Goldman. This man took money to put a name on the list. I was told this by a Dr. Schwartz, in Vienna; he had paid in diamonds to save his wife."[30] So, Schindler, the playboy and draft dodger, saved "his Jews" while making a good life for himself (leaving his neglected wife in the cold), which was more or less what the film said, but somehow got lost in the Schindler veneration.

The Academy Award–winning *Schindler's List* became a huge commercial success. Though no postwar German filmmaker would have allowed himself to make a movie about a "good German," now that it had been done in America, five million Germans flocked to the theaters; another seven million saw the movie on television.[31] These were the 1990s: By now, everyone knew about the death camps, many had visited them, and "Auschwitz" had become a term more familiar than Stalingrad or Pearl Harbor. The film had shown that good could emerge from bad, which led, of course, to the next question: Why had others not acted the same? Why did it take a guy like Schindler to succeed where others had not even tried? Was corruption the only answer? As in all cases of absolute power, corruption was big in Hitler's Reich; as a sub-theme in the film, it raised more questions than it answered. Though I have to admit to some reservations about "good man Schindler," I still add the film to my list of seminal events because of its extraordinary scenes of senseless barbarism in the concentration camps, and the chilling cynicism of those with the absolute power over life and death.

I then return to the 1980s, when, four decades after Zero Hour, dealing with the *past* was still almost exclusively reserved for the formal observances of a growing number of anniversaries. Thus, item number four in my catalogue is the speech by Federal President Richard von Weizsäcker on May 8, 1985, celebrating the fortieth anniversary of the end of the Hitler Reich: "We all, whether guilty or not, whether old or young, must accept the past. We are all affected by its consequences, and held liable for them." (My translation.) It was a good speech, inasmuch as it told people that everyone had to bear some degree of responsibility for what had happened, since everyone had known something, and it echoed my long-held thoughts.

The Weizsäcker speech, widely applauded as signaling a turning point in public awareness of the Nazi crimes, sounds rather mild and conciliatory today, particularly when compared with the official address by the Speaker of Parliament three years later. Philipp Jenninger's speech on November 9, 1988, marking the fiftieth anniversary of *Kristallnacht* turned out to be a very unhappy event, indeed: By presenting in a wooden and unfeeling manner the hard facts about German anti-Semitism and the persecution of the Jews, the Speaker, listeners complained, had displayed a shocking lack of tact, for which he was forced to resign from the second-highest office in the land. (Details in Interlude IV.) Honest, but clumsy Jenninger may have annoyed most of Germany's opinion-makers; because of his extraordinary candor and brave intentions, I am happy to add him as number five to my catalogue.

Numbers six and seven may also be missing from a good many lists. Ralph Giordano's angry book, *The Second Guilt,* provides a great many details suggesting that, through several decades, the German successor state to the Third Reich, for reasons of *realpolitik* or opportunism, failed to handle the country's past. His strong views on the unpopular issue of "collective guilt" may also have antagonized many writers and politicians.[32] As a valuable source of information and a veritable icebreaker regarding Germany's much delayed *Vergangenheitsbewältigung,* the book is an important item in my catalogue.

Calmer and not directed by personal victimization during the time of the Third Reich is Gabriele von Arnim's book *The Great Silence*—a successful title that has become a slogan in recent newspaper articles. The book is based on numerous interviews the author had with people of different ages, personal histories and education who, for a variety of reasons, were reluctant to discuss the question of guilt in the Third Reich, or were infuriated about the absence of any personal responsibility in postwar Germany ("…by politicians giving speeches of commemoration the state administers the repression [of guilt]" said somebody).

Gabriele von Arnim had discovered the Great Silence.[33] Reading about her experiences in the early nineties, I felt delighted and vindicated: For the first time, a multitude of voices had corroborated what I, judging only from a distance, had observed or suspected all along.

My eighth and final selection, *Hitler's Willing Executioners*,[34] published in the mid-1990s, is almost certainly on everybody's list. Goldhagen's brazen answer to the question of the extent and depth of German anti-Semitism electrified the German public like few issues had done before. If seventeen years earlier NBC's television series *The Holocaust* had elicited shame, perhaps even remorse, by reminding people of the Jewish pogroms they had quietly tolerated, Goldhagen's book was in an entirely different league as it accused the entire German people of guilt by complicity, or worse. Most historians rejected the work as being sensational rather than scientific, pointing out its great number of mistakes.[35] Germany's postwar generations, however, who flocked to the young Harvard professor's lectures by the thousands, hailed it like the Tables of Moses. The extraordinary interest stirred up by Goldhagen's voluminous book revealed something that nobody had quite realized before: the fundamental shift in perception, even acceptance, of the history of the Third Reich. These were the 1990s: The Cold War was over, the two Germanies had reunited without any major éclat—though much to the consternation of the intellectual left, whose entire political stock had been invested in the existence of that mean German-German border as a permanent punishment for Auschwitz. The men who had been young officers or functionaries in the Third Reich, and who had quickly become the new managers of the Federal Republic's "economic miracle," had retired during the eighties. The levers of power had shifted from the Hitler generation to the baby boomers, with a second postwar generation already graduating and taking a critical look at their country's past and future. Goldhagen became the timely agent who satisfied a new hunger for information with his own phenomenal desire to disclose. Though historians claimed that most of what he revealed had been said before, the sheer mass of his evidence impressed most of his readers. Generational resentment among many Germans was suddenly buoyed by the realization that their fathers, these paragons of wealth and virtue, had actually been *responsible* for the *Verbrecherstaat* (criminal state) that now caused their sons so much shame and contrition. They had been *there* and done nothing about it.

Goldhagen's basic thesis—that the Holocaust could never have happened without the people's fundamental agreement with the policies of the Hitler government—is, of course, very close to my own argument. What is debatable is the degree of anti-Semitism that led people to become accessories to the highly complex, Europe-wide process of the Final Solution. "In order to ensure their own survival, the destruction of the Jews seemed (in the eyes of the Germans) a necessary national project," says Rudolf Augstein, editor-in-chief of the German weekly *Der Spiegel*, adding that Goldhagen's claim that "they had hated the Jews with a passion that had worked itself up to a national psychosis is, of course, pure nonsense."[36] (My translation.) Despite Goldhagen's shocking accusations, the question of the depth and intensity of German anti-Semitism will never be answered conclusively. Whether the people were indeed "Hitler's Willing Executioners," as his book's polemical title suggests; whether most of them never fully realized the cumulative effect of their tiny individual contributions to the lethal outcome, as many would later claim; or whether they co-operated "to prevent worse,"[37] a favored excuse by those directly involved: it seems increasingly beside the point. The bond between *Führer* and *Volk* was near-absolute; everything else followed from there. Even if Goldhagen's sensationalism leads him to much more aggressive conclusions, his revelations have been instrumental in opening the door to that basic fact.

*   *   *

As the Nazi Reich has proven, if a small clique of political strongmen—even through a perfectly legal democratic process—gains power over a population with highly developed societal structures and a deep commitment to civil obedience, that clique would have little trouble winning control over all social and political institutions, including the opposition parties.[38] Neither would such a regime, if history is any guide, have much to fear from the Christian Churches, whose leaders have rarely felt compelled to endanger their spiritual or physical survival by bluntly challenging new secular powers. Which leaves the military.

The Wehrmacht is the one institution of the Third Reich about which opinions are more deeply divided today than about any other component of the Nazi state. It took more than three decades for Germans to accept the truth about the Holocaust; it took five to raise serious questions about the extent of the Wehrmacht's involvement. Says Augstein: "I know what it cost to include the Wehrmacht ... as one of the parties responsible for the crimes of the Nazi dictator. [The effort] succeeded. That was a ... breakthrough."[39] (My translation.) The satisfaction of the *Spiegel*'s editor-in-chief refers to a controversial exhibition that traveled Germany from 1996 to 1999. Entitled "War of Destruction—Crimes of the Wehrmacht 1941 to 1944," it was the work of the Hamburg Institute for Social Research and its founder Jan Philipp Reemtsma. Born in 1952, Jan Philipp, multi-millionaire heir to the Reemtsma cigarette fortune, bade farewell to his family's business in order to dedicate his life and money to more people-friendly missions, among them the financing of the institute. From the day of its opening, the Wehrmacht exhibition stirred up a huge controversy, drawing hundreds of thousands of viewers and even provoking a parliamentary debate. Once steeped in glory, Hitler's famous war machine, which invented the blitzkrieg and surpassed Napoleon's triumphant campaigns, was belatedly tarred with the Nazi brush. Commented Reemtsma: Its reputation will never be the same.

If "the Nazis" had always been a rather vague notion in numbers and identities, the Wehrmacht[40] with a total war-time conscription of 20 million men had deep roots in the population. Children grew up knowing that their fathers or grandfathers, brothers or uncles had once fought in a big war, though things were not often talked about and details remained hazy. But even if they knew little, most of the young did not think badly about their elders. They may have changed their minds after having seen the exhibition. Why, and why so late?

The second question has already been answered: The Cold War had ended, and the levers of power were transferred from the war generation to the postwar one. Naturally, the veterans, who had rebuilt the country and run it successfully for four decades, did not give up without a fight. (When minor mistakes in the exhibition's documentation were later discovered, an exhausted Reemtsma reacted by withdrawing.[41]) The split between the generations, however, was not caused by the exhibition; rather, the exhibition was caused by the split, which had begun in the late eighties, and deepened with the powerful emotional invocation of Auschwitz. Originally, Auschwitz—or the Holocaust which it symbolizes—had had little to do with the Wehrmacht and everything to do with the SS. To close the circle, the connection between the two uniformed forces had to be established, which is what the exhibition set out to accomplish.

On March 30, 1941, less than three months before the attack on the Soviet Union, Hitler called his docile army commanders into the Reich Chancellery to inform them about the forthcoming war of destruction (*Vernichtungskrieg*), which would not be conducted along the lines of a conventional war. Subsequently, during Germany's "epic struggle" in the East, the verbal and physical assaults against millions of civilian Jews and Slavs (*Untermenschen*, or sub-humans, in Nazi parlance) fused with the "official" campaign against the Jewish-Bolshevik Red Army, thereby turning a four-year war against Europe's largest, multi-ethnic nation into an ideology-driven slaughter in the name of the survival of the master race. A total of 3.5 million German and nine million Red Army soldiers did not survive the most bloody campaign in world history. Civilian numbers are vague. An estimated ten million Soviet citizens died from hunger, disease or forced relocation; almost one million during the four-year blockade of Leningrad alone. Of roughly 3.15 million German prisoners of war, 1.1 million did not survive their captivity. Hunger, ill treatment, and deliberate murder killed 3 million Russian prisoners out of a total of 5.7 million.[42]

While few adult German civilians could later claim not to have heard of Nazi atrocities in the East, it is difficult to conceive that any Wehrmacht soldier fighting on Russian soil failed to hear rumors, or even to witness instances, of such actions. To be sure, most of the crimes against civilians were perpetrated by the SS. How many Wehrmacht commanders succeeded in keeping their troops away from the bloody work of the *Ordnungspolizei* (Order Police) and the SS *Einsatzgruppen*, which operated closely behind the battle lines, nobody will ever know. As Haffner points out, the reaction of Wehrmacht officers to the conduct of the SS differed widely between Poland and the Soviet Union: While there were strong remonstrations by Colonel General Blaskowitz, the first military commander in occupied Poland (who subsequently lost his job), about the murderous persecutions of Poles by the SS, the Wehrmacht's moral rectitude turned considerably weaker two years later in Russia.[43]

Most historians will probably agree that the Jewish genocide, the single most notorious chapter of World War II, though high on Hitler's priority list, was not a publicly declared war aim, or something that millions of German soldiers (excluding the SS) would have expected to get involved in at the time of their enlistment. Indeed, none of the great powers went to war over Germany's racial policies, which were viewed as an internal

matter not warranting external interference. It was the Reich's hegemonic politics, brazenly threatening the balance of power in Europe,
which finally got the Allies to declare war on Germany.

If that threat was obvious to others, it was far from evident to the ordinary German, who, after months of anxious war talk, was positively
shocked when England and France declared war after Germany's invasion of Poland on September 1, 1939. Fourteen at the time, I hardly
remember where I was when the invasion began and the war started. But
I clearly remember my personal circumstances on September 3, when the
radio announced that England and France had come to the defence of the
Poles. Six years of National Socialist indoctrination had put an entirely
different spin on Germany's wars of aggression against Poland and,
subsequently, the Soviet Union: "Bereft of its colonies after World War I,
Germany was the only major power lacking secure supplies of food and
raw materials. Her dependence on imports made it militarily vulnerable.
Poland and the Ukraine, on the other hand, possessed vast lands right
across Germany's Eastern border, populated by Slavs and Jews, whom
fate had predestined to serve the 'superior Germanic race.'" The
conquest of new *Lebensraum* (living space) was declared a matter of
national survival and, according to every orator from Hitler and
Goebbels to generals, school principals, parsons and priests, sanctioned
by providence itself. If that sounds preposterous today, for *Das Volk ohne
Raum,* or The People Without Space—after the title of a book by the
Nazis' most celebrated novelist, South African writer Hans Grimm—it
was the quintessential truth, a dogma of National Socialist ideology. The
lines of a Hitler Youth song still ring in my ears: "A hunger has been set
into the eyes / New lands, new lands will we conquer." Not only was new
Lebensraum a vitally important goal, it was also a noble one. We had all
learned in school about the long and proud history of the Teutonic
Knights and the Hanse, the society of merchants that had opened up
Europe's Eastern seaboard by bringing trade and culture to an area
thinly populated by Slavic tribes. It was a German tradition, a mission
really, to enlighten the primitive peoples with our superior culture, even
if that meant the supreme sacrifice of war. Hadn't history's greatest
conquerors—Alexander, Caesar, and Napoleon—carried the fruits of
their civilizations wherever they went?

Whether Hitler's mind indeed entertained such romantic notions is hard to assess. Almost certainly, however, both the conquest of *Lebensraum* and the expulsion and enslavement of Jews and Slavs had been competing for his attention since the earliest planning stages, and many years before that. *Lebensraum* had already seemed a *fait accompli* after the first months of a rapid advance. But then came the massive and entirely unexpected Russian counteroffensive on December 6, 1941, that changed everything. As mentioned in an earlier chapter, when Hitler the politician became convinced that the war against the Soviet Union could no longer be won, he turned into Hitler the mass murderer.[44] Plans for *Lebensraum* were shelved while the "solving of the Jewish problem" attained high priority, with details for the Final Solution ready to be presented at the Wannsee Conference only forty-five days later. Although further great advances were made along the southern Russian front during the summer of 1942, the German army was ultimately stopped at the Volga River towards the end of that year.

After the disastrous defeat at Stalingrad in early 1943, and during the protracted German retreat, *Lebensraum* slowly disappeared from Nazi propaganda, replaced by wild exhortations against "Bolshevist Red Army hordes," with images of Genghis Khan and a Holy War for the salvation of the *Abendland* (Western civilization). Hitler's vicious *Kommissarbefehl* of June 6, 1941, the order to shoot on the spot any captured Bolshevik commissar, may or may not have been followed by all, or even most, Wehrmacht officers. But in the increasingly brutal fight against partisans—a vast underground war governed by fear rather than rules and conventions—whole villages were burnt, their populations rounded up and destroyed. The fact that three million Red Army prisoners perished, mostly through starvation or deliberate maltreatment, strongly suggests that the Führer's obsessive hatred of Jews and Slavs did not go unanswered by the army, many of whose soldiers had been exposed to years of Hitler Youth indoctrination prior to their enlistment.

Hannes Heer, the director of the exhibition, summarizes his personal reaction: Firstly, there is the horrible realization that this war was conducted precisely as Hitler had conceived and planned it. Secondly, there still is an immense wonderment: How could people, within days, become mass murderers and, under the circumstances of war, consider everything legitimate, (including) the murder of the Jews (and) the murder of prisoners. When I search for an explanation, I tell myself: At the moment when emotions and compassion die, all else becomes possible. Thirdly, I also react with surprise. I feel pity when I see the damage done to that generation ... I have seen perpetrators (in the pictures). But it became increasingly clear to me: They also are victims. And they have been damaged in several ways: through the violation of standards ... and moral conventions, and through the exorbitant strains of this war, not only the physical but also the psychological ones, like the death of their comrades.[45] (My translation.)

The specific message of the exhibition "War of Destruction—Crimes of the Wehrmacht 1941 to 1944," and the predictable controversy it stirred up, were consequences of a major social and political shift that had been going on for years. Since the end of the 1960s and the student revolt, a vocal group from the intellectual left had tried to block, or influence, a number of major political or military decisions on the grounds that Germany had a permanent responsibility for the crimes of the Third Reich. Their claims that West Germany not only had the right, but the moral obligation to pursue policies different from those of the Western Alliance—choosing the "third way," as it were—caused great difficulties for the German chancellors of the 1970s and 1980s.[46] With the growing awareness of the Holocaust in the 1980s, demands for "politics of redemption"—including the acceptance of a permanent division of the two Germanies and the official recognition of East Germany—were increasingly raised by West German writers, journalists and politicians on the political left. During the 1990s, the "Holocaust" became widely supplanted by the narrower term "Auschwitz." A powerful emotional trigger, heavily laden with unforgettable torment, it has grown into a moral imperative that illuminates much of German creative thinking, influences the country's cultural and social endeavors, and maintains a strong voice in domestic and foreign affairs. Under the current coalition government of Federal Chancellor Gerhard Schröder's Social Democrats and the Green Party, tensions over Germany's moral place in the world have not eased. Under NATO obligation, German soldiers took part in the liberation of Kosovo from Serbian nationalists, their first military action since World War II. The pride and satisfaction about that operation, however, was soon overshadowed by political and moral misgivings. Now, the looming military conflict between the developed world and various Muslim dictatorships with their starving populations has opened up another rift in Germany's coalition government. Given the lessons of Auschwitz, what are the country's primary duties? Is the half-century-old dictum that no German soldier should ever participate in another war (outside NATO commitments) still valid? Or have reunification and restitution to world power status brought about political and military responsibilities which a nation of eighty-two million can no longer shrug off? German foreign policy has become a high-wire act as the government tries to strike a balance between the contradictory demands of its Allies and neighbors: Don't dominate us with your political and economic might, but carry your weight. The result is a society where political leadership and social innovation are hampered by indecision, and cutting-edge technologies are seen as a threat to the nation's uneasy peace with the *past*.[47] The way out of this impasse is the European Union. Since the Fifties, Germans have been looking forward to a new European identity that would allow them to finally shake off their national legacy. As Europe grows into "Euroland," and a dozen currencies convert to the Euro, one question lingers: Will the "United States of Europe" they are all marching towards (without anyone holding the compass) be a federation of equals, or will the mighty nation in the center, simply by volume and numbers, unbalance the grand design?

Among the population, the conflict between those who want to "move on", and others who insist that the country cannot, and must not, extricate itself from its *past* is still much alive. Though there are no clear political or societal lines, one may assume that a majority—made up of the very old and the very young, the political right-of-centre, and many of the centre, plus the success-oriented, managerial part of the baby boomers—wants to step out of the shadow of the Hitler Reich. They are opposed by a smaller, but highly vocal, intellectually influential group of baby boomers—some still mentally connected to the 1968 student revolt—who want to embrace Auschwitz as Germany's single most compelling issue. Their message is: NEVER FORGET. It is a solemn promise and timeless obligation in the land of the perpetrators that seems impossible to contradict. Yet, a growing number of Germans feel weary of a too literal, too oppressive observance of the country's indelible guilt.

"Everything is Auschwitz today"; and "I keep my mouth shut—you can't say anything anymore" were remarks I picked up during a recent trip to Germany. Is the Great Silence of guilt and shame of the earlier decades about to change into a silence of intimidation in the wake of the heated debates about the singularity and moral authority of Auschwitz? Thoughtful and well-meaning people have involved themselves in arguments one would find disturbing, if the moral rectitude of the protagonists were not so eminently established. The acceptance speech by the winner of Germany's most distinguished literary award, Martin Walser, on October 12, 1998, became a landmark in an escalating war between tolerance and free speech, and the "opinion soldiers, who force the writer into the opinion service with their morality pistol at the ready." The hard-hitting address by the seventy-one-year-old novelist (once an early proponent of the collective guilt argument) antagonized many of Germany's leading intellectuals, but also found sympathy and support. "I want to understand," said Walser, "why, in this decade, the past is being presented like never before." Searching for answers, he believes he has discovered "that frequently it is no longer memory, the lest-we-forget, that is the motive, but the instrumentalization of our shame for current purposes. Always good and honorable purposes, but instrumentalization nonetheless."[48] (My translation.) No speech in recent memory has provoked a similarly vicious and divisive controversy in Germany as that of this stubbornly independent novelist.

The German government, meanwhile, continues to commemorate days and events relating to the crimes of the Third Reich. According to the federal center for political education, there are presently 2,000 museums and historic sites in Berlin, at former concentration camps, and elsewhere in Germany, all devoted to the memory of the Holocaust.[49] Unlike many other countries, Germany has no Remembrance Day or Veterans Day. Instead, the *Volkstrauertag* (People's Day of Mourning), a Sunday in mid-November, is dedicated to all those whose lives were ended by the violence of war—the murdered, the bombed, the fallen. There is also January 27, the day in 1945 when Auschwitz was liberated by the Red Army; it has now been declared a National Remembrance Day for the Victims of the Holocaust. Finally, there is the two-acre Holocaust memorial currently being built near the *Reichstag* in the heart of Berlin. Because of its vast dimensions, abstract design and uncertain message in the land of the perpetrators, the project was approved by Parliament only after ten years of arguments that did nobody credit, and left everyone with a bad aftertaste.

Now that Holocaust studies are mandatory in schools, including visits to Auschwitz or other places of sorrow, the anti-Semitism of old has largely disappeared in Germany. In its stead, a new philo-Semitism is beginning to grow. Though confused and sentimental, it is also an expression of young people's urgent desires to make amends, to do better than their elders. "Memory" may have created its own traumatized youth, a new class of victims desperately yearning for understanding and love from the legitimate ones. Whether this new devotion to Hebrew culture, folklore and Klezmer music is the beginning of something genuine and durable, or a misguided and mawkish blind alley, only the future will tell. Jewish-Canadian author Erna Paris rejects this trend: "More than fifty years after the war, the new generations are shadowboxing with memories that seem unassimilable to both Jews and gentiles, and the standoff appears to be deepening, as repentant Germans try, in growing numbers, to atone for the deeds of their parents and grandparents, and Jews become increasingly uncomfortable with their entreaties and their appropriation of 'Jewish space.'" Concluding that "some lines cannot be transgressed," she quotes the director of the New Synagogue in Berlin: "certain absolutions cannot—will not—be made."[50] Wickert, seeing things from the side of the German baby boomers, is equally negative: By trying to convert to the mosaic faith, finding out they were Jewish in a former life, or choosing Jewish girls' names "[m]ore and more Germans discover their Jewish heritage—an ersatz identity that permits the assimilation of the Holocaust from the side of the victims."[51] (My translation.) Perhaps, turning sorrow and repentance into a kind of Weltschmerz—*"felix culpa"* (happy guilt), as Hannah Arendt mockingly called it[52]—seems slightly narcissistic and a bit over the top. Still, I find it hard not be touched by those efforts, which may be kitschy, but are surely harmless. In the end, of course, it must be the victims and their children and children's children who will be willing to forgive, where mankind will never be able to forget.

*   *   *

In the East Berlin district of Treptow lies the huge Soviet war memorial where Berliners and tourists can quietly walk about or sit in contemplative silence. There is no comparable site in Germany's capital to commemorate the country's six million soldiers killed in two world wars.[53] Nor is there a memorial in the centre of Hamburg to remind the city's busy residents of their 40,000 fellow citizens incinerated in a few nights of unspeakable horror.[54] Instead, since 1993, the *Neue Wache* (New Guardhouse) at Berlin's famous boulevard Unter den Linden has served as the country's "Memorial for the Victims of War and Totalitarianism." Its Pantheon-like open-ceilinged hall is empty but for the bronze figure of a mother cradling her dead son, by German sculptress Käthe Kollwitz. Like the People's Day of Mourning, the *Neue Wache* is dedicated to all those whose deaths were caused by the violence of war or its aftermath, the racial laws of the Hitler regime, or the wilful murders at the hands of the former East German government. The solemnity of the memorial and the inclusiveness of its message make it noble and inspiring for many; somewhat vague for others.

Since the earliest postwar years, Germans have felt uncomfortable with ceremonial bombast when remembering their own soldiers or citizens killed in World War II. Large war memorials were declared passé, something no progressive German would like to be erected in his rapidly rebuilt city center. Many municipalities found their own solutions by simply adding "1939–1945" to already existing World War I sculptures; churches and chapels engraved the names of their communities' fallen soldiers on a commemorative wall. In 1964 a modest four-by-seven-foot bronze plaque with the inscription "To the Victims of Wars and Totalitarianism" was unveiled in the *Hofgarten* of West Germany's former capital city Bonn, for foreign dignitaries to place their wreaths. Since then, "inclusiveness of victims" has become the hallmark of German memorials, with the twenty-five-line citation at the *Neue Wache* probably the most comprehensive.

After the war ended, there was little understanding among Germans of the true extent of the catastrophe, no real sense of the unimaginable number and range of victims; just a terrible mental and physical chaos with all values void. As Hitler and the Third Reich were eradicated from the people's minds like phantoms that never were, the Wehrmacht, Nazi Germany's most impressive symbol, vanished too; not deliberately, not maliciously—just so. Soldiers came home, were welcomed and urged to integrate as quickly as possible into the drab postwar society. Of the ones who were dead, little was said. An aunt of mine dedicated a corner of her bedroom to the memory of her boy; her friends thought her "house altar" tacky. Perhaps people were too worn-out, or they did not know how to feel any more grief in the face of the terrible accusations that rolled over them like a landslide. Choked by an overwhelming sense of sorrow—their losses useless, their sacrifices made for a criminal Führer, embarrassed, rudderless, crushed—Germans' collective soul closed up like an oyster. There were millions they had loved and wanted to mourn; millions more they had never known, yet were expected to mourn. For neither was there the strength or the time—perhaps not even the will. The measure of exhaustion surpassed the measure of loss. The rest was denial—and an overpowering desire to forget.

Years from now, when the Holocaust memorial in the heart of Berlin is completed and accepted by a relieved public, Germans may find the generosity—or maturity—to finally come to terms with themselves. Somewhere, far from the busy heart of the capital, they might then build a simple yet dignified site there to remember those who died for something they desperately wanted to believe in, who did not choose their lot, yet were asked to pay the ultimate price. One cannot help but be reminded of the hauntingly beautiful Vietnam memorial in Washington. Long and difficult arguments preceded its construction, but once completed, it contributed much to America's healing. Granted, the Wehrmacht's campaign in Russia was of a different scope and kind than the Vietnam war; and, unlike the American people, no German ever marched in protest against Hitler's war. Yet, the silence surrounding the homecoming soldiers, who had caused— yet also suffered—such terrible harm, was strangely similar in both countries: No grief counsellors for battered souls, no welcoming parties for heroes whose honor had been soiled by the corrupted ambition of their leaders.

*　　*　　*

Whenever I am in Germany I visit the charming village of Münstertal in the foothills of the Black Forest, and its tranquil cemetery nestled close to the walls of the old monastery church of Sankt Trudpert. In the center of the cemetery stands a stone monument of a grieving mother and her fallen son, bearing the names of Münstertal's soldiers killed in World War I and the dates they fell; the same family names again and again, sometimes the same dates. Next to the sculpture lies an iron slab of

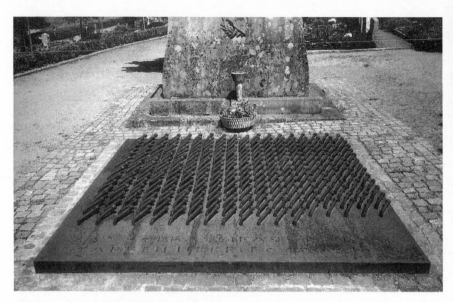

War memorial for the fallen of Münstertal 1939–1945

contemporary simplicity, more than two square metres in size. On the narrow side is the inscription "1939–1945," but there are no names. The World War II memorial of Sankt Trudpert cemetery has 265 nails for 265 fallen men. The nails are thick and stand in orderly formation, as though still marching. Their heads are bent. In Sankt Trudpert, even the nails must bear the grief.

CLOSING WORDS

Language is the foremost medium to reflect the social make-up of a people. It is a living thing, constantly shaped and amended by the expressions, trends, and lifestyles of a society. Therefore, if indeed postwar Germans wished to purge themselves of disagreeable memories of the Nazi era, what simpler way to do so than by cleansing the language? Here, then, is what you would find in the 1980 "anniversary edition" of the *Duden*, the German equivalent of the *Oxford Dictionary* or the American *Webster's*:

Hitler, Adolf: no entry.

Nor do the H's mention Himmler, boss of the SS, SD, and Gestapo, creator of the SS state and the man behind the genocide of six million Jews. The *Duden* does, however, list Hindemith, a contemporary composer of modest fame, who was disliked by the Führer. Still under the same letter, one fails to find any reference to Hindenburg, Germany's commander-in-chief in World War I and president of the tottering Weimar Republic who, in 1933, had the misfortune to appoint Adolf Hitler as Reich Chancellor in a coalition government. Nor, under "G," are there any entries for Nazi ministers and party bosses Joseph Goebbels and Hermann Göring, although, thank God, I did find Goethe, Germany's most famous bard, in the heavily edited "Go"section. Equally invisible is Mussolini, the Italian fascist leader and Hitler's closest ally, whereas the name of Spain's fascist dictator Francisco Franco, who wisely stayed out of the war, is duly listed. Foreign contemporaries enjoy a somewhat uneven attention: Churchill and Chamberlain are reduced to an "English family name," while all American presidents of the twentieth century are designated as such. Stalin is correctly, if somewhat modestly, described as "Soviet statesman."

If the selection of worthies whose names warrant inclusion in the *Duden* is baffling, so is the treatment of places whose fame (or shame) has turned them into household words. After the word "Konzentration" (concentration), demanding five lines of explanation, we find "Konzentrationslager" (concentration camp), "Abk. KZ" (abbr. KZ), followed by several lines of variants of the verb "konzentrieren" (concentrate). Similar brevity pertains to another place: "Nürnberg" (Nuremberg), synonymous with Nazi party rallies, race laws, and war crimes tribunals, is tersely identified as a city in central Franconia. It is followed by "Nürnberger Trichter," a mythical device used to funnel wisdom into dumb heads—unfortunately without further instructions.

Granted, the format of this particular edition of the foremost dictionary of the German language is limited to 700 pages, compared to the 1,700 pages of my *Webster's*. But for a German dictionary to list Stalin and Franco and omit Hitler and Mussolini suggests an unpleasant editorial bias. Worse, the omission of the infamous trio Himmler, Göring, and Goebbels reveals the taboos of a venerable publishing house hoping to eradicate the *Dritte Reich* (unlisted) by simply expunging its main characters. After all, if correct spelling is the *Duden's* raison d'être, its users should not be left unaided about names like Adolf (not Adolph) Hitler, Joseph (not Josef) Goebbels or Hermann (not Herman) Göring (also spelled Goering, according to the faithful *Webster's*, which lists them all).

Though the passage of time has not diminished the world's fascination with the Hitler era, the *Duden* has stayed its course. In its 1996 "completely revised and enlarged" 900-page edition, the Nazi elite still remains unmentioned, while in the admirably denazified "Go" section, Goethe and van Gogh now rub shoulders with Gorbachev.

Notes to the Postscript

1   Wickert, Ulrich, *Deutschland auf Bewährung* (Germany on Probation), (Munich: Heyne, 1999), 275.

2   Herf, Jeffrey, *Divided Memory: The Nazi Past in the Two Germanys* (Cambridge, Mass.: Harvard University Press, 1997), 225.

3   Wesel, Uwe, *Geschichte des Rechts* (History of Law) (Munich: C.H.Beck, 1997) 511.

4   Mitscherlich, Alexander and Margarete, *Die Unfähigkeit zu trauern* (The Inability to Mourn) (Munich: Piper, 1967), 68.

5 Kurt Schumacher, the leader of the opposition in Parliament, denounced Adenauer publicly as "the chancellor of the Allies," an insult the elderly Adenauer could never entirely shake off.

6 Herf, Jeffrey, op. cit., ref. 2, 206.

7 Giordano, Ralph, *Die zweite Schuld oder Von der Last, Deutscher zu sein* (The second guilt or on the burden of being a German) (Hamburg: Drömer, 1987), 123.

8 ibid. 96.

9 Wickert, Ulrich, op. cit., ref.1, 93.

10 Herf, Jeffrey, op. cit., ref. 2, 204.

11 Ryder, A.J.: *Twentieth-Century Germany: From Bismarck to Brandt* (London: MacMillan, 1973), 483.

12 In the hilarious 1959 Peter Sellers satire, *The Mouse that Roared*, the Duchy of Grand Fenwick tries its best to start, and lose, a war with the United States in order to later reap billions in American aid.

13 The German philosopher Karl Jaspers arrived at the following conclusion: "… there is no moral collective guilt, but a collective political liability (for all citizens)." Jaspers, Karl, *Wohin treibt die Bundesrepublik?* (Munich: Piper, 1988), 69. This statement is amplified by Wickert's discussion of Jaspers's principles: "… man is bound to a collective and, by necessity, becomes liable for the consequences of all state actions of that collective." Wickert, Ulrich, op. cit., ref. 1, 294. (My translations.)

14 Wesel, Uwe, op. cit., ref. 3, 514.

15 Giordano, Ralph, op. cit., ref. 7, 150.

16 That same year, the "Ulm *Einsatzgruppen* trial" had revealed the fact that huge crimes were still left unredeemed. (Wesel, Uwe, op. cit, ref. 3, 517.)

17 ibid, 518.

18 According to the sculptured documentation at the navy war memorial Laboe near Kiel, the *Kriegsmarine* lost an incredible 120,000 ships in World War II.

19 Novick, Peter, *The Holocaust in American Life* (New York: Houghton Mifflin, 1999), 91.

20 Title of a book by Arnim, Gabriele von, *Das grosse Schweigen* (The Great Silence) (Munich: Kindler, 1989).

21 Mitscherlich, A. and M., op. cit., ref. 4, 71ff.

22 Hochhuth, Rolf, *Der Stellvertreter* (*The Deputy*) (Reinbek bei Hamburg: Rowohlt, 1963).

23 In contrast, Peter Weiss's play "*Die Ermittlung*" (The Investigation), first published in 1965, renders a highly stylized interpretation of the Auschwitz trial

without any theatrical props or dramatic acting, relying entirely on the power of the language. (Weiss, Peter, *Die Ermittlung* (Frankfurt: Suhrkamp, 1991.)

24 op. cit., ref. 22, 178. In 1959 German authorities issued an order of arrest against SS physician Dr. Josef Mengele (the *Doctor*), together with a ten million DM reward. (*Enzyklopädie des Nationalsozialismus* [Stuttgart: Klett-Cotta, 1997]). A demand for his extradition was rejected by the Argentine government. (Arendt, Hannah, *Eichmann in Jerusalem* [Munich: Piper, 10th ed., 2000], 386.) In spite of these alleged initiatives, the name of Dr. Mengele remained generally unknown in Germany until decades later.

25 Wickert, Ulrich, op. cit., ref. 1, 23ff.

26 Hartung, Klaus, *Runter mit dem Zeigefinger* (Down with the index finger), *Die Zeit*, No. 5, 2001.

27 Novick, Peter, op. cit., ref. 19, 133.

28 Little, Franklin H., *Den Holocaust erfinden* (To invent the Holocaust), *Freiburger Rundbriefe*, No. 2, 1997, 102. Reprinted from: Holocaust and Genocide Studies, Vol. IX, No. 2, 1995.

29 Novick, Peter, op. cit., ref. 19, 133.

30 Laurence, Charles, "There never was a Schindler's list," *The Ottawa Citizen*, October 18, 1997. (From the *Daily Telegraph*.)

31 Wickert, Ulrich, op. cit., ref. 1, 213.

32 Giordano, Ralph, op. cit., ref. 7.

33 Arnim, Gabriele von, *Das grosse Schweigen* (The Great Silence) (Munich: Kindler, 1989).

34 Goldhagen, Daniel Jonah, *Hitler's Willing Executioners: Ordinary Germans and the Holocaust* (New York: Alfred Knopf, 1996).

35 Finkelstein, Norman G. and Birn, Ruth Bettina, *A Nation on Trial: The Goldhagen Thesis and Historical Truth* (New York: Henry Holt & Company, 1998).

36 Augstein, Rudolf, *Der Soziologe als Scharfrichter* (The sociologist as executioner), *Der Spiegel*, April 15, 1996. Reprinted in Schoeps, Julius H., ed., *Ein Volk von Mördern? Die Dokumentation zur Goldhagen-Kontroverse um die Rolle der Deutschen im Holocaust* (A people of murderers? The documentation to the Goldhagen controversy about the role of the Germans in the Holocaust) (Hamburg: Hoffmann & Campe, 1996), 107ff.

37 Arendt, Hannah, op. cit., ref. 24, 222.

38 Starting out as Reich Chancellor of a minority government, it took Hitler exactly fifty-three days to force through the *Reichstag* (Parliament) the *Ermächtigungsgesetz* (Enabling Act), which disenfranchised all opposition, and deprived parliament of its political rights.

39 Augstein, Rudolf, op. cit., ref. 36.

40 In 1935, Hitler introduced general conscription. With only minor protests from England, France, and Italy, he ignored the Treaty of Versailles and increased the total strength of the German peace-time army (*Reichswehr*) from 100,000 to 550,000 men of the newly organized Wehrmacht. At the same time, he began openly to build up the *Luftwaffe*.

41 At the time of writing, the exhibition reopened in Berlin. It provoked a demonstration by 3,500 right-wing demonstrators, and fights between the police and left-wing groups trying to interfere with the march of the skinheads.

42 Numbers of German and Russian prisoners of war from *Militärisches Forschungsamt*, Potsdam.

43 Haffner, Sebastian, *Anmerkungen zu Hitler* (Notes about Hitler) (Munich: Kindler, 1978) 169.

44 ibid, 180. See also Interlude IV, ref. 6.

45 Heer, Hannes, *Am Abgrund der Erinnerung* (At the abyss of memory), *Die Zeit*, No. 22, 1999.

46 Wickert, Ulrich, op. cit. ref., 1, 226ff.

47 In a recent interview with *Die Zeit* (No. 49, 2001), Hubert Markl, outgoing president of the Max-Planck Society (MPG), and the *Deutsche Forschungsgemeinschaft* (Germany's leading research institution and research funding agency, respectively), regretted the co-operation between the Nazi regime and the Kaiser-Wilhelm-Gesellschaft (predecessor of the MPG) in unethical research. He also noted that he was the first president of the MPG who had not seen an MPG member receive a Nobel prize during his five years in office. See also Chapter Five, n 3.

48 Walser, Martin, *Die Banalität des Guten* (The banality of good), *Frankfurter Allgemeine Zeitung,* No. 236, 1998.

49 Rürup, Reinhard, *Ideologisierter Holocaust?*, *Die Zeit*, No. 34, 2000.

50 Paris, Erna, *Long Shadows* (Toronto: Knopf, 2000), 22.

51 Wickert, Ulrich, op. cit., ref. 1, 288.

52 Koenen, Gerd, *Und in den Herzen Asche* (And ashes in the hearts), *Spiegel special*, No. 1, 2001.

53 The *Luftwaffe* has its own memorial in Fürstenfeldbruck, near Munich, the Navy at Laboe, near Kiel, and the Army in Koblenz.

54 Hamburg's 36,918 firestorm victims of July 1943 are buried in four huge mass graves arranged in the form of a cross and covered by lawn in the city's largest cemetery. A dozen long wooden bars, each carrying the name of a city section erased by phosphorus bombs, divide the grassy expanse. Simplicity, silence, and

a heart-rending anonymity. No flag or coat of arms of the city, whose busiest parts were once populated by those now dead—no legend to tell their fate. Just a bunker-like structure with a sculpture by Gerhard Marcks showing a grim Charon as he ferries a mourning family across the Styx.

BIBLIOGRAPHY

Albrecht, Jörg, *Das Erbe* (The Legacy), *Die Zeit*, July 1, 1994.

Arendt, Hannah, *Eichmann in Jerusalem: Die Banalität des Bösen* (Munich: Piper, 1964).

Arnim, Gabriele von, *Das grosse Schweigen* (Munich: Kindler, 1989).

Augstein, Rudolf, *Der Soziologe als Scharfrichter* (The sociologist as executioner), *Der Spiegel*, April 15, 1996.

Böhm, Kleine-Brockhoff, Willeke: *"Das deutsche Bankgeheimnis"* (The German Bank Secret), *Die Zeit*, No. 34, 1998.

Cartier, Raymond, *Der Zweite Weltkrieg* (Munich: Piper, 1979).

Cornwell, John, *Hitler's Pope: The Secret History of Pius XII* (London: Viking, Penguin Group, 1999).

Eban, Abba, *My People* (New York: Random House, 1984).

Engelmann, Bernt, *Einig gegen Recht und Freiheit* (Gütersloh: C. Bertelsmann, 1975).

Enzyklopädie des Nationalsozialismus (Stuttgart: Klett-Cotta, 1997).

Finkelstein, Norman G. and Birn, Ruth Bettina, *A Nation on Trial: The Goldhagen Thesis and Historical Truth* (New York: Henry Holt & Company, 1998).

Fischer, Ursula, *Zum Schweigen verurteilt: Denunziert – verhaftet – interniert (1945–1948)* (Berlin: Dietz, 1992).

Gailus, Manfred, *Für Gott, Volk, Blut und Rasse* (For God, folk, blood and race), *Die Zeit,* No. 44, 2001.

Gilbert, G. M., *Nuremberg Diary* (New York: The New American Library of World Literature, 1947).

Giordano, Ralph, *Die zweite Schuld oder Von der Last, Deutscher zu sein* (Hamburg: Drömer, 1987).

Goldhagen, Daniel J., *Hitler's Willing Executioners: Ordinary Germans and the Holocaust* (New York: Alfred Knopf, 1996).

Greenhous, Harris, Johnston and Rawling, *The Crucible of War, 1939–1945: The Official History of the Royal Canadian Air Force,* Volume III. (Toronto: University of Toronto Press, 1994).

Haffner, Sebastian, *Anmerkungen zu Hitler* (Munich: Kindler, 1978).

Hartung, Klaus, *Runter mit dem Zeigefinger* (Down with the index finger), *Die Zeit*, No. 5, 2001.

Heer, Hannes, *Am Abgrund der Erinnerung* (At the abyss of memory), *Die Zeit*, No. 22, 1999.

Herf, Jeffrey, *Divided Memory: The Nazi Past in the Two Germanys* (Cambridge, Mass: Harvard University Press, 1997).

Hilberg, Raul, *The Destruction of the European Jews: New Viewpoints* (New York, 1973). Quoted by Jäckel, Eberhard in Schoeps, Julius H., ed., *Ein Volk von Mördern?* (Hamburg: Hoffman und Campe, 1996).

Hochhuth, Rolf, *Der Stellvertreter* (*The Deputy*) (Reinbek bei Hamburg: Rowohlt, 1963).

Ignatieff, Michael, *The Warrior's Honour* (Toronto: Viking, 1998).

Jaspers, Karl, *Wohin treibt die Bundesrepublik?* (Munich: Piper, 1966).

Johnson, Paul, *Eine Epidemie des Hasses*. In: Schoeps, Julius H., ed.: *Ein Volk von Mördern?* (Hamburg: Hoffmann & Campe, 1996).

Kalshoven, Hedda, *Ich denk so viel an Euch: Ein deutsch-holländischer Briefwechsel 1920–1949* (Munich: Luchterhand, 1995.) From a review by Gabriele von Arnim, *Die Zeit*, No. 8, 1996.

Kershaw, Ian, *Hitler, 1889–1936* (London: Penguin Press, 1998).

Klee, Ernst, *Deutsche Medizin im Dritten Reich* (Frankfurt: S. Fischer, 2001); *Die Zeit*, No. 44, 2001.

Koenen, Gerd, *Und in den Herzen Asche* (And ashes in the hearts), *Spiegel special*, No. 1, 2001.

Kogon, Eugen, *Der SS-Staat: Das System der deutschen Konzentrationslager* (Munich: Kindler, 1974).

Kohrs, Ekkehard, *Eine falsche Rede* (A faulty speech), *General-Anzeiger*, November 11, 1988.

Laurence, Charles, "There never was a Schindler's list," *The Ottawa Citizen*, October 18, 1997.

Lewy, Günther, *The Catholic Church and Nazi Germany* (Da Capo Press, copyright 1964, First Da Capo Press Edition 2000).

Little, Franklin H., *Den Holocaust erfinden* (To invent the Holocaust), *Freiburger Rundbriefe*, No. 2, 1997. Reprinted from: Holocaust and Genocide Studies, Vol. IX, No. 2, 1995.

Lukacs, John, *The Hitler of History* (New York: Vintage Books, 1998).

Markl, Hubert, *Ich ging bis an die Grenze* (I went to the limits), *Die Zeit*, No. 49, 2001.

Mauch, Christof, *Schattenkrieg gegen Hitler: Das Dritte Reich im Visier der amerikanischen Geheimdienste 1941–1945* (Stuttgart: Deutsche Verlags-Anstalt, 1999).

Middlebrook, Martin, *The Battle of Hamburg: Allied bomber forces against a German city in 1943* (London: Allen Lane, 1980).

Mitscherlich, Alexander and Margarete, *Die Unfähigkeit zu trauern* (Munich: Piper, 1967).

Novick, Peter, *The Holocaust in American Life* (New York: Houghton Mifflin, 1999).

Overy, Richard, *Das Reich des Bösen*, *Spiegel special*, NO. 1, 2001.

Paris Erna, *Long Shadows* (Toronto: Knopf, 2000).

Ritter, Gerhard, *Carl Goerdeler und die deutsche Widerstandsbewegung* (Stuttgart: Deutsche Verlags-Anstalt, 1955).

Rürup, Reinhard, *Ideologisierter Holocaust?*, *Die Zeit*, No. 34, 2000.

Ryder, A.J., *Twentieth-Century Germany: From Bismarck to Brandt* (London: MacMillan, 1973).

Salomon, Ernst von, *Der Fragebogen* (Reinbek bei Hamburg: Rowohlt, 1951).

Sebald, W.G. *Luftkrieg und Literatur* (Munich: Hanser, 1999).

Ullrich, Volker, *Goldhagen und die Deutschen* (Goldhagen and the Germans), *Die Zeit*, No. 38, 1996.

Volkswagenkommunikation, Unternehmensarchiv, Wolfsburg, Ed.: *Erinnerungsstätte zur Geschichte der Zwangsarbeit im Volkswagenwerk*.

Wahl, Torsten, *Naziakten wechseln wieder den Besitz* (Nazi Files Change Hands Again), *Leipziger Volkszeitung*, May 28, 1994.

Walser, Martin, *Die Banalität des Guten* (The banality of goodness), *Frankfurter Allgemeine Zeitung*, No. 236, 1998.

Weiss, Peter, *Die Ermittlung* (Frankfurt: Suhrkamp, 1991).

Weizsäcker, Richard von: *Vier Zeiten* (Berlin: Siedler, 1999).

Wesel, Uwe: *Geschichte des Rechts* (Munich: C.H.Beck, 1997).

Wickert, Ulrich, *Deutschland auf Bewährung* (Munich: Heyne, 1999).

INDEX

Photographs are indicated by italicized page numbers